LETTERS ON APPLIED TACTICS

LETTERS ON APPLIED TACTICS

TWENTY-FIVE TACTICAL EXERCISES

DEALING WITH

THE OPERATIONS OF SMALL DETACHED FORCES
OF THE THREE ARMS

WORKED OUT BY

MAJOR-GENERAL GRIEPENKERL

TRANSLATED
FROM THE SEVENTH GERMAN EDITION BY
KARL von DONAT
LATE LIEUTENANT 33RD (EAST PRUSSIAN FUSILIER) REGIMENT
GERMAN ARMY

The Naval & Military Press Ltd

Published by

The Naval & Military Press Ltd
Unit 5 Riverside, Brambleside
Bellbrook Industrial Estate
Uckfield, East Sussex
TN22 1QQ England

Tel: +44 (0)1825 749494

www.naval-military-press.com
www.nmarchive.com

In reprinting in facsimile from the original, any imperfections are inevitably reproduced and the quality may fall short of modern type and cartographic standards.

PREFACE

THE late Captain R. Maxwell (89th Regiment), who was the original translator of these Letters, wrote in his Preface :—

" It is necessary to inform readers of this translation that, in order to render these Letters useful to British officers unacquainted with the organisation of the German Army, the imaginary forces, whose operations are dealt with in the following pages, are to be considered as organised on British lines. The expression ' battalion,' therefore, throughout this translation may be taken to imply 8 companies, each 100 strong; ' squadrons,' 100 sabres; and ' battery,' 6 guns. The various space and time calculations have consequently been modified. . . . With the exception of alterations thus involved, and of details in connection with ammunition supply, etc., the translation is literal.

" In places, however, the German organisation betrays itself, *e.g.*, in the constantly-recurring expression ' two companies '—the nearest equivalent for the German company (nominally 250 strong on war footing, which, however, for tactical purposes may be reckoned as 200 rifles). The four-company organisation of the German battalion also leaves its impress on the distribution of the outposts in the last few letters, though these are perhaps the most valuable in the book. . . ."

In this new edition (the seventh German and sixth English) I have retained whatever it was possible to retain of Captain Maxwell's translation and plan. The German *Felddienst Ordnung*, 1908, (G.F.S.R.) has been translated by the Imperial General Staff, War Office, under the title *The Field Service Regulations of the German Army*, 1908. This book should be consulted as well as the British Regulations, for every officer should know the tactics of the leading nations, if not even the organisation of their armies.

Roman numerals indicate Battalions, Squadrons, and Batteries; thus, "II/15th Hussars" stands for "second squadron of the 15th Hussars"; "E.F.S.R." stands for "English Field Service Regulations."

K. VON DONAT.

January, 1912.

AUTHOR'S PREFACE TO THE FOURTH EDITION

THE fact that a fourth edition is called for of a collection of tactical problems of such dimensions as the present, which demands of students both assiduous labour and no small amount of time, affords a proof that my method of assisting my brother officers of all ranks of the German army in their tactical studies has met with wide approval. There is, therefore, no occasion for me to introduce any important changes in the arrangement or matter of the work. In the present edition such alterations only have been made as have been necessitated by the appearance of several tactical works bearing on my subject, and of new regulations. I have also subdivided into several short exercises one of the problems, which, in the opinion of many of my readers, was too lengthy.

Readers of the book will be interested to know that it has met with notice in several foreign countries. A French translation, by Captain Richert, of the École supérieure de Guerre, under the title of *Thèmes tactiques gradués*, has been published by L. Baudoin (Librairie Militaire, Paris). A translation into Japanese (published by authority of the Japanese War Office), by Professor K. Shiba, of the Staff College in Tokio, is to appear next month at Tokio.

THE AUTHOR.

HILDESHEIM,
December, 1896.

PREFACE TO THE FIFTH EDITION

I HAVE not found it necessary to make any important changes in the fifth edition. On the contrary, I have been assured by those officers for whose benefit these "Letters" were originally written, viz., junior regimental officers, that they have above all things appreciated the simplicity of the problems offered for solution, the thorough way in which they are worked out, and the gradual progression from easy exercises to more advanced ones. I trust, therefore, that senior officers will make allowances for intentional repetitions and apparently superfluous explanations. Though the work as a whole is practically the same as in the earlier editions, I have had to considerably modify the Sixth Letter in accordance with recent changes in the Order of Field Service, the new Field Artillery Training, and recently published tactical works.

It gives me great pleasure to announce that the unparalleled success of the work, and notably the manner in which it has been received in foreign countries, has far exceeded my utmost expectations.

A translation into French by Commandant Richert has already gone into a second edition. A translation has been made into English, under the title of *Letters on Applied Tactics*, by R. Maxwell, late Captain 89th Regiment (London, Hugh Rees and Co.), and the work has been rendered in Roumanian by Lieut.-Col. A. Saegiu of the Headquarter Staff, under the title *Teme Tactice Pe Harta* (Bukarest, Thoma Basilescu).

A translation into Japanese has also appeared, with a characteristic preface, from which I will here quote one or two passages.

General Prince Akihito, Chief of the Headquarter Staff of the army during the war between China and Japan, and a recognised military authority in the Japanese army, places on the title-page of the translation the following profound maxim of Confucius—"Right and Left have a common origin" (spring from one source).

Viscount Soroku Kawakami, Head of the Imperial Japanese General Staff, whose death has been recently announced, writes in the preface to the translation of *Letters on Applied Tactics* as follows :—

"A Chinese sage has said that tactical refinements are too immaterial to admit of expression by word of mouth or writing, and that they can only be flashed, as by thought-transference, from one mind to another; not by dull printed characters. This, however, requires considerable modification. A teacher must, above all things, be clear and intelligible. He must give the pupil general principles and show him how to apply them. A student frequently is unable, after flogging his brains and applying to his instructor, to comprehend the situation, and the removal of such difficulties is the aim, not only of military science, but of all science.

"Captain Shioda and Professor Shiba have asked me to write a preface for their translation of *Letters on Applied Tactics*, written by an officer in the Prussian army.

"I have read the translation and am of opinion that the work outlines the principles of Tactics remarkably well, not merely from a theoretical point of view, but in accordance with practical requirements, and in strict conformity with the most up-to-date regulations on the subject. I consider the book indispensable to the coming generation of officers, as a perusal of it will not only prove instructive, and give them an insight into the niceties of the art of Tactics, but teach them to think for themselves—which is far more important.

"Of such individuals, however, who think it beneath them to study their profession—the less said the better!"

That this new edition may meet with the same favourable reception as its predecessors is the wish of

THE AUTHOR.

Engers on the Rhine,
September, 1900.

PREFACE TO THE SIXTH EDITION

SOME years having elapsed since the appearance of the fifth edition, it has become necessary to introduce numerous modifications in the present edition, though the general cast of the book remains unaltered. The comments on the various exercises have been somewhat abbreviated, and the work has been brought up to date with the latest tactical regulations. Though no change of importance has been made in the exercises, they have undergone a process of recasting in accordance with recent changes in Tactics, and new matter has been introduced bearing on Machine Guns and heavy Field Artillery, so far as they enter into the problems here dealt with.

In addition to the translations of the work into foreign languages mentioned in the preface to the fifth edition, a Greek translation has been published under the following title :—

Ποικίλα Τακτικὰ Θήματα vom Leutnant Ἄντων Φ Πραντοῦνα.

THE AUTHOR.

SAARLOUIS,
September, 1904.

AUTHOR'S PREFACE TO THE SEVENTH EDITION

SINCE the sixth edition was published most important regulations have been issued to the Army, foremost among which are the new *Field Service Regulations*, and the *Infantry* and *Field Artillery Drill Books*. The Service Regulations forming the basis of this book, a complete revise of the "Letters on Applied Tactics" was urgently needed, so as to make them harmonise with the many changes caused by these "Regulations." The whole arrangement of the book, leading from the more elementary to the more difficult problems, the simplicity of the problems, and the thoroughness in discussing them, have been preserved as much as possible; but the problems and discussions have been suited to the altered views in tactics, to the new war material, and to the new means of intercommunication. The alterations in the book are less numerous in the problems dealing with the various march orders than in those dealing with attack and defence and outposts orders.

I hope that the "Letters on Applied Tactics" in this new edition will continue to fulfil their object of facilitating *independent study* by junior officers in the art of leading troops.

THE AUTHOR.

THORN,
September, 1908.

CONTENTS

FIRST LETTER
INTRODUCTORY

	PAGE
Object of the Letters	1
Course of study recommended prior to working out the Exercises	4
The value of the Models of Orders	6
Advice on the subject of working out Tactical Problems	6
Requirements to be satisfied by Orders	8
First Exercise (*Orders for a March*)	13
Model for Orders for a March	15
Example of Orders for a March	16

SECOND LETTER
ORDERS FOR A MARCH

Points to be considered in selecting the road by which to move	18
How the nature of the country will affect the march	19
Distinction between disabling and destruction of a line of railway	20
The situation as regards the enemy	20
Time required for the execution of the March	22
Coming to a Decision	24
Regulating Command of Cavalry	25
Cyclist orderlies	27
The Distribution of Troops	28
The Order of March	29
The hour at which the Orders are issued	30
The information concerning the enemy	31
The intentions of the Commander	31
The time of starting	33
The reconnoitring that has to be performed during the March	34
The Advanced Guard and the Main Body	36
The Second Line Regimental Transport	38
Varying arrangements for Second Line Regimental Transport	38
Place of the Officer commanding the Detachment	40
The reasons for the measures adopted	41
The object of showing the troops on the map	42
Calculation of road space occupied	42
The Orders complete	44
Second Exercise (*Flank March*)	45

THIRD LETTER
FLANK MARCH

	PAGE
The object of a Flanking Detachment	47
Comments on the network of roads	47
How the enemy will probably advance	49
Is a Flank Guard necessary?	51
The Distribution of Troops for the Flank March	54
Best place for the Rifle Battalion in the Column of Route	54
Distribution of the Artillery	55
Artillery Brigade Ammunition Columns	57
Tabulating the Distribution of Troops, mode of issuing the Orders	57
Calculating the time for starting	58
Preparing for the start	59
The Orders for assembling the troops at the starting-point	60
The actual Orders for the March	61
Third Exercise (*Billets and Flank March*)	62

FOURTH LETTER
MARCH QUARTERS AND FLANK MARCH

Points to be considered prior to billeting	64
Comments on the network of roads	65
Reconnoitring and Screening by Cavalry	67
Is a Flank Guard necessary?	68
Our own intentions and the attitude of the Enemy	69
The Distribution of Troops for the Flank March	70
How the Outposts are to join the March Column	71
How to billet the troops for the night	72
The assembly before the March	75
Calculation to find the hour of starting	75
The Orders for readiness to march	78
The Orders for the March	79
Comparison between the first three Exercises in respect of various measures adopted for the protection of the Flanks of the line of March	79
Fourth Exercise (*Change of Direction of a March*)	80

FIFTH LETTER
CHANGE OF DIRECTION OF MARCH

Points to be considered prior to issuing the Orders	82
The network of roads	82
The issuing of Orders during the March	84
Decision arrived at by the Commanding Officer	88
The duty of the Advanced Guard	90
The Orders for changing the March direction	92

CONTENTS

	PAGE
Reasons for the Orders	93
Comparison between the first four Exercises as regards disposal of Second Line Regimental Transport	95
Fifth Exercise (*Protection of a Convoy*)	96

SIXTH LETTER
PROTECTION OF A CONVOY

Difficulty of protecting a Convoy	97
Arrangements for the protection of a Convoy	98
Choice of a road by which the Convoy will move	101
Calculation to find the hour of starting of the Convoy	102
Distribution of the Escort	103
The Orders for assembling the Force and the Orders for the March	105
Measures that would be adopted under different circumstances	106
Sixth Exercise (*Advanced-Guard Orders*)	108
Model for Advanced-Guard Orders	109

SEVENTH LETTER
ADVANCED-GUARD ORDERS

The measures to be adopted by the Officer commanding the Advanced Guard	111
Place of assembly of the Advanced Guard	112
The Distribution of Troops	114
Calculation to find the hour for the Advanced Guard to start	115
The Orders sent to the Outposts and to the Reinforcing Troops	118
The Advanced-Guard Orders proper	119
Remarks on the Advanced-Guard Orders	120
Seventh Exercise (*Orders for Retreat*)	122
Model of Orders for Retreat	123

EIGHTH LETTER
ORDERS FOR RETREAT

Choice of road for the Retreat	125
The Mission of the Detached Force	126
Decision as to the manner of conducting the Retreat	127
The Outposts in Retreat	129
Employment of the several arms in Retreat	130
The rôle of Infantry and Cavalry in a Retreat	130
The Artillery and Engineers in a Retreat	131
The Machine-Gun Detachment in a Retreat	132
Distribution of Troops for the Retreat	133
Points to be considered in framing the Orders for Retreat	134
Distance between the Main Body and the Rear Guard	135
Position of the G.O.C.	135
The Detachment Orders	137
Eighth Exercise (*Rear-Guard Orders*)	140

NINTH LETTER
REAR-GUARD ORDERS

	PAGE
Points to be considered by the Officer commanding the Rear Guard prior to issuing his Orders	141
Cavalry in a Retreat	142
Selection of a line on which to delay the Enemy	144
Points in which the Distribution of the Troops in a Rear Guard differs from that in an Advanced Guard	146
Relation of the Rear-Guard Orders to the Detachment Orders given in the previous Letter	148
The Rear-Guard Orders	151
Ninth Exercise (*Retreat of a Flanking Detachment*)	153

TENTH LETTER
RETREAT OF A FLANKING DETACHMENT

Comments on the road by which the Detachment has to march, with regard to the object to be attained by the Flanking Detachment	155
The task of the Flanking Detachment	156
Decision arrived at by the Officer commanding the Detachment	160
The Orders for being ready to march	161
Distribution of Troops for Retreat	162
The Orders for Retreat	165
Tenth Exercise (*Retreat after Defeat*)	166

ELEVENTH LETTER
RETREAT AFTER A DEFEAT

The various lines of Retreat	168
Points to be considered before issuing the Orders	169
Distribution of Troops in the Retreat	174
The Orders	175
Eleventh Exercise (*Orders for a March. Recapitulation*)	177

TWELFTH LETTER
ORDERS FOR A MARCH FORWARD. RECAPITULATORY

Object to be attained by the March	179
Points to be considered in connection with the Advance	179
The Detachment Orders	183
Twelfth Exercise (*Orders for Attack*)	184
Hints for an Order for attack on an enemy already deployed in a position prepared for defence	185

THIRTEENTH LETTER
ORDERS FOR ATTACK

	PAGE
Position of the various portions of the column on the March at the moment when the Orders are issued	186
The situation as regards the enemy	187
Flank attack or Frontal attack?	188
Main attack and Secondary attack	189
Points to be considered before deciding which Flank to attack	190
Frontage of a force in attack	193
Position of the G.O.C. when he issues his Orders for attack	194
One Order or separate Orders?	194
Termination of the March phase	197
Employment of Artillery in attack	198
Employment of Infantry in attack	200
Position of Readiness, unfolding and deploying	200
Distribution of frontages	202
The General Reserve and the Engineers	204
Employment of Cavalry in attack	205
The Dressing Station and supply of ammunition for Infantry and Artillery	207
Position of the G.O.C. during the action	208
Signalling and Infantry Telephone Detachments	209
The Detachment Orders	210
Distribution of the attacking force just before the assault	212
Thirteenth Exercise (*Orders for a March and Orders for Attack*)	215

FOURTEENTH LETTER
ORDERS FOR A MARCH. ENCOUNTER ACTION

Distribution of Troops	217
Place of the Machine-Gun Detachment	218
Detachment Orders for the March	220
Points to be considered before the attack	221
Encounter Action	222
The Advanced Guard in an encounter action	224
The Machine-Gun Detachment	224
Detachment Orders for Unfolding for the attack	225
Detachment Orders for the attack	228
Observations on the Detachment Orders	229
Fourteenth Exercise (*Orders for occupying a Defensive Position*)	230
Model of Orders for the occupation of a Defensive Position	231

FIFTEENTH LETTER
ORDERS FOR THE OCCUPATION OF A DEFENSIVE POSITION

Position of Readiness or Defensive Position?	232
Criticism of the position selected	234
The Machine-Gun Detachment in the Defence	234
The Artillery and the Infantry	234

CONTENTS

	PAGE
Obstacles in front of a position; their effect	235
The flanks and the ground in rear of the position	237
The frontage of the position	237
Division of the position into sections	238
Section Reserves and General Reserve	239
The Engineers	241
Arrangements with regard to supply of ammunition	241
Position of the Officer commanding	241
The Detachment Orders for occupying the position	242
Distribution of the defending force	244
Fifteenth Exercise (*A Retreat. Recapitulation*)	248

SIXTEENTH LETTER

RETREAT

Decision arrived at by the G.O.C.	250
Infantry Telephone	253
Shortened March Column	253
Orders for assembly	254
Orders for the Flank Guard	256
Sixteenth Exercise (*Retreat*)	257

SEVENTEENTH LETTER

RETREAT

Points to be considered in connection with the Retreat	258
The Detachment Orders for Retreat	259
Seventeenth Exercise (*Position of Readiness*)	259
Hints for issuing Orders for the occupation of a Position of Readiness	260

EIGHTEENTH LETTER

A POSITION OF READINESS

Selection of a Position	262
Advanced Posts and Advanced Positions	264
Position of Readiness	267
Occupation of the "Framework" of the position for defence	268
The Machine Guns	269
How Cavalry is employed when a position of readiness has to be occupied	269
Position of readiness of the Artillery	270
The preparations for defence	271
Dressing Station	271
Detachment Orders for taking up the position of readiness	272
Eighteenth Exercise (*Defensive Position*)	273

NINETEENTH LETTER

POSITION FOR DEFENCE

	PAGE
The Machine-Gun Detachment in Defence	274
The occupation of the position	275
The General Reserve	275
Rôle of Cavalry in the defence	276
The Dressing Station	276
Position of the Detachment Reserve S.A.A. carts	276
Detachment Order for occupying the position	277
Nineteenth Exercise (*Attack made by a Flanking Detachment*)	278

TWENTIETH LETTER

ATTACK MADE BY A FLANKING DETACHMENT

Forming an opinion on the various Reports received	280
Decision arrived at by the G.O.C.	282
Forming an opinion on the enemy's position	283
Action of the Artillery in the attack	286
Action of the Infantry in the attack	287
Action of the Cavalry in the attack	287
The Orders for attack	288
Twentieth Exercise (*Advanced-Guard Action*)	289

TWENTY-FIRST LETTER

ADVANCED-GUARD ACTION

(Encounter of two forces, both in motion)

What plans can be formed on receipt of the reports from the Cavalry	291
Comparing the value of various positions	292
Space and time calculation in connection with the two opposing forces	292
Employment of Cavalry in reconnoitring in front of a position of readiness	297
The dismounted service of Cavalry	297
The Orders for the Cavalry	299
Reports, Cyclists and Telephone Lines	300
Form and requirements of reports	301
Orders for taking up the position of readiness	304
Solving the Problem under different assumptions	306
Twenty-first Exercise (*Orders for an Advanced Guard to take up an outpost line and occupy billets*)	307
Model for Orders for an Advanced Guard to take up an outpost line	308

CONTENTS

TWENTY-SECOND LETTER
ORDERS FOR AN ADVANCED GUARD TO TAKE UP AN OUTPOST LINE AND OCCUPY BILLETS

	PAGE
Advanced-Guard Orders and Outpost Orders	310
Position of the Commander when he issues his Advanced-Guard Orders	311
Strength of the Outposts	312
Selection of the line of observation	312
Procedure in case the enemy attacks	313
Quartering of the Main Guard	313
The Cantonment Commandant and the officer for Cantonment duty	314
The Second Line Regimental Transport with Outposts	314
The Advanced-Guard Orders	315
How to show on the map the way in which the Main Guard is quartered, and division of the village into districts	316
The Inlying and Outlying Guards and their sentries	317
Alarm Posts and Alarm Rendezvous	318
Twenty-second Exercise (*Outpost Orders, and showing the outpost position on the map*)	319
Model for Outpost Orders for Mixed Outposts	319

TWENTY-THIRD LETTER
OUTPOST ORDERS

Position of the Commander of the Outpost when issuing his Orders	321
Task of the Outpost Cavalry	321
The Outpost Company	323
Depth of the Outpost Position	323
The Outpost Reserve	325
Supplies for Outposts	326
The Outpost Orders	327
The Commander of the Outposts rides round the Outposts	328
Action of the Outpost Cavalry by night	328
Maintenance of the touch by means of Cavalry	328
The Outpost after Orders	329
How to show the Outposts on the map	329
Positions of the Outpost Cavalry in detail	330
Detail of the positions of the Outpost Companies, and of the Reserve by day	331
Twenty-third Exercise (*Outpost Orders*)	333

TWENTY-FOURTH LETTER
OUTPOST ORDERS

The nature of the country to be observed by the Outposts	335
The Orders of the Commander of the Detachment	336
Lines of observation to be occupied by the Outpost Cavalry and Infantry respectively	337
Arrangements for the Outpost Squadron	338

CONTENTS

xxiii

	PAGE
Division of the line of observation into sections for the Outpost Companies	339
The Outpost Orders	340
Positions of the Outpost Cavalry in detail by day	342
Positions of the Outpost Companies in detail	342
Twenty-fourth Exercise (*Outposts during a pursuit of a defeated enemy*)	343

TWENTY-FIFTH LETTER
OUTPOSTS DURING A PURSUIT OF A DEFEATED ENEMY

Object to be attained by the Outposts	345
Points of difference between the present and previous Outposts	346
Regulating Command within the Outpost Line and of other protective bodies	347
Points to be considered for billeting the Advanced Guard	347
What is to be done in case of an alarm	348
Advanced-Guard Order for billeting and for placing Outposts	349
Showing on the map the measures for security	350
Twenty-fifth Exercise (*Attack on an Entrenched Position*)	352

TWENTY-SIXTH LETTER
ATTACK ON A FORTIFIED POSITION

Principles bearing on the defence of a river line	353
Surprise and Feint	356
Night attacks	358
Heavy Artillery of the Field Army	360
Light Field Howitzers	360
Attack in two columns	361
The Advanced-Guard Orders for attack	364

IN CONCLUSION

Self-set Exercises	368

MAPS
(IN POCKET AT END)

General Map of Metz and neighbourhood, scale $\frac{1}{100,000}$

Ars.-a.-d.-Mosel, scale $\frac{1}{25,000}$

Verny
Gravelotte } Scale $\frac{1}{25,000}$
Metz

LETTERS ON APPLIED TACTICS

FIRST LETTER

INTRODUCTORY

I HAVE often been asked by young officers preparing for the Staff College entrance examination, to set them tactical exercises and to look over their solutions. In doing so, my observations on the various solutions sent me had for the most part to be put in writing. Hence was evolved, in course of time, the following series of letters; my main object in compiling which was to assist young officers in preparing for examination who have no opportunity of obtaining advice from qualified senior officers in the garrisons where they happen to be quartered.

The study of the Regulations and tactical text-books forms only a part of the preparation necessary for an examination, for *essays* on applied tactics are not required, but *application* of theoretical principles in the solution of problems, which generally involve the framing of orders. The art of framing orders is not, however, a natural gift, nor can it be gained from any text-book, for the framing of orders involves the *solution of tactical problems*, to do which in a correct manner, without having passed through the Staff College course, is only granted to very few exceptional geniuses. My experience shows me that the *study necessary to prepare for an examination must begin with the simplest possible situations*, leading *gradually* to more difficult problems, hence must be *carefully and systematically* arranged, and *the elementary principles at the same time thoroughly investigated.*

In a great measure your studies must consist in your going over the same ground that was traversed by you in preparing for your examination for a commission in the Army, and refreshing your knowledge of subjects which you have forgotten. My object is to conduct you, by the following letters, to a point from which you may continue your studies *unaided*.

Having applied to attend the Staff College entrance examination, a General Staff officer of the Army Corps will set you a certain number of tactical problems a few weeks before your attendance. *It would be a fatal error on your part to assume that the working out of these few problems is sufficient preparation for that examination.* Anyone who in the most important of all the subjects, in Tactics, wishes to feel reasonably safe, must spend *very much more* labour on it. I therefore advise you to work out the problems given here *before* you solve those set by the General Staff officer and to look upon his problems as a kind of preliminary examination, as it were.

The problems solved in the following pages are *extremely simple*, for most problems that have been set in recent examinations are not difficult, and experience shows that *simple* problems are *the most instructive*, provided they are *thoroughly* worked out. They are undoubtedly more instructive than complicated situations, which too often lead to unnatural solutions.[1] The paragraph, moreover, of the syllabus dealing with the entrance examination distinctly says : " An exercise in applied tactics should be *as simple as possible* and of a kind obliging the candidate to come to a decision and give his reasons for it." In discussing the

---

[1] "Situations of war which depend on many and complicated hypotheses are much less useful for manœuvres than those which are very simple and can be grasped easily and unhesitatingly. *Even from the most simple situation of war may be evolved many problems requiring decisions.*"—*German Man. Regl. (M.O.),* 1908, para. 47.—*Trans.*

INTRODUCTORY

following exercises I have *designedly* gone into considerable detail, and I am prepared to admit that I might in many places have dealt more briefly with my subject; but my experience shows me that undue conciseness of style is apt to puzzle a beginner, or, at any rate, give him more trouble in comprehending what is said. *I have made a point of discussing at some length subjects which led to misunderstandings and mistakes* on the part of officers who have already worked through these exercises.

These letters are meant in the first instance for those who are preparing for entrance into the Staff College. They have, however, been of service to officers desirous of making themselves efficient for " Staff Tours," " Regimental Exercises," and similar tactical exercises, or who have merely wished to refresh their theoretical knowledge. They are intended merely to act as a *guide*, and to incite you to make your own way towards higher military culture; *they make no higher pretensions*.

The scene of operations in these exercises is the neighbourhood of Metz. This locality was the most convenient for me; and, besides this, the four maps on a scale of 1 : 25,000 are easy to read and admit of many changes in the scene of operations, which is desirable in the case of beginners. A study of this district will also assist you in following, at some future date, the history of the war of 1870, comprising, as it does, those blood-stained fields which, from August to October of that year, were the scene of so many glorious deeds of the German army.

Instead of making all the exercises dependent on one General Idea, I have purposely devised a different situation in the case of each exercise, with a view to affording you frequent opportunities of rapidly becoming familiar with a tactical situation.[1] I have in most cases considered Metz as an unfortified town, for the obvious reason that, *as the fortifications are not shown on the map, I have had to leave them wholly out of the calculations.*

[1] *German Man. Regl.*, 1908, para. 48.

Before commencing to work out the following exercises, I advise you to prepare yourself as follows: First, study the general principles governing the employment of the three arms in the field as given in the latest edition of the *Tactical Guide*[1] in use at the Royal War Schools, and it will be sufficient if you master the contents of that work. In the case of an arm to which you do not belong, you must get a clear idea of the formations employed for assembly, march, manœuvring, and attack. After this, I advise you to devote special attention to Part II of the *Infantry Training*,[2] which contains principles regulating the action of the other arms as well; and he who does not belong to the infantry should most carefully study the tactics of infantry, which is the paramount arm. Part IV of the *Field Artillery Training*[3] also requires special attention. In it many of the rules given in the *Infantry Training* are repeated word for word, giving you thus a clear insight into what the ruling ideas about tactics are now. This preparation, supplemented by a perusal of the musketry instructions and of the *Field Service Regulations*, will enable you also to answer the question in formal tactics,[4] as expressly required by the previously mentioned syllabus for the examination. The *Field Service Regulations* must, in particular, be thoroughly mastered, and you should finally work through the "Principles of Attack and Defence," the attack and defence of "Localities," and "minor warfare" in the *Tactical Guide*. I consider this preparation quite sufficient, and warn you against the study of advanced tactical and strategical works, which will only tend to confuse you. I shall often take occasion in the following letters to refer you to passages in the "Training Books" and in the

---

[1] "Leitfaden für den Unterricht in der Taktik auf den Königlichen Kriegs-Schulen."—1910.
[2] German official publication. Same as Part IV of *English Infantry Training.—Trans.*
[3] German official publication. Same as chap. VIII, *English Field Artillery Training.—Trans.*
[4] Formal tactics are the drill of each arm.—*Trans.*

comprehension of the map is not sufficient for tactical ends, least of all for the working out of exercises. You must be able to project on your mind an accurate and vivid picture of the country in question—imagine, for instance, that you stand upon some particular height, and ask : How will the surrounding country appear according to the map ? What localities are in sight ? What roads, and how many of them ? And, in particular, how far distant is the visible horizon ? Where do woods, rows of trees, heights, and villages conceal the country behind them ? etc. This naturally requires care and much practice. The more defective the map, the more care is necessary. You will be somewhat spoiled by the very excellent maps on which we shall work together, but at first that does not matter.

3. **Realise accurately your own position and that of the enemy.** Imagine, for instance, that you are in command, halting at the place mentioned in the data, surrounded by your staff. You must now see the troops in formation on the country before you, your own as well as the enemy's. *The more vivid your imagination, the better will be your tactical work.* Be then perfectly clear about what your orders are. This will form the basis of your appreciation. How must I act to carry out the superior's intention in harmony with the rest ?

4. **Read the proper sections in the " Tactical Guide,"** or in the *Field Service Regulations* and the Training Books. By these means you will, of course, work somewhat more slowly, but the time which you spend on this **will repay you. As a matter of principle verify every point on which you are in doubt by referring to the above works.**

5. **When dealing with movements of troops, calculate the time required to march** to the important points mentioned in the data, not only for your own troops, but for those of the enemy as well, by measuring the distances. *In the case of positions, measure their frontage and depth.*

6. **Consider the counter measures likely to be adopted by the enemy,** while, for instance, you are marching yourself,

or taking up a given position. In this matter the beginner is apt to commit the fault of considering the enemy as too inactive; thinking, for instance, that he remains at rest, while in accordance with the general situation he must be moving. Ask yourself: *What are probably the enemy's intentions? How strong is he according to the reports received?* Remember that *the enemy is most likely going to do that which you will like the least.*

7. **Arrive at a definite decision.** Are you to act offensively or defensively, are you to contain the enemy or to avoid him altogether? (*G. Inf. Tr.*, para. 273.)[1] As above indicated, great weight will be attached to this at the examination. No half-measures. For instance, when you have decided to act offensively, attack with the utmost energy with all your troops; if you wish to retreat, do not again come to a standstill after the first few miles without the weightiest reasons. Be **perfectly clear** in your own mind **what you intend to do,** and carry it out with determination (*G. Inf. Tr.*, paras. 272 and 273).[2]

8. **Consider the distribution of your troops** (*G.F.S.R.*, para. 45).[3] Write the details provisionally in your rough note-book and see whether you have disposed of all the troops allotted to you. The beginner may easily forget some portion or other; as the result of my own experiences, I especially advise caution in the distribution of the cavalry.

9. **Now, and not before, compose the actual orders.**[4] In doing this use my models until you are quite certain to forget nothing. Write the orders also in the note-book, and then test them carefully point by point to see if they answer the following requirements:—

(*a*) **Each set of orders must be logically arranged.** My

---

[1] *E.F.S.R.*, I, sect. 99, and *E. Inf. Tr.* sect. 121.—*Trans.*

[2] *E. Inf. Tr.*, sect. 121.—*Trans.*

[3] i.e. *German Field Service Regulations.* These have been translated by the Imperial General Staff and can be bought for 1s. at any bookseller's; the corresponding paragraphs of the *English Field Service Regulations* will be found in Part I, sects. 23 and 27.—*Trans.*

[4] In connection with the framing of orders, see *E.F.S.R.*, Part I, chap. II.

INTRODUCTORY

models ensure this at first; later on you will yourself have acquired the necessary practice. Never hesitate to deviate from my models when you have a reasonable ground for doing so. Be careful to break up the orders into numbered paragraphs, and combine into one paragraph passages relating to one subject, giving precedence to the most important matter (*G.F.S.R.*, para. 51). (*E.F.S.R.*, Part I, sect. 10 (3)).

(*b*) **Each order must be as short as possible.** Short sentences are easy to understand; a discursive mode of expression, a long-winded, elaborate style, is unmilitary. Test your orders then, to see whether you cannot strike out a superfluous word, or whether a simpler or more serviceable phrase does not occur to you—**grudge every word.** You will thus at first have much to alter in your note-book, but this is as it should be. There is an old saying that *an order which has not suffered many corrections in the notebook is worth nothing.* Experience shows that a wordy order is always abbreviated by those to whom it is dictated; this is, of course, quite inadmissible, for those with whom you deal are often not in a position to judge whether in altering the phrasing they do not also alter the sense. If, then, evil consequences are to be avoided, the orders must be so issued as to be written down *word for word.* Reasons for a given disposition have no place in the orders, for if the orders are well put together they justify themselves. Besides, as a rule a justification of the dispositions you have made is specially asked for, and then you have the desired opportunity of stating in conclusion the reasons for your measures. Instructions for the care of the sick and wounded, for supply and replenishing ammunition, are embodied in **operation orders** only **exceptionally**—namely, when it is a question of issuing the orders briefly and rapidly. **As a rule,** these matters are regulated by **"Special Orders,"** supplementing the operation order and being issued **only** to the troops directly concerned. **"Routine Orders"** regulate interior economy, returns, police measures, furnishing of orderlies, cyclists, etc. (*G.F.S.R.*, para. 52). (*E.F.S.R.*, paras. 10–14).

(c) **Each order must be perfectly clear and intelligible.** If misunderstandings arise, the chief fault lies with the issuer of the order. He ought to have framed it so as to leave no opening for mistakes. It is, in fact, true that the quality of the order is mirrored in its execution. *In practice* the orders must be suited to the individuality and visual range of the recipient, though in working out exercises *on paper* all subordinate officers are assumed to be perfect.[1] Still, it is as well to consider the question : What knowledge can the recipient have of the general circumstances ? Will he understand my point of view from the wording of the orders, and thus comprehend the orders in my sense ? You should therefore put yourself in the recipient's place, and consider what you yourself would do if you received an order in such and such terms, and had to execute it yourself. Clearness must not be sacrificed to brevity ; hence choose rather a longer phrase, if there is the possibility of being misunderstood by too short an expression. *Brevity must never lead to superficiality*. Terms which easily give rise to misunderstandings, since their significance depends on the actual point of view of the observer—as, for instance, *right, left, in front of, behind, on this side, on the other side* —are to be avoided. Replace them by points of the compass, thus—not " to the left of Verny," but " west of Verny." You should not refer to " the southern outlet " of a village unless there is only *one* such. In dealing with larger places, doubts easily arise ; it would be still more objectionable to choose intermediate points of the compass and speak, for instance, of the S.S.W. outlet ; it is better to say "at the outlet towards X," or " at the outlet of the pathway to X," if there are several such outlets. Roads must always be described by two places, and in a manner indicating at the same time the direction in which it is intended to march. You must not say, therefore, " the Metz road," but " the road from Verny to Metz," if the inten-

---

[1] Write your orders with the firm conviction that they will be read by at least one idiot, who will try and misunderstand them.—*Journal R.U.S.I.*, July, 1896.

frequently going deeply into different sorts of tactical situations and inwardly digesting them, you will create and sharpen the faculty of forming a *tactical judgment*.

You must not look askance on the notes and models for framing orders which I shall give you. You have, doubtless, often been warned against cast-iron rules in tactics—*and rightly so*. And yet it is necessary that you should study a number of models of orders in order to prevent your forgetting important details as a beginner. These notes and models of orders are therefore to be considered as aids to memory, nothing more. I shall show you that it is frequently justifiable and necessary to deviate from these models, and shall so frame the exercises as to counteract any tendency on your part to fall into a set form of framing orders. The form in which orders are cast is, generally speaking, of secondary importance, when once you have mastered the essence of the matter, though our customary forms are not founded on caprice, but on most practical considerations. The art of framing orders consists in giving orders suitable for the attainment of the object in view, whatever it may be, and this must frequently involve deviations from the ordinary form. In the issuing of orders in practice I am opposed to the use of set forms, which I look upon as merely the tools of the trade. **It is one thing, however, for a senior general officer, of long experience, both in war and peace, to issue orders; and quite another when a beginner has for the first time to be taught the use of all the implements usually employed in the art of framing orders.**

I recommend that all tactical exercises should be worked in the following manner—the processes being gone through in the order below stated :—

1. **Read the exercise through carefully several times** with the map in your hand. The longer the exercise the more care is necessary.

2. **Study carefully on the map the ground under consideration,** especially the network of roads. A general

INTRODUCTORY

Field Service Regulations, and you will soon perceive for yourself that it is easier to *understand* the principles detailed in the above works than to *apply them to the case in hand. Do not mind the trouble of looking up every single paragraph I refer you to of the " Training Books " and of the " Field Service Regulations."* If you bring yourself to applying always the paragraphs cited by me to the problem in hand, you will gain quite another insight into the *spirit* of these regulations than by simply reading them.

Accustom yourself also to work by the clock, noticing the time taken from the moment when you first set eyes on the data and the map to the last stroke of the pen, and *make a rule of finishing each exercise at a sitting*. With practice you will be able to work quicker and quicker. At the examination the time allowed you is short, but if you feel sure of being able to finish in the time you will do your work with greater confidence and better. In such case also you will be able to bestow more attention on composition, style, and handwriting. *An intrinsically good tactical exercise loses by a faulty style of expression or illegible handwriting, and is apt to be judged unfavourably.* An experienced examiner can tell by the style of your work whether you have had sufficient practice in solving tactical problems or not. It is not essential that your solutions should exactly tally with those which I give. Nothing is further from my intention than to give what are called " patent solutions." Many tactical measures are a matter of opinion. In practice the same object may be attained by very different means, and it frequently happens that there is no objection to a measure in itself, but that possibly some other measure may offer more advantages. In examinations, staff tours, etc., the examiner will thank you more for a judicious decision, *intelligently carried out* and *clearly reasoned*, than for a solution whose sole merit is that it exactly coincides with his own, for even a solution correct in itself may be spoilt in the working out. By comparing, however, your solutions and your views with mine, and by

tion is to march to Metz. Unusual expressions, *foreign words especially, are to be avoided.*

(*d*) **No order must be couched in uncertain terms**; for an ambiguous order is loosely carried out. All modifying expressions, such as " as far as possible," " as well as you can," " according to circumstances," must be rejected; for the commander must accept the whole responsibility and shift none of it on to the shoulders of his subordinates. Precise orders give a subordinate confidence in undertaking a dangerous task with determination, for they appeal to a subordinate's most necessary quality, namely, his military obedience. The more difficult the position, the clearer and more definite the order must be. It would be most reprehensible in the drawing up of an order, intentionally to choose an obscure, ill-defined, or ambiguous expression under which to hide one's own indecision.

(*e*) **The orders must not in their arrangement trespass on the province of the subordinate.** This is an error only too often committed both in the field and in the solution of exercises. Beware of it! Your orders must only contain what your subordinate cannot of himself arrange for the carrying out of your intentions (*G.F.S.R.*, para. 50).[1] The details of the execution must be left to him, especially if your orders are somewhat long in transmission, and if the circumstances which you have presupposed have quite changed on arrival of the orders. By means of your orders, place before your subordinate his *task*—the execution of it is *his* affair (*G. Inf. Tr.*, para. 275).[2] The higher the commander, the shorter and more general may his orders be. In practice you could always interfere later, were it absolutely necessary—as, for instance, if your subordinate were making a mistake which would absolutely jeopardise the attainment of the object you have in view (*G. Inf. Tr.*, para. 276).[3]

---

[1] *E.F.S.R.*, Part I, sects. 12 (2) and 13 (2).—*Trans.* [2] *Ibid.*

[3] Initiative of subordinates must not degenerate into arbitrary action. Initiative within proper limits is the source of great success in war.—*Trans.*

(*f*) **The orders must not arrange anything too far in advance**; in fact, not further than can be seen with certainty at the moment of framing the orders. Arrangements of this kind seldom get executed, for the commander cannot foresee the next counter-measures of the enemy, or various unexpected contingencies, and he would be only too often forced to recall his first orders, and then follow " order, counter-order, and disorder." Moreover, frequent changes in orders already issued weary the men, shake their confidence in their commander, and tend to make subordinates uncertain in their demeanour. Elaborate directions for various hypothetical cases are to be avoided in orders. It is possible that one of these cases may occur, but it is equally likely that something unforeseen may happen also, and then the subordinates cannot tell what is to be done. Nor will it do to say in the orders that one " expects this " or " presumes that." If, later on, the presumption is not verified, the subordinates see the error of their leader, and that shakes their confidence. On the other hand, it is nearly always of importance for the subordinates *to recognise clearly the general object aimed at by the order, i.e.* the intention of the commander, so *that they may themselves strive to attain it, should the general situation demand a procedure different from that originally directed.*

(*g*) **In each order, particulars of time and place must be so exactly given** that error is impossible. I refer you to the appropriate Instructions on this subject contained in *Field Service Regulations*, which I need not repeat here (*G.F.S.R.*, paras. 96–106).[1] In giving particulars of time, I recommend you to write the minutes very distinctly; in the case of hard names of places—as, for example, French or Polish names—you must compare them letter by letter with the map.

Further, simple as they are, it is only too easy, unwittingly, to transgress the rules as to Form laid down in the *Field Service Regulations*. Take pains from the beginning

[1] *E.F.S.R.*, Part I, sect. 9.—*Trans.*

INTRODUCTORY

in this, for an error committed out of mere carelessness is always very annoying. Besides, these precise rules in our *Field Service Regulations* are the *result of exhaustive experience in war*, and not mere superfluous trivialities. *If they are not accurately followed, mischievous misunderstandings may easily result.*

When you have carefully worked out the distribution of the troops, and the orders in your note-book, copy them both very clearly, the more clearly the better, and I here recommend you to *underline the opening words* of each paragraph to emphasise them. The examiner ought to be able, in a measure, to take in *at a glance* a well-expressed order. This distinctness has, in addition, no small value in actual service; all ranks see at once what they have to do, and *the orders are more easily and quickly understood*.

I will now give you a very easy exercise, namely, an order for a March or Advance.

FIRST EXERCISE.

(See maps Metz and Verny.)

A Red Division in an enemy's country bivouacs on the night 2/3.7.00 south of Liéhon (southern edge of Verny map). At 9.30 p.m. Colonel A., commanding 98th Infantry Regiment (I, II, III Battalions)[1] receives the following order: "In addition to your own regiment there will be placed under your command to-morrow the following troops:—

        Ist and IInd Squadrons 9th Dragoons.
        7th Field Battery R.A.
        1st Field Company R.E.
        Sect. A, 1st Field Ambulance.
        ⅓ Artillery Brigade Ammunition Column.

You will block to-morrow morning for some days the railway traffic at the station of Peltre. The division remains in its present

---

[1] In abbreviating the designations of troops, battalions of infantry and squadrons of cavalry are numbered in Roman figures; batteries of artillery, regiments of cavalry, etc., in Arabic figures.—*Trans.*

bivouac to-morrow. Hostile cavalry patrols have been seen this afternoon south of the unfortified town of Metz; and according to trustworthy reports, hostile infantry and artillery are bivouacked near Antilly (northern edge of Metz map).

Required:—

(1) The orders issued by Colonel A. on the evening of 2.7.00.
(2) Reasons for the measures adopted.
(3) The troops to be shown on the map an hour and a half after leaving the bivouac.[1]

---

[1] To save marking the map, a piece of tracing-paper may be laid over it; the troops being drawn on the tracing-paper, instead of on the map.—*Trans.*

MODEL FOR A MARCH ORDER.

(*G.F.S.R.*, para. 53.)[1]

OPERATION ORDER No......   *Copy No.*.......

BY

COLONEL C., COMMANDING DETACHED FORCE.

Reference: *House.*
Map used.   *Place.*
    Date.

1. *Advanced Guard:*[2] O.C.
   Infantry.
   Machine-Gun Detachment.
   Cavalry.
   Artillery.
   Engineers.
   Field Ambulance (rarely).

2. *Main Body* (in order given): O.C.
   Cavalry (orderlies or troops).
   Infantry.
   Artillery.
   Infantry.
   Machine-Gun Detachment.
   Engineers.[3]
   Field Ambulance.[3]
   Artillery Brigade Ammunition Columns.

3. *Right (Left) Flank Guard:* O.C.
   Same as Advanced Guard.

1. Information as to *the enemy* and *our other forces.*
2. *Intention of O.C. Detachment.*
   (In the most general terms.)
   Distribution in margin.
3. *Order for the Advanced Guard.*
   (Time of starting;[4] place whence it will start;[4] road by which it will march; reconnoitring to be performed; communication to be maintained with parallel columns,[4] etc.; any special duties.)
4. *Order for the Main Body.*
   (Either the distance to be preserved between it and the advanced guard,[4] or place and hour of starting.)
5. *Order for the Flank Guard.*
   (As No. 3, but with special mention, as a rule, of reconnoitring duties. Sometimes the point at which the flank guard is to be detached is mentioned.)
6. *Orders for the Outposts.*
   (Instructions as to how they are to join the column of route.)

[1] *E.F.S.R.*, Part I, sect. 12 (4).—*Trans.*
[2] Should be seniority of arms and units.—*E.F.S.R.*, Part I, sect. 12 (8).
[3] *E.F.S.R.*, Part I, sect. 27 (2).—*Trans.*
[4] *Ibid.*, sects. 67 (2) (3) and 68 (1) are at variance with this.—*Trans.*

	7. *Order for the 2nd Line Transport*[1] *and Supply Columns.*
	(Distance to be preserved between it and the main body, or special arrangements.)
	8. *Position of the officer commanding:—* at the beginning of the march.[2]
Manner of communicating the orders to the troops (*G.F.S.R.*, para. 55).[3]	C., *Colonel.*
Hour of issue.	

NOTE.—If the cavalry is not attached to the advanced guard, but is constituted "Independent Cavalry," it will form No. 1 in the Distribution of Troops (with an officer detailed to command it). The third paragraph in the actual order would then be *Order for the Independent Cavalry* (time of starting; place whence it will start; road by which it will march; reconnoitring to be performed; communication to be maintained with parallel columns, etc.). Even so, however, there must always be sufficient protective cavalry attached to the advanced guard to provide for its own immediate security on the march.

If no outposts are mentioned in the problem, No. 6 will be omitted.

EXAMPLE OF A MARCH ORDER.

Copy No. 1.

OPERATION ORDER No. 1.
BY
COLONEL A., COMMANDING DETACHED FORCE.

Reference:	*Bivouac North of Z.*
$\frac{1}{100.000}$ Ordn.	11.5.00.
1. *Advanced Guard:* Lt.-Col. B. I/Battalion 1st Infantry Regiment. Machine-Gun Detachment.	1. *The enemy's* infantry has been seen near X and Y, and his cavalry patrols north of W. *Our 3rd Division* will march to-morrow from M on N.

---

[1] *E.F.S.R.*, Part I, sect. 12 (7) footnote.—*Trans.*
[2] *Ibid.*, sect. 12 (4) last but one paragraph.—*Trans.*
[3] *Ibid.*, sects. 9 (1) xi and 12 (4) last paragraph.—*Trans.*

INTRODUCTORY

Ist (less 1 troop), IInd, IIIrd Squadrons 1st Dragoons.
1st F.C. R.E.

2. *Main Body* (in order given): Lt.-Col. C.
1 Troop 1st Squadron 1st Dragoons.
II/Battalion 1st Infantry Regiment.
1st Field Battery R.A.
III/Battalion 1st Infantry Regiment.
Sect. A, 2nd Field Ambulance.
Field Artillery Brigade Ammunition Col.

3. *Right Flank Guard:* Major F.
1st Company 1st Rifles.
IVth Squadron 1st Dragoons.

Dictated to representatives of (or verbally to the assembled)
O.C. Cavalry
  ,, Artillery
  ,, Engineers
  ,, Infantry
  ,, Rifles
  ,, Field Ambulance
at 11.15 p.m.

2. *The Detachment* will march to-morrow on O. (distributed as per margin).

3. *The Advanced Guard* will start at 6.15 a.m., and move by the main road through P on O, reconnoitring towards D, E, and F, and keeping up communication with the 3rd Division.

4. *The Main Body* will follow the advanced guard with half a mile distance.

5. *The Right Flank Guard* will start at 5.45 a.m., and move, viâ S, to T, reconnoitring through V and W in the direction of U.

6. *The Outposts* will stand fast until the vanguard has passed through the outpost line.

7. *The 2nd Line Transport* will follow the main body at 1¼ mile distance as far as G, where it will remain till further orders.

8. *Reports* will reach me (or, my position will be) at the head of the main guard.

A.,
Colonel.

N.B.—All words printed in italics in the above orders should be underlined by you in writing such orders

SECOND LETTER

ORDERS FOR A MARCH

ACCORDING to my experience, you will have required some three or four hours to work out this exercise if you did as I advised; this is, however, not too long. Quicker work will come with practice.

If a detachment has to execute works within striking distance of the enemy, and at the same time protect the working party, as in the present case of interrupting the traffic on a railway, it should take up a position at such a distance between the scene of operations and the enemy as to protect the working party from the enemy's fire. The operations may thus be carried on for some time, or even possibly completed, *while fighting is going on in front*. Protection must be secured not only from infantry fire, but especially from artillery. *This principle will regulate the distance of the covering detachment from the scene of operations.* It is very advantageous if the latter is covered from view and fire by a line of heights sufficiently to the front, as in the present case. In such a case the greater part of the detachment occupies these heights; a smaller part—in the present example a field company of Engineers, supported, if necessary, by some infantry—undertakes the duty of interrupting the traffic. The covering heights stretch from Mercy-by-Metz to Basse Bévoye; these heights, then, are the *goal of the detachment*.

The *best route thither* is the high road by Haute Grève. The more westerly road by Chérisey, Orny, Chesny is longer because of its frequent windings, and is also worse, especially in the Hospital Wald. While in bivouac at Liéhon, one cannot in the least tell the nature of the section between Orny and Chesny. In practice one can sometimes resolve such doubts by reconnoitring, but in working out orders with the map it is better to remain prudently on a main road, even if it be somewhat longer. Slight détours matter little, for the troops march with more comfort, and therefore with more speed, and are less tired. Even the advantage of approaching Peltre by the less exposed route through the Hospital Wald should not tempt you to enter on this doubtful road. Again, you could advance by the main road past Haute Grève and then branch off to Peltre viâ Chesny. If you only had in view a march to the station of Peltre, this way is about as long as the high road and almost equally good. Since, however, the heights to the north of Peltre are the objective of the greater part of the detachment, there is no reason to choose this last-named way rather than the preferable main road; but there is no reason why you should not order the working party to branch off viâ Chesny.

For the purpose of the march you must consider not only the road itself, but the surrounding country. First, you have on your left flank[1] the Hospital Wald, then later, on your right flank, the wooded patches east of Mécleuves, the great wood of Champel, as well as the woods west of Ars-Laquenexy. The rest of the country on both sides of the route is fairly open to view. As soon as your patrols have penetrated to the north of Haute Grève, and in especial somewhat later to the elevation marked 270.8 south-east of Pierrejeux (*G.F.S.R.*, para. 103 (3)), they can survey the country before them to some distance. The distant line of heights to the north between Mercy-by-Metz and Basse Bévoye bounds their view. On reaching these heights, however, a wide prospect is opened as far as Metz and the heights of Belle-Croix. Now, what can the enemy see? You can scarcely prevent his patrols reaching the

---

[1] Whether advancing or retiring, the left or right are always as you face the enemy.—*Trans.*

heights of Mercy-by-Metz. Thence they can observe your advance as soon as you descend the elevation marked 270.8 south-east of Pierrejeux, and also later on when you reappear on the higher parts of the main road.

Moreover, the enemy will try to push his patrols as near as possible to your column on both flanks, under cover of the woods; you must keep these circumstances before your mind in framing orders for reconnoitring and screening.

Your own position is much simplified by the fact that the troops are collected in one bivouac; therefore you have only to march them off. The exercise says nothing about the rest of your troops (and nothing about outposts); so you need not trouble yourself about these; still less need you inquire why you have to interrupt the railway at Peltre, whereas it might equally effectively—or even more effectively—be done elsewhere. Take the exercise as it is; do not import difficulties—*beginners often do so.* If the exercise says distinctly, as in this case, that the railway must be interrupted at the Peltre Station, you must take your measures accordingly.

In the exercise I have intentionally used the word "block" (disable) with regard to the railway, adding " for a few days." Thereby I desired to point out to you that there is a difference between complete " destruction " of the line and " temporary interruption " of the traffic (*G.F.S.R.*, paras. 549 and 550).

In the case of a " destruction," which generally requires many hours to accomplish, the covering body must keep the enemy away from the working party for a much longer time than in the case of a simple "interruption." If a " destruction " is interfered with by the approach of the enemy, an attempt should be made to carry out one or more " interruptions." An interruption " *for some days* " demands somewhat extensive works, and this explains why, in the present instance, a detachment of this strength is employed for this purpose.

We know that the enemy on the afternoon of the 2nd

July has bivouacked with infantry and artillery near Antilly; it is probable, therefore, that he will remain there for the night. The cavalry which he has sent in advance, viâ Metz, will either return to the main bivouac at Antilly or encamp nearer to Metz. In any case, the information about the enemy is rather indefinite. You know nothing of his strength, and so must be prepared for superior numbers. The statement "with artillery" indicates that at least two or three battalions are bivouacking at Antilly, for artillery seldom accompanies smaller bodies of infantry than this. The enemy's immediate destination is, apparently, the unfortified town of Metz, for he is not likely to pass by so great a town with its many resources. This is shown further by the fact of his having sent cavalry in advance to Metz. One can then assume with some certainty that on the morning of the 3rd July the enemy will be **en route from Antilly to Metz.** We cannot tell when he receives news of the advance of our detachment, and whether this will cause him to leave his former route and march direct against us, leaving Metz to the west, but you must reckon with the possibility. The enemy's cavalry, being in its own country, may have been informed by the country-folk that there are troops south of the town, or it may itself have noticed some portion of your cavalry. In either case it will push its reconnoitring next morning further towards the south, and then the opposing cavalries will soon come into contact. If our cavalry proves superior, we *may* hope to conceal from the enemy the advance of our detachments: this is uncertain, however, and *such uncertainty is the rule in war*. That is just the difficulty of commandership, that we but seldom know, with any certainty, the movements, strength, and intentions of the enemy, and must fall back on *conjectures* founded on the often scanty information received. Learn the art of always dexterously sketching out for yourself, from the various and more or less trustworthy sources of information available, a mental picture of the whole situation, and so much the better will your arrangements be. The reports received from your cavalry will, in practice, first establish whether your conjectures were accurate—therefore the great importance of well pushing forward cavalry reconnaissance. Bear in mind, moreover, that troops " in a friendly country " are, as a rule, better provided with information than are troops " in an enemy's country."

You can now calculate by what hour the detachment can reach the heights of Mercy-by-Metz, and when the hostile infantry can do the same. To do this you must first be clear on what the rates of marching are.

A small column, composed entirely of infantry, may under favourable circumstances, for short distances, march at the rate of 4 miles per hour.[1] Cavalry employed on reconnoitring duty, in which it for the most part alternately walks and trots, moves on an average 5 miles per hour. At the same time it will, as a rule, be able to advance more rapidly the first few miles, enjoying as it does greater security, *until it has established touch with the enemy*. Thereafter it has to take into consideration the necessity of advancing under cover, and must make longer halts for the important duty of obtaining a good view. This causes the cessation of continuous forward movement. I specially direct your attention to this, because beginners are prone to overestimate the pace at which reconnoitring cavalry moves.

A larger column—and yours is one—marching for long distances under favourable conditions and including halts, you will find, marches at the average rate of $2\frac{1}{2}$ miles per hour (*G.F.S.R.*, para. 353). To determine your rate of marching you must therefore ask yourself the following questions :—

1. Am I dealing here with a *large* column ?
2. Is the distance *long* ?

---

[1] The calculations in what follows will be worked out in conformity with British Regulations, see *E.F.S.R.*, Part I, sect. 26, and not as in the original. —*Trans,*

3. Have I to allow for *halts*, or is the distance too short to allow for more than the ordinary brief halt, included in the ordinary rate, shortly after starting?
4. Are the *other* conditions favourable?

The first question can be answered in the affirmative, but not so the second, for I measure the distance on the map from the bivouac south of Liéhon to the heights of Mercy-by-Metz as being roughly 7½ miles. That is a *short* distance; and this settles at the same time the third question, whether you have to allow for more than the ordinary halts. It is *unnecessary* in this case, and moreover highly desirable that it should be so, for we wish to reach the heights, if possible, *before* the enemy. The other conditions can be looked upon as being favourable. You have to deal here therefore with an easy short march *without* any long halts, enabling you to assume a rate of 3 miles per hour.

We must expect a slower rate of march than 2½ miles per hour when the attendant circumstances are unfavourable, such as long, continuous stretches of uphill road, bad state of roads, unfavourable weather (heat, wind, slippery ice), exhaustion of the troops after a forced march, or when performing a night march, etc. There is much more than can be calculated, in consequence of which no hard-and-fast rules can hold good, and we must be guided by the circumstances in each individual case. According to Bronsart von Schellendorff (*Duties of the General Staff*), when the thermometer stands at 77° Fahr., we must allow about 5 minutes extra time in marching each mile; in greater heat correspondingly more. Night marches last about half as long again as day marches of equal length. Sandy or slippery ground causes an extra delay of 3 to 5 minutes on each mile marched, heavy rain or snow 2 to 3 minutes, a strong head wind 6 to 9 minutes. In hilly country, when it is a case of a road ascending a valley rather steeply, add 5 to 10 minutes, according to the gradient, on each mile covered.

SECOND LETTER

When measuring the distances on the map, I advise you to leave a good margin, taking particularly into due consideration the curves in the road. Should you overestimate the distance by $\frac{1}{2}$ mile, this corresponds to 10 minutes in time. To be 10 minutes late may be awkward; but, on the other hand, to arrive 10 minutes before the time makes no great odds. I now take 500 m. off the scale of the map with a pair of compasses, measuring the distance liberally.

This done, it is seen that the head of the infantry column could reach the end of its march in $7\frac{1}{2}$ miles $\div 3 = 2$ hours 30 minutes. The enemy has from Antilly to the heights of Mercy-by-Metz 10 miles $\div 3 =$ roughly $3\frac{1}{4}$ hours. *Under the supposition that both parties march off at the same time without making any long halt,* Colonel A. could thus reach the goal of the march 45 minutes earlier than the enemy.

To make arrangements at this stage as to how the detachment is to occupy the heights of Mercy-by-Metz, or for a portion of it to diverge just above Chesny, in the direction of Peltre, would be to fall into the mistake of "making arrangements too long beforehand." *Let the troops begin the march first; the rest comes at a later stage, and is thus the subject of later and fresh orders.* We do not yet know whether we shall reach the heights without a fight, or whether we shall get as far as the mouth of the branch road to Chesny.

It is unnecessary to detach a flank guard, as at the outset we have only cavalry opposing us. Not till a later stage in the proceedings can the enemy's infantry become dangerous, so that cavalry alone is sufficient for information and protection on both flanks. The detachment therefore marches on *one* road, in accordance with the principle that one should concentrate one's strength as far as possible in *one* column, in the case of detachments like this, and only break them up when absolutely necessary.

As the outcome of the above considerations we arrive at

the following **decision**: The detachment to march as early as possible, so as to attain the objective before the enemy; and in *one* column, by the **high road** to the heights of Mercy-by-Metz. The cavalry to trot on ahead.

With regard to the latter, note that on account of the conformation of the country, it is desirable to dislodge the enemy's cavalry as soon as possible from the heights of Mercy-by-Metz. Perhaps also our cavalry, by fighting dismounted, can hold the heights until their own infantry come up (*G.F.S.R.*, para. 195, and *G. Cav. Tr.*, para. 363).[1] As to whether the above tasks can be successfully carried out or not is an open question; but in any case the cavalry must hurry on far ahead. For the proper performance of its duty cavalry requires great freedom, but nevertheless it must not wholly lose touch with the infantry in rear, for it must be sufficiently at hand at any possible development of the fight. This being premised, you now have the choice either of placing the bulk of your cavalry directly under the commanding officer of the detachment, and then pushing it forward far beyond the advanced guard, or of assigning it to the advanced guard as "advanced guard cavalry" (*G.F.S.R.*, para. 165). In the present problem sound reasons may be advanced for either course.

For placing the cavalry directly under the commander of the whole detachment the following is to be said: The cavalry must, for the reasons I have above detailed, gain a footing on the heights of Mercy-by-Metz as soon as possible. To do this the cavalry needs a certain freedom in its movements, which it cannot possess if it is attached to the advanced guard. Besides, every advanced guard commander is naturally prone to use cavalry solely in providing for the security of the march; whereas the commander of the whole force, owing to the broader view taken by him, will accord it far greater freedom. The latter also is in a better position to judge when the occasion requires his intervention to prevent the cavalry getting out of hand.

---

[1] *E.F.S.R.*, Part I, sect. 3 (1), and *E. Cav. Tr.*, sect. 141, p. 187.

I also place the cavalry under the commander of the whole, when its mission lies outside the sphere of the advanced guard, or temporarily, at all events, lies far in advance of it.

For "Advanced Guard Cavalry" there speaks the consideration that, in the present case, our cavalry will in all probability very soon encounter that of the enemy; and, if it then finds itself unable to make headway without assistance, the advanced guard will have to reinforce it, in which case it were better that both bodies should, from the outset, be under the command of one and the same person. In other words, the assumed proximity of a strong hostile cavalry might constitute an argument for employing the cavalry in the advanced guard. Moreover, its numerical weakness might be adduced as an important reason for attaching the cavalry to the advanced guard. When placed under the commander of the detachment, there would remain only about a squadron and a half for independent cavalry, as it would first have to furnish one troop for the advanced guard, one troop for the main body, and men for orderlies. So weak a force of cavalry as this would be wanting in independence, being deficient in the necessary fighting strength.

For guidance, I give you the following points to consider:—

> *A detachment should employ its cavalry generally as advanced guard cavalry, unless it is exceptionally strong in that arm.* By "exceptionally strong" I mean three or more squadrons, when one squadron or less would be sufficient to provide for the safety of the march. It is a downright mistake to send forward an independent cavalry unless there is sufficient of that arm, in addition, to ensure the safety of the march.
>
> Cavalry is placed under the commander of the detachment when there is some independent task for the cavalry outside the sphere of the advanced guard,

be it with reference to place or time. There is always a danger, however, that the cavalry may misuse its independence, get beyond control, and not be at hand when required. If the independent cavalry of a detachment is less than two squadrons, it is a rare and exceptional case, requiring specially careful justification.

In connection with the distribution of the cavalry, bear in mind that, considering the paucity of that arm, and the difficulty of the task before them, as few men as possible should be withdrawn from the squadrons. We are rather spoiled by having such a great amount of cavalry in peace time during our manœuvres, the detachments in most cases having attached to them more than twice the number of cavalry they would have in war. On active service the few squadrons attached to infantry must be spared in every possible way, if they are to continue fully active from day to day for weeks or months.

As we have a first-class road to march on, free use may be made of cyclists, thus sparing the cavalry and using it only for carrying messages across country, which it would be awkward for cyclists to do, as they are confined to roads (*G.F.S.R.*, paras. 81 and 564).[1] Four cyclists attached to the cavalry will suffice.

The officer commanding the detachment must be satisfied with a N.C.O. and three to four men in attendance on him, and in addition two cyclists; but it is not necessary to mention this in the operation order.

A lieutenant of cavalry or army service corps is attached to the staff of each regiment on active service to command and superintend the second line regimental transport (*G.F.S.R.*, para. 443).[2] The officer commanding the advanced guard takes the few orderlies he may require from the cavalry allotted to the advanced guard, for *there must*

---

[1] *E.F.S.R.*, Part I, sects. 3 (3), 20 (1), 88 (3), 157 (6) refer to cyclists generally.—*Trans.*
[2] *Ibid.*, sect. 28.—*Trans.*

always be some cavalry with the advanced guard (*G.F.S.R.*, para. 166).[1]

It will seem inconsistent with the above if I advise to allot to the main body a whole troop, which would then march at its head, so that the commander of the detachment may have in hand some cavalry of which he can dispose in case of need. To have a troop of cavalry at the head of the main body is especially desirable in flank marches; or when traversing an enclosed country in which, in spite of reconnaissance to the front, hostile bodies might suddenly appear and endanger the main body; or, lastly, when it is probable that the main body will have to move and engage the enemy in another direction than the advanced guard—a case which sometimes happens—in which event a paucity of cavalry would be distinctly prejudicial (*G.F.S.R.*, para. 166).

The advanced guard takes from $\frac{1}{3}$ to $\frac{1}{8}$ of the infantry,[2] though tactical units must never be broken up to attain this exact proportion. In this case a battalion is suitable. The rest of the infantry is with the main body. Of artillery there is only a battery present, which will naturally accompany the main body; and, in consideration of its safety, cannot be at the head of it, but should have a battalion in front of it. In compliance with the regulations given in the *Artillery Training*, a portion of the light ammunition column has been allotted to the detachment.[3] The field company of engineers is, as a rule, with the advanced guard (*G.F.S.R.*, para. 170).[4] If all goes on well, it can, by being so placed, turn off towards Peltre, and begin its work there earlier than it could if it were in the main body. It is an exception when engineers remain with the main body of a small mixed force. The engineers of the advanced guard

---

[1] *E.F.S.R.*, Part I, sect. 66 (3) and (4).—*Trans.*
[2] *Ibid.*, (2).—*Trans.*
[3] *G. Art. Tr.*, para. 450; *E.F.A. Tr.*, chap. VII., sect. 78; and *E.F.S.R.*, Part I, sect. 160.—*Trans.*
[4] *E.F.S.R.*, Part I, sect. 66 (3) and (4).—*Trans.*

ORDERS FOR A MARCH

march either with the vanguard or with the main guard (*G.F.S.R.*, para. 171).[1]

The bearer division, as a rule, remains with the main body, marching at the tail of it. There is seldom more than one bearer division with a small mixed force; and it is not required until the fighting has become severe at some particular spot, thereby entailing many casualties. Until this happens the wounded are sufficiently attended to by the surgeons and stretcher-bearers accompanying the troops (*G.F.S.R.*, paras. 478, 481, 486, and 488).[2]

The officer commanding the advanced guard decides the order of march of his own command. In framing orders, all you have to do is to assign to him his troops, mentioning them by arms in the conventional order (*G.F.S.R.*, paras. 55, 364).[3]

The officer commanding the whole force himself decides, as a rule, the order of march of the main body, drawing attention to the paragraph in the orders referring to the main body under the heading of " Distribution of Troops " by the words " Main body (in order of march)." The commander of the main body is responsible for the proper time of starting of each unit; he superintends the march, maintains connection with the advanced guard and any flank guard, and arranges for any necessary protection of the flanks.

The distribution of troops having now been decided, I give it you in the alternative, according as you have decided on " independent cavalry " or not.

---

[1] *E.F.S.R.*, Part I, sect. 66 (4).
[2] *Ibid.*, page 44 note; Part II, chap. x.
[3] *Ibid.*, sect. 12 (8).—*Trans.*

SECOND LETTER

DISTRIBUTION OF TROOPS.

1. *Advanced Guard:*[1]
   Lt.-Col. B.
   I/Battalion 98th Inf. Rgt.
   1st Sqd. (less 1 troop) and IInd Sqd. 9th Dragoons.
   16th Field Co. R.E.

2. *Main Body* (in order of march): Lt.-Col. C.
   I Troop 1st Sqd. 9th Dragoons
   II/Battalion 98th Inf. Rgt.
   7th Field Battery R.A.
   III/Battalion 98th Inf. Rgt.
   Sect. A, Field Ambul.
   ⅓ Art. Brgde. Ammunition Col.

or

1. *Cavalry:* Major C.
   Ist Sqd. 9th Dragoons (less 2 troops).
   IInd Sqd. 9th Dragoons.

2. *Advanced Guard:*[1] Lt.-Col. B.
   I/Battalion 98th Inf. Rgt.
   I Troop 1st Sqd. 9th Dragoons.
   16th Field Co. R.E.

3. *Main Body* (in order of march): Lt.-Col. C.
   I Troop 1st Sqd. 9th Dragoons.
   II/Battalion 98th Inf. Rgt.
   7th Field Battery R.A.
   III/Battalion 98th Inf. Rgt.
   Sect. A, Field Ambul.
   ⅓ Art. Brgde. Ammunition Col.

In conclusion, you should test *whether every unit belonging to the force has been disposed of*. With regard to the abbreviations of the designation of troops, battalions and squadrons of cavalry should be numbered in Roman figures.[2]

"Place, Date, Hour of Issue" can now be given, "Bivouac south of **LIÉHON**, 2.7.00, 10 p.m."[3] The hour of issue is that when the hour is completed and issued, not that when you *begin* writing it. Since it was 9.30 p.m. when the officer commanding received the order on which this problem is based, he could scarcely issue his own orders before 10 p.m. He must first attentively read the order

---

[1] *E.F.S.R.*, Part I, sect. 12 (8).—*Trans.*

[2] *G.F.S.R.*, para. 105. For abbreviations, see *F. S. Pocket Book*, 1908, pp. 6 to 8.—*Trans.*

[3] Different in *E.F.S.R.*, Part I, sect. 12 (4) last sentence and sect. 9 (1) (xi).

received, and study the map before drawing up the orders for his detachment. Meanwhile the officers to receive the orders for the several units are being assembled, and not till all are present can the order be dictated. All this requires time—which you must take into account.

No. 1 reads: "Hostile infantry and artillery are bivouacked near **ANTILLY**. Hostile cavalry patrols are reported south of **METZ**. Our division remains in its present bivouac to-morrow."

Thus the information concerning the enemy is repeated almost word for word as in the original orders received from headquarters. You must not, however, always do this. The point is to give your subordinate officers what is essential for them to know in order to be able to execute their individual tasks in accordance with your intentions. Anything more is superfluous; unimportant details must be omitted. Very *unfavourable* news, the gravity of which might be magnified by subordinates, should, whenever practicable, be either wholly omitted or, at any rate, referred to in very circumspect terms. Good news, on the contrary, should be given special prominence. Never lose sight of the fact that your orders pass through many hands, and that despondent men, who can unfavourably influence the "moral" of the troops, are everywhere to be found. The troops of the detachment must be told by the order that our division remains in its bivouac to-morrow.

No. 2. "The Detachment will march to-morrow morning on **MERCY-BY-METZ**."

You observe how little concerning the enterprise you have in hand need be mentioned to subordinates; enough, however, to ensure that each in his place (even if something unforeseen occurs) shall, without further prompting, adopt the line of action which will be correct, and suitable to the general situation; you not premising too much as to your intentions. If it thereafter proves impossible to carry out the enterprise in hand (supposing, for example, Peltre is found to be already occupied by an enemy in superior force), your subordinates will not notice the failure of the undertaking, and you prevent manifold rumours getting about. It is only too easy to shake the confidence of your troops in you as leader by issuing indiscreet orders, and the harm, once done, is with difficulty made good; in addition to which it nearly always perceptibly impairs their fighting efficiency. Besides, *your plans should be kept as secret as possible.* First reach the heights of Mercy-by-Metz, if you can; it is then time enough for your subordinates to know what is really intended. The commanding officer is, however, justified in giving more detailed information concerning his intentions, etc., to some of his subordinates, *e.g.* the senior field-officer, and especially to the officer commanding the cavalry. The latter will thereby know to what points to call special attention in his reports. Again, suppose that, in the case before us, the officer commanding the cavalry sees that it is doubtful whether it will be possible to carry out the blocking of the railway as planned. If he had been taken into the confidence of the commanding officer he would, at all events, try to effect a minor interruption of the line with the means at his disposal—possibly in the neighbourhood of Peltre—possibly somewhere else.

It is further advisable that the officer commanding the detachment should send for the officer in command of the engineers overnight, and discuss with him the task before him. The latter will thus have the opportunity of making some preparations, even possibly during the night.

As to a possible retreat, no orders are issued, although the commanding officer will consider what he intends to do if he meets unexpectedly an enemy in greatly superior force. The troops must think only of " Forwards "; and, certainly not at the beginning of the affair, of " Retreat." Moreover, it is wholly unnecessary at this stage to mention any arrangements for a retreat, because one generally retreats (if at all) to that place from which one set out, which in this case is the bivouac of our division. Often also the halting-place of the second line regimental transport is an indication of whereto retreat is eventually intended.

No. 3. You will now have to settle the hour when the detachment is to start from the bivouac, which, as you know, will be determined by the consideration that you have to reach the heights north of Peltre *as soon as possible*. The desirability of reaching some place or another as quickly as possible is an element in almost every tactical problem; but I must warn you against fixing *too* early an hour for marching off in this as in other problems. *Avoid, especially in consideration for the mounted arms, starting the troops until an hour after daybreak.* The march should, as a rule, begin even later, in order to give the troops as much as possible of the absolutely necessary night's rest, unless possibly, by way of exception, it is desirable to avoid marching in the middle of the day in very hot weather. In general, one starts from a bivouac rather earlier than from quarters. At the beginning of July the sun rises about 4 a.m. You should therefore fix 5 a.m., at the earliest, as the hour of starting. Even so, the mounted arms will have to begin their day's work soon after 3 a.m. It is not likely that the enemy on his part will start much earlier than 5 a.m. *Precise regulations for the hour of starting do not exist.* If the tactical situation, or the state of the weather, or the length of the march demand it, we must of necessity start accordingly earlier (*G.F.S.R.*, para. 338). Special reasons must be adduced when an exceptionally early start is made.

Average figures in round numbers for sunrise and sunset you will find tabulated in the appendix to the *Field Service Regulations*.[1]

From this point onwards the orders will differ, according as you have allotted the cavalry to the advanced guard or

---

[1] This table is not given in the English edition of the *G.F.S.R.*, nor is it found in the *F.S. Pocket Book* of 1908.—*Trans.*

not. In the latter case No. 3 should run: "The cavalry will trot on ahead at 5 a.m. to MERCY-BY-METZ—reconnoitring towards COLOMBEY, BORNY, QUEULEU, and SABLON. The HOSPITAL WALD and the large wood of CHAMPEL are to be observed."

The reasons for the cavalry moving forward at a trot have been already given. Although you specify Mercy-by-Metz as the goal of their efforts, yet doubtless the officer commanding the detachment recognises in his own mind the improbability of their being able to trot continuously that distance. As soon as they begin to get the touch of the enemy, however, their rate of progress will gradually get slower. The further afield you fix the goal of their efforts, the more energetically are cavalry likely to act. They will, at any rate, *try* to reach it quickly. Possibly they succeed in doing so—so much the better then. There is an established axiom in military matters that a General should require of his troops what is next door to impossible. By this means the possible is performed. But there must be no over-driving!

Borny is given as a point to be reconnoitred, because of the main road leading thither viâ Vallières;—Colombey, to secure the right flank in good time;—Queuleu and Sablon as a matter of course.

More extensive reconnoitring than this is not necessary to begin with. Should it, however, become necessary to push the cavalry even further towards Antilly, I should manage it by means of a *new* order—probably given on the heights of Mercy-by-Metz. The reconnoitring thus goes on, as it were, *by instalments*. The advantage of this course is that it will counteract any tendency of the cavalry to get out of hand, besides giving the commander of the detachment a guarantee that the reconnaissance of the first few miles of country will not be slurred over. Thus our motto is "*give the cavalry a large order*," yet for all that with certain qualifications. By specially mentioning the Hospital Wald and the large wood of Champel in the order, we ensure greater attention being given to examining these localities. As to *how* this is to be done—whether by patrols or by larger bodies—is the business of the officer commanding the cavalry. In fact, at the time the order is made out, the officer commanding the detachment is not in a position to pronounce on this point. The more cavalry the enemy displays in these localities next morning, the more *we* must send thither (*G.F.S.R.*, paras. 195, 118, 146).

There is no doubt that in giving these directions about searching the woods you are somewhat interfering with the independence of the cavalry commander. He probably recognises the necessity, without your telling him, of examining large woods lying close to the route to be traversed. Nevertheless, it is desirable to insert this clause, so as to be perfectly certain that both flanks of the line of march will be carefully reconnoitred. In practice the amount of independence allowed a subordinate depends on his personal character, a factor which is wanting in the theoretical solution of a problem. Yet, even in practice, the supreme commander is sometimes justified in encroaching on the initiative of his subordinates, *even when their efficiency and zeal is undoubted* (as, for instance, in the present case, where certain instructions are given about the way the reconnaissance is to be carried out); for the general continuity of the arrangements as a whole, the unity of leadership, and *the supreme commander's own views and intentions outweigh all other considerations*. The freedom which is necessary to a subordinate in arranging the details of how he intends to execute your orders, on which I laid stress in my first letter, must not be carried too far. *Still, it is not so bad to err on this side as to hamper him with useless details. You must have very good grounds for interfering in your orders with a subordinate's freedom of action in executing them.*

I would not advise you to say *merely*, "The cavalry will reconnoitre towards the line Colombey–Sablon." Provided a cavalry leader holds the same views on the situation as the commander of the detachment, such an order may be sufficient for an intelligent cavalry officer; he would act in accordance with the intentions of his commander. But whether this can be safely presumed in any case is an open question. The commander of the whole will be more on the safe side if he does not only indicate a general line towards which reconnaissance must be directed, but definite directions in which he wishes reconnaissance to be carried out. He then knows for certain that parties have been sent in those directions (localities), whereas the former wording of his order would not procure him that certainty (*G.F.S.R.*, para. 120).[1]

It will not infrequently occur that the supreme commander, if he has it very much at heart to reconnoitre in any particular directions, will order officers' patrols out, *but he must not make a practice of doing this* (*G.F.S.R.*, para. 146).[1] As a rule, all such arrangements are equally well made by the cavalry commander, or by the commander of the advanced guard; and the whole conduct of the reconnoitring thereby remains more in one hand; nor does the subordinate officer get in a habit of relying on the commander to do his work for him. I do not think it necessary in this case to start the cavalry much before the infantry, as the former will soon get ahead by moving at a trot. Nor need the place of departure be specified—seeing that the cavalry are in the bivouac. Their line of route also is left open, so as to give them a free hand in the matter.

No. 4. "The Advanced Guard will start at the same hour for **MERCY-BY-METZ**, viâ the main road through **HAUTE-GRÈVE**."

Note that the commander of the advanced guard has a definite route prescribed to him. For all other particulars, however, such as the measures to be taken for the protection of the march, and for keeping up the connection with the cavalry in front—also the order of march of his command—it rests with him to make his own arrangements.

---

[1] *E. Cav. Tr.*, chap. VII, sects. 145 and 146.—*Trans.*

If you have put your cavalry in the advanced guard you must express No. 3 thus: "The Advanced Guard will start at 5 a.m. for MERCY-BY-METZ, viâ the main road through HAUTE-GRÈVE. The Cavalry will proceed in advance, at the trot, to MERCY-BY-METZ, and, while observing the HOSPITAL WALD and the large wood of CHAMPEL, will reconnoitre towards COLOMBEY, BORNY, QUEULEU, and SABLON."

By such an order you would interfere with the independence of the commander of the advanced guard; but your justification for so doing is that you are doubtful whether his views on the subject of employing cavalry are the same as your own.

No. 5 (or if you have attached the cavalry to the advanced guard, No. 4). "The Main Body will follow at 1600 yards distance."

You can either fix a certain *hour* for the main body to start, or as above, mention the *distance* (in yards) at which it is to follow the advanced guard.[1] The latter is best in practice, because, should any accident delay the start of the advanced guard, the main body still preserves the required distance. The only case in which you should arrange the start of the main body by reference to time is when the advanced guard and the main body have to start from different rendezvous, which lie far apart, and are separated by country where the view is so limited that the head of the main body cannot see the advanced guard start. A distance of about $\frac{2}{3}$ mile is, in the case of small forces consisting of a few battalions only, about sufficient when the enemy is distant and the general situation is as yet little ascertained (*G.F.S.R.*, para. 169). Experience shows that two factors enter into the determination of the distance— on the one hand, the advanced guard must be far enough in advance to prevent any checks to its advance delaying the main body also; on the other hand, the main body

---

[1] *E.F.S.R.*, Part I, sects. 67 (2) and 68 (1) says differently, but probably means to refer to very large advanced guards, *e.g.* one for a division.—*Trans.*

must be near enough to intervene in good time if the advanced guard encounters the enemy. Exceptional arrangements must be made, as you should bear in mind for future reference, in the case of an advance against an enemy who is already established in your vicinity. Here the distance between advanced guard and main body can be reduced, with a view to expediting deployment to the front. But even in such a case it is advisable to have the main body *not too close* to the advanced guard, for as a rule the commander of the force will retain *greater freedom in handling the main body* when that is further in rear.

No. 6 (or if you have attached the cavalry to the advanced guard, No. 5). " The 2nd Line Transport will remain stationary in column of route on the by-road leading from LIÉHON into the main road—the head of the column being at the junction of the two roads mentioned."

The baggage might, in the present instance, almost equally as well be left behind in the bivouac. This is often done when one is *sure* of returning thither again. In the present case, however, this is by no means certain, so it is better not to leave the baggage behind.

As to the distance between the baggage and main body in general, the former must, on the one hand, be kept well in rear, if there is any chance of a fight ; while, on the other hand, it must be capable of being readily brought into billets or bivouac by nightfall, and therefore must not be too far behind. But it is often impossible to foretell where the force will pass the next night. In the present instance the baggage should not be taken far afield. In fact, it would be a downright mistake to drag it about at our heels; for, on commencing the day's march, it is impossible to foresee whether the force may not experience a reverse, and have to make a hurried retreat ; in which case the clumsy wagons would be very much in the way on the main road. The best course here is to let it go a little way, at any rate, so that the wagons may fall into their places, on one road and in one column. One likes to post it *on a by-way, with its head at the junction of the by-way with the main road*, so that it can either readily move to the front or retreat, as in our case here, southwards. It would not be wrong to advance the baggage a little further to the front in the present instance—say to Basse-Grève, as you can be pretty certain that it will not be in the way there. I should not advance it any further than that though; and in any case it must on no account go down the steep descent near Pierrejeux too soon.

With small forces the baggage (or 2nd line transport) usually follows about $1\frac{1}{4}$ miles in rear of the tail of the combatant column on the march. Bear in mind now, for future reference, the following cases which may occur with regard to the baggage:—

(1) It follows the main body at a distance of about $1\frac{1}{4}$ miles.
(2) It follows the main body at the same distance as in (1), but only to some appointed spot, where it awaits further orders.
(3) It marches only a short distance, in order to fall into its order of march properly.
(4) It remains behind in bivouac or billets.
(5) It follows close on the main body without any distance, or else very close in rear of it (in Flank marches).
(6) It does not follow the main body, but marches on a road of its own (in Flank marches).
(7) Instead of following in rear it is sent on in front (in Retreats); or, the troops being temporarily stationary, it is sent back to the rear (in Defence—sometimes, but not so often in Attack).

You have *never* to mention anything about the 1st line regimental transport in operation orders, that is to say, about that part of the baggage which is wanted during action, as that follows each unit *without saying* (*G.F.S.R.*,

SECOND LETTER

para. 438).[1] Mountain warfare forms a rare exception; but *2nd line transport* must always be mentioned. Your vehicles will always follow in the same order of march as the combatant units. The 2nd line transport must be separated from the fighting troops the moment there is a chance of an action coming off; and this, as a rule, will be the case in tactical exercises (*G.F.S.R.*, para. 441).[2]

No. 7 (or if you have attached the cavalry to the advanced guard, No. 6). "I shall be found (reports will reach me) at the head of the main guard.[3]

A.,
Colonel."

The best position for the officer commanding a detachment is between the vanguard and the main guard, where he can await the first reports. So stationed, he is less subject to distractions, and can better exercise supervision, than by being altogether at the head of the column, in which case his attention would be liable to be taken up by comparatively unimportant details. But as soon as he receives news that *touch has been established in earnest with the enemy, he must gallop as far forward as possible.* There he interrogates the advanced guard commander as to what the latter has observed, and it now becomes his duty to see for himself; because the commander's own observation of the situation as regards the enemy and of the country is worth more than reports or information at second hand, or the mere inspection of the map. Others could watch for the commander in case of need, but he alone can issue orders to the whole, and that is the reason why he should be as far to the front as possible, where reports, moreover, will find him soonest (*G.F.S.R.*, para. 164).

---

[1] *E.F.S.R.*, Part I, first footnote, page 26, and *Transport Manual*, 1905, Part I, sect. 1 (1).—*Trans.*

[2] *Ibid.*, sect. 28 (3).—*Trans.*

[3] *Ibid.*, sect. 12 (4) last but one sentence.—*Trans.*

At the foot of the order note briefly how it reached the troops (*G.F.S.R.*, para. 55).[1]

As in the present instance the order is given in bivouac it is only necessary to assemble the officers from the several units to receive it, and dictate it to them. So you write: "Dictated to the officers representing the several units."

With regard to the reasons for the measures adopted, I can be very brief. The person who sets the problem will see, by the reasons adduced by you, whether you have clearly realised *the whole state of affairs* and thoroughly grasped the tactical principles involved. This is shown by the reasons on which you base the measures adopted. Bearing this in mind, write your proof concisely. Aim at expressing yourself very clearly, strictly logically, and with decision, as becomes a military order. In the present problem you might arrange your reasons as follows :—

(1) Show that you comprehend the general situation as regards yourself and the enemy. Your own task. Intention of the enemy.

(2) Give reasons for the decision arrived at. Weighing the pros and cons of different solutions.

(3) Give reasons for the distribution of troops.

(4) Give reasons for each paragraph of your order, so far as is necessary.

Beginners, when starting writing their reasons, often furnish a description of the situation almost identical with the wording of the problem. I hardly need to point out to you that this is altogether superfluous. Clutch your subject at once. State at once in your first sentence what you think your object is.

While you are writing the reasons, it will sometimes occur to you—especially if you are a beginner—to alter, for the better, some points or expressions in the orders. This is one of the chief advantages in writing your reasons

[1] *E.F.S.R.*, Part I, sect. 14 (4) last sentence and sect. 9 (1) (xi.).—*Trans.*

for the measures adopted. The act of giving your reasons in writing compels you to think out so thoroughly the various reasons, that, very likely in the course of doing so, you arrive at more correct decisions. Thus the subsequently written reasons act as a crucial test whether your work was sufficiently thorough when you drew up the orders. *It is on this account I advise you to give reasons, based on sound tactical principles, for all orders framed by you.*

A few words, in conclusion, as to the estimate of the length of the column which is involved. The order of march, drawn to the scale of the map, will show at a glance the position of the several portions of the force at the given time, and, above all, the road space occupied by the whole column. This latter the commander should thoroughly realise in two cases: firstly, when, *during a march*, a fresh order may have to be issued; for instance, when some alteration has to be made in the distribution of the troops in view of a change of direction, or when, while on the march, orders for attack, or for occupying a position, may have to be made out; secondly, when fresh orders will be required to distribute the troops to different places of bivouac or billets *at the termination of a march*.

The road space occupied by the several tactical units are given in round numbers in the Appendix to *Field Service Regulations*, p. 4.[1] An hour and a half's marching will bring the infantry of the vanguard about $4\frac{3}{4}$ miles, *i.e.* near La Horgne-au-Cheval-Rouge. Let us take this as our reference-point. As an advanced party, at a varying distance in front, is the cavalry of the vanguard maintaining connection with the bulk of the independent cavalry still further in front. The order of march of the detachment is then :—

[1] Pages 186 to 188 in the English edition by the *Imperial General Staff, War Office*. The corresponding numbers for British estimates of lengths of units are given on pp. 29 to 31 of *Field Service Pocket Book*, 1908. The length of a battalion is given there as being 660 yards; it must be 610 according to the length of a brigade, which is given as 2530 yards.—*Trans.*

ORDERS FOR A MARCH

		Yards.	Yards.
Vanguard	Point (1 officer and 4 to 6 men Infantry) .	0	
	Distance . . .	400	
	2 Cos. Infantry	100	
	Field Co. R.E.	300	
			800
	Distance, say		400
Main Guard	1 Troop Cavalry . . .	30	
	6 Cos. I/Battalion (with 1st Line Transport)	500	
			530
	Distance, say		1600
Main Body	1 Troop Cavalry . . .	30	
	II/Battalion	600	
	Battery R.F.A.	400	
	III/Battalion	600	
	⅓ Field Ambul. . . .	120	
	⅓ Ammunition Col. . . .	350	
			2100
	Total road space .		5430[1]
	Say 3 miles.		

Therefore to deploy on the head of the vanguard, the whole force would require about 1 hour.

If 2nd line transport followed, its distance, 1¼ miles, and its length would have to be allowed for. For numbers see Appendix to *Field Service Regulations*, p. 4 (English translation of *G.F.S.R.*, pp. 186–188).[2]

The tail of the advanced guard will thus be on the main road somewhere near point 270.8, the head of the main body about Basse-Grève, the tail of the main body near point 263.2, while the 2nd line transport has not yet left Liéhon. I have not allowed for possible halts. A space and time calculation can never be more than *approximately* correct, which, however, is sufficient for practical purposes. A few hundred yards over or under estimated is of no importance as a rule. On this account your estimate need

---

[1] The road spaces and distances are given as in *Field Service Pocket Book*, and are in round numbers; they are, of course, different to those given in the original, which are based on German organisation.—*Trans.*

[2] *F.S. Pocket Book*, pp. 29-31.

not precisely agree with that above given; for instance, your "distances" might be different to mine, thereby giving a different "total road space." I have left it for you to decide how far the cavalry—independent or otherwise—is in front of the head of your vanguard.

I will now put together for you the orders (already detailed) in the form in which they should be written by you.

Copy No. 1.

OPERATION ORDER No. 1.

BY

COLONEL A., COMMANDING DETACHED FORCE.

Reference:
Ordn. $\frac{1}{25.000}$ or $\frac{1}{100.000}$

Bivouac South of
LIÉHON,
2.7.00.

1. *Cavalry:* Major D.
    1st Sqd. 9th Dragoons (less 2 troops).
    IInd Sqd. 9th Dragoons.

2. *Advanced Guard:*
    Lt.-Col. B.
    1 Troop 1st Sqd. 9th Dragoons.
    1st Field Co. R.E.
    I/Battalion 98th Inf. Rgt.

3. *Main Body* (in order of march): Lt.-Col. C.
    1 Troop 1st Sqd. 9th Dragoons.
    II/Battalion 98th Inf. Rgt.
    7th Field Battery R.A.
    III/Battalion 98th Inf. Rgt
    Sect. A, Field Ambul.
    ⅓ Art. Brgde. Ammun. Col.

1. *Hostile* Infantry and Artillery are bivouacked near **ANTILLY**. Hostile cavalry patrols are reported south of **METZ**. *Our division* remains in its present bivouac to-morrow.

2. *The Detachment* will march to-morrow morning on **MERCY-BY-METZ**.

3. *The Cavalry* will trot on ahead at 5 a.m. to **MERCY-BY-METZ**— reconnoitring towards **COLOMBEY, BORNY, QUEULEU,** and **SABLON**. The **HOSPITAL WALD** and the large wood of **CHAMPEL** are to be observed.

4. *The Advanced Guard* will start at the same hour for **MERCY-BY-METZ**, viâ the main road through **HAUTE-GRÈVE**.

5. *The Main Body* will follow at 1600 yards distance.

ORDERS FOR A MARCH

6. *The 2nd Line Transport* will remain stationary in column of route on the by-road leading from **LIÉHON** into the main road—the head of the column being at the junction of the two above-mentioned roads.

7. *Reports* will reach me at the head of the main guard.

Dictated to officers representing the various units,[1] at 10 p.m.

A.,
Colonel.

If the cavalry be allotted to the advanced guard, the orders must be altered as previously mentioned. I again remind you that all words printed in italics in the above orders should be underlined by you in writing such orders, and names of places should be written in block capitals.[2] In writing a tactical exercise, begin a new page with the orders for the sake of distinctness.

SECOND EXERCISE.

(See maps Metz, Verny, and Ars a. d. Mosel.)

The 16th Division, in its own country, bivouacs on the night 5/6 July, 1900, between Retonféy and Glatigny (map Metz, east of Retonféy). A flank guard under Colonel A, consisting of:—

I/Battalion.	Ist, IInd, and ½ IIIrd 1st Dragoons.
II/Battalion.	1st Field Battery R.A.
III/Battalion.	" A " Battery R.H.A.
IV/Battalion (Rifles).	1st Field Co. R.E.
	Sect. A 1st Field Ambul.
	⅔ Art. Brgde. Ammun. Col.

has gone into close billets in Colligny late in the evening of the 5th July.

---

[1] According to *E.F.S.R.* each unit should be stated, *vide F.S.R.*, Part I, sect. 9 (1) (xi.) and sect. 12 (4) last sentence.—*Trans.*

[2] *E.F.S.R.*, Part I, sect. 9 (1) (iv.).—*Trans.*

SECOND LETTER

At 11 p.m. Colonel A. receives the following order from the G.O.C. 16th Division:—

16th Division.   **D.H.Q. GLATIGNY,**
                                                                     5.7.00.

The enemy has crossed the **MOSELLE** at noon to-day near **NOVÉANT** with a column of all arms, and occupied **FÉY, CUVRY, POUILLY,** and **FLEURY** with a few infantry. Isolated cavalry patrols of the enemy have appeared north and east of the **HOSPITAL WALD. METZ** is not occupied by the enemy. The Division will start for **METZ** viâ **LAUVALLIÈRE** at 5.15 a.m. to-morrow. You will cover the march again to-morrow as a left flank guard, marching by **COLOMBEY,** and making arrangements for your detachment to have passed the ravine of the **VALLIÈRES** brook by 7 a.m. The 2nd line transport of the division will assemble on the main road from **GLATIGNY** to **PETIT-MARAIS** at 8 a.m. to-morrow with its leading wagon at the latter place.   X.,

In writing by Orderly Officer   *Lieut.-General.*
    at 10.30 p.m.

Required:—1. Colonel A.'s arrangements for 6.7.00.
              2. Reasons for the same.

NOTE.—The woods in the neighbourhood of Metz have very dense underwood, and infantry could only work through them *slowly,* and *in extended order.* As regards the fortifications of Metz, see the remarks in the first letter, according to which you must leave them wholly out of the calculation.

THIRD LETTER

FLANK MARCH

THE data given at the end of the last letter involve a simple advance of a detachment protecting the left flank of a force about to march from Retonféy to Metz viâ Lauvallière.

It is not within our province to inquire why the force does not assume the offensive against the adversary who has crossed the Moselle. The order received from the Lieut.-General in command distinctly states that the division will march on Metz. There are doubtless excellent reasons for this course. Remember the maxim always to confine yourself strictly to the data in the exercise, and never be led astray into the consideration of circumstances outside the scope of those data.

The road by which the detachment will have to march runs from Colligny viâ Colombey to Metz; so the detachment has to cross the precipitous and deep ravine of the "Vallières brook" near Colombey. The Division will have to cross the same ravine at Lauvallière; and at both places precautions must be taken, even if both these first-class roads are in the best condition. The Lieut.-General will be glad when his main body has crossed the ravine; for to be attacked during its passage would place him in an awkward position. In view of this the detachment must so place itself as to cover the passage of the ravine by the main body; not merely marching parallel with it on Metz, but *halting in a suitable place* until the whole of the main body has crossed the ravine (*G.F.S.R.*, para. 178).[1] Where and

---

[1] *E.F.S.R.*, Part I, sect. 70.—*Trans.*

in what manner this halt is to be made it is impossible to say—*at the present stage of the proceedings*—at least with any accuracy; but information will come to hand after the march is begun which will enable us to decide this matter. Pending this, all that can be done is to *begin the march* so as to get the detachment over the ravine in good time, and to make careful provision for reconnaissance. This much, however, can be definitely stated, *that for the purpose of feeling the way* the detachment must not go beyond the " Franz. Denkm." As regards the orders we have to frame, this point therefore may be considered as being, *for the present*, the object to be reached by march. It is evident that the officer commanding the Division has not contemplated the detachment halting east of the Vallières brook, because his order demands Colonel A.'s force to be *over* the brook by a given hour.

The question may have occurred to you, Why did not the Lieut.-General state how far the detachment should go before halting? *There is doubtless some ground for asking such a question.* Inasmuch, however, as he has left his subordinate perfect freedom of action in deciding the details, and has not hampered him with any special requirements, *so it is the duty of the latter to arrive at a right decision for himself.*

The detachment must, as it advances, keep up close touch with the main body, so as always to know exactly how far the latter has got. There will not be much difficulty in doing this, as the country between the two roads for the most part lies open to view, except in the immediate vicinity of the Vallières brook; and there are plenty of good cross-roads, suitable also for cyclists. But besides the high road on which the detachment will march we must also consider what roads may be of importance in facilitating reconnaissance, that is to say, those south of and parallel to the first mentioned. These are:—

(1) The road viâ Marsilly and Aubigny to Colombey.— Patrols moving by this route would have to strike across

country for part of the way, but even so, the road throughout is too near the main road on which the detachment will march to be of much use for reconnoitring and security.

(2) *The road viâ Marsilly and Ars-Laquenexy to Grigy.*—Near Ars-Laquenexy this by-road strikes another main road (chaussée) which, about 1¼ miles south of the route of the detachment, runs also to Metz. But between the two main roads, from Colombey to Borny, and from Ars-Laquenexy to Grigy, there are so many woods and copses that it would be difficult to keep up visual communication between the two roads.

(3) *The road viâ Marsilly and Ars-Laquenexy to Mercy-by-Metz—thence on viâ Grigy or Haute-Bévoye to Queuleu.*—Using this road one gets, near Mercy-by-Metz, a view over the country east of the Hospital Wald. From this point, too, one can, with any luck, prevent hostile cavalry detachments penetrating by the gap between the large wood of Champel and the wood west of Ars-Laquenexy, to observe the advance of our detachment. From Haute-Bévoye also there is a view over the country west of the Hospital Wald, and, what is important, the main road Verny–Pouilly–Metz lies in sight from this point. *It follows from the above that this main road through Mercy-by-Metz promises best for reconnaissance.*

The enemy has crossed the Moselle with columns of all arms about noon on the 5th July. In what strength we do not know; but the fact of his having occupied Féy, Cuvry, Pouilly, and Fleury the same afternoon indicates that probably more of his troops will have crossed the Moselle on the afternoon of the 5th, and perhaps also after sunset. It is therefore not unlikely that he will be in superior strength on the 6th, though at the outset we shall have only his advanced parties to deal with. Apparently, however, the enemy is not strong in cavalry on the right bank of the Moselle. If he were, *more would have been seen of this arm than " isolated patrols "* mentioned in the Lieut.-General's order. It may therefore be presumed that the bulk of the hostile cavalry is, for some reason or other, at present kept back on the west bank of the Moselle. It strikes us very much that, according to divisional orders, the enemy has hitherto abstained from occupying the important town of Metz. It points to his having already gained knowledge of the approach of the 16th Division, and to his intention of attacking it with all his forces as yet east of that town. Advancing in an easterly direction, the Hospital Wald lies directly in his way. He is not likely to pass south of this large wood, as it would involve too great a détour; but will either pass north of it, viâ Peltre or Mercy-by-Metz, or *through* the wood viâ Chesny. At any rate, his patrols will reconnoitre in the direction of the important main roads leading from the eastwards towards Metz, and thereby soon encounter our patrols. If the enemy's patrols once succeed in getting near Ars-Laquenexy or Grange-aux-Bois, the advance of our detachment cannot long remain concealed from their observation, even if not previously made known to them by the inhabitants of the country or otherwise. From this results that *the detachment must be prepared to meet the enemy in serious engagement, and that, moreover, it is a question of gaining with the cavalry as rapidly as possible the country about Ars-Laquenexy and Grange-aux-Bois.*

The enemy may thus be expected to advance on Grange-aux-Bois or on Ars-Laquenexy, either—

(1) viâ Peltre and Mercy-by-Metz, or
(2) viâ Chesny.

On reaching Ars-Laquenexy, it is more to his advantage to advance *west* of the Vallières brook, and try to prevent our main body crossing it, than to the east of the ravine, when he would probably be too late to effect the same purpose. If at all, we shall therefore probably have to fight a general action between Colombey and Borny. But mark here once more, it is a case of *perhaps*, or *probably*; but whether *really* is an open question.

By what time, approximately, can the enemy reach the

FLANK MARCH

line Colombey–Borny ? The distance, as the crow flies, from the nearest of the villages occupied by him, Fleury and Pouilly, is about 5 miles ; by road considerably more. The flank detachment, on the other hand, from Colligny to the Vallières brook has only about 2½ miles to go, so can easily get the start necessary to cross the ravine unmolested and select a position west of it, *provided, of course, the enemy does not begin to move at an exceptionally early hour.*

The more difficulty the hostile cavalry has in reconnoitring, the slower will the troops in the rear of it march. The cavalry of the flank guard must therefore endeavour, when at Mercy-by-Metz, to push back hostile patrols, as well as larger bodies of cavalry on the Hospital Wald. If it does no more than this, our cavalry will have amply done its duty ; for you must realise that the cavalry cannot, as a rule, guarantee *absolute protection, in the full sense of the word*, to infantry marching in rear of or beside it. *Cavalry lacks the power of resistance requisite to ensure protection.* In this instance all it can do is to prevent the enemy's patrols from approaching our column, in other words, if it *screens* the column ; and to give the infantry the earliest tidings when and whence the enemy is coming, in other words, if it *reconnoitres*. Both it will achieve best *by riding close to him* and keeping his cavalry so occupied as to deprive it of the initiative (*G.F.S.R.*, paras. 118, 192, and 194). Four cyclists will be attached to the cavalry as despatch riders. Should the telegraph patrol of the regiment happen to be with the two squadrons (*G.F.S.R.*, para. 556), its duty would be to establish the line from Mercy-by-Metz viâ Grange-aux-Bois to the Franz. Denkmal.

I would *not* in this instance recommend throwing out, with the idea of thereby gaining additional security, a flank guard composed of infantry, to march, say, on Grigy viâ Marsilly and Ars-Laquenexy. Such a flank guard would get too much separated from the detachment by the Vallières brook and the woods west of Ars-Laquenexy, and thus exposed to the danger of being **destroyed *in detail.***

Let us assume, for the sake of argument, that you *have* detached, say, half a battalion, with some cavalry, as a flank guard to the detachment, marching viâ Marsilly and Ars-Laquenexy on Grange-aux-Bois. The enemy approaches by way of Mercy-by-Metz, and the four companies make an attempt to delay him somewhere near Grange-aux-Bois, while the rest of the detachment is taking up a position for defence at the Franz. Denkmal. No doubt the four companies will delay the enemy some time. It will take the enemy's cavalry some time, much more time than is the case during peace manœuvres, to see what force they have to deal with. This uncertainty imposes caution, and with it *delay*, on the enemy. But now for the other side of the picture. In the long run the enemy perceives the weakness of the flank guard, and then the four companies have to retreat, exposed to the annihilating fire of modern weapons. In what state will they rejoin their main body? Does the advantage to the detachment justify this sacrifice? *Would it not have been just as well to rely solely on the cavalry reporting the approach of the enemy?* As soon as it came to an engagement, *i.e.* to the enemy's attacking the detachment in position, the rôle of any hitherto existing flank guard (if there had been one) would become identical with that of "advanced posts" in front of a defensive position. Every improvement in modern fire-arms lends extra weight to the already cogent objections to advanced posts (*G. Inf. Tr.*, para. 407).[1]

Note here, for future reference, that when the enemy's presence is reported on the flank of your line of march, and you are in doubt *whether you ought to throw out a special flank guard composed of some infantry or not, you must weigh* :—

(1) Whether, all things considered, a small infantry flank guard is necessary for you *to gain time*.

(2) Whether there is a suitable road for such a flank guard.

[1] *E.F.S.R.*, Part I. sect. 108 (10)

FLANK MARCH

(3) If this be the case, *how far apart* are the two roads under consideration. It is most exceptional for a " detachment " to send out an infantry flank guard more than $1\frac{1}{4}$ miles.

(4) Whether the two roads are separated by ravines, woods, etc., exposing the flank guard to the danger of being destroyed before support could reach it from the main body of the detachment.

After weighing these points, you will more often than not decide to dispense with an infantry flank guard of this small size ; unless, as a special case, and not likely to occur often, you deem it important to divert the enemy's attention from the main column by throwing out such a flank guard. *Where cavalry will answer the purpose, infantry should not be employed*, the latter, owing to its slow movement, having difficulty in rejoining the column from which it is detached. You see thus that the Division, for certain reasons (*G.F.S.R.*, para. 181), has detached a *large* flank guard, but the latter must be satisfied with covering its own exposed flank by cavalry.

In the present exercise protection both can and must be provided by cavalry. To fetter this arm to the advanced guard would be a positive blunder. It can here, being *in sufficient strength*, operate outside the sphere of the advanced guard, with an *independent* mission, and push *far out* in search of the yet *far distant* enemy.

The above considerations lead us to the following decision: the detachment to march in one column to the Franz. Denkm., as a preliminary measure ; pushing forward the cavalry to Mercy-by-Metz viâ Ars-Laquenexy.

What is to be done at the Franz. Denkm., whether we will take up a position of readiness or a defensive position there or elsewhere, it is impossible to say yet while the detachment is still on the march ; no mention, therefore, must be made of this in the order ; it would be matter for a fresh order, based on the reports meanwhile coming in. *For the present* all we can do is to get the detachment on the way. Still less do we know how long the detachment will remain in position, though we know at what time the Division is going to start, and can calculate from this about what time the Division will be safe. But such a calculation is *never absolutely reliable*, as unforeseen delays may upset them at any moment.

The next point to be considered is the distribution of troops.

Considering the general situation, it is highly improbable that the advanced guard will soon become engaged, but we cannot be certain of it, *since in war, even with the best of information at one's disposal, all is uncertain*. We must therefore be prepared for everything, and arrange the composition of the advanced guard accordingly. It is as well to assign the rifle battalion to the advanced guard, so as to have with the main body one regiment complete.[1] The rifle battalions are generally used like any other battalion of infantry, for we are, as a rule, not able to take full advantage of their better marksmanship and greater mobility, it being rarely possible nowadays to retain and save them for any particular purposes. They would therefore be frequently in a place other than that where their employment would be most desirable. For this reason I advise you always in a detachment to place the Rifles if possible in the advanced guard, if, like here, you thereby keep the tactical units intact in the main body. If it is a case of our having to *attack*, the undoubtedly superior fire effect of the Rifles will prepare and support the attack of the other troops, for their good marksmanship is bound to make itself felt in the long-drawn-out fire action. If it is a case of our standing on the *defensive*, an opportunity often occurs of putting the Rifles in a place where they can find a field of action suitable to their special qualities. I would not have less than *one* battalion in the advanced guard, for we must get a considerable body of infantry on the west side

[1] The other three battalions form one regiment of three battalions, like the British Grenadier and Coldstream Guards.—*Trans.*

of the Vallières ravine as early as possible. If, however, this consideration were not so important in this case, you could make the advanced guard weaker in infantry; because, as a rule, the rôle of an advanced guard is not so important in a flank march as in an advance—*consequently it need not be so strong*. The advanced guard must, besides, have the necessary cavalry; but only sufficient to furnish patrols to reconnoitre the Colombey road, and the country close to and on each side of it, and to maintain connection with the main body of the division, as well as with the independent cavalry; the number of these patrols can be kept at the lowest, because for the two latter purposes cyclists might as well be employed. I would assign a troop to the advanced guard, perhaps two, but not more than two, for we must be careful to economise in cavalry, whenever possible, so as to have a superiority in that arm where it is more needed.

The next point for consideration is whether one of the two batteries should be detailed for the advanced guard. You may take note here that it is a general principle to keep the field artillery together in larger units, if there is no urgent reason for splitting them, because isolated batteries coming into action against a superior enemy often suffer heavy loss, if not complete annihilation. The artillery, moreover, needs to be protected by the other arms. We have, in the present instance, only one battalion in the advanced guard, and should, as a rule, be *most reluctant* to attach artillery to such a small body of infantry; because small detachments which have, like an advanced guard, to operate independently for some time, are often compelled to spread themselves over a front *out of all proportion* to their strength, and consequently are unable to afford sufficient protection to artillery. There is the less justification for attaching guns to the advanced guard in this case, in that the main body of the flanking detachment will be near enough at hand to be able to despatch quickly one or both of the batteries to the front at a trot. A mixed force, comprising two batteries which has only one battalion in the advanced guard, keeps, *as a rule*, both batteries with the main body—the more so, as the artillery is thereby kept united. It is only advisable to give the advanced guard a battery in the very exceptional case of the advanced guard having to *gain a footing* somewhere *with as little delay as possible*. Say, for example, the object is to secure a position on a height, or some other section of ground, with as little delay as possible; keeping the enemy at a distance, meanwhile, by long-range artillery fire, or compelling him to deploy prematurely. Here the intervention of artillery *a few minutes* earlier is in some cases such an advantage, that one would not hesitate to put a battery in the advanced guard, and put up with the risk it incurs by being for some time insufficiently protected. At all events, there must be adduced very sound reasons for justifying such a measure.

If you wish to separate the batteries, and should one of them be a horse-artillery battery, as I have purposely assumed to be the case in this exercise, it had better remain with the main body, for the advanced-guard battery needs less mobility, as it mostly comes into action close to the road of march. The greater mobility of the horse-artillery battery finds its application in that it is able to bring quickly the desired support from the main body to the front. Should it have occurred to you to send the horse-artillery battery with the cavalry ahead, I would be unable to agree with that course. Two squadrons—and more will not be available—are so weak a protection for one battery as *to render your decision exceedingly hazardous*.

The field company of engineers goes with the advanced guard, as its services may be required during the passage of the Vallières ravine. Should it, later on, have to strengthen a position occupied for defence, this forward position will enable it to begin work earlier.

It will be well in this case to keep a troop of cavalry with the main body of the detachment, and not be satisfied

FLANK MARCH

with a few mounted orderlies, because the *left flank of the main body of the detachment* must be adequately protected by patrols, the protection afforded by the advanced cavalry or by the few patrols of the advanced guard being not enough in this case. The troop for the advanced guard and that required for the main body will be taken from the IIIrd Squadron, so that the other two squadrons remain intact.

Portions of an artillery brigade ammunition column are often detailed to individual batteries; these portions march, as a rule, behind the field ambulance.[1]

On the subject of orders, I explained in the previous letter that frequently *two* sets of orders for a march instead of one can be issued. Always bear in mind that it is most desirable for the troops to know overnight, if possible, what time they must be ready to begin the march next morning. The company[2] commanders, etc., can in that event make their arrangements better on matters of interior economy, such as the issue of rations, access to baggage, etc., than if the order reaches them almost like an alarm-order, just before the fall-in for the start.

If you issue two sets of orders, then by the first, issued overnight, you *assemble the troops for the start* only; the second, the *order of the march proper*, being promulgated verbally or dictated shortly before marching off. *This method of issuing orders is that which is most employed in the field*, especially when in the vicinity of the enemy. The advantage of it is that the *manner in which the troops are to be employed* and the *choice of roads* is left open up to the moment of starting. On the following morning the officers commanding units are assembled some 10 or 15 minutes before the actual time of starting, to receive the orders for the march.

In the field, orders as a rule are issued, both for divisions and detachments, *late* at night; as, usually, the reports on

---

[1] See *E.F.S.R.*, Part I, sect. 27 (2) last sentence.—*Trans.*
[2] Equal to a British double-company.—*Trans.*

the events of the day and the orders of superior commanders have to be waited for. The officers detailed to receive the orders often have to wait for hours together before they can be issued. All are worn out with the exertions of the day, and will be glad when at last they can ride away, but even then must betake themselves to their respective commanding officers, who generally will have to be awakened. In short, picture to yourself vividly all the circumstances of the situation, and you will realise how desirable it is that orders which have to be issued in the middle of the night should be *as simple as possible*. How easy it would otherwise be for fatal mistakes to arise. Issuing orders by word of mouth has also the undeniable advantage that it is possible to explain and clear up any doubtful points.

The detachment is in close billets during the night, that is to say as many men as possible are put in the buildings of Colligny, the remainder, not finding room there, bivouacking close outside the village (*G.F.S.R.*, para. 405).[1] The units are certainly less concentrated and not so easily supervised as in camp, still matters are arranged with a view of separating units as little as possible. There is therefore no need for assembling the troops outside the village previous to starting, which, moreover, would greatly inconvenience the troops. The least inconvenience would be caused to the troops if the order fixes *the time at which the troops should be ready to march;* then each unit can patiently await its turn to fall into its proper place in the march-column.

In calculating the hour of starting you must bear in mind that, in accordance with the orders from Divisional Headquarters, the detachment—though not its baggage—must be across the Vallières brook by 7 a.m. The distance by road from Colligny to the Vallières brook is roughly $2\frac{1}{2}$ miles = about 50 minutes' marching; because from the same reasons as in the previous exercise you can assume

[1] *E.F.S.R.*, Part I, sect. 54.—*Trans.*

FLANK MARCH

a rate in this short march without a halt of about 1 mile in 18 minutes. The point of the vanguard will require that time to march the distance. But we must calculate, in addition, the total road space occupied by the detachment in order of march, which will be (given more roughly than in the previous letter) as follows :—

Rifles	600 yards.
3 Battalions	1800 ,,
1 Troop Cavalry (of the Main Body)	25 ,,
2 Batteries (one of which H.A.)	860 ,,
1 Field Co. R.E.	300 ,,
1 Sect. Field Ambul.	125 ,,
$\frac{2}{3}$ Art. Brgde. Ammun. Col.	500 ,,
Distance between Point and Advanced Party	200 ,,
,, ,, Advanced Party and Support	400 ,,
,, ,, Support and Main Guard	400 ,,
,, ,, Main Body and Main Guard	800 ,,
	6010 yards.

Marching 1760 yards in 18 minutes = roughly 1 hour.

Thus the detachment must march off 1 hour 50 minutes before 7, *i.e.* at 5.10 a.m. Commanding officers to assemble to receive orders at 4.45, and the detachment to be *prepared to* march off by 5.10 a.m. The orders will be best issued where the road from Colombey enters Colligny. As soon as the orders have been given and the commanding officers have rejoined their units, the march can begin.

A very much later time is chosen for the 2nd line transport than for the troops, so that the latter have left the village some time when the baggage-wagons set out, in order that, during the departure of the troops, the streets in the village may be free from vehicles. On the other hand, the 2nd line transport must assemble early enough to start in good time (*G.F.S.R.*, para. 442).[1] It is, further, highly

---

[1] *E.F.S.R.*, Part I, sect. 12 (7).—*Trans.*

desirable to assemble it on the road *as part of the column of march*, to which end it must be *stated* in the orders, where the head or tail of the baggage column must stand, because this is the simplest way of setting the transport *en route*, and saves the heavy wagons the necessity of much turning or leaving the road.

I take this opportunity of impressing on you that, *as a rule*, all the 2nd line transport of a Division is massed, and marches *in one* body (*G.F.S.R.*, para. 441).[1] The Divisional Commander has therefore expressly stated in his order where the 2nd line transport of the Division will assemble. It is the business of the flank detachment to see that its own 2nd line transport joins in time that of the Division.

The first order would run :—

Copy No. 1.

OPERATION ORDER No. 1

BY

COLONEL A., COMMANDING FLANK DETACHMENT.

Reference:
Ordn. $\frac{1}{100.000}$

HORSE SHOE INN,
COLLIGNY,
5.7.00.

1. *The Detachment* will be ready to start to-morrow at 5.10 a.m.

   The 2nd Line Transport will stand in column of route at 7 a.m. on the road **COLLIGNY–PETIT MARAIS** with its tail at **COLLIGNY**.

2. *Orders to Commanding Officers* will be issued at 4.45 a.m. at the exit of **COLLIGNY** leading to **COLOMBEY**.

Dictated to representatives of the several units at 11.15 p.m.

A.,
Colonel.

---

[1] *E.F.S.R.*, Part I, sect. 28 (2) and (3).—*Trans.*

FLANK MARCH

The actual orders for march run as follows :—

Copy No. 1.

OPERATION ORDER No. 2

BY

COLONEL A., COMMANDING FLANK DETACHMENT.

Reference:
Ordn. $\frac{1}{100,000}$.

Northern exit of
COLLIGNY,
6.7.00.

1. *Cavalry:* Major B.
   1st and IInd Sqds. 1st Dragoons.

2. *Advanced Guard:*
   Lt.-Col. C.
   1 Troop 1st Dragoons.
   1 Field Co. R.E.
   IV/Battalion (Rifles).

3. *Main Body* (in order of march): Lt.-Col. D.
   1 Troop 1st Dragoons.
   I/Battalion.
   "A" Battery R.H.A.
   1st Field Battery R.A.
   II/Battalion.
   III/Battalion.
   Sect. A, Field Ambul.
   $\frac{2}{3}$ Art. Brgde. Ammun. Col.

1. *The Enemy* has yesterday afternoon occupied **FÉY, CUVRY, POUILLY,** and **FLEURY.** His cavalry patrols have shown themselves near the **HOSPITAL WALD. METZ** was not occupied by the enemy.

   Our Division will march to-day viâ **LAUVALLIÈRE** on **METZ.**

2. *The Detachment* will march to-day, as a left flank guard, provisionally to the "**FRANZÖSISCHES DENKMAL,**" west of **COLOMBEY.**

3. *The 1st and IInd Squadrons* will immediately advance at the trot to **MERCY-BY-METZ,** viâ **ARS-LAQUENEXY,** reconnoitre in the direction of **CHESNY, ORNY,** and **POUILLY,** and try to prevent hostile cavalry gaining ground east of the **HOSPITAL WALD.**

4. *The Advanced Guard* will start at once by the road through **COLOMBEY** to the **FRANZÖSISCHES DENKMAL,** keeping up connection with the Division, with **CRIGY** and **BORNY.**

5. *The Main Body* will follow at a distance of a mile.

6. *The 2nd Line Transport* of the detachment will join that of the Division by **PETIT MARAIS**.

7. *Reports* to the head of the main guard, where I shall be.

A.,
Colonel.

Verbally to the assembled commanding officers at 5 a.m.

THIRD EXERCISE.

(See general map and the maps Metz and Verny.)

A detachment (see diagram below) under Colonel A. is in an enemy's country, and on the 1st August, '00, is on the march by the road passing through Vigy (general map north of St. Barbe) and St. Barbe (map Metz). On the afternoon hostile cavalry patrols have fallen back, viâ Nouilly, Lauvallière, on Planchette, towards Metz. The enemy is reported to have a large number of troops in bivouac west of Borny. At 5 p.m., when the head of his vanguard has reached Petit Marais (north of Retonféy), Colonel A. decides to billet his troops in the villages of Gras, Cheuby, Erpigny, St. Barbe, and Avancy, and to throw out outposts (4 companies I/Durham Light Infantry, 2 troops 1st Squadron 7th Hussars) on the line Poixe–Croix-Bellevue.

At the same moment an orderly officer of the 15th Division hands to the Colonel the following order :—

"The 15th Division is marching to-morrow from Rémilly (general map) viâ Sorbey on Metz. The detachment will join the 15th Division at Laquenexy to-morrow at 8 a.m."

Required :—

1. The order of march of the detachment on the 1st August, '00, in the form of an estimate of the road space occupied.

2. The arrangements for billeting the detachment for the night (omitting the outposts).

FLANK MARCH

3. The arrangements made by Colonel A. for the 2nd August, '00.
4. Reasons for the measures adopted.

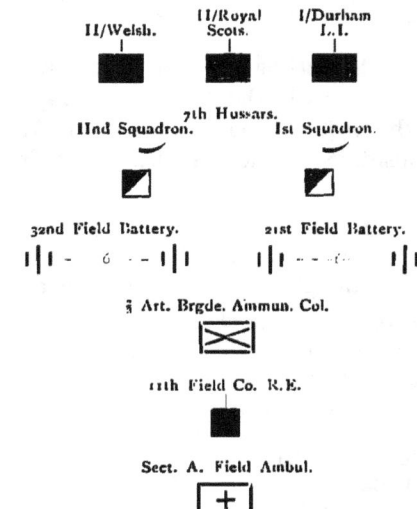

FOURTH LETTER

MARCH QUARTERS AND FLANK MARCH

TO work out the estimate of the road space occupied by the detachment, the "Distribution of Troops," that is to say, the order of march on the 1st August, must first of all be considered. The Distribution of Troops might be as follows:—

1. *Advanced Guard.*
   I/Durham Light Infantry.
   1st (less 1 troop) and 11nd Sqds. 7th Hussars.

2. *Main Body* (in order of march).
   1 Troop from 1st Sqd. 7th Hussars.
   II/Royal Scots.
   21st Field Battery R.A.
   32nd   ditto.
   II/Welsh Regiment.
   11th Field Co. R.E.
   Sect. A, Field Ambul.
   ⅔ Art. Brgde. Ammun. Col.

If you have put another battalion in the advanced guard, or less cavalry in the main body, or the engineers in the advanced guard, it is all the same as regards the steps to be taken for billeting the troops at night. A good deal might be said for such dispositions, and in such case your numbers only will slightly differ from mine.

With regard to the distribution of the troops among the various villages, the important question is, where are the several portions of the column of march at 5 p.m., when the officer commanding the detachment decides to halt; our object being to make such arrangements for billeting the

MARCH QUARTERS AND FLANK MARCH

troops that, if possible, there may be *no need for anyone to retrace his steps*. It is on this account that I have asked you to make an estimate of the road space occupied by the detachment on the march.

As soon as the exercises will become more difficult, it is advisable to put one's own and the enemy's troops on the map in colours which will wash off; this will make matters much clearer and better shows the whole situation.

Most of the cavalry is pushed out to the south-west, nor has their exact position at this time any bearing on the question of billeting them for the night.

The first principle to be observed in billeting the troops is, as mentioned before, that no unit shall have to go back if it can be possibly avoided. The second must now be laid stress on, viz. that *the troops should be distributed among the villages in such a manner as will best facilitate re-forming the column of march to resume the advance the next day*, provided that, as in this case, the direction and purpose of the next day's march *can* be foreseen. *Billeting the troops, therefore, is*, in a sense, *the beginning of the next day's march.* Therefore the first thing to do is to consider how the detachment will advance on Laquenexy on the 2nd August, and the C.O. must settle this in his own mind before he allots the billets.

The main body will naturally march by the main road as far as the cross-roads north of Colligny; thence either to the south edge of Ogy, and from there, by the by-road running due south, direct to Laquenexy; or viâ Colligny and Villers-Laquenexy to Laquenexy. Other roads which likewise enter into the question are :—

(1) The road viâ St. Barbe, Gras, Retonféy, Flanville, and Ogy.

(2) From Servigny-by-St. Barbe, viâ Noisseville, Montoy, and Coincy, and then either through Ars-Laquenexy or through Marsilly.

(3) From St. Barbe, viâ Cheuby, Glattigny, Vaudreville, Maizery (general map), and Colligny.

These three roads may be considered, tactically speaking, roads parallel to the line of march. The first is at no point more than about 1600 yards from the main road; for the most part nearer. On account of the numerous bends it is about 2 miles longer. The second is nowhere more than 2 miles from the main road, but is inconvenient, as it crosses the deep ravines of Noisseville, Montoy, and Coincy. The third road is not only considerably longer than the main road, but much worse, so that we should hesitate to march troops or vehicles by it without previously reconnoitring it.

Of great importance are further the high roads running through Lauvallière, Planchette, Colombey, and Ars-Laquenexy respectively towards Metz, and, consequently, towards the enemy. Study the country traversed by these roads, and you will see that, from the following points, extensive views are to be obtained:—

(1) From Amitié Brauerei, a view to Belle Croix.

(2) From Haut-Montoy, a view to Toten-Allee.

(3) From a point on the main road south of Coincy, or from the high ground near Aubigny, a view to the high ground west of Colombey, and the woods south-west of that place.

It is much more difficult to find a point whence a good view can be had on the high road through Ars-Laquenexy to Grigy. On the three first-mentioned roads (those leading to Metz viâ Lauvallière, Planchette, and Colombey) a comparatively small force of cavalry will suffice for reconnaissance; but the high road through Ars-Laquenexy requires very careful watching.

The country west of the high road, by which the main body will march, is, on the whole, easy to see over as far as the Vallières brook, for the valleys of Noisseville, Montoy, and Coincy can be easily observed by a few patrols. It is not so easy to watch the Vallières ravine itself, and the view is very restricted by the woods south-west of Colombey. After all, though, the line of heights east of the Vallières brook affords such a commanding view that, so long as our cavalry is there, the detachment is secure from surprise. If the enemy attacks from the westward, the villages of Retonféy, Flanville, St. Agnan, Ogy, and Marsilly are so favourably situated in the vicinity of our line of route that, by defending them, the enemy's advance could be checked a considerable time.

The mission of the detachment is accurately defined by the fact that it has to be at Laquenexy by a *certain* time; so the point is to decide how we shall utilise the roads at our disposal. All the hostile patrols have fallen back towards Metz, so that is the direction from which the enemy may be expected; moreover, reports state that there is a large bivouac of hostile troops near Borny. It is therefore a *flank march* that the detachment will have to make on the 2nd August.

To provide for protection and reconnaissance on the threatened flank devolves on the cavalry, which must go out in advance towards Metz on the most important roads, viz. those through Lauvallière, Planchette, Colombey, and Ars-Laquenexy. The cavalry must set out as soon as possible, especially on the main roads, passing through the two last-named places, to find out the exact whereabouts of the hostile force reported to be near Borny. Dividing the cavalry is thus quite unavoidable, as so often with detachments operating independently, however desirable it might be to keep the cavalry more together. Small patrols will not do here; they must be readily supported by closed bodies, whole troops or squadrons or cyclists, if the enemy shows great activity. Therefore in this case too the cavalry is to *reconnoitre* in the first instance, and in the second to *screen* the march of the detachment, the parties, sent towards Lauvallière and Planchette, carrying out the screening duties more *defensively* (*G.F.S.R.*, para. 196),[1] and those sent towards Colombey and Ars-Laquenexy more *offensively* (*G.F.S.R.*, para. 195).[1] The details for this are left to the cavalry commanders.

[1] *E. Cav. Tr.*, sect. 154.—*Trans.*

As we have the enemy on our flank, you might well ask whether a special flank guard, composed of infantry, should be thrown out. In this case it *is* desirable, as, should the enemy attack, we must not only have early information of his approach, but must hold him back as long as possible, until the main body either has formed up for action, or has gained a sufficient start on its march south. It is a question of *gaining time* which cavalry, on account of their small power of resistance, cannot gain for us unaided. Infantry is therefore needed, supported, if necessary, by artillery.

If the main body of the detachment is to march by the main road through Colligny, there can be no other road selected for the flank guard than that viâ Gras, Retonféy, Flanville, etc. The flank guard will thus be near enough to the main road for it to be easily supported. There are no obstacles between the two roads, and the view from one to the other is unimpeded. The road Noisseville–Montoy, etc., is *too far from the road by which the main body will march*, and is, moreover, *too near the enemy*, seeing that we have no occasion to seek an engagement, or to provoke the enemy to attack, but shall be well content if we can effect a junction with the 15th Division without having to fight. On this account, also, it would not be advisable to make the main body march by way of Retonféy and Ogy, and the flank guard possibly by Noisseville and Montoy, with the mistaken idea that the flank guard would thus be favourably placed to prevent the enemy crossing the Vallières brook. Neither would I recommend that the cavalry should *march parallel* with the main body by the road viâ Noisseville and Montoy, because the cavalry ought to go *straight* to the place where the enemy is reported to be.

The exercise does not say whether the enemy is in occupation of Metz, but it may be surmised from the fact that his patrols have fallen back on that town. The troops near Borny may consequently be considered as pushed out from Metz. The enemy will either retire, or stand fast, or advance.

If he retires, there is nothing in the way of preventing our intended junction with the 15th Division,—if he remains where he is, we shall perhaps attack him in close company with the 15th Division,—if he advances, the detachment must seek to avoid the danger of being beaten in detail; *but in any case we must try to effect a junction with the 15th Division without loss of time.*

The following are the lines by which the enemy may advance:—

(1) *By way of Lauvallière.* In that case we make efforts to push on the march, leaving the flank guard to follow as a rearguard.

(2) *By way of Planchette* on Flanville or St. Agnan. The flank guard, possibly reinforced, may make a stand until the detachment has got sufficient start in the direction of Colligny. Here again it will be a kind of rearguard action, only in this case the flank guard will probably have to hold its ground *much longer* than in the first case.

(3) *By way of Colombey.* It is more likely that the enemy will advance on this line than any other, because he is already present in some strength near Borny; *that is to say, on this road.* But it is hardly possible to imagine that he will move troops by this road without at the same time engaging the 15th Division with other troops going by the road Grigy–Ars-Laquenexy, as otherwise he would probably come between two fires. In this case the detachment would, in all probability, have to assume a vigorous offensive (having first effected a junction with the 15th Division), to drive the enemy back into the Vallières ravine. Should the junctions have not yet been effected, a delaying action must be fought. In *both* cases, however, the flank guard has to fend off the enemy until the main body is deployed and ready for action.

(4) *By way of Ars-Laquenexy only.* In this case the enemy will collide with the 15th Division, which we must support.

You must not now, however, because of the importance

of the flank guard, be led astray into making it too strong, still less is it advisable to cut up your detachment into two columns of about equal strength. Where large forces are concerned, the latter arrangement has, doubtless, the advantage that one half of the force can more effectually and quickly support the other if both are on parallel roads,—provided that the lateral distance between the two roads is less than half the depth of the column which would be formed by the entire force,—that the roads do not cross one another,—and that no impassable ground lies between them. In the case of a small *detachment*, however, a division into two columns tends to *fritter away its strength*. *The less disseminated a force is, the stronger it is;* for bodies once detached are for the time being out of hand, and one is never sure whether they are not being committed to an engagement *contrary to the intentions of the supreme commander;* whereas troops kept united in one column on the march can be applied in accordance with one fixed purpose. Before splitting up your force always ask yourself the question, *What is the least amount of troops* that can do the work? and detach only what is *absolutely necessary*. A flank guard of a few companies must suffice for such a detachment as we are here concerned with, the more so in view of the fact that the main body will not require long to form up for action.

In flank marches such as this the advanced guard, *as a rule*, plays an *un*important part; in the present instance, especially, it is difficult to suppose that we can encounter the enemy right in front of us, as he would, in that case, be pushing in between the 15th Division and the detachment. This is most improbable, because, remaining stationary as the enemy is in the neighbourhood of Metz, and in a country friendly to him, he is sure to receive information from the inhabitants, magistrates, etc., and cannot remain in ignorance of the advance of a division viâ Sorbey.

Two companies are sufficient for the advanced guard;

the other six of the same battalion can be detailed for the flank guard, so that a battalion in all is employed to protect the march. It would be permissible to detail a half-battalion for each purpose, but I prefer the first-mentioned distribution, as the flank guard may be involved in an obstinate fight ; moreover, as it is not impossible that the flank guard may have to be supported by a battery from the main body, it may be as well to allot it two extra companies for the greater security of the guns. It is desirable to take both flank guard and advanced guard from *one and the same battalion*, so that the main body may consist of complete battalions. At first no artillery must be attached to either flank guard or advanced guard, as they are both too weak. If the support of artillery is required, the guns can always be moved up from the main body in time, care being taken to provide for their safety while so moving. It is best, therefore, to keep the two batteries with the main body. There is no need for *engineers* with either flank or advanced guard, as no special obstructions are likely to be met with, and there would hardly be time to prepare any locality for defence.

With small detachments, and Colonel A.'s detachment being comparatively a small one, it is not desirable to impose again the fatiguing duty of forming the advanced or flank guard on the outposts, which have had no rest all night. The outposts usually stand fast until the new vanguard has passed through the line, when they close on the road and take their place in the column. Thus the outposts cover the rendezvous of the other troops, and are not withdrawn *till the cavalry of the vanguard has gained ground sufficiently to the front*. By this means you effect the desired relief easily and naturally. A *larger* body (Division) keeps its advanced guard composed of the same troops for some time, and makes no change in its composition until a unit has become so weakened by casualties that it becomes necessary to relieve it by a fresh one. This is rendered possible, because the advanced guard is so big that it can detail its component units for the heavier duties in due rotation. *Small* detachments, on the other hand, cannot adopt this procedure, and have to detail a new advanced guard each day, as above shown. It is best to detail the protective bodies for the next day to enter upon their duties just before beginning the fresh march.

If we have touch of the enemy's patrols, it would be a mistake to withdraw the outposts *too soon, as their withdrawal will inform the enemy that we are about to march off.*

Cavalry and flank guard have in this instance the same duty, and the closer the connection they keep up with each other the better will that duty be performed, and it is desirable, when the relative ranks permit of it, to assign the command of the flank guard to the officer commanding the cavalry. If, however, you wish to place the cavalry under the commander of the whole detachment, such a course might be justified by the need for sending out the bulk of the cavalry in advance in the direction of Metz. In that case, however, you must give the flank guard *some* cavalry, a troop at least, and this causes your cavalry to be rather disseminated. I therefore prefer the first-mentioned distribution (*i.e.* treating the cavalry as part of the flank guard), the more so because it will tend to counteract any *abuse of liberty by the cavalry, while not restricting its necessary freedom of action.*

The advanced guard can make shift with very little cavalry, as it only has to examine the country in close vicinity of the main road; for this purpose 1 N.C.O. and 6 troopers are enough. Communication with the 15th Division will be kept up by cyclists. The rest of the troop I would assign to the main body.

The distribution of troops for the 2nd August will be issued to the troops the night before, so that everybody may know in ample time to what portion of the column he belongs, and where he has therefore to fall in.

The 1$^\text{st}$ Squadron, which was on outpost duty, is named to furnish the troop for the main body and advanced guard, since it may be assumed that the two troops of this squadron on outposts will push out their reconnaissance in the direction of Metz before the march is begun, and that some time will therefore elapse before they are re-formed. The IInd Squadron thus remains intact for the purpose of reconnoitring towards the right flank.

The cavalry hitherto employed on outpost duty must have a fixed time and place of assembly appointed, that it may be placed at the disposal of the officer commanding the cavalry, and got in hand in good time for the purpose of covering the march. It should assemble, half an hour after the march begins, at the point where the road from Retonféy to Noisseville intersects the main road from Petit Marais to Lauvallière, this being about the centre of the line on which it has hitherto been operating as outpost cavalry. By this arrangement orders can reach it in proper course, and we do not have patrols and orderlies from the outpost companies wandering about, not knowing where they are to re-form after the detachment has marched off; for the result of the arrangement suggested is that the troop-leaders can give out early in the morning where the place of assembly is to be (*G.F.S.R.*, para. 274). It would be a mistake to recall the outpost cavalry before the detachment has got under weigh, as its duty is to *reconnoitre with the utmost vigour* while the other troops are being assembled.

The I/Durham Light Infantry will join the tail of the infantry in the column of march.

Having thus far explained the advance for the morrow, I will now consider the arrangements for billeting the troops. To this end I must once more review the various considerations which will influence the manner in which we must billet the troops; these are—firstly, the existing order of march when the detachment halts on the evening of 1st August,—care being taken that no unit has to *retrace* its steps to reach its quarters for the night; nextly, due convenience for continuing the advance,—care being taken that no unit has to make a *détour* to take up its place in the column next day; finally, the order of battle,—care being taken to arrange for the units under one command being quartered *as near one another as possible*. It must also be borne in mind that, the more distant the enemy, the more regard can be had for the *convenience* of our troops; but that *in the vicinity of the enemy tactical requirements prevail*, *i.e.* infantry occupies the villages nearest the front, which are the most exposed to attack; cavalry is billeted more towards the rear or flank, where they are safer and the horses get more rest; and artillery must *never* be billeted *by itself, nor yet too much to the front*. When the enemy is very near, troops are more closely packed into the villages, to which end all available sheds and stables should be utilised (*G.F.S.R.*, paras. 376 and 377).[1]

As four companies of the I/Durham Light Infantry and two troops of the Ist Squadron are on outpost duty, we shall billet the other half-battalion of the Durham Light Infantry and the other half of the Ist Squadron at Gras.

Infantry and artillery will be best on the main road, while cavalry can occupy the billets furthest from the road; so the IInd squadron will be quartered in Cheuby, where it is in safety, and can rest, as there is plenty of stabling.

The best place for the six companies of the flank guard will be on the road by which they will march next day, viz. at Erpigny; the two companies for advanced guard, which belong to the same battalion, being close by, in the houses on the western outskirts of St. Barbe. The II/Welsh Regiment and the two batteries may be quartered in St. Barbe, where the artillery are ensured security, as well as ample stabling for their numerous horses (280).

The engineers and the section field ambulance can remain either in the hamlets of Soleil d'Or and Point du Jour, where there will be plenty of room for them, or in Avancy.

[1] *E.F.S.R.*, Part I, sect. 45.—*Trans.*

The ammunition column will proceed to Avancy. The officer commanding the detachment will select his quarters so as (1) to be able to communicate his own orders rapidly—therefore in *as central a position as possible ;* and (2) so that reports from the front or orders from superior authority may readily reach him—therefore *on the main road.* St. Barbe meets both requirements.

Second Line Transport accompanies the respective units (*G.F.S.R.*, para. 444).[1] That of the outpost troops will either remain in Gras, or,—as the enemy is at present sufficiently distant, and there is no reason to fear a sudden attack,—it can, at any rate for a few hours, be placed at the disposal of the outpost companies.

If you have adopted a different order of march to mine, the arrangements for billeting the troops will likewise be different ; you can make the proper alterations yourself. Perhaps, in reasoning out the matter, you have not taken into account the question of *continuing the march on the morrow*, on the grounds that you do not consider it possible to foresee the exact manner in which it will be done, since circumstances may have altered before the time of starting comes. In practice, of course, we cannot always tell, at the time the troops go to their quarters for the night, what will be the exact arrangements for the march on the following day ; but when, as in the present instance, we can, it would be a mistake not to take advantage of it. The fact of the enemy's patrols having fallen back on Metz clearly indicates that there is not much likelihood of anything happening before to-morrow's march begins ; *else the enemy would show more activity in reconnaissance.*

The hour of beginning the march is fixed by the requirements laid down in the data, viz. that the detachment is to arrive east of Laquenexy by 8 a.m. From what we have discussed in the previous letter, it would be wrong to have *one* point of assembly, such as St. Barbe, or Petit Marais, for the whole detachment ; for we must, so far as is pos-

---

[1] *E.F.S.R.*, Part I, sect. 12, p. 26 footnote, and sect. 28 (1).—*Trans.*

sible, avoid causing any unit an unnecessary détour, which the flank guard would have to make if all had to rendezvous at either of the two above-named points.

Two companies from St. Barbe and cavalry from Gras will form the advanced guard; they can start from Petit Marais. From Petit Marais to Laquenexy it is a little over $5\frac{1}{2}$ miles, or 1 hour and 50 minutes' march. The advanced guard must therefore be assembled by 6 a.m. to start at 6.10 a.m.

The main body will be composed of cavalry and four companies from Gras, a battalion and the two batteries from St. Barbe, the outposts, and, in addition, the engineers, the field ambulance section, and the ammunition column. All these units assemble in column of route on the road St. Barbe–Petit Marais with its head where the road from Gras joins that main road. I assume that the advanced guard companies precede the main body about $\frac{1}{2}$ mile; they push out half a company $\frac{1}{4}$ mile as advanced party with an infantry point about $\frac{1}{4}$ mile ahead of it. The total distance from the point to the head of the main body is thus about a mile. The distance from Petit Marais to the head of the main body being about $\frac{1}{2}$ mile, the main body must be assembled by 6.15 a.m. to start at 6.25 a.m.

The outposts do not affect the question, as they will march by the shortest way to the main road, and probably join the main column as it passes Retonféy.

The flank guard, to be composed of the infantry from Erpigny, and cavalry,—some from Cheuby and some from Gras,—can start from Gras. A special order must be sent to the two troops of the 1st Squadron on outposts at their place of assembly. We must fix the time for the flank guard to start, so that it will march *approximately* level with the advanced guard, remembering to give it some start, as the road it has to march on winds considerably. I let it start at 5.45 a.m. (*G.F.S.R.*, para. 176).[1]

The 2nd line transport, in the present instance, had

[1] *E.F.S.R.*, Part I, sect. 70.

better follow immediately in rear of the main body, so as to reduce the length of the column and pass from in front of the enemy as soon as possible. Perhaps it has occurred to you to send it by the road through Cheuby, Glattigny, etc., thus by a road parallel to that of the main column and away from the enemy ; this is not advisable, for, as we have seen above, this road is too bad for ponderous wagons. No doubt this is a disadvantage, but bear in mind that there are so many by-roads running eastwards from our main road, that we can always withdraw the baggage by one of them as soon as it appears, by the reports from the front, that we cannot avoid an obstinate engagement with the enemy. I do not consider it necessary to provide any special protection, in the sense of a small rearguard, for the baggage in this case, as it can be sufficiently protected—in case of being attacked, for instance, by hostile cavalry—by men who have fallen out, unable to march, or by the rearmost troops of the main body. Avoid causing any vehicle a détour. The main body in column of route is over a mile long, and therefore extends from the junction of the Gras road with the St. Barbe-Colligny road to about where this latter road branches off from the main Metz–Avancy road. The vehicles of the 2nd line transport must therefore have moved up by 6.40 a.m. to the main road St. Barbe-Colligny, ready to join in their proper place in the column. But no wagon must be allowed to enter the road before the fighting troops of the main body have passed. It is the business of the officer commanding the baggage to see that each unit takes its proper place in the column (G.F.S.R., para. 442).[1]

[1] *E.F.S.R.*, Part I, sect. 28.

FOURTH LETTER

OPERATION ORDER No. 3
BY
COLONEL A., COMMANDING DETACHED FORCE.

Copy No. 1.

Reference:
$\frac{1}{100.000}$ *Ordn.*

ST. BARBE,
1.8.00.

1. *Advanced Guard:*
    Capt. B.
    1 N.C.O., 6 men I/7th Hussars.
    2 Companies II/Royal Scots.

2. *Main Body* (in order of march).
    1 Troop I/7th Hussars.
    II/Welsh Rgt.
    21st Field Battery R.A.
    32nd   do.
    I/Durham L.I.
    11th Field Co. R.E.
    Sect. Field Ambul.
    Ammun. Col.

3. *Right Flank Guard:*
    Lt-.Col. C.
    I/7th Hussars (less 1 troop).
    II/7th Hussars.
    II/Royal Scots (less 2 companies).
    Detachment of Cyclists.

1. To-morrow will stand in column of route ready to start:

    The Advanced Guard by 6 a.m. with its head at **PETIT MARAIS**.

    The Main Body by 6.15 a.m. with its head at the point where the road from **GRAS** joins the main road **ST. BARBE–COLLIGNY**.

    The Right Flank Guard, under whose orders will be placed all the cyclists of the detachment, by 5.45 a.m. with its head at the eastern outlet of **GRAS**.

    The 2nd Line Transport will join the column independently, the wagons of the various units being ready by 6.40 a.m. with their heads close to the **ST. BARBE–COLLIGNY** road. No wagon is allowed to enter that road except by order of the commander of the whole baggage.

2. *The Infantry of the Outposts* will close in on the road **ST. BARBE-COLLIGNY** at 6.15 a.m. *The Cavalry of the Outposts* will assemble at 6.40 a.m. at the intersection of the **RETONFÉY–NOISSEVILLE** road with the main road from **PETIT MARAIS** to **METZ**.

3. *Officers commanding units* will attend to receive orders at 5.45 a.m. on the knoll north-east of **GRAS**.

        A.,
        Colonel.

Dictated to officers representing the several units at 10 p.m.

MARCH QUARTERS AND FLANK MARCH

OPERATION ORDER No. 4

BY

COLONEL A., COMMANDING DETACHED FORCE.

Reference:
$\frac{2}{100.000}$ *Ordn.*

Knoll N.E. of **GRAS**,
2.8.00.

Copy No. 1.

1. *The Enemy* is reported to be in bivouac near **BORNY**; his patrols fell back on **METZ** yesterday afternoon.

2. *The Detachment* has to join, at 8 a.m. near **LAQUENEXY**, the 15th Division, which is advancing viâ **SORBEY**.

3. *The Advanced Guard* will march off at 6.10 a.m. on the road to **LAQUENEXY** viâ **COLLIGNY** and **VILLERS-LAQUENEXY**, and will endeavour to open communication with the 15th Division.

4. *The Main Body* will follow at $\frac{1}{2}$ mile distance.

5. *The Right Flank Guard* will march off at once, viâ **RETONFÉY, FLANVILLE,** and **OGY**, for **LAQUENEXY**, reconnoitring towards **METZ** by way of **LAUVALLIÈRE, PLANCHETTE** and **COLOMBEY, ARS-LAQUENEXY**.

6. *The 2nd Line Transport* will follow the main body without any distance.

7. *Reports* will reach me at the head of the main guard.

Verbally to the assembled
commanding officers at
5.45 a.m.

A.,
Colonel.

The knoll north-east of Gras is fixed upon as the place for issuing the final order, because from that point a commanding view is to be had over the country under consideration, which is always an advantage in explaining matters, should any of the subordinate officers ask questions or require explanations—a thing which in reality not infrequently will occur, *in spite of the clearest orders.*

In conclusion, I will ask you briefly to review the exercises we have up to now worked out. In the first we dealt with a simple advance, with nothing but hostile cavalry to expect on our flank; so the attention of our own cavalry, especially towards the parts threatened, was sufficient, and a flank guard was not wanted.—In the second exercise we had hostile *infantry* to expect on one flank, though so distant that we could depend on reconnaissance with cavalry alone warning us in good time to occupy a suitable position. A flank guard was unnecessary here too.—In the third exercise, the present one, we had again a case of a flank march, the enemy on this occasion, however, being so near that an engagement was quite possible. In this instance, owing to favourable roads and the favourable nature of the country lying *between* the roads under consideration, *a flank guard* was not only allowable, but *necessary*, in order to gain for the main body the time necessary for taking counter measures.—In the next exercise we shall again have the enemy on our flank, but under somewhat different circumstances to any we have yet had to deal with.

FOURTH EXERCISE.
(See general map, and maps Metz and Verny.)

A detached force in its own country, under Colonel A., composed as follows:—

> I/Battalion.
> II/ do.
> III/ do.
> Rifle Battalion.
> 1st and IInd Sqds. 1st Dragoons.
> 1st Field Art. Brgde. with Ammun. Col.
> 1st Field Co. R.E.
> Sect. A, 1st Field Ambul.

is on the march, on the 3rd June, 1900, from Tennschen (general map, east of Metz) to the unfortified town of Metz, which is garrisoned by portions of the 3rd Division. The cavalry of the detachment is pushed out in a south-westerly direction towards the railway from Metz to Saarbrücken (Remilly).

At 8.30 a.m. an orderly-officer from the 3rd Division hands to Colonel A. the following message:—

"Reliable information states a hostile Division to be advancing west of the Französische (French) Nied. The 3rd Division wil provisionally maintain a defensive attitude, until the arrival of reinforcements expected from Diedenhofen. A small force of our Division has occupied the suburbs of Plantières and Queuleu. Cavalry is reconnoitring towards Courcelles-on-the-Nied (a. d. Nied)."

When at 9 a.m. the advanced party of the vanguard has arrived about Amitié brewery (south of Noisseville), the following report from an officer's patrol reaches Colonel A., who has ridden forward to the brewery :—

"High ground east of **AUBIGNY**,
"3.6.00.
"8.35 a.m.

"Hostile column of all arms advancing from **COURCELLES-ON-THE-NIED** on **ARS-LAQUENEXY**, hostile advanced guard infantry shortly reaching **CHAMBERDINE**. Have noticed a squadron halted at the churchyard of **ARS-LAQUENEXY**, which is patrolling towards **COLOMBEY**. An inhabitant of the country reports that last night a hostile force of 6 battalions and several batteries were bivouacked south of **SORBEY**. Remain in observation."

Required :—
1. The distribution of troops during the march on the 3rd June.
2. The arrangements made by Colonel A.
3. Reasons for the arrangements made.

FIFTH LETTER

CHANGE OF DIRECTION OF MARCH

WITH regard to the network of roads entering into the problem, we must firstly consider the main roads running to Metz—then those leading towards the enemy. If it continues its march on the road on which we find it, the detachment will have, on passing Amitié brewery, to descend into the deep and precipitous ravine of the Vallières brook, and then ascend the heights of Belle Croix. The latter constitutes a striking point in the country. Thence towards the south the country can be seen, beyond the road from Borny to Colombey, as far as the woods south-east of Borny;—towards the south-east to beyond the Todten-Allee (though Colombey itself cannot be seen, nor the bottom of the Vallières ravine between Colombey and Lauvallière) ;—towards the west the Metz road as far as Bordes is hidden from view from the south by the spur close alongside of it marked 219 and 214. The roads south of the main road through Belle Croix have not much importance for the detachment, *as we have no occasion to seek an engagement by moving in the direction of the enemy;* but it is far different with the roads to the north, by which we may reach Metz perhaps without fighting. These are :—

(1) The road viâ Noisseville, Nouilly, and Vallières. This excellent road soon after leaving Noisseville descends into the valley of the Vallières brook, running parallel with and on the north bank of the brook as far as the village of Vallières, after that south of it. An enemy approaching from the south cannot see this road until he gets on the

CHANGE OF DIRECTION OF MARCH

break of the southern slope of the valley, immediately overhanging the brook.

(2) The road viâ Gras and Servigny-by-St. Barbe to the main road Metz–Freisdorf (general map). This road has some bad places between the villages of Gras and Servigny-by-St. Barbe.

(3) The road from Petit Marais viâ St. Barbe, then Metz–Freisdorf main road—a long distance, to be sure. As soon as the enemy reached the heights of Belle Croix or Amitié, he could see a column of troops marching on the Metz–Freisdorf main road on the far horizon.

Roads leading in the enemy's direction, or, which amounts to the same thing, available for his advance against our detachment, are:—

(1) The main road viâ Colligny.

(2) The road through Retonféy and Ogy.

(3) The road through Montoy and Coincy to Ars-Laquenexy.

(4) The road from Belle Croix to Colombey by Todten Allee.

(5) The road from Belle Croix through Grange-aux-Bois to Ars-Laquenexy.

(6) The road from Borny through Grigy and Ars-Laquenexy.

Hostile infantry, at all events, moving by roads (1), (2), or (3) would hardly arrive in time to disturb the march of the detachment, though *possibly cavalry* advancing on these roads might do so. Road (6) runs from Grigy to the vicinity of the villages of Queuleu and Plantières, which are held by detachments from the garrison of Metz. The enemy will not be long in ascertaining that these villages are being held, so he will avoid taking this road, and confine himself to roads (4) and (5). The detachment, on the other hand, can employ all these roads in reconnoitring, to ascertain the direction of the enemy's march, and to this end the eastern and western roads will be of great value, lying as they do on both flanks of the advancing enemy (*G.F.S.R.*, para. 127).

FIFTH LETTER

After working out the two previous exercises, you will now be quite clear, without my specially directing your attention to it by asking you for an estimate of road space, as to the position of the various portions of the column on the march when the orders reach them, which the officer commanding the detachment must now issue, basing them upon the report received from the officer's patrol. Perhaps you have marked your own and the enemy's troops on the map in colours that can be washed off.

According to the special idea, Colonel A. has ridden on in advance to Amitié brewery, whence he gets a commanding view, especially towards the west and south-west. Besides his Adjutant, an orderly-officer, some mounted orderlies and cyclists, probably the officers commanding the artillery, the field company of engineers, and the advanced guard would have ridden forward with him. The above-mentioned commanding officers thus can receive the orders *verbally* and *at once;* but the orders will have to be sent to the cavalry, the main body, and the 2nd line transport. As we have to transmit *important* orders, they had better be in writing. *Officers* are sent to carry them, if at the same time they are to give verbally any further information that may be desirable. Should this not be the case, the orders can be carried in writing by cyclists or mounted orderlies. It is permissible to convey orders *verbally* if it is a question of a *short message only*, if, as in this case, it were only necessary to send a notice to the 2nd line transport to turn off into the Metz–Freisdorf road. As, however, it is necessary to mention the general situation as regards the detachment, in order to make *the whole state of affairs* clear to the recipient, there can be no question that *written* orders are preferable (*G.F.S.R.*, para. 46).[1] In our case here I would send a cyclist to the main body and 2nd line transport with a written order.

If you give an order *verbally, don't be in a hurry*. It often happens to an aide-de-camp, rushing off at a gallop,

---

[1] *E.F.S.R.*, Part I, sect. 9 (1) (i.).—*Trans.*

to be in doubt already after covering the first few yards what the full text of the order was, and it is shown in practice that *errors in the names of villages* occur too easily. It is best in this case to make the bearer not only repeat the order, but to show him also the names of the places on the map; he then not only remembers them better, but can also show them more readily to the recipient of the order, thus saving sometimes most valuable time.

Instead of *one* operation order addressed to your several units collectively, you might now give *several separate* orders, one to the cavalry, one to the advanced guard, one to the main body, one to the artillery, and one to the 2nd line transport; in all five, some verbally, and some in writing. To ensure the thorough combination, however, of all I prefer one operation order for all; for the several subordinate commanders can much more clearly understand their own respective duties, if each knows what the others are about, and *they will make their dispositions fit better into the general plan of action*. In this case, as the orders are heard by the officers commanding advanced guard and artillery as they are being dictated to the Adjutant and orderly-officer, it actually will take less time to issue one operation order than several separate ones.

It is often advisable in the first instance to issue brief orders or extracts from orders, and to allow the complete order to follow (*G.F.S.R.*, para. 54).

We will suppose that for deliberating on the situation and giving out the orders only 10 minutes are required—this is very little, and presupposes a very able commanding officer—and that during this time the detachment continues its march. The officer commanding the advanced guard, as we said before, receives the orders at once, that is, at 9.10 a.m., being on the spot. He sends a mounted officer to the cavalry commander. Two cyclists carry the order to the main body, and after delivery proceed with it to the 2nd line transport with the same object. The first point to settle now is therefore the position of the main body and 2nd line transport at 9.10 a.m.; next, their positions when they receive the order.

I assume the following, leaving to you the necessary calculations :—

The advanced party of the vanguard has nearly reached the eastern edge of the village of Lauvallière.

The head of the main body is about $\frac{1}{4}$ mile east of the Retonféy–Noisseville road junction.

The tail of the main body is about $\frac{1}{4}$ mile east of Petit Marais.

The head of the 2nd line transport is something like $1\frac{1}{4}$ miles east of Petit Marais.

A cyclist (better two) will by such a good road reach the head of the main body in a few minutes, at a time therefore before it has quite reached the road junction Retonféy–Noisseville; the cyclist can reach the 2nd line transport while it is with its head still east of Petit Marais, it having not yet covered the $1\frac{1}{4}$ miles to that place by that time.

The report states that the infantry of the advanced guard of a hostile column composed of all arms reached Chamberdine at 8.40 a.m. Regarding the strength of the said column, we have only the report of an inhabitant to depend on, to the effect that six battalions and several batteries of the enemy had bivouacked the previous night near Sorbey. This is such a definite statement that perhaps it is correct, but only *perhaps*, for all such kind of reports should be received with caution, even when made by our own countrymen, and are not deserving of much attention, unless *corroborated*, or, at all events, as in this case, have *some colour lent them* by the reports of our cavalry. Much of the information received on active service is either false, or else most inaccurate and contradictory, and the only intelligence that is really trustworthy is that transmitted by *a reliable officer, and based upon what he has distinctly seen with his own eyes from not too great a distance.* All that is certain from the news to hand in the present instance is that the enemy is advancing, and has got pretty

CHANGE OF DIRECTION OF MARCH

near the detachment ; but this is enough to compel the commanding officer to come to an important decision. There are several questions to which we have no answer. We have received information from Metz that a hostile division is on the march northwards to the west of the Französische Nied. What connection has the hostile detachment whose advance is reported with this division ? If it is its advanced guard, where is the main body of the division ? or if it is a flank guard, whereabouts is its main body ? or is the enemy marching in two columns of equal strength ?

If the enemy has continued his advance in the same direction without a halt, and there can be little doubt about this, he will be arriving at Chagny-la-Horgne about 9.5 a.m. Thence he will probably, as we saw when considering the network of roads, continue his advance either towards Colombey or on Grange-aux-Bois. From his advanced squadron he has, at the very least, learnt that it has gained touch with our patrols, and it is quite possible that he has further received information of the advance of Colonel A.'s detached force. The fact of the hostile squadron having halted at the churchyard of Ars-Laquenexy, and provisionally patrolling only to Colombey, leads to the conclusion that, in consequence of news received, it intends exercising *great caution* as to how it prosecutes its reconnaissance. As, moreover, the churchyard of Ars-Laquenexy is on the road to *Colombey*, and the enemy's patrols are *for the most part* moving on the latter village, it may be reasonably assumed that the hostile column is to march on Colombey. It is strange that the officer's patrol has seen only *one* squadron of the enemy. From this it would seem either that the enemy is very weak in cavalry, or that he is employing some of his cavalry elsewhere ; for instance, in the neighbourhood of the great wood of Champel, or of the woods west of Ars-Laquenexy, to reconnoitre towards his left flank and towards Metz. At all events we have, *for the time being*, the advantage of being *superior* to the enemy *in cavalry* in the neighbourhood of Colombey. This circumstance will not only retard the enemy's reconnaissance—as he will have to advance cautiously—but also his advance as a whole. This, however, means *gaining time* for Colonel A.'s detachment. If matters turn out as unfavourably as possible for us, the head of the enemy's column passing Chagny-la-Horgne at about 9.5 a.m., may appear on the high ground south of the Französisches Denkmal in 36 minutes, *i.e.* at 9.41 a.m., and then open fire, with his artillery pushed forward, in the direction of Belle Croix.

If Colonel A. simply continued to advance on the same road as before, the head of his main body would be somewhat west of Lauvallière by 9.41 a.m., and so the main body and the 2nd line transport might have to ascend the height of Belle Croix under the enemy's fire. The inevitable result of this would be an engagement with the enemy. But the detachment has nothing to gain by *bringing about such a conflict on its own responsibility*, and it has the less reason to do so, since it cannot at all be foreseen to what such an action may lead under the present circumstances and how the detachment can afterwards disengage itself from the enemy. Any leader, however, who without a *definite object* engages in a combat *which is avoidable* commits an error. It must, moreover, be remembered that we know that the 3rd Division in Metz will remain on the defensive until reinforced from Diedenhofen. The detachment would act contrary to this distinctly expressed intention if it would rush into an action with an enemy probably much superior to it; for the moment the detachment would get into difficulties; the 3rd Division would be bound to come to its rescue. The above reasoning leads to the conclusion that the detachment must *diverge* from its previous line of march. But if the main body, after arriving with its head west of Lauvallière at 9.41, would continue its march now *across country south* of the Vallières brook, turning Belle Croix in the north, it would of course be soon covered by the heights of Belle Croix; but its march would

CHANGE OF DIRECTION OF MARCH

not only be very uncomfortable and slow, but it would also have the Vallières brook as an obstacle on its right, which might cause the main body to find itself in a very tight corner should the enemy press on vigorously.

The best plan therefore is for the main body to continue marching *north* of the Vallières brook by turning off beforehand at the road junction east of Noisseville, and marching through that village *into the Nouilly valley*, where it will be perfectly covered from the view of the enemy. To cover the main body, the hitherto advanced guard must occupy a good position south of the brook, namely, at Belle Croix, to delay the enemy, should it be absolutely necessary (*G.F.S.R.*, para. 178).[1] But the advanced guard should cause this delay if possible even *without engaging its infantry*.

The main body may be considered out of danger when the tail of it has reached the village of Vallières ; this will not be until 1 hour 40 minutes (a little over 5 miles) after 9.10 a.m., that is to say, at 10.50 a.m. Until *at least* 10.50 a.m., therefore, the advanced guard has to hold the enemy in check. But as the enemy may possibly begin to make himself felt at 9.45 a.m., it follows that, on behalf of the *main body only*, the advanced guard may have about 1 hour's fighting before it. Now we have to consider the 2nd line transport. If you purpose to make it likewise diverge by way of Noisseville, the advanced guard will have to hold its ground proportionately longer. It is more convenient to move the transport out of danger further to the north ; and, as the road between Gras and Servigny-by-St. Barbe is too bad, to send it from Petit Marais viâ St. Barbe to the main Metz–Freisdorf (Vrémy) road. On the assumption that the head of the baggage column reaches Petit Marais about 9.40 a.m., it will be safe in St. Julien about 2 hours after that (6 miles).

The fact has now to be reckoned with, that in reality tactical operations *require very much more time* than would appear from our peace manœuvres, where we sometimes

[1] *E.F.S.R.*, Part I, sect. 70 (3).—*Trans.*

carry out several distinct attacks in the course of a forenoon. In reality, our opponent, when operating in a country hostile to him, requires *a long time* to carry out his reconnaissance, owing to his uncertainty as to, and ignorance of, the general situation; especially when, as here, he is inferior in cavalry. Again, the circumstance that the enemy in this case will have to be doubly cautious, owing to the proximity of Metz and the awkward obstacle presented by the Vallières ravine, will gain time for our detachment. Time is also required for his deployment and for the artillery preparation of his attack. In short, not until some hours have elapsed, probably, would the enemy be able to think of an attack on Belle Croix; that is, supposing he decides to do so at all, *which is quite uncertain*, as, before undertaking an offensive movement against the detachment, he must detach troops in the direction of Metz in sufficient strength to cover his left flank. Yet it would be a false conclusion to say, "The enemy will not attack—we can continue the march undisturbed"; for you must ever reckon with the possibility of his attacking.

Colonel A.'s advanced guard should begin by taking up the favourable position of Belle Croix *in readiness* for possible contingencies. As the advanced infantry of the vanguard was just entering the village of Lauvallière at 9.10 a.m. it will take about 24 minutes to reach Belle Croix (under $1\frac{1}{4}$ miles).

The principal duty of the advanced guard is *to gain time* without committing itself to an obstinate and bloody infantry engagement, if such can be avoided. To enable it to accomplish this, it is best to reinforce it by the three batteries, whose fire will compel the enemy to deploy early and to advance for some distance slowly in extended order. Our object, thus, is to conduct the fight at the outset with artillery fire only; which will, moreover, probably mislead the enemy as to the strength of the force holding Belle Croix, as, usually, the presence of several batteries implies a considerable force of infantry acting with them. I admit that one battalion is rather a small escort for the three batteries, but this does not matter, considering the strength of the position, as the guns have a good line of retreat if seriously endangered, or, in case of need, infantry reinforcements can easily be sent up from the main body. There would be no trouble in carrying out the latter measure, as there are plenty of passages across the Vallières brook, which the infantry would, moreover, be able to ford should this become necessary. At the outset there is no need to reinforce the infantry of the advanced guard.

The *decision* therefore is : The advanced guard, with the addition of the three batteries, to take up a position of readiness at Belle Croix ; the main body to turn northwards viâ Noisseville ; 2nd line transport viâ St. Barbe.

You will, perhaps, wonder why I have hitherto occupied your attention so much with calculations. It is by no means "*colourless theory,*" for the correct estimation of space and time is the foundation on which correct tactical decisions have to be based, and is a process which cannot be practised enough in working out tactical problems. A pair of compasses is thus the most important aid to any officer in command of troops. That instrument will save him making grievous blunders, although it has no pretensions to the absolute accuracy of a mathematical calculation, which is thoroughly reliable. In tactics, moreover, such calculations can never be absolutely accurate. We are too much dependent on accidents, which may upset the most careful calculations. Without, therefore, attributing an *exaggerated* value to the product of these latter, there can be no question as to the advantage of these estimates of space and time. Remember the manœuvres in which you have taken part, and how easy it is, for instance, for a General, brought up in the cavalry or artillery, to wax impatient over the " incredible slowness " of infantry ; and how natural it is for a commander brought up in the infantry often to wonder how it is reports from the cavalry are so long in reaching him, or why artillery cannot change position in a moment. Just calculate how long it would take the three batteries, in the present instance, to reach Belle Croix under the most favourable circumstances.

I will assume the existing distribution of your troops to be as follows :—

DISTRIBUTION OF TROOPS.

1. *Advanced Guard:* Lt.-Col. C.
   Ist Sqd. and IInd Sqd. (less 1 troop) 1st Dragoons.
   1st Field Co. R.E.
   Rifle Battalion.

2. *Main Body* (in order of march): Lt.-Col. D.
   1 Troop IInd Sqd. 1st Dragoons.
   I/Battalion.
   1st Field Art. Brgde.
   II/ and III/Battalions.
   1st Field Ambul.
   Field Art. Brgde. Ammun. Col.

Copy No. 1.

OPERATION ORDER No. 2

BY

COLONEL A., COMMANDING DETACHED FORCE.

Reference: **AMITIÉ BRAUEREI,**
$\frac{1}{100,000}$ *Ordn.*   3.6.00.

1. *A Hostile Column* of all arms is advancing from **COURCELLES-ON-THE-NIED** to **ARS-LAQUENEXY**.

   Our 3rd Division is holding weakly the suburbs of **PLANTIÈRES** and **QUEULEU**.

2. *The Detachment* will turn off northwards, and continue to march to **METZ**.

3. *The Advanced Guard* will at once be reinforced by the 1st Field Artillery Brigade, and will take up a position near **BELLE CROIX** to delay the enemy until further orders. It will watch **ARS-LAQUENEXY** and **LAQUENEXY** through **GRIGY, COLOMBEY,** and **COINCY**, along the **VALLIÈRES** brook.

4. *The Main Body* will proceed, via **NOISSEVILLE, NOUILLY,** and **VALLIÈRES**, to **LES BORDES**.

5. *The 2nd Line Transport*, escorted by 2 companies of the III./Battalion, will proceed, viâ **ST. BARBE, KRUG** near **VRÉMY**, to **METZ**.

6. *The Artillery Brigade Ammunition Column* will be at the disposal of the Officer Commanding Artillery Brigade.

7. *Reports* to **BELLE CROIX**, where I shall be.

Verbally to C.O. Advanced Guard,
„ Artillery.
In writing by 2 cyclists to
C.O. Main Body, Copy No. 2,
„ 2nd Line Transport, Copy No. 3,
„ 3rd Division, Copy No. 4,
at 9.10 a.m.

A.,
Colonel.

N.B.—*No* distribution of troops here, as that was given in the orders issued overnight.

I have given you here the whole order without any preliminary observations, so as to afford you a general idea of the measures I think it necessary to adopt. I will now go through the paragraphs of the order one by one.

No. 1. There is no occasion to mention in the order the report concerning a hostile squadron having halted by the churchyard of Ars-Laquenexy, for you cannot be sure it is still there at the moment the order is issued. Your cavalry, whom the information principally concerns, will have meanwhile long ago observed for themselves whether the hostile squadron is remaining halted there or no.

No. 2. The words " turn off northwards " forthwith summarise your general intention, so they are not redundant; although in subsequent paragraphs the fact that the detachment will turn off northwards is repeated, together with instructions as to how it is to be done.

No. 3. As soon as the enemy's direction of advance has been ascertained, you must endeavour, above all things, to watch his movements from a position on his *flank ;* for nothing more can be learnt from a position in front when once you are engaged with the infantry of his advanced guard. Every party of our cavalry must see clearly here that their *main task* consists in preventing the enemy from becoming aware of the direction of our march having been changed; they must therefore *veil* this movement by driving away the hostile patrols (*G.F.S.R.*, paras. 195 and 197). Send the *bulk* of the cavalry towards that flank of the enemy which is most dangerous *to you* (in this case his right flank, because of Colombey), to find out all they can and to veil your own march. The other flank, in this case less dangerous to you, because of the proximity of Metz, must be watched by weaker bodies—troops and patrols. The closer the enemy's infantry approaches, the more will your cavalry close in on the flanks of your position (*G.F.S.R.*, para. 131). For the most part, however, it is better to leave the cavalry commander a free hand as to the details of the distribution of his command—at any rate, when the enemy is yet distant—for he, being in touch with the enemy, is in a better position to judge of such matters. You can leave him, provisionally, the freedom he has hitherto had, although you are dictating the roads to be *especially* watched by the advanced guard. As the officer commanding the detachment remains at Belle Croix, close to the officer commanding the advanced guard, *both* these officers will receive information from the cavalry patrols simultaneously.

The advanced guard is left to make its own arrangements for taking up a position near Belle Croix, but is instructed to hold out "till further orders," because the officer commanding the detachment will require it to stand fast until the main body and 2nd line transport are in safety. By what time this will be accomplished may, of course, be estimated approximately, but not with absolute certainty, as unforeseen delays may occur. The commander of the whole force will always be able to note the position of the main body and transport, and generally to supervise *the whole force;* while the advanced guard commander can *devote his whole attention* to the enemy's advance and *the fighting*.

No. 4. The senior officer present and in charge of the main body while the commander of the whole detachment is for the moment absent arranges for the new direction of the march to be initiated; he will inform the officers commanding the various units about the fresh orders received. I consider it unnecessary in this case for the main body to form a *new* advanced guard, because of the proximity of Metz.

No. 5. It now becomes necessary to give the 2nd line transport a *special escort*. This must be considered an *exceptional* measure, justified by the necessity for protecting the transport, which might at any moment be attacked by *strong bodies* of the enemy's cavalry moving northwards through Colligny or Marsilly (*G.F.S.R.*, para. 434).[1] Two companies are ample for the purpose, and it is most convenient to select the two rearmost companies in the main body, which can wait at Petit Marais until the transport arrives there. As to which two companies of the III/Battalion it will be, Colonel A. can hardly say. On this account Colonel A. says " two companies."

No. 6. As regards the artillery brigade ammunition column, you will find the particulars in the *Artillery Training*.

In conclusion, compare the various measures which we have adopted, in the exercises so far worked out, with regard to the 2nd line transport. The first exercise dealt with a simple advance—a collision with the enemy being probable—so the transport *remained behind* at a suitable place, after proceeding a short distance, only just enough to get the wagons into their places.—In the second exercise we had to do with a flank march, and the transport is moved up to the Division.—In the third exercise— again a flank march—the 2nd line transport had to follow *close on the main body* without special escort. If, however, there had been suitable roads for it to travel on, on the side further from the enemy, we should have caused it to

[1] There is no mention made of this particular procedure in the *E.F.S.R.*—*Trans.*

move by them. It had to follow close on the main body without any distance, so as to reduce as far as possible the length of the column.—But in the present, the fourth exercise, there is *a serviceable road running parallel,* on which the transport is at once placed under escort, as soon as the enemy threatens the flank.

FIFTH EXERCISE.

(See Map Ars-on-the-Moselle.)

A convoy of provisions intended for troops in the unfortified town of Metz, occupying a road space of 1¼ miles, escorted by

I/ and II/Battalions,
I/ and II/1st Dragoons,

under Colonel A., after an exhausting march in its home country halts for the night 1/2 August, 1900, in and south of Marieulles, where it arrives late in the evening. During the march the following intelligence had come in:—

1. A railway official from Novéant has learned that the enemy reached Gorze with a force of all arms about 4 p.m., his outposts standing at Schl. Ste. Cathérine.[1]

2. The cavalry which had been pushed out towards Corny reported the following at 9 p.m.: "Met east of Corny hostile cavalry patrols, who withdrew on Corny. Came under infantry fire from Corny and Zgl. south of it."[2]

Colonel A. places outposts for the night, consisting of the II/Battalion and a troop of I/1st Dragoons, on the line Bois-le-Comte–Wald von Arry. All the bridges over the Moselle between Corny and Metz have been destroyed by the Metz garrison.

Required:—

The arrangements made by Colonel A. for the 2nd August, with reasons for the same, assuming that up to the time of starting no fresh information is to hand respecting the enemy.

---

[1] St. Catherine Castle.   [2] Zgl. = Ziegelei = brick-kiln.

SIXTH LETTER

PROTECTION OF A CONVOY

THE *protection of a convoy* demands measures somewhat different from those usually adopted for the protection of an ordinary march. This follows from the fact that a convoy is always more or less slow and clumsy, and that it is not easy to bring it into a place of safety, should the enemy attack it. The difficulty of escorting it increases in proportion to the length of the convoy, especially when, as nearly always happens on service, *but few troops* can be detailed for this comparatively unimportant duty. On coming in contact with the enemy, a very little is enough—say rifle bullets or a shrapnel shell taking effect on the wagon teams—to throw the whole convoy into confusion, and cause a check, to say the least, extremely inconvenient, *generally very dangerous*. With drivers organised as soldiers, these difficulties can perhaps be, comparatively speaking, easily got over; but in dealing with impressed, possibly disaffected country folk, with their own horses, nothing but the most uncompromising severity of the officers, N.C.O.'s, and men appointed to supervise the convoy can *maintain the order which is so vitally important.* Such officers, etc., are responsible for the order of the convoy, and for it keeping strictly to one side of the road, so as not only to leave room for other traffic, but that any broken-down wagons may be readily drawn out of the column and repaired; subsequently joining the tail of the convoy with as little delay as possible. If, as is usually the case, it would take too long to repair a wagon, the soldiers superintending the convoy have to transfer its contents to other wagons, or destroy them if necessary, rather than they should fall into the enemy's hands. Such interruptions as this involve *a loss of time*.

From the above considerations it follows that, with a view to the protection of the convoy, arrangements must be made to prevent it, as far as possible, coming in *contact with the enemy*. In this case, the principles usually regulating the strength, distance from the main body, etc., of detachments intended to provide for its security on the march must lapse. *The protection of a convoy demands exceptional measures*. On encountering the enemy it must, at any rate, be possible to bring the convoy into a place of safety in good time. This generally involves taking a *new road*, though it may even be necessary sometimes *to turn right about*. Should matters take the most unfavourable turn, and the loss of the convoy appear inevitable, the escort must, at all events, make every effort *to gain* at least sufficient *time* for either destroying it or rendering it unserviceable. When a convoy has to be protected, the detachments thrown out in the direction of the enemy have the *brunt of the fighting*. They must therefore be exceptionally *strong*, and the *distance* between them and the convoy must, as a rule, be *greater* than that of an ordinary advanced or flank guard from its main body.

The escort should be distributed so that *at least half* the available infantry is thrown out in the direction of the enemy, whether as advanced, rear, or flank guard, supported by the bulk of the cavalry, and by artillery in the *exceptional cases* when guns form part of the escort. The circumstances of each case alone can decide how far these troops should push out towards the enemy, or, in other words, the distance between them and the convoy. The main body will consist of the convoy itself, with *about half the infantry* as its immediate escort, marching part immediately in front, part in rear of the convoy. Thus about a quarter of the total infantry is at the head of the main body, followed by the convoy, while a quarter of the infantry forms the tail of the column; though tactical units must not be broken up to obtain these exact proportions. The infantry marching at the head and tail of the convoy has also to furnish the *personnel* to superintend the drivers. For this purpose cavalry is more suitable, but we have generally so little of it that we have to make shift with infantry and cyclists.

The above general principles being premised, we will now turn to the special case in hand, which, you are doubtless aware, involves dealing with a flank march. According to the information received, the enemy's main body arrived at Gorze on the afternoon of 1st August, and our cavalry has definitely ascertained Corny to be held by the enemy. The statements of the Novéant railway official are therefore probably correct.

It is doubtful whether it will be possible for the convoy to reach Metz if the enemy crosses the Moselle on the morning of the 2nd August, and succeeds in striking in between it and that town. It seems probable, however, that the enemy, having heard of the presence of hostile troops on the march to Metz from the south, intends to attempt doing this very thing.

He will probably march *on Féy*. A flank guard must therefore be thrown out between the convoy and the enemy, and suitable measures adopted to prevent, or at any rate delay, him gaining possession of Féy, which is an important junction of roads; that is to say, we must threaten his exit from the valley of the Verchot brook. *Thus Féy is the important point.*

That hostile infantry will pass Féy, by moving through St. Blaise, for instance, can hardly be supposed. It is possible, of course; but the road is bad, and very steep, so that the enemy's rate of progress would be slow. At all events, we should know *in good time* through our cavalry if the enemy begins to move in this direction, as from the slopes of St. Blaise the whole Moselle valley lies in full view. Should the enemy's *infantry* advance in any strength by way of St. Blaise, the flank guard must quit Féy, and move as quickly as possible on Schl. Grosyeux,[1] there afresh to oppose him. The commanding officer must undoubtedly contemplate the possibility of this, and can even send on an officer to look about for a position, possibly the wood of St. Jean. No mention of it, however, should be made in the order, which should inform the flank guard solely that Féy should be held. Should large bodies of hostile *cavalry* move by St. Blaise to turn the flank of our flank guard, it would be unfortunate, as from St. Blaise the whole country for a long way to the east can be seen, and *therefore the convoy would be visible*, though protected against cavalry, *however strong*, by the infantry marching with it.

It may occur to you that the flank guard might take up a *flanking position*. The enemy's line of advance is the main road from Corny to Féy, which is, of course, commanded from the neighbourhood of Sommy. If the flank guard takes up a position here, facing south, the enemy must attack it before marching on Féy. In such case, however, the most important condition for a flanking position is wanting, viz. *security for the threatened right flank*, and so the position could easily be rolled up. Besides, the flank guard is not strong enough to occupy such a position properly, and the retreat on Augny is difficult; while the dense Bois de la Goulotte would also impede the retreat. I am therefore opposed to a flanking position, and prefer the simpler plan of occupying Féy.

Neither am I in favour of taking the offensive, *i.e.* attacking Corny, *although the idea is a tempting one*. We do not know enough of the general situation. Suppose that the enemy during the night puts more infantry into Corny. Our infantry attacking that place might then find themselves in an awkward predicament, and the safety of the convoy be imperilled. Besides, I do not consider it suitable to the object in view *to provoke an engagement, so long as it is possible to meet the case by other means*.

[1] Grosyeux Castle.

PROTECTION OF A CONVOY

We have now to decide when, approximately, the enemy will reach Féy. His cavalry, which is already across the Moselle, will probably resume their reconnaissance as early as possible next morning, and may be expected in the neighbourhood of Féy soon after daybreak. In opposition to it our cavalry has to perform chiefly *the duty of screening ;* and the event will show whether it will succeed in driving away the enemy's patrols from the neighbourhood of the St. Blaise, and preventing them getting a view from the hills over the country between the Moselle and the Seille. It is not likely that any infantry which may already be in Corny will march by itself to Féy. It will await the arrival of reinforcements from Gorze, keeping the defile open meanwhile. Thus, apart from the cavalry, the main consideration is the troops from Gorze. Assuming the distance from Gorze, viâ Novéant, to Féy as about $6\frac{1}{4}$ miles—a distance which the enemy can cover without a halt—the head of the enemy's column, starting from Gorze at 5 a.m. (and he can scarcely start much before that), can reach Féy about 7 a.m., which is assuming that he experiences no delay in crossing the Moselle. Accordingly it is desirable to get the convoy past Féy *or the country east of that village* by 7 a.m.

Perhaps you suggest the advisability of pushing on to Metz during the night. This, however, must be objected to, as the convoy did not reach Marieulles till *late* in the evening, after a tiring march, so that both men and horses are worn out and stand in urgent need of rest. An *immediate* start is thus out of the question, though the march must be resumed *early* next morning. The *latest* hour of starting can be approximately calculated, basing the calculation on the rate the convoy itself can march, as it is the convoy we are most concerned with.

The shortest way to Metz is the high road through Féy and Augny ; but, as has been above shown, the convoy would run most risk by this road. I therefore prefer the road past Sabré, then following the high road for the convoy, while the escort proceeds to Féy. The greater the distance the convoy puts between itself and Féy, and the sooner it does it, the better. The convoy may be considered pretty well out of danger as soon as it has passed the cross-roads west of Cuvry. As we calculated above, the enemy can hardly reach Féy before 7 a.m., so it *will do* if the convoy gets past the above-mentioned cross-roads *by that hour*. Thus we come to the conclusion that it will be possible to solve the problem *without* crossing the Seille. Otherwise you must get the Seille between the convoy and the enemy —a course which I do not consider necessary in the case before us.

The convoy is $1\frac{1}{4}$ miles long. Half of the infantry, *i.e.* a battalion, accompanies it, throwing out two companies as an advanced guard. The 2nd line transport of the troops had better move with the convoy, and we may assume the road space occupied by it as about 300 yards.

I will take the distance from the head of the vanguard to the tail of the main body as about $2\frac{1}{2}$ miles = about 50 minutes. The distance by road from the north-eastern exit of Marieulles to the cross-roads west of Cuvry is, roughly, $3\frac{3}{4}$ miles = about 70 minutes; thus the vanguard must start, say, 2 hours before 7 a.m., *i.e.* at 5 a.m. This is the *latest* time of starting. It would be well, however, to start rather earlier than this, as one can never be sure when the enemy will start, and *delays* may occur with the convoy, in spite of the road being good. I would therefore start at 4 a.m. The tactical situation does not, of course, admit of much regard being had to the convenience of the troops, nevertheless I would not start *earlier* than 4 a.m., as after the long march of the previous day men and horses require some rest. Bear in mind, that to start at 4 the camp must be astir before 3 o'clock.

The convoy may be considered *perfectly safe* as soon as it has passed the practice-entrenchment (Übungs-Schanze) at the junction of the road from Augny with the main road Pournoy–Metz. From the cross-roads west of Cuvry to this point the tail of the main body has about 2½ miles to march = 50 minutes. If therefore you start at 5 a.m. you will have to check the enemy at Féy for these 50 minutes—after which the flank guard can continue its march on Augny. The earlier we start, the more chance we have of being able to get to Metz *without any fighting*. The flank guard also ought to get to Féy in good time, so as to establish itself there; it will therefore march off *at the same time* as the advanced guard. The battalion which was on outpost duty will march with the convoy; the I/Battalion marches to Féy. The officer commanding the II/Battalion settles where the companies of the battalion are to march (say how).

Colonel A. therefore arrives at the following *decision* :—
The convoy to begin its march at 4 a.m., moving by the high road through Sabré to Metz; a left flank guard to hold Féy until the convoy has passed the practice-redoubt on the roadside.

There must naturally be some cavalry with advanced guard and main body, not so much to reconnoitre the route as to keep touch with the flank guard. A troop, however, must suffice for this purpose, so that we may have as much cavalry as possible out towards Corny. This troop again to be so subdivided that the larger part of it goes to the advanced guard, to serve as advanced party of the vanguard and to keep up connection; while the smaller part of the troop moves at the head of the main body. Cyclists will be used for the same purpose and for keeping order within the convoy and 2nd line transport. The rest of the cavalry will belong to the flank guard.

The I/Battalion and the cavalry will be billeted in Marieulles for the night, but will furnish a guard over the convoy, which will bivouac south of Marieulles.

The 2nd line transport may *precede* the convoy on the march, *and I prefer this arrangement*, because thus the numerous wagons will fall into one column in the easiest and simplest manner; a more convenient arrangement, to say the least, than making the whole convoy pass the transport on the road.

To prevent the column being too long, the advanced guard need be only some 500 yards in front of the main body. The II/Battalion must also be instructed to furnish the personnel necessary to superintend the convoy. The convoy should be divided into groups of 10 wagons, with a N.C.O. and a few men to each, the whole being, if possible, under a mounted officer.

A word as to the position of the officer commanding the detachment. As concerns the convoy, all that he need trouble about is to satisfy himself, from time to time, of its satisfactory progress. Whatever else may have to be seen to in respect of the convoy may be entrusted to the officer commanding the II/Battalion. The officer commanding the detachment has a *far more important duty* to perform, viz. keeping an eye on the action of the left flank guard. He must remain in its vicinity, and watch the enemy's advance, but must refrain from interfering with the free action of the commander of the flank guard, even should there be fighting. The officer commanding the detachment must ever strive to *keep an eye over the whole force*, and leave details to others; thus only can he appreciate the right moment to order the flank guard to break off the fight. His closest attention must be given to the difficulties of the retreat of the flank guard, since its line of retreat is to a flank (the right flank), taking at the same time into his consideration whether the four companies of the tail of the main body will eventually have to occupy a position for the flank guard to fall back on, after the convoy is in safety.

The following orders are therefore issued :—

I.

OPERATION ORDER No. 4

BY

COLONEL A., COMMANDING CONVOY AND ESCORT.

Reference:
$\frac{1}{100.000}$ Ordn.

MARIEULLES,
1.8.00.

1. *Advanced Guard:*
    Major N.
    1 Troop I/1st Dragoons.
    2 Cos. II/Battalion.

2. *Main Body* (in order of march): Lt.-Col. B.
    1 N.C.O., 8 men I/1st Dragoons.
    II/Battalion (less 6 cos.).
    2nd Line Transport.
    Convoy.
    4 Cos. II/Battalion.
    Lt.-Col. M.

3. *Left Flank Guard:*
    I/1st Dragoons (less 1 Troop).
    II/1st Dragoons.
    I/Battalion.

Dictated to representatives of
C.O. 1st Squadron,
  ,, IInd Squadron,
  ,, I/Battalion,
  ,, II/Battalion,
  ,, Convoy,
  ,, 2nd Line Transport,
at 11 p.m.

1. *The Detachment* will be formed up to morrow at 4 a.m. in readiness to march off as follows (Distribution in margin):—

    The Main Body with *2nd Line Transport* at the exit from **MARIEULLES** to **SABRÉ**, in column of route with the tail of 2nd line transport at **MARIEULLES**, the wagons closely drawn up to the left side of the road. The advanced guard 500 yards in front.

    The Convoy at the same hour in the bivouac.

2. *Issue of Orders* at 3.45 a.m. tomorrow at the exit from **MARIEULLES** to **VEZON**.

A.,
Colonel.

SIXTH LETTER

II.
OPERATION ORDER No. 5
BY
COLONEL A., COMMANDING CONVOY AND ESCORT.

Copy No. 1.

Reference:
$\frac{1}{100.000}$ *Ordn.*

Exit from **MARIEULLES**
to **VEZON**,
2.8.00.

1. *The Enemy* is said to have reached **GORZE** with a force of all arms yesterday afternoon, and is holding **CORNY** and **ZGL.**[1] south of **CORNY**.

2. *The Detachment* will march to-day on **METZ**, which is held by troops of our own country.

3. *The Advanced Guard* will start at 4 a.m., moving by the main road through **SABRÉ** and the cross-roads west of **CUVRY** to **METZ**, and keeping communication with the garrison there.

4. *The Main Body* will follow at 500 yards' distance. The II/Battalion will furnish the party to supervise the Convoy.

5. *The Left Flank Guard* will at once occupy **FÉY**, and hold it till further orders; reconnoitring by **CÔTE-DE-FAYÉ** in the **VERCHOT** valley, and by **ST. BLAISE** towards **CORNY**. All hostile patrols to be driven back on the **MOSELLE** valley.

6. *Reports* will reach me with the left flank guard.

Verbally to the assembled officers commanding units at 3.50 a.m.

A.,
Colonel.

There is another solution of the problem which I am far from altogether condemning, viz. for *the bulk* of the detachment to move on Féy, under the officer commanding, leaving half a battalion for the immediate escort of convoy and 2nd line transport. This solution practically turns *the detachment itself* into a left flank guard. Four companies would be sufficient protection for the convoy, at a pinch, against any enterprises of the enemy's *cavalry*,

---

[1] Zgl. = Ziegelei = brick-kiln.

and the convoy is safe from his infantry until such time as it may have fought its way through the detachment itself. Think out this plan for yourself, and weigh its attendant advantages and disadvantages.

In conclusion, let us consider what sort of a decision Colonel A. would have come to had the special idea been as follows :—

The convoy is advancing viâ Marieulles and Féy on Metz. When the main body reaches the southern outskirts of Marieulles, a report is received to the effect that the enemy is marching on Corny and that his advanced guard has already arrived there. In this case we should at the beginning of the march have thrown out an advanced guard consisting of a battalion, with the bulk of the cavalry, well in front (a mile to a mile and a quarter in advance), the other battalion moving with the convoy. On receiving the report, the officer commanding decides to *make the convoy change direction towards the east*. The convoy is ordered to move by Sabré and provide for its own security. It accordingly throws out a *small advanced guard on its own account*, while the troops till now composing the advanced guard and the cavalry take up a position at Féy *as a left flank guard*, subsequently following viâ Augny *as a rear guard*. Thus what was originally an advance *becomes first a flank march, and then a retreat*.

Had it been stated in the exercise that the enemy was already in occupation of Féy, and the woods to the east of it, it would be of course hopeless to try to reach Metz by the west bank of the Seille. The convoy would have to make a complete wheel, and endeavour, *covered by the hitherto advanced guard*, to move on a wide arc viâ Pommérieux and Verny. You see that all these exercises are more or less similar to the exercise discussed in the last letter. It would be good practice to work out the appropriate orders in the above-described circumstances.

I should also recommend you to settle for yourself what would be the distribution of troops and the other arrangements, if, in this exercise, the troops at your disposal had been

(1) 1 battalion and 1 squadron.
(2) 3 battalions, 3 squadrons, and 1 battery.

SIXTH EXERCISE.

(See general map, and maps Gravelotte and Metz.)

A detachment under Colonel B., in its own country, is billeted for the night 2/3 August, 1900, in and north of Maizières-bei-Metz (general map on the railway north of Metz). It is protected by outposts under Lt.-Col. A. These consist of the I/Battalion and the 1st and 2nd Troops I/14th Hussars, and are standing on the line Point du Jour (south-east of Norroy le Veneur)–Ladonchamps–La Maxe.

The following reports are received by Lt.-Col. A. in the afternoon of 2nd August:—

Small hostile infantry post at the Maschinen House[1] south-west of Plappeville.

Hostile infantry at Lessy.

At the cemetery[2] of Longeville-bei-Metz a section of hostile infantry.

At St. Georges hostile infantry; some infantry posts on the heights east of St. Georges and on the St. Quentin.

Hostile cavalry patrols at Woippy and Saulny.

No enemy at Plappeville and Ban-St. Martin.

The open town of Metz is going to be occupied on the forenoon of 3rd August by a friendly division coming from Bettsdorf (general map, north-east of Metz).

At 3 a.m. the following order comes from Colonel B.—

A hostile detachment of all arms is at Moulins-bei-Metz and St. Ruffine.

The enemy is said to be expecting reinforcements from Verdun.

The main body of the detachment will advance to-morrow at 5 a.m on Lessy, marching from Maizières-bei-Metz by Woippy, Le Coupillon, and Plappeville.

The outposts will form the advanced guard together with the

---

[1] Engine house. [2] Khf. = Kirchhof = churchyard or cemetery.

remainder of the I/ and II/14th Hussars, the 1st F.A. Battery, and the 1st Field Co. R.E., all in Amelange.

Reconnoitring towards the line Longeville-bei-Metz–Châtel St. Germain.

2nd line transport of the outposts will remain at the northern exit of St. Remy.

Required:—
1. Appreciation of the situation by Lt.-Col. A.
2. Arrangements made by Lt.-Col. A., with reasons for them.
3. The order of march of the advanced guard to be shown on the map 40 minutes after starting, indicating clearly how the cavalry is employed.

MODEL FOR ADVANCED GUARD ORDERS.

Copy No......

OPERATION ORDER No......
BY
.... COMMANDING ADVANCED GUARD.

Reference Map.   *Place. Date.*

1. *Advanced Guard Cavalry:* C.O.
   Cavalry.

2. *Vanguard:* C.O.
   Cavalry.
   Engineers.
   Infantry.

3. *Main Guard* (in order of march): C.O.
   Cavalry.
   Infantry.
   Machine-gun detachments.
   Artillery (sometimes last).
   Infantry.
   Engineers.
   Section Field Ambul. (seldom in the case of detachments).

1. Information concerning *the enemy* and *our own troops in other quarters.*

2. Task of the *Advanced Guard.*

3. Order for the *Advanced Guard Cavalry* (time and place of starting, road by which to march, what reconnoitring is to be performed, and any special duties).

4. Order for the *Vanguard* (as in 3).

5. Order for the *Main Guard* (distance in rear of vanguard, or place and time of starting).[1]

6. Order for the *Flank Guard* (as in 3).

7. Order for the *Outposts.*

8. Order for the 2nd *Line Transport* (very seldom).

[1] Note the difference in *E.F.S.R.*, Part I, sects. 67 (2) and 68 (1).—*Trans.*

4. *Right or Left Flank Guard*: C.O.
   Cavalry.
   Engineers.
   Infantry.

9. Position of the *Officer commanding* advanced guard.

Signature,
Rank.

Issued : how, to whom, and at what hour.

REMARKS.—Should a flank guard have to be furnished *by the main guard*, it is best, to make the orders more readily intelligible, to detail the flank guard in the Distribution of Troops; but if it is to be furnished *by the vanguard*, the latter must be made strong in proportion, and the order relating to it must contain the necessary instructions as to its sending out a flank guard.

The Distribution of Troops is necessary only for large forces. In *small* advanced guards it may be omitted, *but in that case the orders must contain all necessary instructions.*

SEVENTH LETTER

ADVANCED-GUARD ORDERS

LIEUT.-COLONEL A.'s position, as defined in the exercise, is a somewhat *exceptional* one; for the officer commanding a detachment usually fixes time and place of assembly of the advanced guard. Again, it is unusual, and must appear strange, after the preceding letters, for the outposts to be detailed for advanced guard; this being contrary to the general rule that the outposts stand fast until the vanguard of a fresh advanced guard has passed their lines. We have thus to deal with *an exceptional state of affairs*. This is a not uncommon procedure, not only in exercises, but in practice; especially when an officer commanding a detachment desires his advanced guard to start in good time, and is uncertain whether his other infantry can be brought up in time enough; or when, for some reason, this latter is not to be used as advanced guard.

In other respects the problem is easy, so that I can discuss it briefly. I shall subsequently refer to the manner in which the exercise is expressed.

I do not propose to enter on the question of the detailed distribution of the outposts in the present case, as I shall deal with outposts later on.

The measures adopted by Lieut.-Colonel A. on receiving Colonel B.'s orders must comprise the following :—

(1) The outpost troops must be concentrated somewhere before the march is begun.

(2) While they are assembling reconnaissance of the enemy must be going on.

(3) The troops detailed to reinforce Lieut.-Colonel A.'s

command must be acquainted when and where they have to arrive.

(4) Advanced guard order.

The place of assembly must be on the road by which the advanced guard will march, not visible from the hills held by the enemy, and so selected that all the advanced guard troops can reach it without inconvenience, or having any considerable détour to make. The choice lies between the north outskirts of Ladonchamps and the north outskirts of Maison Rouge. The advantage of the latter is that many of the roads leading from the outpost position into the road on which the advanced guard is about to march meet in its vicinity; thus facilitating the assembly. On the other hand, this place is so near the enemy's position that the *security* so indispensable for a place of assembly *is not ensured.* It would be dangerous to assemble there, and it would be more prudent for the advanced guard to assemble somewhat further from the enemy, *i.e.* on the northern outskirts of Ladonchamps, which is about the centre of the outpost line.

In conformity with the instructions contained in preceding letters, you will doubtless have studied for yourself the entire *network of roads* affecting the advance, as well as *the country between the roads.* There is therefore no need for me to discuss the various roads with such minuteness as before, and I shall confine myself to observing that the road between Woippy and Le Coupillon lies *very low*, and that between Le Coupillon and Lessy it is completely commanded by the heights *on either side.* It would be a serious matter for the advanced guard to be attacked unexpectedly from the heights on either side; we must therefore reconnoitre on *a broad front. The road, in fact, presents great difficulties to the advanced guard.*

The enemy holds the very commanding position of St. Quentin and the heights west of Plappeville, whence he has an extensive view; consequently he cannot fail to perceive the advance of our detachment.

ADVANCED GUARD ORDERS

If the enemy retires, the advanced guard must follow him to Maison Neuve, west of Moulins-bei-Metz. If he offers resistance, it will depend on the reports received whether the advanced guard attacks him (which it could not do, unless he were very inferior numerically), or only begins and prepares the attack until such time as the main body arrives to carry it out. It is not likely that the enemy will leave his excellent position and *advance against* the detachment. The only thing that might cause him to do so would be if he had received considerable reinforcements. In such case Lieut.-Colonel A. would have to endeavour, wherever the advanced guard happened to be at the moment, to check the enemy until the main body has made ready for action. *Meanwhile, all he can do is to begin the march, though prepared for all these contingencies.*

From the moment the enemy observes the advance of the detachment, he is debarred, failing some new development of affairs, from himself advancing *on Metz*. According to the information received from Colonel B., there is only a *detachment* of the enemy at Maison Neuve. This information is probably correct, for otherwise the enemy would have ere this made a move towards gaining possession of such an important town as Metz, from which he is only about 4 miles distant. The rest of the information to hand concerning the enemy further leads us to the conclusion that his outpost line extends from Longeville-bei-Metz, past the machinery house south-west of Plappeville, to St. Georges. His outpost line is about 3 miles long, according to which he has *at least* a battalion on outpost duty. The whole of this line would be much too extensive for a detachment to occupy as a defensive position, and *is not therefore so advantageous* as it appears at first sight ; irrespective of the fact that the northern and eastern slopes of the hills favour an attack, owing to the thickets and woods clothing them, and the villages of Plappeville and Lorry-bei-Metz. The right flank of the position, of course, rests on the Moselle ; but the left flank is quite open, and this is the more unfortunate for the enemy, *as his line of retreat on Gravelotte runs from this flank*. To menace the left flank by advancing on St. Georges will touch the enemy at a very sensitive point, and *perhaps compel him to abandon the whole position;* provided, of course, that he does not intend an obstinate defence; especially as the deep and precipitous Montveau valley in the rear of the position renders *his retreat extremely difficult*. In short, Lieut.-Colonel A. can say to himself that, if it is only *a weak detachment* that is holding the position, the easiest way to overcome the resistance is by sending part of the advanced guard against St. Georges. At any rate, the attempt must be made.

By detaching part of the advanced guard in the direction of Lorry, we gain possession of the commanding ground west of the low-lying road we are about to march by. Cavalry alone would not suffice for this purpose, as, should the enemy advance viâ Lorry, he must be held until the advanced guard has deployed for action from column of route. You will rightly appreciate the circumstances which in the present case have justified the formation of an infantry flank guard, comparing them with those existent in former exercises (*G.F.S.R.*, para. 181).

You would probably find out very little by sending all the cavalry of the advanced guard straight against the enemy's *front*—towards Plappeville, for instance—as it would very soon encounter hostile infantry. The cavalry should aim at the enemy's flanks, and in moving against his *left* flank it will find the plateau west of Lorry more favourable to its action than the slopes of St. Quentin near the Moselle valley would be. *The bulk* of the cavalry will therefore be employed against the enemy's left flank, only a few *patrols* being required to *watch* Plappeville and Ban St. Martin.

Conformably with the above considerations Lieut.-Colonel A. comes to the following *decision:* Assembly near Ladonchamps; advance by the road ordered, detaching a right

ADVANCED GUARD ORDERS

flank guard towards St. Georges; and employing the bulk of the advanced guard cavalry in the direction of St. Georges.

The two troops on outposts must remain in observation while the outpost infantry are concentrating, so will be more or less extended when the forward movement is begun, subsequently concentrating little by little. On this account they had best be employed on some unimportant duty in vanguard and flank guard, and for reconnoitring towards Ban St. Martin; while the $1\frac{1}{2}$ squadrons arriving fresh and compact from Amelange move as advanced cavalry on Lorry. To detail, however, two fresh troops for vanguard and flank guard would mean *disseminating the cavalry* at the commencement of the operation; and you would have, to begin with, only one squadron as advanced cavalry.

Let us detail two companies, with some cavalry, as a flank guard; two companies, with the necessary cavalry, as vanguard; there remains for main guard half a battalion, the engineers, and the battery. This would settle the distribution of troops.

I assume that Nos. 7 and 8 Cos. were on the right flank of the outpost line. It is not necessary for these two companies to rendezvous near Ladonchamps, but, to save them unnecessary marching, they may start from some other place, on the road by which they will march to Woippy; for instance, from the cross-roads 650 yards west of Ste. Anne.

We thus calculate the time by which the advanced guard troops must be assembled:—From the northern outskirts of Ladonchamps to the southern outskirts of Maizières-bei-Metz is 3 miles, which can be traversed in one hour, so the head of the main body will reach the northern outskirts of Ladonchamps about 6 a.m. But there should be a distance of about $\frac{1}{2}$ mile between the advanced guard and the main body, and the road space occupied by the former is somewhat over a mile; then $\frac{1}{2}$ mile + a little over 1 mile = a little over $1\frac{1}{2}$ miles = say 35 minutes; so the advanced guard must start about 35 minutes before 6 a.m., *i.e.* at 5.25 a.m. This calculation of the time of starting can, of course, be only *approximately* correct, and therefore the proper distance must be got in the course of the march.

I arrive at the length of the column on the march by counting the distances between the main guard and vanguard, and between the latter and the advanced party as about 400 yards each. The *G.F.S.R.*,[1] in paragraph 172, prescribe a distance of ¾ to 1 mile to intervene between the main guard and vanguard when *large* forces are concerned and when the nature of the country admits. But with a small advanced guard, as in our case, you need not adhere to these distances; yet I would advise you not to reduce them too much, for there is no question that one of the consequences of our present armament is that the various protective bodies must be pushed proportionately further in advance of each other than was formerly necessary.

The infantry detailed for right flank guard should start rather earlier than the vanguard, as it has to march by a more roundabout and indifferent road, and must be clear of Woippy when the vanguard arrives there, so as *to prevent the two bodies meeting in the village itself.* This procedure is, at any rate, both simpler and safer than to cause the flank guard to traverse the village by a different road to the advanced guard. As the flank guard forms vanguard and main guard, just like the advanced guard, it will occupy about 1200 yards road space, and may start say 15 minutes before the vanguard.

Lieut.-Colonel A. receives his orders at 3 a.m., and had best issue his orders *for the assembly at once,* as they have to be sent to Amelange, for the information of the reinforcements quartered there, and the compilation, etc., of the orders and assembling the troops takes time. The outpost companies have also their preparations to make; the orders, moreover, for the outpost cavalry must be couched in very definite terms as regards these two troops, to *ensure*

---

[1] No prescriptions are given in the *E.F.S.R.*—*Trans.*

ADVANCED GUARD ORDERS

their joining the vanguard and right flank guard respectively *at the right time*. Nor need these troops, in so doing, return to Ladonchamps or to the west of Ste. Anne. It will do if they join their respective commands in and near Woippy, as meanwhile the advanced cavalry will have got far enough to the front to have taken up the reconnaissance and observation of the enemy along the whole line.

The news that the enemy is expecting reinforcements from Verdun had better not be communicated to the subordinate officers;—*why cause them anxiety before it is necessary?* If the news is correct, it will be time enough to tell them later on. On the other hand, they should be informed that a division of our own troops is coming up and will occupy Metz in the course of the forenoon, as this is *favourable* news, promising an assured line of retreat, should the enemy be encountered in superior force. On the other hand, the orders should direct the attention of the advanced cavalry towards Gravelotte; in order to ascertain, by reconnaissance, whether it is a fact that reinforcements for the enemy are on the march from Verdun. If a single patrol succeeds haply, by a wide détour, in working round the enemy's flank as far as Gravelotte, which is far enough on the road to Verdun, it will be able to transmit invaluable information. It is, moreover, advisable that *no one* but the officer commanding the advanced cavalry should know of the disquieting report concerning the enemy's reinforcements—it being communicated to him verbally. He will then give his patrols special instructions to report to him even if they observe nothing on the Verdun road (*G.F.S.R.*, para. 66).[1]

The following therefore would be the orders issued by Lieut.-Colonel A. :—

[1] *E.F.S.R.*, Part I, sect. 16 (6).—*Trans.*

I.
ORDERS SENT TO THE OUTPOSTS.
OPERATION ORDER No. 3

Copy No. 1.

BY

LIEUT.-COLONEL A., COMMANDING THE OUTPOSTS.

Reference:
$\frac{1}{100.000}$ *Ordn.*

Bivouac north of
ST. REMY,
3.8.00.

1. *Nos. 1, 2, 3, 4, 5, and 6 Cos. I/Battalion* will be formed up, in readiness to march off, at 5.20 a.m. at the northern outskirts of **LADONCHAMPS**. *Nos. 7 and 8 Cos.* at 5.5 a.m., at the cross-roads 650 yards west of **STE. ANNE**.

2. *No. 1 Troop of I/14th Hussars* will resume the reconnaissance, as before, through **WOIPPY** at 4 a.m., and *No. 2 Troop* through **SAULNY** at the same hour. No. 1 Troop will join the vanguard under Major S., at 5.40 a.m., at **MAISON ROUGE**; No. 2 Troop the right flank guard, under Captain P., at 5.45 a.m., at the old church of **WOIPPY**.

3. *The 2nd Line Transport* will wait for further orders on the northern outskirts of **ST. REMY**.

4. *Company Commanders to attend for orders* at 4.45 a.m. on the southern outskirts of **STE. AGATHE**.

Copies despatched to the outpost companies by cyclists. Verbally to the reserve of the outposts; at 3.10 a.m.

A.,
Lieut.-Colonel.

II.
ORDERS SENT TO THE REINFORCING TROOPS.
OPERATION ORDER No. 4

Copy No. 1.

BY

LIEUT.-COLONEL A., COMMANDING OUTPOSTS.

Reference:
$\frac{1}{100.000}$ *Ordn.*

Bivouac north of
ST. REMY,
3.8.00.

1. The II/14th *Hussars, the remainder of* I/14th *Hussars, the* 1st *Field Battery R.A., and the* 1st *Field Co. R.E.*, will form to-day, together with the outposts under my command, the

ADVANCED GUARD ORDERS

Advanced Guard of the Detachment, and will be formed up, in readiness to march off at 5.20 a.m., on the northern outskirts of **LADONCHAMPS**.

2. *Captains and Mounted Officers to attend for orders* at 4.45 a.m. on the northern outskirts of **STE. AGATHE**.

Copies despatched by Lieut. G. to O.C.'s concerned at 3.15 a.m.

A.,
Lieut.-Colonel.

III.

ORDERS FOR THE ADVANCED GUARD.

Copy No. 1.

OPERATION ORDER No. 5

BY

LIEUT.-COLONEL A., COMMANDING ADVANCED GUARD.

Southern Outskirts of
STE. AGATHE,
3.8.00.

Reference:
$\frac{1}{100.000}$ *Ordn.*

1. *Advanced Cavalry:*
   Major N.
   II/14th Hussars.
   I/14th Hussars (less 2 troops).

2. *Vanguard:* Major S.
   1st Troop I/14th Hussars.
   Nos. 1 and 2 Cos. I/Battalion.

3. *Main Guard* (in order of march): Major W.
   1 N.C.O., 4 troopers of 1st Troop I/14th Hussars.
   Nos. 3 and 4 Cos. I/Battalion.
   1st Field Battery R.A.
   Nos. 5 and 6 Cos. I/Battalion.
   1st Field Co. R.E.

1. *A Detachment of the Enemy* is reported to be at **MAISON NEUVE**, west of **MOULINS-BEI-METZ**, and small bodies of infantry at **LONGEVILLE-BEI-METZ**, the **MASCHINEN HO.** south-west of **PLAPPEVILLE**, and **ST. GEORGES**.

   Our Detachment starts from **MAIZIÈRES-BEI-METZ** at 5 a.m. A Division coming from **BETTSDORF** by **ANTILLY** will occupy **METZ** this morning.

2. *The Advanced Guard* will move on **MAISON NEUVE**, west of **MOULINS-BEI-METZ**.

3. *The Advanced Cavalry* will start at 5.25 a.m. and move by **WOIPPY, LORRY-BEI-METZ**, and **ST. GEORGES** on **MAISON NEUVE**, west of **MOULINS-BEI-METZ**, and will reconnoitre towards

SEVENTH LETTER

4. *Right Flank Guard:*
Captain P.
2nd Troop I/14th Hussars.
Nos. 7 and 8 Cos. I/Battalion.

LESSY and SCY. An officer's patrol is to be sent on GRAVELOTTE.

4. *The Vanguard*, starting at the same time, will move viâ **WOIPPY, LE COUPILLON,** the **KRIEGSSTRASSE, PLAPPEVILLE,** and **LESSY** on **MAISON NEUVE,** and send patrols viâ **BAN ST. MARTIN** in the direction of **MAISON NEUVE.**

5. *The Main Guard* will follow at ½ mile distance.

6. *The Right Flank Guard* will start at 5.10 a.m. for **WOIPPY** by the direct road, thereafter moving viâ **LORRY-BEI-METZ** and **ST. GEORGES** on **MAISON NEUVE.**

7. *Reports* to the head of the vanguard.

Verbally to the assembled commanding officers at 4.50 a.m.

A.,
Lieut.-Colonel.

N.B.—If you had not given the distribution of the troops in the margin, paragraph 3 of your order, for instance, would have to read: "The Advanced Cavalry (Major N., II/14th Hussars and I/14th Hussars less 2 troops) will start, etc." Paragraphs 4, 5, and 6 would be altered similarly.

It would be perfectly correct to issue *one* set of orders only for assembling the troops, applying both to the outposts and to the troops in Amelange; which might also, to simplify matters, contain the distribution of troops. Moreover, we might put the bulk of the cavalry in the *same* heading with the right flank guard. This would entail some modification of my arrangements for the distribution of the cavalry. I am, however, opposed to this measure, because the *freedom of action*, so requisite in this case for the cavalry, would be interfered with by making them conform to the slow-moving infantry following the same route. Again, less than a troop might be detailed to the right flank guard (say 1 N.C.O. and 9 men = 3 patrols), with a view to making the advanced cavalry as strong as possible. The vanguard, however, cannot do with less than a complete troop.

As the name "Maison Neuve" appears in two places in the tract of country entering into the exercise, care is necessary to prevent any misunderstanding (*G.F.S.R.*, para. 101).[1]

When you get an exercise like this, in which there are several points which seem to you irreconcilable with actual service conditions, I advise you to adopt a cautious way of expressing yourself in writing your solution, since you can scarcely see why the person who set the exercise has expressed it in such and such a particular way. Avoid anything which might be interpreted in a sense unfavourable to you, and twice rigorously stick to the wording of the exercise. I have *raised this point*, in this exercise, *on purpose* to warn you against this error. *The less this exercise has pleased you, the more glad am I.* In the case before us the following questions might reasonably be asked :—

(1) Why are the outposts taken for the advanced guard?

(2) Why does not the officer commanding the detachment himself fix the place and time for the advanced guard to start?

(3) Why does not he himself send the reinforcing troops at the right time to Lieut.-Colonel A.?

(4) Why does not he give definite directions for the way reconnaissance is to be carried out?

(5) Why does not he advance viâ Lorry and St. Georges, instead of by the route selected, which is low-lying and difficult to deploy from?

---

[1] *E.F.S.R.*, Part I, sect. 9 (1) (iv.).—*Trans.*

SEVENTH LETTER

SEVENTH EXERCISE.

(See general map and the map Verny.)

The 3rd Division is encamped about Grigy and Borny. It had pushed out a detached force, under Major-General A., composed of—

    I/Battalion.
    II/Battalion.
    III/Battalion.
    Rifle Battalion.
    1st Machine-Gun Detachment.
    1st Dragoons.
    1st Field Battery and "A" Battery R.H.A.
    1st Field Co. R.E.
    Sect. A. 1st Field Ambul.
    ½ Art. Brgde. Ammun. Col.

towards Delme (south edge of general map), which on the 1st July, 1900, is obliged to fall back, viâ Solgne, before the enemy in superior force, and occupies close billets for the night in Pontoy, with outposts (I/Battalion, 3 N.C.O.'s, 36 troopers I/1st Dragoons) on the line Liéhon–Haute-Beux. Nos. 1 and 2 Cos., with 1 N.C.O. and 12 troopers, are posted south of Liéhon; Nos. 3 and 4 Cos., with 1 N.C.O. and 9 troopers, at a point on the main road due east of Liéhon; Nos. 5 and 6 Cos., with 1 N.C.O. and 12 troopers, at Haute-Beux. The reserve of the outposts, consisting of Nos. 7 and 8 Cos., with 3 troopers, is at Petit Grève.

Connection has been established by the cavalry telegraph line from Pontoy with the outposts of the Division at Jury le Petit, telephone connection leading thence to Divisional Headquarters.

At 10 p.m. the Colonel commanding the dragoon regiment reports from Liéhon as follows:—

"The enemy followed with a column of all arms by the main road to Solgne, where he halted. Several companies of infantry and 2 to 3 squadrons dragoons marched by Sécourt on Vigny. Enemy's outposts are on the line Ancy-bei-Solgne–Pagny-bei-Goin. A squadron of hussars at Luppy. Hostile cavalry patrols followed as far as Beux–Silly-en-Saulnois and Goin."

This report having been communicated to the Division by telegraph and telephone, Divisional Headquarters issued the following order at 10.45 p.m.—

ADVANCED GUARD ORDERS

"The Division intends to accept battle on the 2nd July in a position west of Mercy-bei-Metz. General A. will continue his retreat, and, without becoming engaged seriously, check the enemy's pursuit."

Required :—

1. The orders issued by General A. for the retreat on the evening of 1st July.
2. Reasons for the same.

MODEL FOR ORDERS FOR RETREAT.

Copy No......

OPERATION ORDER No......
BY
.... COMMANDING ....

Reference:
Map used.

Place.
Date.

1. *Troops sent on in advance:* O.C.
   Cavalry (seldom).
   Artillery (seldom).
   Engineers (often).
   Infantry.

2. *Main Body* (in order of march): O.C.
   Ammun. Col.
   Field Ambul. ⎫ or *vice*
   Engineers   ⎭ *versa.*
   Infantry.
   Artillery.
   Infantry.
   Cavalry.

3. *Rear Guard:* O.C.
   Cavalry (in considerable strength).
   Artillery (always, if possible).
   Engineers (seldom).
   Infantry.
   Machine-Gun Detachment.
   Cyclist Detachment.

1. Information as to *the Enemy* and *our forces* in other quarters.

2. *Intention of the Officer commanding.* Distribution of the troops in margin.

3. *Order for the 2nd Line Transport.* (Generally well on ahead; place and hour of starting; route; sometimes escort.)

4. *Orders for the Troops sent on in Advance.* (Place and hour of starting; route; special duties, *e.g.* preparing for blocking road, blowing-up bridges, etc.)

5. *Order for the Main Body.* (Place and hour of starting; either to follow the troops sent on in advance or special route.)

6. *Order for the Rear Guard.* (Distance to be observed, or place and hour of starting; reconnoitring especially to the side

4. *Right (or Left) Flank Guard:* O.C.
   Same as rear guard.

    roads, or often enough to say, "Patrols to keep in touch with the enemy." Special duties.)

7. *Order for the Flank Guard.*
   (Same as 6.)

8. *Order for the Outposts.*

9. *Position of the Officer commanding at the beginning of operations.*

                            Signature.

Manner in which the order is communicated to the troops. Hour of issue.

REMARKS.—In using the expressions "right flank," "left flank," "wing," "flank guard," and the like, *the direction facing the enemy* is assumed (*G.F.S.R.*, para. 98).[1]

[1] *E.F.S.R.*, Part I, sect. 9 (1) (vi.).

EIGHTH LETTER

ORDERS FOR RETREAT

THE exercise asks you to describe the arrangements for a simple retreat; and bear in mind that *the detachment is not demoralised by any recent actions*. General A. has orders from headquarters 3rd Division to continue his retreat; the *direction* of which is left to him to decide, as he has no precise orders on this subject. If the detached force retires direct to its rear by the main road, it will, if the enemy follows—which is to be expected, as he has followed up to now—mask the fire of the main body from its commanding position. It must therefore *clear the front* of the position probably taken up by the main body, and has the choice of retreating round the right or the left flank of it, *i.e.* either towards Basse-Bévoye or towards Mercy-bei-Metz. The lie of the roads is all against the latter alternative; so it is better to retire first of all by the main road, and then viâ Chesny and Crépy on Basse-Bévoye. The road through Orny and the Hospital Wald is unsuitable, being further to go. The shortest way, the cart-track leading from the northern exit of Pontoy to the main road, is also impracticable, as the portion south-west of Mécleuves is too steep to be sure that some accident might not happen to the vehicles accompanying the troops. Even if you had not noticed the closeness of the contours at this point, the zigzag course of the main road would call your attention to the steepness of the slope just here. Thus, although there is no reason why one should not use cart-tracks, as such, or even field-paths, provided they are in good repair, to march on, yet they should be avoided when they have bad places like this, especially when, as in this case, there is no pressing need for taking a short cut.

It will thus be better to leave Pontoy by the western outlet, and get on the *main road* at Haute-Grève. Tactical considerations favour this route, as the outposts are sufficiently advanced to prevent the enemy obtaining a *clear* view.

In pursuance of orders from headquarters, the enemy's advance has to be *delayed* as far as possible, without allowing ourselves to become obstinately engaged. This can be done by the rear guard from time to time taking up a position, *to force the enemy to deploy*, immediately continuing the retreat as soon as this object is attained. When and where such positions are to be taken up cannot be foreseen at the time of issuing the order, and must be arranged next day, while on the march, and on the spot, or be left wholly to the discretion of the officer commanding the rear guard. Best of all is to compel the enemy, by taking up a position behind a formidable *obstacle*, to lose time in deploying, or make a wide détour. There is no such position, however, in the present case, so we must be content with *at all events* causing the enemy *some* delay by *destroying the road* at suitable points (*G.F.S.R.*, para. 187).[1] First of all the bridges over the stream flowing by Chérisey can be destroyed, *i.e.* the bridge on the main road south of Basse-Grève (a difficult job), and the two bridges near Chérisey. The enemy will have to make them passable, at any rate, for his vehicles, which will cause some delay. The bridges over the St. Peter brook, near Crépy, should, on the other hand, *not* be destroyed by the detachment, as they come within the sphere of the main body, and we cannot be sure whether it would fit in with the plans of the commander of the 3rd Division to destroy them. The engineers may, however, prepare a position, to serve as it were as a rallying position, at the entrance to the Hospital Wald north of Orny.

" The 2nd line transport should be sent on as far in advance

---

[1] *E.F.S.R.*, Part I, sects. 73 (1), 71 (3).—*Trans.*

as possible, so that it may not retard the retreat of the troops. Two hours' start is none too much for it, though it cause some inconvenience to the troops, to be obliged to have the baggage wagons packed so early. *The safety of the march far outweighs all considerations as to convenience.*

The information as to the enemy is as explicit as can be expected in the field. As to his strength we have, of course, no accurate information, though we know *for certain* that a *strong* force is resting for the night at Solgne, and a *small* force of infantry (four to six companies though) is with a few squadrons of cavalry in Vigny. Thus the enemy is marching in two columns *at least*, and will advance on the morrow by the main road and a parallel road to the west of it, it may be viâ Vigny on Chérisey, or viâ Liéhon. It is not likely that the western column will advance viâ Pournoy-la-Grasse, and round the west side of the Hospital Wald, as that would entail the separation of the two columns during their march by the Hospital Wald. The western column will therefore probably move by Orny.

It is worth remarking that, whereas dragoons were noticed in the western column, hussars were ascertained to be near Beux, from which it may be inferred that the pursuing enemy has more cavalry than our detachment. At any rate, we may count upon cavalry pursuing next day viâ Pontoy, as it is to the advantage of a pursuing enemy to cover *a wide front*, so as to work round our flanks (*G.F.S.R.*, para. 186).[1] As to *what strength* the enemy's cavalry is in, east of the main road, is uncertain. It is, however, improbable that the enemy has *exactly one squadron* of hussars, and no more.

It is, moreover, quite possible that the enemy has sent detachments to the important line of railway leading to Saarbrücken (through Remilly and Herlingen) to secure it as early as possible. A distant patrol must watch in that direction (*G.F.S.R.*, para. 123).[2]

---

[1] *E.F.S.R.*, Part I, sects. 72 (5), 112 (1), 113 (2).—*Trans.*
[2] *Ibid.*, Part I, chap. VI generally.—*Trans.*

The portion of the enemy's force which most embarrasses General A. is that which is advancing *west* of the main road, as this, should it succeed in making a rapid movement on Chesny, will be in a position to harass the retreat of the detachment on Crépy. Counter-measures must therefore be adopted, *i.e.* we must detach a flank guard composed also of infantry; in connection with which it becomes a matter for consideration whether such flank guard shall be furnished by the main body of the detachment, or by its rear guard. The *most obvious* plan is to detail for this purpose those companies which are already on outpost duty south of Liéhon. Consequently they will naturally form part of the rear guard. It is, therefore, best to entrust all the arrangements to the rear guard. But, in any case, the orders must be so worded as to direct the attention of the rear guard to the necessity for checking the enemy's advance on the Hospital Wald, as General A. cannot absolutely depend on his rear-guard commander holding the same view as himself. This formation of a flank guard is inconsistent with the principle I have previously taught you, that flank guards should not, as a general rule, be used if they would be separated from the main column by natural features. In this case, the flank guard would, as a matter of fact, for some time be so cut off by the eastern portion of the Hospital Wald. The circumstance, however, that the enemy's advance has to be delayed justifies a breach of the general rule. Thus we see that in tactics there are many exceptions to general rules, that *all theoretical principles have but a very qualified value,* and that *the special circumstances of each individual case are invariably determinative.*

All the protective measures for the retreat should be *under one uniform command.*

The question may be asked whether any counter-measures should be taken in respect of the hostile cavalry which is reported to be in Luppy. As the country east of the main road is commanding, thus facilitating observation on the part of the enemy, we must endeavour to check an advance on the part of his cavalry in this quarter. Our cavalry might drive away hostile patrols, though it is open to doubt whether the enemy may not possess such a marked superiority in cavalry that our cavalry may not be able to accomplish this end *unaided*. It would be fruitless to detach two or three companies of infantry to assist the cavalry. This measure would fail to attain the desired end, since the enemy's cavalry would merely have to take a wide sweep to get past the infantry, which could not prevent them doing so. In this case also, therefore, we must confine ourselves to observation by means of cavalry, transmitting information promptly to divisional headquarters.

The outcome of the above considerations is the following *decision* on the part of General A. :—Fall back viâ Chesny on Basse-Bévoye, the rear guard moving on a *broad* front, and the transport being sent on in advance.

The principal point to be observed in the distribution of troops is that a rear guard should generally be *stronger* than an advanced guard, so as to have a fairly strong first line to oppose the enemy, should it become necessary to face him once more (*G.F.S.R.*, para. 182).[1] Two battalions are not too much in this case. The officer commanding the rear guard is thus enabled to take up, *with part of the troops under his own command*, a rallying position for those others of his troops most exposed to the enemy, and no delay is caused to the main body of the detachment. If troops are left in support of the rear guard *by the main body, while it really intends to continue its retreat*, more troops are exposed to be beaten *in detail* by the enemy, and *the danger arises that, contrary to the original intention, the whole force will be involved in action, if these other troops are to be extricated in their turn.*

Unlike an advance, where *the outposts* generally stand fast at first, and then join the main body, in a retreat the outposts usually join the rear guard, and *hold as long as*

[1] *E.F.S.R.*, Part I, sect. 71.—*Trans.*

possible the line they have occupied during the night. The object of this is to keep the enemy in ignorance *till the last moment* as to the *retirement of the troops in rear.* It will not much matter if this causes the outposts to get rather too far behind, for they can soon recover their proper position, *as small bodies can get over the ground quicker than can a large mixed force.*

It would also be possible to form up some other portion of the rear guard, in a sort of rallying position, and make the outposts pass through it ; but it would take more time to get into column of route this way, besides which it is a somewhat more complicated manœuvre, and therefore less suitable to the object in view. The whole column must be *well on the move* when the troops nearest the enemy, in other words the outposts, *begin* to fall back. We have to take into the bargain the disadvantage that the same troops which have borne the brunt of fatigue during the night will again have the most arduous duties to perform next day.

Suppose the I/, II/, and III/Battalions belonged to the Grenadier Guards or were the regiment of Coldstream Guards, the I/Battalion being on outpost duty, it would not be right to apportion the Rifle Battalion to the rear guard ; one other battalion of the same regiment, the IInd, should be detailed, so as to keep as much as possible the tactical units intact. For the same reason the IIIrd should march at the tail of the main body, in this case nearest the rear guard.

All the available cavalry should be placed in the rear guard, as this arm has not only to maintain touch with the enemy, but also specially watch the parallel roads, and promptly oppose any attempt on the part of the enemy to pass our flanks. It will have to maintain touch not merely with the enemy's advanced parties, but in particular with his *main body*, as otherwise the enemy might be pursuing us with only a detachment, while the bulk of his force is either, it may be, stationary, or taking some new direction,

ORDERS FOR RETREAT

or even retracing its footsteps. The stronger the pursuing cavalry, the more arduous the duties of our cavalry, which will have to make *unusual exertions, and make the most of its numbers.* It would be a pity for a single trooper to be absent when such important duties lie before the cavalry. In the case of a small force it is, as a rule, desirable to leave the execution of all measures for information as well as for protection to the *officer commanding the rear guard*, to whom all information concerning the enemy is then sent also, *direct and at first hand.* When the enemy, however, is so distant that cavalry intended to maintain touch with him must be left *very far behind*, thereby virtually losing all connection with the rear guard, or when our cavalry has to keep touch with some movement of the enemy *very far towards* a flank, the cavalry may be independent, and placed directly under the officer commanding the detachment. But even then there should be a sufficiency of cavalry with the rear guard, *more than would be allotted to an advanced guard under similar conditions.* Here all three squadrons should be allotted to the rear guard, a few troopers being enough for the main body. To detail more cavalry to the main body is in this case not necessary, for to keep in touch with the 3rd Division, for instance, we can use both telegraph and telephone. Patrols on the flanks of the main body are here not wanted. The officer commanding the rear guard must be perfectly free to dispose of his cavalry in his own way, the officer commanding the detachment merely informing him in what direction he may consider *it specially* important to reconnoitre.

Should the strength of the force render it in any degree possible, artillery should be attached to the rear guard, as this arm can force the enemy to deploy at a great distance, thereby frequently *gaining time* without the co-operation of the other arms, for the enemy not only loses time in deploying, but must quit the roads and move across country in extended order, which entails a slower rate of progress. Thus frequently a battery, or even two, may be allotted

EIGHTH LETTER

to a rear guard composed of only one battalion of infantry —a measure which would be considered exceptional if it were an advanced guard instead of a rear guard.

It will frequently happen that *the officer commanding the detachment* will have an opportunity of covering the retirement of the rear-guard artillery by the fire of the artillery of the main body. If you had any intention of dividing your artillery, the fact that a battery of *horse artillery* is with the detachment would have caused you to consider how it may best be utilised. In the *very exceptional* cases in which a detachment comprises a horse battery, its place in a retreat is, *according to tactical principles, with the rear guard*, since it can, thanks to its superior mobility, extricate itself more readily from difficult situations. To detail the horse battery to the cavalry would be rather risky, considering the smallness of that arm in this case.

Only under the *most exceptional circumstances* would there be no artillery at all in a rear guard, such as when demoralisation has set in, or when the roads are so very bad that it would be *almost a certainty* that the guns would be lost. Guns would not then be attached to the rear guard unless it were absolutely necessary to *sacrifice them to save the other arms*.

If there is a *machine-gun detachment* available, as in the case here, it will likewise be detailed to the rear guard, the same as all the *cyclists* belonging to the detachment; it is always much to be desired not to be forced to engage strong infantry in action, so that the retreat may be carried out rapidly and as unobserved as possible by the enemy. Artillery, machine-guns, and cyclists, by their greater mobility, easily make good the start the infantry had which was put in motion first.

As previously stated, engineers are very frequently sent on ahead in retreat; for all operations conducted by them, no matter of what nature, require some *preparation*, and a *reasonable time* must be guaranteed them when any result worth having is looked for. On this account they are, as

ORDERS FOR RETREAT

a rule, quite out of place in the rear guard at the beginning of a retreat, for in such a position they would seldom have the necessary time. If not sent on in advance, they should at least move at the head of the main body, either in front of or immediately behind the field ambulance. When they have finished their work, say, for instance, *prepared* a bridge for blowing-up, a few of them remain behind to carry out the *actual demolition* or to remain on guard at the spot, subsequently joining, as a rule, the rear party of the rear guard.

In certain cases engineers are sent on in carts, to save time and labour. As, however, from 20 to 25 ordinary farm wagons would be required to transport a company on war strength, and probably wagons will have to be requisitioned from Pontoy for the transport of the sick, etc., it is doubtful whether this measure could be carried out, and I prefer not to count on it, but merely desire to mention its possibility (*G.F.S.R.*, para. 187).

The exercise expressly asks for General A.'s orders for retreat issued on the evening of 1st July, 1900, in order to make you employ the method of issuing orders for a march with only *one* order. We assume, therefore, that no fresh information is likely to come to hand during the night or early in the morning; so that all the arrangements for the march can be settled overnight and one order be issued, embodying all these arrangements.

We must so arrange that the detachment (with the exception of the outposts, which must stand fast till the officer commanding the rear guard sends them the order to retire) shall be in Pontoy ready to march off at an appointed time. These instructions, applicable to the whole detachment, may be contained in the paragraph of the order detailing the object to be attained by the detachment.

Every subordinate commander must be informed that the 3rd Division intends standing on the defensive west of Mercy-bei-Metz; for this will tell him, on the one hand, that he will there find *support* in case of need; and, on the other, that he must not dawdle about *longer than necessary* in front of this position. The two first headings of the order may in that case be merged into one paragraph.

The order for the 2nd line transport is framed on the same lines as in an advance, with the sole distinction that the road to be taken by it must be carefully defined. It must be sent far enough to the rear to be out of the way if an obstinate engagement takes place on the heights of Mercy-bei-Metz. I select Pépinières, near the eastern churchyard of Metz,[1] as a position for it, and I would send it to the rear by the main road, as at present it is impossible to foresee where the detachment will pass the next night. If the officer commanding the 3rd Division has sent his baggage *further* back, he will cause the necessary orders to be given to the baggage of the detachment as it passes through the position, since the officer in charge of the baggage has in any case to report his arrival to him. It would not be correct to order the 2nd line transport to retire " to Metz," for Metz is a large place, and one might be a long time finding it there. A definite and unmistakable place must be appointed.

The order for the engineers must be so worded that the officer commanding the field company shall know exactly what is expected of him, while perfectly free to *distribute his company as he deems best to the various tasks*. For the officer commanding the detachment to interfere in *details* would not only be superfluous, but *positively harmful*. As, in the case before us, the engineers have a special duty entrusted to them, there must be a separate heading of the order for them.

For the main body, too, the route to be followed must be distinctly stated, to prevent any possibility of a misunderstanding, especially as in this case the main body has to move by a different road to the baggage. The hour of starting is left to General A.'s discretion, so he fixes 5 a.m., and sends the engineers and transport off two hours earlier.

[1] On map Metz. Ost Khf. = Ost Kirchhof = eastern cemetery.

The distance between the main body and the rear guard is, as a rule, *much greater* in a retreat than that between main body and advanced guard in an advance, to minimise any danger caused by possible hindrances to the march of the main body, and remove the main body out of range of the enemy's artillery fire. The distance, in the case of detachments of this strength, may be 1 mile to 1¼ miles. In this case it is, for example, desirable for the main body to have got well through Chesny before the enemy's artillery can reach the height marked 270·8, south-east of Pierrejeux (*G.F.S.R.*, para. 184).[1]

Orders, as a rule, are so worded as to make the officer commanding a rear guard *far more independent* than an officer commanding an advanced guard, for most of the measures to be adopted by the former are dependent on the manner in which the enemy presses the pursuit. *A small force in retreat* has to make its actions conform to a far greater extent to those of the enemy than has a *strong force* which is *advancing*. Moreover, in a retreat the officer commanding the detachment will often be at a far greater distance from the rear guard than he would be from an advanced guard in an advance, *as it is often necessary for him to ride on ahead.* "After once the column is on the march he should not attempt to assist in all conceivable details, for this is the duty of the subordinate commander. By abdicating his functions at the right time he will best achieve success" (Schlichting). The only way I should feel inclined to interfere with the rear-guard commander's freedom of action in the present case would be to direct him to cause the outposts to hold their ground as long as possible, as otherwise he might possibly call them in too soon.

When the march begins, the commanders of both main body and rear guard will watch in company, from some point affording a good view, whether the enemy is pressing the pursuit, and, if so, in what manner. The best point

[1] *E.F.S.R.*, Part I, sects. 71 (4), 72 (8).

for this purpose will be the high ground by Haute-Grève, but later on the officer commanding the detachment will probably hurry on in advance, firstly to the point 270·8, and then to other suitable points, till finally he has to make arrangements for forming up the detachment according to the orders he receives from headquarters of the 3rd Division. Thus in a retreat the position of the commanding officer is far more undetermined than in an advance. In the orders he can only make known his *first* position, and care must be taken, by leaving mounted orderlies or cyclists behind, that when he quits his position, reports, etc., are forwarded on to him by the shortest route. General A. must never lose sight of the importance of maintaining communication with the 3rd Division, and will, during the night, *report* by the cavalry telegraph to the supreme commander what he has decided on doing (*G.F.S.R.*, para. 556).[1] It is, moreover, advisable to send a staff officer to divisional headquarters, so as not only to report, but also when questioned to give verbal information on the general situation and intentions of the detachment, for it is expressly stated in the *German Field Service Regulations*, para. 556, that transmission by cavalry telegraph is by no means reliable. About $4\frac{1}{2}$ miles of line can be laid by one patrol using the stores of one cavalry regiment. You had better read what is said about cavalry and infantry telephone detachments in *German Field Service Regulations*, para. 555. I cannot give you at present any more details about these detachments, the subject being still in an experimental stage; but I am dealing with these detachments as I am sure of their being finally established.

The detachment orders issued by General A. will be as follows:—

[1] *E.F.S.R.*, Part I, sect. 17.

OPERATION ORDER No. 3

Copy No. 1.

BY

MAJOR-GENERAL A., COMMANDING DETACHED FORCE.

Reference:
$\frac{1}{100,000}$ *Ordn.*

PONTOY,
1.7.00.

1. *Sent on in Advance:*
   Major G.
   1st Field Co. R.E.

2. *Main Body* (in order of march).
   Ammun. Col.
   Field Ambul.
   Rifle Battalion.
   III/Battalion.
   1 N.C.O., 6 troopers II/Sqd.

3. *Rear Guard:* Colonel B.
   1st Dragoons (less details).
   "A" Battery R.H.A.
   1st Field Battery R.A.
   I/Battalion.
   II/Battalion.
   Machine-Gun Detachment.
   Cyclists of the Detached Force.

1. *The Enemy* has followed us with a force of all arms to **SOLGNE**; infantry of his, with two or three squadrons of dragoons, is in **VIGNY**; his cavalry patrols were seen on the line **GOIN–SILLY-EN-SAULNOIS–BEUX**. A hostile squadron of hussars has been ascertained in **LUPPY**.

2. *The Detachment*, with the exception of the outposts, will be in **PONTOY** at 5 a.m. to-morrow, ready to march off and withdraw on the 3rd Division, which will be holding a position west of **MERCY-BEI-METZ**.

3. *The 2nd Line Transport* will be in column of route at 3 a.m. to-morrow, with its tail at the western exit of **PONTOY**, and move by the main road, through **GRIGY**, to **PÉPINIÈRES** at the east churchyard, south of **PLANTIÈRES**, where it will await further orders.

4. *The Field Co. R.E.* will leave **PONTOY** at 3 a.m., prepare for demolition the bridge on the main road south of **BASSE-GRÈVE**, and the two bridges near **CHÉRISEY**, and prepare a rallying position on the border of the **HOSPITAL WALD**, north of **ORNY**.

5. *The Main Body* will start at 5 a.m., moving by the main road through **HORGNE-AU-CHEVAL-ROUGE**, thence viâ **CHESNY** and **CRÉPY** to **BASSE-BÉVOYE**.

6. *The Rear Guard* will follow at a distance of 1¼ miles, keeping touch of the enemy by patrols, and reconnoitring towards **VIGNY** and **LUPPY**. Should the enemy attempt to advance, he must be delayed, but the rear guard must not become seriously involved. The rear guard will detach a flank guard, which will move viâ **ORNY** and **CHESNY**. An officer's patrol is to be sent viâ **ALBEN** towards the **SAARBRÜCKEN** railway.

7. *The Outposts* will remain in their present position as long as possible. The infantry telephone detachment will at once establish connection between **PONTOY**, **PETIT GRÈVE**, and the 3rd and 4th Cos.

8. *All the Cyclists* of the Detachment will join the rear guard.

9. *Reports* will reach me from 5 a.m. to-morrow near **HAUTE-GRÈVE**.

A.,
Major-General.

Dictated to representatives of all units.
By Cavalry Telephone to H.Q. 3rd Division at 11 p.m.

There could be no objection to fixing an *earlier* hour for the *start* of the main body, for in a retreat more than in any other movement it is desirable to assure the main body's safety by a very early start. In that case, however, you must make the rear guard stand fast awhile, which means increasing the distance between main body and rear guard, *as otherwise you will not satisfy the requirement of the exercise to the effect that the enemy's advance must be delayed as much as possible.* The 2nd line transport and engineers, too, would, in such case, have to make a correspondingly earlier start. Such an arrangement is, of course, attended by the danger that the rear guard would be left to its fate more than is required by the general situation in this instance, for it would be a difficult matter to afford it opportune support. In practice, the amount of fatigue the troops have been called upon to undergo the previous day has an important bearing on the hour of starting, for it is absolutely essential for their efficiency that they should have a sufficient period of rest, though it may frequently amount to only a few hours.

It might appear, at first sight, advisable to cause the main body to halt, and stand on the defensive somewhere between Pontoy and Basse-Bévoye, with a view to rendering support, if necessary, to a rallying position taken up by the rear guard; but the objection to this course is that such an arrangement is very apt to tend to fatal errors, as it would make it far more difficult for the detachment to disengage itself from the enemy. It may have occurred to you to halt the ammunition column at some place or other with the object of placing it at the disposal of the batteries should they come into action. I consider this permissible but not absolutely necessary, for a likely artillery combat here can only be of short duration, and for such the ammunition with the batteries is sufficient.

It would be incorrect for the officer commanding the detachment to be present with the rear guard. He could only be so for a very brief space, for what principally concerns him is to direct the movements of the main body. It is possible that an order might arrive from headquarters of the 3rd Division to change the direction of the detachment's march; and, if so, it would take too long to reach him if he were with the rear guard. *It is the officer commanding the rear guard who is immediately concerned with the enemy.*

Similarly I should not approve of the outposts being assembled in the vicinity of Haute-Grève, since that would more imperfectly satisfy the principal requirement of the detachment's task, viz. to delay the enemy's advance.

EIGHTH EXERCISE.

In continuation of the Seventh Exercise, describe the arrangements made by Colonel B., commanding the rear guard, on the supposition that no fresh information is received concerning the enemy up to 5 a.m.

NINTH LETTER

REAR-GUARD ORDERS

THE first thing that will have occurred to Colonel B., as to the officer commanding the detachment, is that, in order to conceal the resumption of the retreat from the enemy as long as possible, both the outpost cavalry, which takes up its duties again at daybreak, and the infantry battalion on outposts must maintain their positions until the main body of the detachment has got under weigh and gained a start. As a preliminary measure, it will suffice if by this means the enemy is delayed till the main body has passed the high ground by Haute-Grève; provided that we find an opportunity of getting ready some means of causing the enemy a *further delay*. This can be done by the rear guard halting for a *short time* in a suitable position, and compelling the enemy to deploy.

The main body has about $\frac{3}{4}$ mile to traverse from the western outskirts of Pontoy to Haute-Grève, so, as you can calculate, will have got a sufficient start by 5.30 a.m., up till which time the outposts must hold their ground. The enemy has, from Solgne or Vigny, as the case may be, to the line held by our outpost companies, about $2\frac{1}{2}$ miles to go. He will, however, be under the necessity of proceeding here with caution, *i.e.* slowly, since the opposing forces are at such close quarters; therefore, assuming that he is not on the move much before 5 a.m., he can hardly attack the outposts before 5.30 a.m., so in all probability the latter will begin their retreat *unmolested*. There would be no advantage in causing the outpost companies to remain *thus isolated* a moment longer than necessary, as they should arrive as early as possible, and *without being closely pressed*, at the first position in front of which we intend forcing the enemy to a serious deployment of his force. In the fight that will probably thereupon ensue our infantry should not become too closely engaged; as, once engaged, this arm is with difficulty extricated. The fighting might easily assume an obstinate character (though the detachment orders enjoin us to avoid it), and, if so, it would be difficult to extricate the infantry from a perilous position, owing to its slowness of movement. Only the flank guard and the rear party, if possible, should be engaged at this first position, the infantry of the main guard remaining under cover in readiness for whatever result may ensue, and, above all things, close to the main road, so as to be able to resume the retreat promptly when the time comes, or, *if absolutely necessary*, take up a rallying position for the flank guard and rear party to fall back on. It is most essential to a thorough comprehension of the problem before us to realise that the intended resistance must be *of brief duration, to be immediately succeeded by a resumption of the retreat*. If this were not the case, *i.e.* if we were purposing to offer a longer resistance, it would be better for the officer commanding the rear guard to issue an order for taking up a position of readiness, instead of an order for retreat; subsequently directing the resumption of the retreat by means of *another order*.

Any of the cavalry not engaged in reconnaissance or in warding off the hostile cavalry patrols can fight dismounted. Suppose, for example, the enemy comes under the fire of dismounted cavalry posted in the gardens of Orny or of Pournoy-la-Grasse (their horses being at hand close by in the village), he cannot at first tell whether he has not to deal with infantry, and so he will have to feel his way cautiously. In a retreat, therefore, the fire of dismounted cavalry, able by means of their horses to withdraw rapidly from a position of danger, can greatly conduce to *deceiving, and consequently checking*, the enemy. Our cavalry may

REAR-GUARD ORDERS

also by similar tactics be of great service in Pontoy, or, possibly, in the Hospital Wald, or in the Bois Cama, by causing the enemy to think there is a considerable force of infantry opposed to him, especially if he sees formed bodies of infantry here and there. Thus it is the duty of the cavalry of the rear guard to act so as *never to lose touch with their own infantry, and always to be ready to take their part in the impending conflict.* As soon as a close touch of the enemy is gained, the co-operation in combat of the cavalry takes *precedence of its other functions, but even then the reconnaissance must not be interrupted.* In the case before us, however, it is *very far from easy* to satisfy both requirements. It calls for great *ability and prudence* in *the commander*, not to let slip the right moment for retiring over the Chérisey brook.

The principal part in the action will, however, be played by the batteries which, protected by cyclists and machine-guns, should be so placed as to command the main road (*as being the principal line of route*) and the country to the west of it, which will probably be traversed by the other column of the enemy.

Breaking off an action, once seriously entered on, is one of the most difficult tasks a commander has to deal with. General von Verdy, in his studies on service in the field (Vol. III), especially calls attention to the fact that during the large manœuvres the breaking off of an action as well as rear-guard actions, present to us pictures which are *not like anything we would witness on active service.* " On the manœuvre field, deployed divisions, nay even whole army corps, break off an action at greatest ease, and we often see them getting into column of route and withdrawing with surprising rapidity. There we see none of the delays in transmitting orders ; these are delivered by the shortest route ; the commanders to whom the orders are to be delivered are rapidly found ; it is exactly known who is commanding at this or that spot; the orderlies carrying the orders remain unhurt ; commands have never changed hands once or twice owing to death or wounding. The orders are carried down to the group leaders in the firing line without the bearers of the orders being molested by hostile projectiles. Owing to all this the movements proceed quite smoothly, the dissolving influence of the action is got rid of in the shortest possible time, order is once more established, and the withdrawal is carried out with surprising rapidity." I have quoted for you the description of this experienced General *in order that you may thoroughly think out for yourself the difficulties of such a task in actual warfare.*

On receiving the orders, Colonel B. must first and foremost consider whether it is advisable for him to do anything *during the night*. The orders, however, direct the outposts to stand fast as a preliminary measure, and tell the remaining troops composing the rear guard where to assemble, so Colonel B. can postpone making any further arrangements till next morning, for *nothing more can be done during the night than has been already seen to in the detachment orders.* All he need do is to establish the telephone connection as ordered; and this connection, in all probability, will have to be removed next morning from Petit Grève to Haute-Grève.

Colonel B. can wait to see whether news of importance may not come in even up to the moment of starting. On the following morning he will thus be *better off* than the officer commanding the detachment was on the previous evening, inasmuch as he will know this much, at least, that the enemy has not set out on his march at an abnormally early hour (for, were it otherwise, the outposts would have already reported it). He will therefore be in a position to *decide definitely* what measures to adopt for checking the enemy; whilst the officer commanding the detachment had to confine himself to making arrangements for the troops beginning the march.

To attempt the first resistance in a position *south* of the Chérisey brook is not advisable; for, if the enemy pressed his attack, it is doubtful whether the outpost companies could make good their retreat over the brook. A stand may well be made, though, along the line Orny–Basse-Grève–Pontoy, having the little brook of Chérisey in front of us. The infantry of the right flank guard, quite irrespective of the participation of the cavalry, may defend Orny; the infantry of the rear party Basse-Grève and Pontoy; and the batteries and the machine-guns fire from the high ground by Haute-Grève; thus the enemy comes under the fire of a position nearly $2\frac{1}{2}$ miles in extent. It will be impossible for him to tell at first sight in what strength it is occupied, so he will have to advance cautiously, thus *losing time*, before getting a clear idea of the situation, and deciding on a resolute assault. Imagine yourself in the position of the officer commanding the enemy. Formerly, before the introduction of smokeless powder, the puffs of smoke gave him, at any rate, some idea of his enemy's strength—nowadays he merely hears the report of fire-arms in various directions along a line some $2\frac{1}{2}$ miles long. By degrees he receives more definite reports from the various parts of the battlefield, and as the situation slowly unfolds itself he can decide what to do. *But all this takes time*, and his artillery, at all events, is *still further delayed* by the demolition of the bridges. We can confidently rely on having no difficulty in checking the enemy until the main body of the detachment has got the wished-for start of $1\frac{1}{4}$ miles, where it will be, for a time, sufficiently protected by the high ground 270·8 south-east of Pierrejeux. If he can manage to deceive the enemy still longer, Colonel B. need not be particular about scrupulously preserving the distance laid down in the detachment orders, of $1\frac{1}{4}$ miles from the main body; for, as was pointed out in the last letter, *the longer the hostile artillery is in reaching the spur south-east of Pierrejeux*, the easier the retirement of the main body of our detachment. Colonel B. will be fully justified in thus understanding his duty; for *obedience in an officer*, especially one in command of a considerable force, bears a different meaning to obedience in the rank and file. Colonel B. should not so much place a *literal* interpretation on the order as carry it out in accordance with the *spirit of it*, and in accordance with the intentions of the officer commanding the detachment, which in this case are to *check the enemy;* while it is of no consequence—provided this is done—if the distance between the rear guard and the main body of the detachment be greater or less than that laid down in the detachment orders.

It would be a mistake to lay down in advance in what manner the rear guard is to retire from the first position, *and whether it is to take up another position later on*, or whether the main guard should occupy a rallying position. It is impossible to settle how long the resistance is to be protracted, or in what manner it is to be made, until we have got a clear perception as to the degree of vigour with which the enemy is pursuing. *Such points as these will be dealt with in later orders*. Of course, subordinate officers must not be left in ignorance in what direction they are to retire, when driven back by superior numbers; since it is doubtful whether, when once the action has commenced, orders to this effect would reach them in time enough to be acted upon. In the present instance, therefore, *as an exceptional case*, there can be no doubt that the line of retreat should be indicated before the action begins, for in this case it is equivalent to *making known the route by which to march*. The *Field Service Regulations*, para. 58, do not apply to this case.[1]

The above considerations will lead Colonel B. to the following decision: take up a position for a short time on the north side of the Chérisey brook, and compel the enemy to deploy.

The rear guard may now be divided into Main Guard, Rear Party, Right Flank Guard, and Cavalry of the Rear Guard. The employment of the cavalry is subject to the following considerations: on the main road we shall not

[1] *E.F.S.R.*, Part I, sect. 113 (2).—*Trans.*

be long in encountering the enemy's advanced guard, and little information will be obtainable in this quarter; it is enough if we establish the fact that the enemy is pursuing, so far as applies to the main road, as before. On the other hand, it is important to reconnoitre both the parallel roads, with a *wide* sweep towards the enemy's *flanks*. Our cavalry is not likely to attain much *by force*, so must confine itself to warding off hostile patrols, and dashing up to the enemy's columns from *the sides* in more or less strength; taking care, at the same time, not to lose touch with its own infantry.

The road which most lends itself to an enemy threatening Chesny is the *western* parallel road; the greater part of our cavalry must therefore be employed in its vicinity. The eastern one is less important, as for the time being we suppose that by it next day one or more squadrons of the enemy's hussars may advance; so in this direction we can do with less cavalry. In order to guard against the danger of unduly disseminating the cavalry, which is liable to arise when a force is retreating with a broad front, the available squadrons are apportioned, some to a *main*, some to a *secondary* duty; the bulk of the cavalry, allotted to the former, being kept more concentrated, while weaker bodies can perform the secondary duty. From this it follows that two squadrons should be detailed to reconnoitre west of the main road, while one will do for the main road and the road east of it. As the 1st Squadron is already, for the most part, posted on the main road during the night, it is best to entrust to it the duty of watching the main road itself and Beux, and sending patrols towards the Saarbrücken railway. In the present instance, therefore, it is perfectly correct for the officer commanding the rear guard *himself* to detail the 1st Squadron for this duty; whereas, as you are aware, it would be more proper to leave the selection of the squadron to the officer commanding the regiment. Besides, it is an advantage to have the two *fresh* squadrons for the *main* duty. In the flank guard the cavalry should work in close co-operation with, and be supported by, the infantry; therefore it is best for both cavalry and infantry to be *united in one command*. You must not mind that in this case the actual rear-guard cavalry consists of only one squadron, while that of the flank guard is two squadrons strong.

Of infantry, Colonel B. has the II/Battalion (concentrated), and the I/Battalion (at present on outpost duty); the former will form the heart of the rear guard, viz. the main guard; the latter the rear party and the flank guard. It naturally fits in for Nos. 1 and 2 Cos. to join the flank guard, similarly for Nos. 3, 4, 5, and 6 Cos. to form the rear party; but there is room for doubt as regards Nos. 7 and 8 Cos. Four companies are enough for the rear party, nor is the main guard short of infantry; but it would be a good thing to strengthen the important flank guard, which will probably have a great deal of trouble with the western column of the enemy, which is already well advanced, and *superior to it in numbers*. Nos. 7 and 8 Cos., therefore, may be allotted to the right flank guard, joining Nos. 1 and 2 Cos. at Orny. The latter, though they need not become unsteady, even though the enemy press them as they fall back, will find it then easier to retreat across the Chérisey brook.

The batteries and machine-gun detachments will for the moment accompany the main guard.

With regard to the issuing of orders on the part of subordinate commanders, I have a few remarks to make which I purposely omitted making in the seventh letter. The procedure adopted there was in strict conformity with the *Field Service Regulations*, which lay down that, as a rule, the subordinate commander should not repeat the whole of the orders received from superior authority, with his own additions thereto, but *independently* issue clear and suitable orders on necessary points (G.F.S.R., para. 57).[1] A subordinate commander is usually obliged to confine

[1] *E.F.S.R.*, Part I, sect. 12 (11).

REAR-GUARD ORDERS

himself to issuing brief assembly orders or orders to be ready for starting, and then giving all further instructions verbally. In conformity with these regulations, independent, verbal advanced-guard (or other) orders might *invariably* be issued, but that the paragraph quoted proceeds to say that " In larger formations orders to the troops will *usually* be based on divisional orders." " Divisional orders," however, correspond generally to the " detachment orders " of these exercises, which deal with smaller bodies. So it is on detachment orders that advanced or rear-guard orders, etc., must be based, but only when, as, for instance, in the present exercise, it can safely be assumed *that the detachment orders have reached all the troops in question.*

With regard to the march orders, it is optional for Colonel B. whether he sends a separate order to each of the scattered portions of his command, or whether they all receive the one set of orders, applicable to the rear guard as a whole. According to the principles laid down in the fifth letter, the latter course is preferable, so that in this case the commanding officer of each unit may at once obtain an insight into what the rear guard has to do, for thus is unity of action among the various portions of the rear guard best ensured.

I have purposely given no model of rear-guard orders, as it is good practice for you to adapt the models of advanced-guard orders and orders for retreat to the purpose, in doing which you should not experience any special difficulty.

It will be as well for Colonel B. to inform his subordinates, first of all, that up to the moment of issuing his orders no fresh information concerning the enemy has come to hand, so that they may all know that the situation remains as described in the detachment orders. Next, each commanding officer must be acquainted with Colonel B.'s intention not to retreat forthwith, but, first of all, compel the enemy to deploy. To prevent, however, any misconception as to the character of the intended action,

Colonel B. again lays stress on the necessity for avoiding any obstinate fighting.

The main guard, which has later on to halt and stand prepared for whatever may turn up, will proceed as far as the hollow about 700 yards north of Haute-Grève, where it will be under cover, and can remain for the most part in column of route. It can, however, first of all follow close on the main body of the detachment, without any distance, so as to arrive at the proposed position as soon as possible, the distance being gained later on.

The order for the rear party can be very short. All it has to say is the hour at which the rear party is to start, and the position it is to occupy at the outset. Any further orders will reach it later on.

The order for the right flank guard should enter somewhat more in detail, as this body will be detached to such a distance from Colonel B.'s position that some freedom of action should be accorded to it in respect of selecting its own time for resuming its retreat beyond Orny; and it must receive instructions in advance in what direction the said retreat is to be made. The officer commanding the right flank guard should also know when the outposts are to be withdrawn, and at what hour, consequently, Nos. 7 and 8 Cos. will be at his disposal. It is left to him to employ these two companies as he thinks fit. It should also be especially impressed on the right flank guard that it is not to confine itself to merely keeping touch of the enemy, but that it is expected of it to *reconnoitre boldly* towards the left flank of the enemy's advance.

There will be some difficulty in ensuring that the bridges prepared by the engineers for demolition are actually destroyed at the right moment. If it were done too soon, it would be disastrous for the cavalry in particular, compelling them to make a wide détour. It would be impossible for Colonel B. himself to decide the right moment; he must therefore make the commanders of the right flank guard and rear party responsible for it, making special mention of it in the orders, so that there may be no misunderstanding on such an important point.

Colonel B. will at first be with the officer commanding the detachment, near Haute-Grève, whence he can give the order to bring his batteries into action, and can supervise as far as may be necessary all other operations. The telephone connection will now be established in such a way as to enable Colonel B. to be in communication with his rear party. Efforts should be made to establish similar connection with the right flank guard, but not before it has arrived at Orny; an order later on should deal with this (vide *G.F.S.R.*, para. 47, last sentence).

Copy No. 1.

OPERATION ORDER No. 1

BY

COLONEL B., COMMANDING REAR GUARD.

Reference:
$\frac{1}{100.000}$ *Ordn.*

Western Outskirts of
PONTOY,
2.7.00.

1. *Main Guard* (in order of march): Lt.-Col. S.
   1st Field Battery R.A.
   "A" Battery R.H.A.
   Machine-Gun Detachment.
   II/Battalion.
   1 N.C.O., 4 Troopers, I/Sqd.

2. *Rear Party:* Lt.-Col. E.
   I/Battalion (less 4 cos.).
   1 N.C.O., 8 Troopers, I/Sqr.

3. *Rear-Guard Cavalry:*
   Major N.
   I/1st Dragoons.

1. Up to the present, no further news has been received of the *enemy*.

2. *The Rear Guard* will endeavour to compel the enemy to deploy at the **CHÉRISEY** brook, without itself becoming involved in an obstinate engagement; thereafter following the main body of the detachment to **BASSE-BÉVOYE**.

3. *The Main Guard* will at first follow the main body of the detachment without any distance, as far as the hollow 700 yards north of **HAUTE-GRÈVE**, where it will await further orders.

4. *The Rear Party* will start at 5.30 a.m., and hold **BASSE-GRÈVE** and

4. *Right Flank Guard:*
Lieut.-Colonel K.
Nos. 1, 2, 7, 8 Cos.
I/Battalion.
1st Dragoons (less 1 sqd.).

PONTOY, to delay the enemy till further orders. Telephone connection is to be established in **HAUTE-GRÈVE.**

5. *The Rear-Guard Cavalry* will keep touch of the enemy by means of patrols on the main road, and viâ **BEUX.** An officer's patrol is to be sent viâ **ALBEN,** in the direction of the **SAARBRÜCKEN** railway.

6. *The Right Flank Guard* will check the enemy in **ORNY,** and at the **HOSPITAL WALD**; retiring, when compelled to do so by superior numbers, through the **HOSPITAL WALD** and **CHESNY.** Nos. 7 and 8 Cos. I/Battalion will be under Colonel K.'s command after 5.15 a.m Colonel K. will begin his retirement, viâ **CHÉRISEY,** with Nos. 1 and 2 Cos. I/Battalion at 5.30 a.m. The flank guard will keep touch of the enemy towards **VIGNY,** and recognoitre viâ **ALLEMONT.**

7. The responsibility for *destroying the bridges* over the **CHÉRISEY** brook at the right time will devolve on the right flank guard and the rear party.

Verbally to assembled commanding officers, copy sent to the outposts by Lieutenant S., at 4.50 a.m.

8. *Reports* will reach me at **HAUTE-GRÈVE.**

B.,
Colonel.

NINTH EXERCISE.

(See general map, and the maps Gravelotte and Ars-on-the-Moselle.)

General Idea.

A Red Division, operating in an enemy's country, has been defeated on the Deutsche (German) Nied, and crossed the Moselle at the unfortified town of Metz, pursued by a Blue Division.

Special Idea for the Red Detachment.

Late on the evening of the 4th August, 1900, the rear guard of the Red Division encamps at Moulins-bei-Metz, with outposts from the Moselle to the western foot of the St. Quentin. The 3rd Brigade of Infantry (less IV/Battalion) under Major-General C., are billeted in Ste. Ruffine, with the 1st Field Co. R.E.—the rest of the Division being in and about Ars-on-the-Moselle. The enemy has followed as far as Metz. It was not possible to destroy the bridges over the Moselle at Metz, but all the bridges between Metz and Pont-à-Mousson are blown up. A hostile column, consisting of several battalions, with cavalry and artillery, was seen towards evening on the march from Maxe to St. Eloy.

At 10.15 p.m. General C. receives the following divisional orders:—

OPERATION ORDER No. 9
BY
LIEUT.-GENERAL N., COMMANDING RED DIVISION.

Reference:
$\frac{1}{100.000}$ *Ordn.*

Divisional Headquarters,
ARS-ON-THE-MOSELLE,
4.8.00.

1. *Main Body*, etc. etc.

2. *Rear Guard*, etc. etc.

3. *Left Flank Guard:*
   Major-General C.
   III/ and IV/Sqds. 9th Lancers.
   2nd Field Art. Brgde.
   1st Field Co R.E.
   3rd Infantry Brgde. (less IV/Battalion).

1. *The enemy* has thrown a bridge over the **MOSELLE** at **OLGY**. **WOIPPY** is said to be occupied by the enemy. Our patrols came under infantry fire from **LORRY-BEI-METZ** and from the **FRANZÖSISCHE THOR**[1] of **METZ**.

2. *The Division* will continue its retreat viâ **ANCY** on the **MOSELLE**, **GORZE, CHAMBLEY** on **DAMPVITOUX**.

[1] Französ. Thor = French Gate.—*Trans.*

Machine-Gun Detachment.
Art. Brgde. Ammun. Col.
Sect. A. Field Ambul.

3. *The 2nd Line Transport* will stand to-morrow at 3 a.m. on the road **ARS-ON-THE-MOSELLE-NOVÉANT** with its head at the northern entrance of **NOVÉANT**, and march by **GORZE** to **DAMPVITOUX**.

4. *The Main Body* will start at 5.30 a.m. from the southern exit of **ARS-ON-THE-MOSELLE**, and march viâ **ANCY** and **GORZE** to **DAMPVITOUX**.

5. *The Rear Guard* will follow the main body at $1\frac{1}{4}$ miles distance, and with patrols keep in touch with the enemy.

6. *The Left Flank Guard* will stand ready to start at 5.15 a.m. from the western exit of **STE. RUFFINE**, and march viâ **GRAVELOTTE, MARS-LA-TOUR** on **HANNONVILLE-AU-PASSAGE**. The 2nd line transport will remain with the flank guard, and stand at 4.45 a.m. at the western exit of **GRAVELOTTE**.

7. *Reports*, etc. etc.

N.,
Lieut-General.

Dictated to representatives of all units at 9.30 p.m.

Required:—

1. An appreciation by Major-General C. of the situation, and his plan of action.
2. The orders issued by Major-General C.

N.B.—The woods west of Metz have thick undergrowth. Infantry could move through them, off the roads, only in extended order, and slowly.

TENTH LETTER

RETREAT OF A FLANKING DETACHMENT

THE answer to the first question, how General C. proposes to carry out the task before him, affords you the opportunity of explaining your views on the general situation; in fact, the answer to this question furnishes *the reasons* for the orders to be given.

General C.'s orders have to comprise arrangements for a retreat. The *road* by which the detachment will march and the *time* it is to start have been fixed by divisional orders; thus far there are no difficulties.

The first point to be considered is where General C.'s detachment is likely to find positions in which it might resist the enemy. The rugged and precipitous *Montveau valley* is unsuitable for *obstinate* defence, as its west edge is covered with dense thickets and woods. The enemy's infantry could, it is true, advance here but slowly and with much difficulty off the road, but eventually it would work its way through; besides which the various woodland roads and footpaths would facilitate the advance of troops in compact formation.

If the enemy advance viâ Moulins-bei-Metz, he will first of all encounter the rear guard of the Division; if the latter have already started, and if he then wishes to follow the flank guard, he has to traverse a difficult uphill road to the high ground by Le Point-du-Jour before he overtakes it. This high ground could thus, in case of need, be utilised for a brief halt of the rear guard of the flanking detachment. The portions of the enemy's force situated to the north of Metz, in Lorry-bei-Metz and Woippy, would, in advancing, be tied to the roads through Scy, Lessy, and St. Georges, all three of which entail a steep descent and ascent in crossing the Montveau valley, so the enemy's progress would be retarded, and he would have to exercise great caution in view of possible surprises. But as soon as the enemy is once established on the western side of the Montveau valley, the broad patch of wood west of Chatel St. Germain is so near the high ground of Le Point-du-Jour that our detachment would not be able to remain long in occupation of the latter, especially as immediately in rear of it is the deep and precipitous Mance valley. This valley infantry can, of course, cross at any point, but cavalry in compact formation only by the main road, and by a few indifferent field-tracks, and artillery only by the main road. We should therefore endeavour to get this obstacle between us and the enemy, and gain *the heights of Gravelotte and Mogador* as soon as possible, where, with luck, we ought to hold the enemy some time. The main body of the pursuing force, whether it advance viâ Moulins-bei-Metz or further to the north, will be tied to the main road in crossing the Mance valley, and we can sweep the road with our fire, especially from near Mogador.

It is possible the enemy might attempt a détour, such as viâ the Mance mill (rather more than a mile south of Gravelotte), which is invited by the oblique direction of our line of retreat, or north of the main road on Malmaison; but it would cause him to lose time, and we could, if we do not wish to limit ourselves to the simple defensive, either seize the right moment for assuming the offensive, with a view to checking the enemy as he is in the act of laboriously emerging from the Bois des Ognons or La Haye aux Mures, or gain our next position for defence *between Gravelotte and Rezonville*, west of the Gorze brook. Other positions suitable for defence exist in the *high ground west of Vionville*, or the high ground at the various tributary streamlets of the *Yron brook. There is thus no lack of favourable positions, with more or less considerable obstacles in front of them, to check the enemy.*

The road by which the main body is to march is so distant (3 to 5 miles) from that to be followed by the flanking detachment, that we cannot count on any support from the main body or the rear guard. It is, however, the more important to maintain connection, so as always to know how far on their way the main body and rear guard respectively have got. It would not be admissible for the detachment to quit the main road, in order to be nearer the main body, for in so doing it would be leaving open to the enemy the shortest road to Verdun;—nothing could be more fortunate for him. It was not voluntarily that the officer commanding our main body decided not to take this road, and there must have been powerful reasons which led him to select the southern and more roundabout road.

As soon as our detachment has taken up a position, the enemy pursuing it will be on his guard against detaching a considerable force in a south-westerly direction to interrupt the march of our main body, as to do so would too much endanger his flank, especially as he cannot be sure, at so early a stage of the proceedings, what is the strength of the detachment. There is no good road leading to Verdun between the two main roads by which we and our main body respectively are to march; but there are several good cart-roads and field-paths available for the movement of troops,—several in particular running from the northern main road to Puxieux and Chambley. North of the road by which the detachment will march, the road through Malmaison and St. Marcel to Ville-sur-Yron must be considered. According to the principles laid down in my previous letters, it would not be correct for a small force of infantry to move by this road to protect the left flank, for it is too distant from the main road,—on the average 2 miles.

The enemy had continued the pursuit till the evening

as far as Metz. It is noteworthy that a column of all arms had been seen on the march from Maxe to St. Eloy. Coupling with this the news that a bridge has been thrown across the Moselle near Olgy, and the report made in the evening of Woippy and Lorry-bei-Metz being occupied by the enemy, the conjecture becomes almost a certainty, that we have in this quarter to deal with a reinforcement coming to the enemy either from the north (Diedenhofen) or the north-east (Bettsdorf). These fresh troops are already to the *north* of Metz during the night, so will probably next morning take up the pursuit by the *northern* of the two main roads leading to Verdun. Possibly it was this consideration that decided our main body to diverge more to the south.

It may be assumed that it is known to the enemy that the main body of the Red Division is at and near Ars on the Moselle, as from the east bank one can see the road on the west side of the river. A *portion* of the Blue Force will, therefore, in any case move on Ancy. But we cannot say in what direction his main body may pursue, therefore we cannot yet foretell with what force the flanking detachment may have to contend, especially as nothing is known concerning the strength of his reinforcements to the north of Metz. The enemy can be pretty sure that the Red Division is retiring on Verdun. He will therefore endeavour to gain the Gravelotte–Mars-la-Tour road, as being the most direct.

Should the enemy at the same time endeavour to drive our flanking detachment off the Gravelotte–Mars-la-Tour road, he will probably not only pursue along that road, but also utilise the Malmaison–Ville-sur-Yron road for this purpose. *The latter road therefore must be specially watched by us.* From this it follows that the detachment must ward the enemy, from whatsoever direction he comes, off the main body, and give the latter time to reach Dampvitoux. The enemy's advance on the Gravelotte–Mars-la-Tour road must be delayed *by all possible means*. The flanking detachment should not fight unless it be unavoidable, and, if it does, must endeavour, like a rear guard, to prevent the engagement assuming an *obstinate* character. Artillery and machine-guns will, therefore, play the principal part in any such action, and aim at compelling the enemy to deploy *at long ranges*. Any infantry fighting at short ranges, more particularly in villages or woods, should be avoided as much as possible. All this is greatly facilitated by the numerous strong positions for defence available, for the enemy will be unwilling to attack them *in front*, and have to make wide turning movements, *thereby losing time*. The cavalry should lose no time in seeking to get touch of the enemy, and, once gained, must not lose it throughout the day. The reconnoitring should be thorough towards both flanks, especially the left, to discover any turning movements as early as possible, and repulse any attempts on the part of the enemy's cavalry to pass round our flanks. It might be as well to offer a somewhat *protracted* resistance in two positions, for the following reasons :—

The main body has, at the beginning of its march, to cross the plateau of Dornot, which is lofty and has steep slopes ; and, while so doing, must be protected against any attack coming from the north until it has passed Gorze. This means that *the detachment must not leave the heights of Gravelotte too soon*. You will notice here what is a peculiar feature when retreating in more than one column, namely, that *if one column retreats more rapidly than the other, it will be fatal for the latter*. Between Gorze and Dampvitoux the main body will encounter no particular difficulties, but precaution should not be neglected. To prevent the enemy pressing the pursuit from an *easterly* direction, *i.e.* through Gorze, is the duty of the rear guard of the Red Force ; but to prevent him pressing too closely from a *north-easterly* direction, *i.e.* through Rezonville or Vionville towards Chambley or Xonville, is the duty of the flanking detachment, which consequently may again have to offer resistance in the neighbourhood of Vionville until the main body has got a sufficient start.

General C. therefore decides to perform the task before him in the following manner :—The detachment to march at 5.20 a.m. from the western outskirts of Ste. Ruffine (covered by a rear guard, which will halt, if necessary, for a short time at Le Point-du-Jour), and proceed, first of all, as far as the high ground east of Gravelotte, where it will take up a position of readiness, and wait to see in what direction and manner the enemy is advancing. This position to be held, if possible, until the main body has passed Gorze. The cavalry will endeavour to get touch of the enemy at once, some watching the main road and keeping up communication with the rear guard of the main body, while the remainder provides for security north of the main road.

As soon as the main body has passed Gorze, the flanking detachment will fall further back, keeping approximately level with the rear guard of the main body. If the enemy presses forward impetuously, the retirement must be conducted in a formation *deployed* on each side of the main road, either with or without a rallying position. There is an opportunity for such by Rezonville. At Vionville another attempt is to be made to hold the enemy until news is received that the main body has passed through Les Baraques, on which the detachment will fall back on Hannonville-au-Passage.

The 2nd line transport should be sent *well on ahead ;* thereby it is at the same time best protected against hostile cavalry which might advance against the main road from the north, *i.e.* from Malmaison, it may be, or Vernéville.

The 2nd line transport of the 3rd Brigade must start early enough to join that of the troops to reinforce General C.'s command at 4.45 a.m., at the western outskirts of Gravelotte. The Field Company R.E. will leave Ste. Ruffine along with the 2nd line transport of the 3rd Brigade, with instructions to prepare obstructions at suitable points on the road. After passing Gravelotte the massed 2nd line transport of the detachment will have got sufficient start to be able to dispense with a special escort.

The engineers must start very early, so as to have plenty of time for the work to be done by them. Definite orders should be given that the Field Company R.E. be accompanied by *all* its wagons, including 2nd line transport. I should designedly abstain from indicating to the officer commanding the field company any particular localities where the road should be blocked, but leave it to his discretion, as he will be better able to decide *on the spot*. His attention can be directed *by word of mouth* to the intention we have of offering a somewhat protracted resistance near Gravelotte, and again near Vronville.

The several commanding officers are informed upon the general situation only so far as is absolutely necessary.

I.

OPERATION ORDER No. 10   *Copy No. 1.*

BY

MAJOR-GENERAL C., COMMANDING 3RD INFANTRY BRIGADE.

Reference: **STE. RUFFINE,**
$\frac{1}{100,000}$ *Ordn.*   4.8.00.

1. *The 3rd Brigade* will be ready to start from **STE. RUFFINE** to-morrow at 5.15 a.m.
2. *The 2nd Line Transport* of the brigade will be formed up at the western outskirts of **STE. RUFFINE** at 3.15 a.m. to-morrow.
3. *The 1st Field Company R.E.* will march with all its transport at 3.15 a.m. to-morrow by **GRAVELOTTE** on **HANNONVILLE-AU-PASSAGE**. It will take along with it the 2nd line transport of the 3rd Brigade as far as the western outskirts of **GRAVELOTTE**, handing it then over there to the officer in charge of the rest of the 2nd line transport of the detachment. Arrangements are to be made for blocking the road to the greatest possible extent between **STE. RUFFINE** and **MARS-LA-TOUR**.

Dictated to adjutants of   C.,
I/, II/, III/Battalions,   *Major-General.*
verbally to O.C. Field
Co. R.E., at 10.35 p.m.

II.

TO THE OFFICER IN CHARGE OF 2nd LINE TRANSPORT.

STE. RUFFINE,
4.8.00.

1. *The Division* will proceed to-morrow, viâ **GORZE**, to **DAMPVITOUX**; and the flanking detachment, under my command, viâ **GRAVELOTTE**, to **HANNONVILLE-AU-PASSAGE**.

2. *The 2nd Line Transport* of the flanking detachment will start at 4.45 a.m. from the western outskirts of **GRAVELOTTE** and proceed by the main road to **HANNONVILLE-AU-PASSAGE**.

In writing through O.C. Field Co. R.E. at 10.40 p.m.

C.,
Major-General.

III.

TO MACHINE-GUN DETACHMENT, III/ AND IV/SQDS. 9th LANCERS, 2nd FIELD ARTILLERY BRIGADE, ½ ARTILLERY BRIGADE AMMUNITION COLUMN, AND SECT. "A" FIELD AMBULANCE.

STE. RUFFINE,
4.8.00.

1. The III/ and IV/Sqds. 9th Lancers will stand at 5.15 a.m. to-morrow at the **KIRCHHOF**[1] north of **STE. RUFFINE**; Sect. "A" Field Ambulance, 2nd Field Artillery Brigade, and the Machine-Gun Detachment at the same time in column of route, in the above-named order, on the road from **STE. RUFFINE** to **ROZÉRIEULLES**, tail at **STE. RUFFINE**.

2. Issue of orders for the left flanking detachment at the western outskirts of **STE. RUFFINE** at 5 a.m. to-morrow.

In writing by orderly officer. 10.45 p.m.

C.,
Major-General.

N.B.—These individual orders you might, of course, have issued in one comprehensive order.

It now remains to compose *the march orders proper*.

Unlike the previous exercises (in which the rear guard retired *on a broad front,* and therefore required more in-

---

[1] Khf. on the map = churchyard, cemetery.—*Trans.*

fantry), the rear guard of the flanking detachment in this case can move *by one road only*, and has no need to throw out infantry flank guards—therefore one battalion is sufficient. Should you have apportioned two battalions owing to the strong artillery, it would not be wrong. The machine-gun detachment is best detailed to the rear guard.

I am decidedly opposed to making the flanking detachment march by the two parallel roads previously mentioned, because they are too far apart from each other. It is true, we like to use *several* roads in a retreat, especially when larger bodies of troops are concerned, because we can thereby disengage ourselves from the enemy twice as quick and shorten by half the time the rearmost troops will have to resist the enemy, but to detachments of a strength like ours this argument *rarely* applies.

A cavalry non-commissioned officer and twelve troopers (=four patrols) may be attached to the main body of the detachment, so that the necessary patrols may be sent out direct to the flank. To keep touch with the main body of the Division cyclists may be chiefly used on account of the numerous good cross-roads. Of the rest of the cavalry, part· should be allotted to the rear guard of the detachment and part detached northwards. The latter requirement is, as I said before, of special importance, so it will be best to detach one of the squadrons as a *left flank guard*, thereby ensuring it the necessary *independence*. This leaves the other squadron for the rear guard of the detachment. This arrangement separates the two squadrons, it is true ; but it is unavoidable, as their respective spheres of action lie in *different* directions. If *both* squadrons were put in the rear guard—a course I do not recommend—it would still be necessary to detach a considerable portion to the north. In fact, in the present instance circumstances utterly preclude all possibility of the cavalry acting together.

It is an open question whether all the batteries or only two be allotted to the rear guard of the detachment.

In the orders for the retreat it must, above all things, be pointed out to the subordinate commanders that the enemy is in occupation of Lorry and Woippy as well as Metz. Under the head of the commanding officer's intentions it may be intimated that it is only " as a provisional measure " that the detachment is to march as far as Gravelotte ; that is to say, that later on the movement will be continued. It would, however, be wrong to state *now* that the detachment will take up a position of readiness near Gravelotte, since it is possible that, for some reason or other, it may not be necessary to do so after all, *in which case the order would have to be cancelled*. All that General C. has to arrange for in the march order is the retreat to Gravelotte. Anything to be done after that will form the subject of fresh orders.

As to the distance between the detachment's rear guard and main body, precise figures cannot be given—in this case, for example, the point is to cover the main body of the detachment while it is crossing the Mance valley, so while this is going on the rear guard must remain on the high ground by Le Point-du-Jour, which means a distance of *at least* $1\frac{1}{4}$ miles. Reference may be made, in the order, to the necessity for communication being kept up between the rear guard of the detachment and the rear guard of the main body of the Division, although, properly speaking, it should go without saying. The orders may likewise lay down that the cavalry is to lose no time in seeking *touch of the enemy*, for this duty comes, if possible, into even greater prominence in the case of a retreat than in that of an advance.

When the left flank guard (of the flanking detachment) is ordered to move by some particular road, the squadron-leader concerned should not consider himself strictly confined to such road, but should interpret the order as only approximately indicating the general line on which he is to move, parallel to the detachment.—It would be impossible for General C. to remain in one fixed place to

RETREAT OF A FLANKING DETACHMENT

await reports. This, as you have already seen, is a common occurrence in the case of retreats. At the outset he will certainly remain for some time at Ste. Ruffine until not only the main body, but the rear guard likewise has got under weigh. Then, however, he will gallop past the column to the high ground near Le Point-du-Jour, whence he can get a view in all directions. After that he must ride on in advance to Gravelotte, so as to arrive at a decision on the spot as to the position of readiness there to be taken up. He can, therefore, only direct that reports be sent to the main body, with which he will leave instructions where he is to be found. A telephone line will be laid from Le Point-du-Jour to the heights east of Gravelotte, so as to keep in better communication with the rear guard. This will be the duty of the 3rd Brigade. However desirable it may be to keep in like communication with the Division, it is beyond the means of General C. to do so; this would be the duty of the Division.

Copy No 1.

OPERATION ORDER No. 11

BY

MAJOR-GENERAL C., COMMANDING LEFT FLANKING DETACHMENT.

Reference: $\frac{1}{100.000}$

Western outskirts of
STE. RUFFINE,
5.8.00.

1. *Sent on in advance:*
    Major Y.
    1st Field Co. R.E.

2. *Main Body* (in order of march).
    Art. Brgde. Ammun. Col.
    Sect. "A" Field Ambul.
    III/Battalion.
    II/Battalion.
    1 N.C.O., 12 Troopers III/9th Lancers.

1. *The enemy* occupied **METZ, LORRY-BEI-METZ,** and **WOIPPY** yesterday evening.—*Our Division* will move to-day viâ **ANCY** on the **MOSELLE, GORZE,** and **CHAMBLEY** on **DAMPVITOUX.**

2. *The Detachment* will move as a left flanking detachment, retiring to **GRAVELOTTE** in the first instance.

3. *The Main Body* will march off at once, by the main road to **GRAVELOTTE.** An Infantry

3. *Rear Guard:*
   Lieut.-Colonel F.
   III/9th Lancers (less 1 N.C.O., 12 troopers).
   2nd Field Art. Brgde.
   I/Battalion.
   Machine - Gun Detachment.

4. *Left Flank Guard:*
   Major D.
   IV/9th Lancers.

Verbally to the assembled commanding officers at 5.15 a.m.

telephone line is to be established from **POINT-DU-JOUR** to the heights east of **GRAVELOTTE**.

4. *The Rear Guard* will follow at a distance of 1¼ miles, keeping touch of the rear guard of the Division; and will at once obtain touch of the enemy through **MOULINS-BEI-METZ, SCY,** and **LESSY.**

5. *The Left Flank Guard* will go to **MALMAISON,** viâ **CHATEL-ST. GERMAIN** and **MOSCOU;** endeavour to get touch of the enemy in the direction of **LORRY-BEI-METZ;** and watch towards **PLAPPEVILLE.**

6. *Reports* will reach me with the main body.

C.,
Major-General.

TENTH EXERCISE.
(See general map, and map Ars-on-the-Moselle.)

General Idea.

A Blue force, operating in its own country, garrisons Metz; a Red army is concentrated north of Toul.[1]

Special Idea (Blue Detachment).

Information having been received that, on 1st February, 1900, strong bodies of hostile infantry and artillery, with a few cavalry, had crossed the Moselle at Pont-à-Mousson (general map), detachments from Metz had been pushed forward to Arry and Marieulles respectively, to observe that portion of the frontier line lying between the Moselle and the Seille.[2] These detachments have

[1] Some 20 miles S. by W. of Pont-à-Mousson.
[2] The frontier line between France and Germany runs nearly east and west between Pagny-sur-Moselle (2 miles S.W. of Arry) and Sailly (some 11 miles E.S.E. of Arry). Thus Arry is about 1 mile and Marieulles 2 miles on the German side of the frontier.—*Trans.*

RETREAT OF A FLANKING DETACHMENT

instructions to check any attempt on the part of the enemy to advance on Metz. A third detachment is in observation to the east of the Seille, in the neighbourhood of Fleury. In addition the line Freskaty–Übungs-Schanze[1] on the main road—Haut-Boutan (map Verny) is held by troops from Metz. On the afternoon of the 2nd February the detachment from Marieulles, consisting of 3 Battalions, 2 Squadrons, 1 Field Battery, $\frac{1}{2}$ Field Co. R.E., $\frac{1}{3}$ Art. Brgde. Ammun. Col., commanded by Colonel A., had been obliged by a greatly superior force of the enemy to fall back from the woods between Sillegny (general map) and Marieulles, after suffering heavy losses, and had been driven back on Féy, where it had gone into close billets late at night. On arrival at Féy, Colonel A. is informed that scarcely a fourth of the ammunition can be found. Outposts are thrown out (1 battalion, 1 troop cavalry) on the line Vezon–Bury–Pournoy-la-Chétive, each village being held by 2 companies and 9 troopers; the remaining 2 companies being posted at Sabré. The troops till now forming the Arry detachment bivouac, after suffering severe losses, in and about Corny—the enemy pursuing as far as Voisage, in this quarter. Marieulles and Coin on the Seille have not been occupied by him, but Lorry and Loyville are occupied by him in force. Just before evening fell, the enemy had unlimbered two batteries on hill 213, west of Loyville, which had opened fire on the outpost companies at Pournoy-la-Chétive, and a battery of the Fleury detachment had come up and helped to repulse hostile infantry attacking Pournoy-la-Chétive through Coin on the Seille.—No hostile troops had so far been seen east of the Seille. An order arrived from Metz, by a telephone line established between Metz and Féy, to withdraw on the 3rd February, slowly to the line Freskaty–Haut-Boutan, on which the Blue force intends to oppose the enemy's attack on the 4th February. Telephone lines have been established between Féy and Corny, and between Augny and Jouy-aux-Arches.

Required:—

1. The opinion on the situation formed by Colonel A., and how he proposes to carry out the duty assigned him.

2. The orders issued by Colonel A. for the 3rd February.

N.B.—The woods south of Metz have thick undergrowth.

[1] Übungs-Schanze = practice entrenchment; at the junction of the roads Augny-Metz and Marly-Metz.—*Trans.*

ELEVENTH LETTER

RETREAT AFTER A DEFEAT

THE data for this exercise are designedly somewhat longer, and comprise various details which have all to be taken into consideration in working out the solution; this renders the solution a little more difficult. *It is advisable to mark the troops on the map in colours that can be washed off, or with coloured pencils.*

The road in the Moselle valley leading to Metz, viâ Jouy-aux-Arches, is being watched by a special detachment, so Colonel A.'s detachment need not trouble about it, especially as the lofty ridge of Côte-de-Fayé and St. Blaise intervenes, rendering it impossible to act in concert with the neighbouring detachment. All that Colonel A. need do in this connection is to have a look-out kept during the morning of the 3rd, from St. Blaise, to see how matters are going in the Moselle valley, as otherwise the enemy might push on viâ Corny and fall on Colonel A.'s flank, or even threaten his retreat. It may fairly be calculated that the Corny detachment can make a stand for a considerable time even against a superior hostile force, but Colonel A. should inform the officer commanding it of his intentions. A thorough use must be made of the existing telephone lines.

Should the enemy attempt to advance by Marieulles and Féy, the presence of the woods on both sides of the road will oblige him to exercise a certain degree of caution, so as to guard against surprises. We may, therefore, safely assume that he will not enter on this tract of country till it is broad daylight.

In the woods themselves the enemy could advance but very *slowly* on account of the thick undergrowth; practically, therefore, he is confined to the road. West of the road begins the steep ascent to the Côte de la Rique, Côte-de-Fayé, and St. Blaise, and although infantry can move over it, yet their progress would be *slow*, so that the enemy can for the most part use only the narrow tract of country immediately adjoining the road for deployments. This is irrespective of the season of the year, which will further determine the practicability of the country. It is easier for the enemy to advance east of the road from Marieulles to Sabré.

A retreat from Féy to Augny would be covered from view by the spur stretching from Féy to Cuvry; this suggests the advisability of reaching Augny before the enemy can get to that spur.

The country is quite open on both sides of the second important road to Metz, that viâ Pournoy-la-Chétive. If you trace the course of this road north of Coin a. d. Seille, you will see that the village of Pournoy-la-Chétive, which is well adapted for defence, forms the first point for resisting the enemy's advance. The outpost companies standing there could check him here. Between Pournoy-la-Chétive and Coin-bei-Cuvry the road runs across a valley which can be swept by fire from the south edge of the latter village. After this the road climbs the spur Féy-Cuvry, which here, too, offers a good position for a *short* defence. There is yet another good position between Haute-Rive and Prayel, so that thus we can delay the pursuit on this road in several positions, *if necessary;*—bearing in mind the desirability of paying special attention to the road Marieulles–Sabré–Augny, so as not to be *taken unexpectedly in flank* from that quarter. *In fact, as a rule, rear-guard actions like this, fought by small forces in presence of superior numbers, call for great ability and foresight in a commander, to prevent the troops running great risk of being annihilated.* It must be remembered that the best part of the main road through Pournoy-la-Chétive is visible from the high ground east of the Seille. It follows that the artillery of the Fleury detachment can co-operate with Colonel A.'s detachment, unless its attention be taken up in another direction by an advance on the part of the enemy by the right bank of the Seille. As the enemy had not crossed the Seille on the 2nd February, we may reasonably count upon this support from the Fleury detachment during the early part of the morning of the 3rd. It is, however, unlikely that the enemy will endeavour, *the first thing in the morning*, to press his advance along the west bank of the Seille; because, although on the 2nd February he will have got a tolerably accurate idea of how much is opposed to him, yet this knowledge avails him nothing as a means of forming his plan of action for the 3rd, on account of the proximity of Metz, whence, for all he knows, the detachments might have been reinforced. He will, therefore, be apprehensive of an unexpected counter-attack, in which case the Seille on his right flank would be a source of danger.

Concerning the enemy's strength, all that is known is that infantry and artillery, with a little cavalry, have crossed the Moselle at Pont-à-Mousson on the 1st February. As to whether more followed on the 2nd we do not know, though it is probable, for the presence of strong Blue forces near Metz cannot be unknown to him. At all events, the enemy was in superior force all along the line on the 2nd February, and was advancing on a broad front by three roads, in doing which he had already pushed forward strong bodies of troops towards the Seille—that is to say, towards the east. His feeble attempt to occupy Pournoy-la-Chétive the same evening has failed, but has acquainted him with the presence of the troops near Fleury, *with which he will have to reckon the following morning*. The fighting of the 2nd February will have left its mark on him likewise, for even the victor will have experienced no small dissolution of tactical formations in the course of the day's fighting, especially when it is a case of *fighting in woods, always so destructive of order*. Therefore even the victor needs time to recover, and this is where the close pursuit of a beaten enemy, which theory demands,[1] so often fails in practice. To carry it out calls for extraordinary will-power in a commander, so as to finally triumph over human weakness. In this connection bear in mind Colonel A.'s success in forming outposts, and the abandonment of the enemy's attempt on Pournoy-la-Chétive after the failure of the first attack.

Colonel A. is so cut off from the Fleury detachment by the Seille that any concerted action is almost out of the question; still, communication must be kept up through Marly, and he must inform the Fleury detachment of his intentions (*G.F.S.R.*, para. 70).[2] Efforts must be made in the morning to establish telephone connection with the eastern portion of Marly, viâ Grosyeux; the further extension to Fleury would be the business of the Fleury detachment.

The above considerations, therefore, lead to the conclusion that the enemy will probably advance the following morning through Marieulles on Féy, as well as on Sabré; while, on the other hand, it is unlikely that he will advance the first thing in the morning through Pournoy-la-Chétive.

In face of this the situation of Colonel A.'s detachment is far from good. He has opposed to him greatly superior forces. We have proof, however, that the enemy has somewhat slackened his pursuit, in that Colonel A. has been able to post his outposts in due form. Had the enemy *closely pursued till the very end*, it might have become impossible to do so, and the two opposing forces would have passed the night *under arms* in immediate contact, snatching a few hours' rest on the battlefield, with a view to resuming the engagement with daylight.

---

[1] See *Soldier's Pocket-book*, by Lord Wolseley, p. 351, and his remarks on Wellington's failure to pursue.—*Trans.*

[2] *E.F.S.R.*, Part I, sect. 8.—*Trans.*

I leave it to your imagination to conceive the state of affairs that evening in the streets of the village of Féy. It will require the most strenuous exertions on the part of officers of all ranks to restore such order among troops and vehicles of all sorts as to get them in hand for the next morning. Actions in our days, with their increased fire effect, so disorganise the troops, especially the infantry, that nothing but *necessity* can justify requiring a weak detachment, which has fought till dark, and been compelled to retire with heavy loss before greatly superior numbers, to make a resolute attempt at resistance again on the following day. There is, therefore, no need for Colonel A. either to make a stand at Féy or to commit himself to the obstinate defence of any other position, *e.g.* at the Bois de la Goulotte. Nor would it be advisable to make a *protracted* defence of Augny, as the southern border of the village is awkwardly shaped for the purpose, and the enemy's attack would be much facilitated by the Bois St. Jean, and the high ground south and south-west of the village.

Although a *protracted* combat is to be avoided, there is, of course, no reason why measures should not be taken with a view to *forcing the enemy to deploy*, so as to gain time, since it is not until the 4th February that the Division intends fighting the decisive battle. We must therefore try to gain a day.

It is, however, as well to impress upon you that it would be possible thus to act only on the supposition that some sort of order has been restored in the Féy detachment. If, on the contrary, the main body of the detachment consisted of troops no longer fit for battle, time would be absolutely necessary to restore order. It might, in that case, be necessary to reinforce the outposts with some of the most reliable infantry, and with a battery, for a hurried retreat would utterly ruin the "moral" of the troops, and cause an even *greater loss in prisoners and matériel* than would an obstinate rear-guard action.

It is desirable that the retreat from Féy to Augny *be not unduly hurried*. With a view to this the outposts should have orders to stand fast to begin with, and not follow the detachment until the enemy presses on in superior numbers. Here again I must lay emphasis on the point already dwelt upon in the eighth letter, viz. that a premature withdrawal of the outposts informs an enemy who is in close touch with one that the detachment is retreating, *and has the effect of making him start correspondingly earlier in pursuit*.

If, however, the outposts are attacked, they must fall back, doing all they can to delay the enemy as far as possible; to which end, as we have seen, the country between Marieulles and Féy, and between Coin a. d. Seille and Prayel, is favourable; that on the Marieulles–Sabré road unfavourable. The retreat of the outposts when pressed by a superior enemy will always be a difficult operation and cause much loss; *they must therefore be supported by a rallying position*. The oft-named ridge between Féy and Cuvry affords such a position, namely, south and southeast of the Bois Robois. Six companies and the battery will be enough for it. If, in addition, we leave two more companies at the southern border of Féy in support of the outpost companies standing at Vezon, we have done all that is possible to ensure the safe retreat of the outposts. The third battalion, which is still available, may take up another rallying position south of Grosyeux Castle,[1] *e.g.* on height 211·8, ensuring thus in turn a safe retreat for the second battalion and the battery. But for the present it cannot be decided yet whether it will be necessary to occupy that rallying position; Colonel A., at any rate, will send the third battalion for the moment only back to Grosyeux, reserving further orders to himself.

We may now decide *when* the detachment should start. At the beginning of February the sun rises about 7.50, and, to march off at 7 o'clock, the troops must assemble

[1] Schl. = Schloss = Castle.

at early dawn, which is never pleasant, especially after a defeat—but they will have had sufficient rest at least. It is unnecessary to start earlier than this, as the enemy also is in need of rest and can scarcely be in motion earlier.

The 2nd line transport must be sent on in advance, and an hour's start is not too much to give it. It would not be a mistake if you have sent it off earlier. As we do not yet know where we shall pass the coming night, it can go on to Montigny, beyond the point where the main road crosses the railway at the sidings. It will be out of the way there, and can be readily got at if wanted. No special escort is necessary for it.

Next come the measures to be taken for making up the deficiency of ammunition from Metz. With a view to this, the first thing to be done is to empty completely as many infantry small-arm ammunition carts as possible, so far as this has not been already done, and distribute the ammunition among the men, company officers taking the opportunity at the same time of seeing that it is equally divided among the men. The empty S.A.A. carts, together with the empty wagons of the light ammunition column, should proceed without loss of time to Metz to refill from the artillery brigade ammunition columns, and must be back at Augny at the right time next morning. The best position for them then will be at the north corner of the park, where they will not be in the way, and can be brought up to all parts of the ground. I explained in my first letter that arrangements concerning ammunition do *not* come within the sphere of operation orders; in this case, however, the data of the exercise expressly refer to the subject of ammunition; you may, therefore, as an exceptional case, give a "special order" relative to the measures to be adopted for replenishing the ammunition supply. It would, however, not be incorrect to omit to do so, and assume that the battery and battalion commanders have made their own arrangements in the matter (*G.F.S.R.*, paras. 52, 507, 508, 513, 519).[1] You may, however, embody in the operation order also the arrangements for replenishing the ammunition, but in that case you must give your reasons in compliance with paragraph 52 (3)[2] of *Field Service Regulations* for this exceptional procedure.

All the available cavalry must go to the outposts, and by thorough reconnaissance prevent the outpost companies being taken by surprise and prematurely driven in. Connection with the neighbouring detachments must be maintained by cyclists and telephones. The commander of the detachment must be content with a few mounted orderlies.

In framing the orders, great care must be taken not to describe the situation as a desperate one, so as not to dishearten the troops. At the risk of repetition, I must impress upon you that an injudicious order, even if it be imparted verbally, and only to officers, may in certain cases work much mischief. Troops, when in a dangerous situation, judge by the bearing and demeanour of their officers whether the latter consider the situation a desperate one or not. A touch of acting, provided it be not overdone, has a good effect on the rank and file, especially in a retreat. On this account Colonel A.'s order must not omit to state that the enemy has not yet crossed the Seille, that we have been able to keep possession of Pournoy-la-Chétive, that we shall find other friendly troops on the line Freskaty-Übungs-Schanze, and that there are other neighbouring detachments south of Metz who might lend us assistance.

Our orders would, therefore, run as follows :—

OPERATION ORDER No. 3
Copy No. 1.

BY
COLONEL A., COMMANDING DETACHED FORCE.

Reference: $\frac{1}{100.000}$ *Ordn.*

FÉY,
2.2.00.

1. The troops billeted in FÉY will be ready to march to-morrow at 6.50 a.m. All mounted officers will be at the southern exit of FÉY to receive orders to-morrow at 6.40 a.m.

[1] *E.F.S.R.*, Part I, sects. 10, 158, 159, 160; *E. Inf. Tr.*, 1911, sects. 167 and 168.—*Trans.*

[2] *Ibid.*, Part I, sect. 12 (1) and (7).

2. The 1st and IInd Squadrons will come under the orders of the commander of the outposts to-morrow at 6.30 a.m. The 1st Squadron will detail six troopers to report to me.
3. *The Outposts* will stand fast till further orders, continuing in observation as hitherto.
4. *The 2nd Line Transport* will be formed up in column of route at 6 a.m. to-morrow, with its tail at the northern exit of **FÉY**, and proceed viâ **AUGNY** to the gasworks at **MONTIGNY**.

Dictated to representatives
of all units at 10 p.m.

A.,
Colonel.

SPECIAL ORDER.

FÉY,
2.2.00.

There will proceed at once to Metz to refill :—
1. All empty wagons of the light ammunition column.
2. The S.A.A. carts of the infantry after having been previously emptied.

The light ammunition column and S.A.A. carts will be back at the north angle of **AUGNY** park by 7 a.m., and await there further orders.

Dictated to representatives
of all units at 10.10 p.m.

A.,
Colonel.

Copy No. 1.

OPERATION ORDER No. 4
BY
COLONEL A., COMMANDING DETACHED FORCE.

Reference:
$\frac{1}{100.000}$ *Ordn.*

Northern exit of
FÉY,
3.2.00.

1. *The enemy* pursued yesterday to the line **LORRY–LOYVILLE**, but did not cross the **SEILLE**, and an attack made by him on **POURNOY-LA-CHÉTIVE** was repulsed. **CORNY** and **FLEURY** have been occupied by *neighbouring friendly detachments;* and the line **FRESKATY–ÜBUNGS-SCHANZE–HAUT-BOUTAN** by troops from **METZ**.
2. *The Detachment* under my command will continue the retreat on **AUGNY**.

3. *The Outposts* (I/Battalion), reinforced by the I/ and II/Squadrons 1st Dragoons, will remain for the present in their former position, withdrawing before superior numbers of the enemy on **AUGNY**.

4. *The II/Battalion, the Battery, and the sections R.E.* will take up rallying positions for the outposts, namely, one at the southern border of **FÉY**, with two companies and the sections R.E., and another on the ridge south of the **BOIS ROBOIS** with six companies and the battery.

5. *The III/Battalion* will march at once to **GROSYEUX**, awaiting further orders at the southern border there.

6. *Reports* will reach me south of the **BOIS ROBOIS**.

Verbally to the assembled commanding officers at 6.50 a.m.

A.,
Colonel.

Cyclists will at once proceed to the neighbouring detachments, carrying to them a written message of Colonel A.'s intentions.

In paragraph 4 of the Operation Order the commander of the detachment intentionally arranges for a particular detail.

ELEVENTH EXERCISE.

(See general map and Metz map.)

A Blue Division is encamped at Amanweiler, being in a friendly country. The officer commanding intends to throw a bridge across the Moselle at Malroy, to pass his force over; and on the 1st August, 1900, sends a detachment consisting of—

4 Battalions	1 Field Co. R.E.
2 Squadrons	1 Section Field Ambulance
3 Field Batteries	1 Light Ammunition Column

commanded by Major-General A., to proceed viâ Metz (which may be considered an unfortified town), and cover on the right bank of the river the crossing at Malroy on the 2nd.—The detachment goes into close billets on the night 1/2 August in St. Julien-bei-Metz and in Bas-Chêne, with outposts (1 battalion, 2 troops cavalry) on the line Méy–Chatillon-Höhe[1] (north of St. Julien)–the Moselle.

[1] Höhe = height, hill.

The inhabitants report that a hostile column of all arms is advancing from Saarlouis (30 miles N.E. of Metz), viâ Bettsdorf (general map N.E. of Metz) on Metz; on the afternoon of the 1st hostile cavalry patrols were seen near Argancy–Antilly and the Wald von Failly, and hostile infantry requisitioned provisions in Champion and Vigy (general map).

Required :—

1. The arrangements made by Major-General A. for the 2nd August.

2. Reasons for them.

TWELFTH LETTER

ORDERS FOR A MARCH FORWARD

RECAPITULATORY

THE problem set here is merely a *recapitulatory* exercise, involving a simple advance.

To cover the construction of a bridge at Malroy, General A. has two positions to choose between, viz. either the high ground north-west of Charly, or the ridge just south of the Bévotte brook south of Antilly. Both are capable of defence, and cover the bridge *from the enemy's view and fire*,—both would answer the purpose in view,—but the former is rather too near Malroy, being scarcely a mile from that village,—rather *too near* to allow the Blue Division ample room to deploy on the right bank after crossing the bridge. General A. will therefore endeavour to gain the position on the Bévotte brook, with Antilly and Buy as supporting points. This position is nearly 2 miles from the place where the bridge is to be constructed.

The detachment therefore marches to Antilly by the direct main road. It does not lie within the sphere of our calculations to query why the Division intends to cross the Moselle at Malroy, instead of availing itself of the bridges at Metz.

Of the enemy little is known, so we must be content with imagining his situation. The report made by the inhabitants respecting the enemy's advance on Metz viâ Bettsdorf is confirmed by the fact that his cavalry patrols have been seen near Argancy, Antilly, and the Wald von

Failly, and especially by the circumstance of hostile infantry having made requisitions in Champion and Vigy. This latter piece of information enables us to judge *approximately* how far the enemy has already advanced, since such requisitions are seldom made by infantry far in advance of their own outposts. We may therefore assume that the enemy is *in or near Bettsdorf* (general map) (*G.F.S.R.*, para. 472).[1]

If this be a correct assumption, General A. must expect, since the ridge which is his objective is about half-way between Bettsdorf and St. Julien, to encounter the enemy in the neighbourhood of Antilly; that is, assuming he starts at the same time as the enemy; but the earlier the enemy starts the sooner, and the nearer Metz, will he be encountered. In any case we must prevent him approaching the bridge at Malroy.

The enemy's route, too, is along the main road running south-west from Bettsdorf, past Antilly, there being no reason for his deviating perhaps viâ Vigy, and his immediate objective being the important town of Metz. It is most unlikely that he knows *as yet* of the design to throw a bridge across the river at Malroy; if, however, his cavalry patrols arrive on the high ground east of the Moselle, say near Argancy, before ours, they will have an extensive view over the Moselle valley, and see the columns of the Blue Division in the low ground west of the Moselle marching on Malroy. *We must therefore drive off any hostile cavalry which may show itself on the heights commanding the Moselle valley;* the cavalry must therefore form an offensive screen. But it will also be necessary for the enemy to reconnoitre towards his left flank, especially in the direction of the woods about Failly; it is probable, therefore, that he will detach some cavalry from Bettsdorf to pass through Vigy. This, however, is only guess-work; our cavalry must get information on this point, for General A. would not, on the strength of a mere conjecture, be justified

---

[1] *E.F.S.R.*, Part II, sect. 36; *E. Cav. Tr.*, sect. 163.—*Trans.*

ORDERS FOR A MARCH FORWARD

in detaching a strong right flank guard. We must employ *only cavalry* for purposes of protection and information to the east of the line of advance. It must trot ahead independently, and somewhat earlier, and try to gain possession as quickly as possible of the heights near Charly, whence the enemy would otherwise be able to overlook clearly the advance of our detachment. Our cavalry's duty here is separate from that of the vanguard, and must anticipate it (compare with page 25–27).

These considerations lead General A. to the following *decision* :—The detachment to advance by the main road to Antilly, keeping a good look-out towards Vigy and Argancy. Should the enemy be encountered south of Antilly, he must be promptly driven back, if the relative strength of the two forces in any way renders it possible. The distribution of troops and the orders will offer no great difficulties. I do not consider it necessary to have a battery in the advanced guard. If you have apportioned one to it, you must, at any rate, adduce sound reasons. The engineers may be attached to the advanced guard, because on arrival at Antilly they will have to begin to prepare the position for defence without loss of time. It would be therefore best to have them with the vanguard. The data of the exercise state that the detachment is in close billets at St. Julien and Bas-Chêne. The troops are closely packed, and the question might be raised, therefore, whether, to facilitate the start, it would not be better to assemble them first in column of route outside the villages. Against this must be urged that it is always desirable to let the troops have their rest as long as possible, and let each unit only turn out in time to fall into its place in the column (*G.F.S.R.*, para. 336).[1] With a little care on the part of the subordinate commanders, and more particularly of the leader of the main body (*G.F.S.R.*, para. 364), troops need not stir earlier than is absolutely necessary, to avoid having to wait probably afterwards unnecessarily.

[1] *E.F.S.R.*, Part I, sect. 30.—*Trans.*

With regard to the outposts, see my observations in the fourth letter. You will do well to arrange the orders at once so that the outpost cavalry does not remain wandering about too long after the mass of the cavalry has taken over the duty of reconnaissance. I would, for instance, arrange for its moving to Chieulles soon after the cavalry starts. If this appears in the orders, then the officer commanding the cavalry will know how to reattach the two troops to his command in the simplest manner. Instead of Chieulles you could detail some other suitable point (*G.F.S.R.*, para. 274).

The 2nd line transport must be kept back pending the development of events at Antilly, and had better be sent back behind the Vallières brook. To prevent the vehicles blocking the village street while the troops are assembling, it is advisable that they leave the village somewhat later than the troops, so they may stand fast at first (*G.F.S.R.*, para. 337).[1] It is a matter of indifference, in this instance, when they assemble. To facilitate their subsequent movement, they should be formed in column of route on the main road and not be parked in some open space.

I leave it to you to decide whether to issue a separate order the night before, telling the troops when to be ready to march next morning, and then to issue in the morning the actual march order, or whether to issue only one order in the evening embodying both the above orders. I choose the latter.

[1] *E.F.S.R.*, Part I, sect. 30 (4).—*Trans.*

Copy No. 1.

OPERATION ORDER No. 3
BY
MAJOR-GENERAL A., COMMANDING DETACHED FORCE.

Reference: **ST. JULIEN-BEI-METZ,**
$\frac{1}{100.000}$ *Ordn.*   1.8.00.

1. *Cavalry:* Major M.
   I/Sqd. 1st Dragoons.
   II/Sqd. 1st Dragoons (less 2 troops).

2. *Advanced Guard:*
   Lieut.-Colonel B.
   1 Troop II/1st Dragoons.
   1st Field Co. R.E.
   I/Battalion (Rifles).

3. *Main Body* (in order of march).
   1 Troop II/1st Dragoons.
   II/Battalion.
   1st Field Art. Brgde.
   III/Battalion.
   IV/Battalion.
   Sect. "A" 1st Field Ambul.
   Art. Brgde. Ammun. Col.

1. *The Enemy* is believed to be advancing, viâ **BETTSDORF**, on **METZ**. His cavalry patrols have been seen this afternoon at the **WALD VON FAILLY** and near **ARGANCY**, and some of his infantry at **VIGY**.

   Our Division intends to cross the **MOSELLE** to-morrow by a bridge to be constructed at **MALROY**.

2. *The Detachment* will march to-morrow to **ANTILLY** to cover the crossing, and be ready to start at 5 a.m.

3. *The Cavalry* will move at 4.30 a.m. at a trot on **ANTILLY**, reconnoitring towards **BETTSDORF**, **MÉCHY**, and **VIGY**. Any advance of hostile cavalry on the high ground about **MALROY**, **OLGY**, and **ARGANCY** is to be prevented.

4. *The Advanced Guard* will start at 5 a.m. for **ANTILLY**, moving by the main road.

5. *The Main Body* will follow the advanced guard at a distance of 1200 yards.

6. *The Outposts* will close in on the road to **ANTILLY** as soon as the vanguard has passed through the

sentry-line. The outpost cavalry will join the advanced cavalry at 4.45 a.m. at **CHIEULLES.**

7. *The 2nd Line Transport* will assemble at 6 a.m. in column of route on the road in the **VALLIÈRES** valley, with its head where this road joins the main **METZ–ANTILLY** road south of **GERBEREI**,[1] and will await there further orders.

8. *Reports* will reach me at the main guard.

Dictated to the representatives of all units at 10 p.m.

A.,
Major-General.

TWELFTH EXERCISE.

As the head of the vanguard reaches the point (184) on the main road where the road from Chieulles joins it, General A., who is on the Chatillon height north of St. Julien, receives the following message from his cavalry which had trotted on ahead:—

"Enemy has taken up a position on spur extending from point 204·8 on main road to the south-east corner of **CHARLY**, with about 2 battalions, 1 squadron, and 1 battery; he is entrenching on the high ground and in **CHARLY**. His squadron has retired from **RUPIGNY** on the **WALD VON FAILLY**."

Required:—

1. The arrangements made by General A.
2. Reasons for the same.
3. Show on the map the distribution of attacking force just before the assault.

N.B.—The Wald von Grimont and the Wald von Failly have no undergrowth, and can be easily traversed.

[1] Gerberei = Tannery.

Hints for an Order for Attack upon an Enemy Deployed in a Defensive Position.

Copy No......

OPERATION ORDER No......

BY

O.C..............FORCE,

Map used.

Place.
Date.

(No distribution of troops.)

1. Information as to the *enemy* (in detail), and as to *our other forces*.

2. *Intention* of O.C. Detachment (generally a brief statement which flank of the enemy is to be enveloped). An order for the order of the march to come to an end.

3. Order for the *Artillery* (whether to pass the infantry to right or left; first position, first target [as a rule the enemy's artillery]), when to open fire. Artillery officer's patrols.

4. Order for the *Infantry*. Occupation of position of *readiness*. Infantry officer's patrols. For unfolding from column of route state: the space for *deployment*, and the portion of the enemy's position to be attacked. Touch to be kept. Separation of main and minor attacks. Establishing Infantry telephone lines.

5. Order for *Machine-Gun Detachments* which may have been attached. (Position, target, opening of fire.)

6. Order for the *General Reserve*. (The troops to compose it, and what it is to do.)

7. Order for the *Cavalry*. (Protection of one flank by the greater part of it, patrols being sent to the other flank.)

8. Order for the *Infantry Brigade Ammunition Reserve*, and for the *Artillery Brigade Ammunition Column*. Position of *dressing station* of Field Ambulance Section (only when this can be known beforehand).

9. Order for the *2nd Line Transport*.

10. Where *Reports* are to be sent to.

How, to whom, and when issued.

Signature.
Rank.

THIRTEENTH LETTER
(In continuation of the preceding Letter.)

ORDERS FOR ATTACK

(Attack on an enemy already deployed in a position prepared for defence.)

ON receipt of the report from his cavalry, General A. cannot doubt but that he must *attack*, as it would scarcely be possible for the bridge to be constructed at Malroy while the enemy holds the high ground north of Charly. In this case, therefore, it is a simple matter to arrive at a decision at once; still, for your future guidance, let me remind you always to make sure whether the attainment of the desired end really requires you to attack or not; and further, whether such attack has any reasonable prospect of success. Having once come, however, to a decision to attack, then make all your arrangements with a view to utilising to the full the strength of the detachment, for in the employment of such weak bodies as detachments nothing is more reprehensible than half measures.

In accordance with the advice I gave you on a previous occasion, always, before issuing important orders during a march, make an exact calculation as to the position of the several portions of the marching column. In this case General A. scarcely needs to do so, as, looking from his position, he would see vanguard and main guard in the country before him; but it is necessary during staff rides and in working on a map, in order to guard against false ideas.

The head of the vanguard is somewhere about point 190, and the head of the main guard is just leaving Chatillon height (240). If the vanguard has not yet come under the fire of the enemy's artillery, we may expect it at any moment.

The cavalry at this moment will be feeling the enemy along his whole front, and trying to ascertain his strength, the extent and solidity of his position, and how occupied; endeavouring at the same time to drive the hostile cavalry behind its own infantry, clear the heights bordering on the Moselle of the enemy's patrols, and then pass round the enemy's flanks, and get a view of what is behind his position (*G.F.S.R.*, para. 131 (3)).[1] The report received by General A. shows that the cavalry has already accomplished part of its task, thus enabling the G.O.C., at this early stage of the proceedings, to form a fairly clear idea as to how the position is occupied. On the left flank of the position is posted a complete hostile squadron, against which the bulk of our cavalry must now act—the more so as the orders for march especially enjoined observation through Méchy.

Colonel A. knows that, *should the cavalry report prove correct*, he is superior by two battalions, one squadron, and two batteries, so that he has *a fair prospect of success in attacking*. The two extra battalions would not of themselves ensure superiority, for the advantage of being twice as strong in infantry is almost annulled by the fact that the enemy, from his defensive position, can utilise the breech-loading rifle to a far greater extent than can the attacker, who has to advance over open country. Our superiority in *artillery* is, however, of great importance, because it makes it possible to put the enemy's battery quickly out of action, and prepare the infantry attack with artillery fire so thoroughly that it will come off with, comparatively speaking, little trouble. Superiority in cavalry holds out a promise of good information during the action, the enemy being debarred from a like advantage.

The enemy's position, from the main road to the southeast corner of Charly, has a frontage of about 1100 yards,

[1] *E.F.S.R.*, Part I, sect. 92 (1).—*Trans.*

which cannot be held in great strength by the force estimated in the report. There can scarcely be more than a battalion holding Charly, the other being posted west of the village, and for the protection of the battery on the main road, part of both battalions being held in reserve.

It is as well here to state that it is but *seldom in practice* that cavalry can make such clear and precise reports as I have here given you in the data. The information which in this instance is conveyed *in a single report* will, as a rule, appear little by little from a quantity of reports, *some true, some false*. It is thus very often *extremely difficult* on service or in manœuvres *to decide the moment correctly when the situation may be considered cleared up, that is to say, when the time is ripe for deciding on one's plan of attack*—much more difficult than in theoretical exercises.

I take for granted that, in accordance with the advice I gave you in the first letter, you read the sections of the Infantry and Artillery Trainings bearing on the subject of the attack before you began to write out the orders. Both Training Books distinguish between :

1. *Encounter Battles.*
2. Attack on an enemy *deployed* for defence.
3. Attack on an *entrenched* position.

There can scarcely have been any doubt in your mind that in this case the enemy is already deployed, and that therefore the attack must *from the very outset* be a carefully planned one. In particular, the circumstance of the enemy having prepared Charly for defence shows clearly that he has given up all idea of assuming the offensive to begin with ; General A. consequently has the advantage of being able to choose the direction and manner of his attack. But owing to the shortness of time the enemy cannot yet have succeeded in *deliberately entrenching* his position.

General A. is enabled to settle *from the very outset how* he will attack. The plan of attack, where detachments are concerned, is only a question, for the most part, as to whether the *right* or the *left* flank of the enemy is to be attacked. To attack *both* is possible only when the attacker *greatly* outnumbers the defender, for otherwise a detachment runs the risk of extending too far and being broken through by a counter-stroke on the enemy's part. To envelop a flank is at the same time a means of bringing about in the easiest manner the *fire superiority* which is indispensable to the success of the attack (*E.F.S.R.*, Part I, sects. 103 and 102 (3)). Such envelopment, however, must be provided for in the first deployment, either by moving forward from *different directions*, or by *retaining units echeloned* for that purpose. Any attempt to envelop the enemy with infantry already deployed in the first line, and possibly already engaged, would lead to no result except extending the front of the first line, *i.e.* to undue dissemination of it, unless the ground in some wholly exceptional manner favours such a procedure.

Only in *exceptional cases* is one under the necessity of making a *frontal attack only*—generally *when the ground renders it impossible to envelop* the position. With detachments, however, this will seldom be the case, as such small forces require, comparatively speaking, so little space for manœuvre. When limited to a frontal attack, it is necessary to have *strong reserves* following the first line, to fill the gaps created by the numerous casualties caused by the enemy's fire ; this implies *small frontage with great depth.*

With a view, however, to *developing one's superiority to the utmost* in attacking the flank, the troops must be so distributed that the assault is really *decisive* only on the *flank ;* the rest of the enemy's position being merely *kept occupied* by either gripping the enemy firmly, or containing him, or merely threatening him with an attack. The attacking force is therefore divided into a *main* and a *secondary attack*, the former being made as strong as possible, which implies cutting down the number of the troops composing the secondary attack. The art of commanding troops in action, therefore, lies chiefly in *distributing the troops so as to attain best the object in view.* Only if we are strong enough can we attack the enemy also firmly in front, and that is, of course, the most effective means of pinning the enemy's forces to the ground in front. But for a mixed detachment, consisting of three or four battalions, with some cavalry and artillery, a frontage of 1 mile in attack is the very utmost that can be conceded; for, if it be more, not only is unity of command rendered very difficult, but the line would become too attenuated to deliver the decisive assault on the flank with the required vigour (*E. Inf. Tr.*, 1911, sect. 128 (3)).

The secondary attack is generally carried out by the advanced guard; the main attack by the main body. If, however, it be intended to leave a large gap between the advanced guard, carrying out the secondary attack, and the main attack, the advanced guard would, in the case of a detachment, possess far too little power of resistance to permit of this being done without danger; for it would be positively inviting the defender to attack and overwhelm the isolated advanced guard, since it is so weak. In view of this always remember that our (in the German Army) brigade and divisional manœuvres frequently convey a false idea, in that in seeking to gain the enemy's flank the attacker often extends his front most inordinately. The mile of frontage which I have indicated above was the frontage of a whole division[1] in attack in the great battles of 1870 (*E.F.S.R.*, Part I, sect. 104 (3)).

As to *which flank* of the enemy is to be attacked, it depends principally on where the *infantry* can find most cover in their advance; *for all depends on the infantry alone.* If the infantry succeeds in setting foot in the enemy's position, the victory is won; all other measures adopted in attack are of importance solely in so far as they render it possible for the *infantry to assault the position.* Again, the longer the enemy remains in uncertainty as to the direction of the main attack, the more chance of success has the attack, as there is more likelihood of the enemy's

---

[1] The German division is 12 battalions of 1000 men each.—*Trans.*

ORDERS FOR ATTACK

reserves failing to arrive at the right place at the right time.

What assists the infantry attack more than anything is a good *artillery preparation*, to which end all batteries should be brought into action. One will, therefore, in the second place, make the main attack *where the artillery can find a commanding position with a clear field of fire* which promises an effective result.

Besides this, one attacks the flank which is *weakest*, or that which lies *nearest to the enemy's line of retreat*, so as, by threatening it, to compel the enemy to an early abandonment of the position; or that where the *attack can be made in greatest security* with regard to its own flank and rear. There are *other reasons*, mostly of a strategical nature, which may induce one to attack this or that flank, with a view to forcing the enemy to retreat in a certain direction. You thus see that several considerations enter into the question, and that, naturally, it is very rarely that *one flank* will satisfy *all* the above requirements. It rests with a commander, therefore, to select for attack that flank *which combines in itself most of these conditions*.

Consider the nature of the country *in front of both flanks* of the enemy.

If, as may be assumed, the hostile battery is posted on or behind the hill 204·8, there will be infantry pushed out 500 or 700 yards in front of it[1] to protect it—probably at the watershed in a direct line between Charly and Malroy, whence it has a clear field of fire to front and flank up to 800 yards and more. The attacker will come under this fire as soon as he tops the spur west of Rupigny. The enemy's artillery has a very good field of fire from the high ground by 204·8 towards the south and south-west. In brief, *the approach to the position on this side is difficult*.

Matters are more favourable to attacking infantry on

---

[1] *German Infantry Training*, para. 401, says: The infantry position must be at a proper distance in front of the artillery; a distance of about 700 yards is desirable.—*Trans.*

the left flank of the position. Charly stands on a hillside; the southern border of the village, which the enemy is holding, lies rather low. The salient ground between Rupigny and Charly approaches within about 500 yards of the latter village, so that here, therefore, attacking infantry have but a comparatively short distance to advance under the full effect of the defender's infantry fire. *The infantry, therefore, will meet with most cover in attacking the enemy's left flank.*

With regard to the question as to how the artillery can prepare the point to be assaulted by the infantry, both flanks are about the same. The watershed between Charly and Malroy can at first be swept by fire from the Chatillon high ground. But the range is too great, beyond 4500 yards, for the artillery to fight here with decisive effect. A change of position to the height west of Chieulles (2000 to 2100 yards) will be necessary; if a shorter range be desired, there is a position on the spur just west of Rupigny. The attack on the south-east corner of Charly can be prepared from the spur just west of Rupigny, at a range of about 1300 yards. There is, therefore, no special difficulty to be encountered as regards artillery positions in front of either flank.

The enemy's left flank is weaker than his right, because of the limited field for his infantry fire caused by the low-lying position of the south edge of the village of Charly. Besides this, the general situation of Charly, with a hill encircling the village close in front—the way in which the houses form a salient at the southern outlet—and the vineyards bordering the village, are all so unfavourable for defence that Charly cannot be considered a *very strong* supporting point, or one which we need hesitate to attack. At any rate, it would be far more difficult to attack up the glacis-like slope in front of the enemy's right flank.

With regard to the enemy's line of retreat, it is a matter of indifference where we attack, as he has two roads to retreat by, either to Antilly or to Méchy.

It might be worth inquiring whether other considerations might not induce us to attack the enemy's right flank. It must be borne in mind that the high ground about 204.8 is nearest to the point where the bridge is to be made at Malroy, so that we might conclude that *the first thing to be done* is to drive off the enemy from that quarter, and that therefore the main attack should be made there. If purely tactical considerations favour the attack on a flank, but other considerations do not, then *in the majority of cases* the former outweigh the latter, for the first and foremost requirement is, *in general, to rout the enemy*, to which all other considerations are subsidiary; such as, for instance, the compelling the enemy to retreat in a certain direction. In the case we are considering, the Moselle, lying close to the left flank of the attack, imposes the necessity of special caution. Imagine the main attack carried out west of the main road, and then a sudden counter-stroke made by troops hitherto unseen issuing out from the Wald von Failly in the direction of Rupigny and the Moselle—and the detachment would be in a very critical position. It is therefore *safer* to make the main attack on the enemy's left flank, *i.e.* deliver the assault on Charly, while keeping the enemy occupied along the remainder of his front.

The detachment can manage well with the frontage of a mile (which I have said is the utmost allowable), provided it does not extend too far west of the main road—for which indeed, there is no motive. The main attack, advancing viâ Chieulles and Rupigny, may extend to the Wald von Failly, while the secondary attack will advance, keeping east of the main road for the most part, against the hill between the village and the main road.

It is not, however, always the case, as here, that the commander is able, immediately on receipt of the decisive report, to issue his primary order for attack; he will, on the contrary, often have first to ride nearer the enemy himself, to get a good view of the enemy and the country, "which can never be obtained either from reports or maps. In this way he is in a position to adopt his first measures in a practical manner, and to procure for himself, by timely decisions, advantages over the enemy, and to save the troops détours" (*G. Inf. Tr.*, para. 277).[1] Were it not for the excellent view to be had from height 240, General A. would have to take a good look round, say from the high ground west of Chieulles, before he could arrive at his important decision. In the present instance it is specially desirable to issue the orders as soon as possible—seeing that the main guard comes in view of the enemy as soon as it descends from height 240, when also it will begin to feel his artillery fire. Whether the deployment is to be to the right or to the left, or on both sides of the main road, the main guard ought to know as early as possible, before the first shells fall among them. There is, therefore, no time to be lost. Let me here again remind you, whenever making out orders for attack, *before you fix on the place whence the orders are promulgated*, to imagine yourself thoroughly in the commanding officer's position. If you do so, you will easily hit upon the right thing to do.

While the orders are being issued the commander of the detachment will order the main guard to halt, and the main body to move up with its head close to, but still covered by, the Chatillon height. The small-arms ammunition carts of the IInd and IVth Infantry Battalions will be emptied (*G.F.S.R.*, 506 and 508, last para.).[2] Infantry and artillery officers' patrols will supplement cavalry reconnaissance without this being specially ordered (*G.F.S.R.*, paras. 148, 154, and 263).[3]

The (German) *Infantry* and *Artillery Training* books especially emphasise that there is no sealed pattern for an attack order, because there cannot be a sealed pattern for how an action is to be conducted.[4] If I have given you,

---

[1] *E.F.S.R.*, Part I, sect. 93.
[2] *E. Inf. Tr.*, 1911, sect. 168.
[3] *E.F.S.R.*, Part I, sect. 94.
[4] *E. Inf. Tr.*, 1911, sect. 120.

ORDERS FOR ATTACK

in apparent contradiction to this, certain " hints " for an attack order, I need only direct your attention once more to what I have explained on page 6. My hints or models are merely aids to memory; they are given to prevent your forgetting important details. The special circumstances of each case will decide *what* has to be ordered, likewise the *form* in which it is to be done, whether it is to be done in one combined order or in separate orders. The will of the commander must be known by the lowest ranks, the *co-operation of all parts*, which is absolutely necessary, must be guaranteed by the mode in which the orders are issued.

Coherent (" combined ") written orders for attack *can in practice be given only if, as in the present instance, one is enabled, thanks to good cavalry reconnaissance, to form an accurate idea of the enemy's position, as well as, to some extent, in what manner his troops are distributed.* Otherwise, the (" immediate " or " separate ") orders for attack are evolved by *instalments, one after another*, being composed in the saddle, since frequently it is not until the introductory movements are on foot that the actual decision as to how the attack is to be made, and with it the allotment to each subordinate commander of his individual share in the action, is matured in the mind of the G.O.C. Able commanders, however, who are gifted with the power of swift comprehension and prompt decision, will endeavour to issue, *at the very start*, combined orders for the whole detachment; for, as I have frequently explained, such orders are **always** *preferable* for ensuring *the joint action of all ;* as the several subordinate commanders can much better work together towards a common object if they are all simultaneously informed *what duties are imposed on the other component parts of the force.* As a rule, too, it occupies very much *less time* to make out one set of orders than when several separate orders with different wordings are sent to subordinate commanders. According to paragraph **274** of the (German) *Infantry Training*, orders for attack are, as a rule, to be issued by brigades and higher units in writing; all the more is it necessary that detachments, like ours, should issue the orders in writing. The transmission of verbal orders is to be the exception, but even in such cases it is usually best to confirm the order by a staff officer taking it down in writing (*G.F.S.R.*, para. 46).[1]

Taking the above explanations into consideration, you will have in each case to think how many of the hints I have given you for an attack order you can make use of altogether at the moment of issue of the order, without falling into the error of disposing too far in advance. If you have any doubts, you had better issue several orders.

The intelligent co-operation of all concerned is ensured if, instead of sending to them *written* or *verbal* orders, the officer commanding the detachment can assemble his subordinates on some commanding point overlooking, as here, the scene of operations, whence he can point out to them how the land lies, convey his orders *personally, by word of mouth—explaining them, if necessary—answer questions, and remove any doubts*. In the present instance, circumstances forbid this in the case of the officer commanding the cavalry, who has ridden far on ahead, and the officer commanding the advanced guard, whose presence is indispensable at the front. It is possible, however, in the case of the senior artillery officer, and of the officer commanding the field company of engineers, whose place up till now is with the G.O.C., as well as in that of the officers commanding units in the main body. These latter, therefore, must assemble to receive orders at the height 240.

The short time lost in assembling officers commanding units in the main body is compensated for; since, as a rule, *time cannot be said to be lost which is given to wise deliberation!*

At the moment when the report from the cavalry is received, the head of the vanguard, which started at 5 a.m., has covered not quite 2 miles of road. It is therefore about 5.35 a.m. Allow the G.O.C. five minutes for reflection—and

[1] *E.F.S.R.*, Part I, sect. 9 (1) (i.).—*Trans.*

ORDERS FOR ATTACK

that is very little—during which time officers commanding units in the main body are assembling on the Chatillon height. The orders, taking 5 minutes more, can then be issued :—

"**CHATILLON-HÖHE** (height) north of **ST. JULIEN**, 2.8.00, 5.45 a.m."

The information concerning the enemy must be given in considerable detail. Of our own Division there is no news beyond what the subordinate officers have already learnt from the orders for advance; there is, therefore, no occasion to refer to it again.

The intention of the O.C. detachment may be tersely expressed, as the details are contained in the subsequent headings. With regard to the expressions "envelop"—"envelopment," let me remind you that *envelopments* take place on the battlefield itself, consequently under the eyes of, and directly influenced by, the G.O.C. "Turning movements," on the other hand, lie outside the actual field of battle, being executed by troops detached for the purpose, and it is very difficult, if not generally impossible, for the G.O.C. to influence them directly. A detachment attacking is concerned, as a rule, with envelopments only.

The hitherto-existing march order, as such, comes to an end the moment the G.O.C. determines upon committing his whole force to the attack. There must be no uncertainty whatever upon this point, nor the slightest misunderstanding as to the conditions under which the orders are issued. The advanced guard is a protection only while the force is on the march, and therefore has its right to exist only so long as the force which it covers is marching; or while, in exceptional cases, the advanced guard has to engage *unaided* an enemy. When, however, the entire detachment is committed to fight, the advanced guard has fulfilled its object, and the troops composing it must rejoin the several tactical units to which they belong. *The duties of the leader of the main body as such cease. A perfectly clear understanding as to the conditions under which the orders are issued is of such importance in battle that my advice to you is always to expressly notify, through the orders*, that the rôle of the advanced guard, as such, has come to an end.

As we have mentioned, the situation of the advanced guard is difficult in so far as it may come at any moment under the fire of artillery. The best aid will be rendered to it by the artillery coming into action rapidly. A suitable position for that purpose is on the Chatillon height close north of the inn (Krug), on both sides of the main road. If all three batteries simultaneously open fire from here on the enemy's position, they will draw upon themselves the indirect fire of the enemy's battery. So as to avoid crossing with its own infantry, the artillery must be ordered *to move forward to the left* of it.

Unlimbering and opening fire will be expressly ordered by the commander of the detachment, for the commander of the whole must control all the forces under his command for the attainment of his object, firmly repressing any tendency to arbitrary action or independence. But if this object is to be attained, it is further necessary that the artillery receive distinct orders from the G.O.C. At each individual moment of the action it must have orders as to in what direction the G.O.C. wishes its fire directed; for he alone can judge where at each moment the tactical situation requires the co-operation of artillery. *The orders for* the artillery must contain: what is intended, strength of the artillery to be deployed, place where and time when it is to come into action, and the task it is to solve (the commander of the artillery only allots the targets and gives the rate and kind of fire). The artillery must in our case first direct its fire on the hostile battery the moment the latter opens fire on our advanced guard when it becomes visible to the enemy. If the enemy's battery is silent, our artillery will wait with its fire until the enemy's infantry can be seen. It is desirable that the enemy's battery is fought down before our own infantry advances to attack. In our case the artillery commander tells the batteries *their positions*, the targets, superintends the practice of the batteries, endeavours always to understand the plan of the officer commanding the troops, in so far as it has not already been detailed to him in the orders, and keeps an eye on the general course of the action; while his battery commanders are fully occupied with the technical service of the guns, and only *when danger threatens* take it upon themselves to order a change of target. It is, naturally, not only the right, but the duty of every subordinate commander, as also of the officer commanding the artillery brigade, to take it upon himself to deviate from the orders he has received if the situation suddenly changes. *Guns must not, however, change position without the sanction of the officer commanding the detachment.* The only exception to this rule is when the tactical situation demands an immediate **advance,** and then a report of the action taken must at once be made to the superior officer whose sanction has been anticipated. In all other cases the officer commanding the artillery brigade has to notify the G.O.C. when he considers a change of position desirable. Slight movements, however, in order to give more effect to the fire, or for purposes of cover, are not to be considered as changes of position in the above sense.

Some amount of independence with regard to the handling of his batteries must be accorded to the officer commanding the artillery brigade in attack, by indicating to him only *approximately* the position of the guns—the selection of the *exact* position being left in his hands.

The artillery commander can select a position for his guns in the *open*, or *half concealed*, or *completely concealed*. About their advantages and disadvantages you will find details in the *Artillery Training* book. *Effectiveness of fire first; cover from the enemy's fire second*, is a tested axiom, unaffected by all the scientific appliances for indirect laying.

The first artillery position is intended to *open the engagement*, and is, as a rule, 3400 to 4500 yards from the enemy's artillery; whereas to carry out the attack will generally necessitate a change of position to ranges of 2500 yards and under. Hence we proceed in practice as follows:—The position of the enemy's artillery being known, take on the compasses a distance of 3400 yards and look for a suitable position not too far outside this distance from the enemy's artillery, and only under *specially favourable* circumstances further than 4000 yards. The conformation of the country will, of course, often decide at what distance from the enemy our first artillery position will be, as, for instance, in our case here. Longer ranges render it too difficult to observe, without which ranging is impossible. Accuracy of fire, however, is the *most essential preliminary condition for the efficacy of artillery*. What else is desirable for a good position you will find in the *Artillery Training*. The artillery commander is responsible for officer's patrols and scouts being sent out early, therefore either during the advance into position, or at the latest after its occupation. The commander of the detachment is, of course, at liberty to send these patrols himself.

The point is to get into the position *under cover* with the whole artillery brigade *simultaneously*, so as to *surprise* the enemy *as much as possible by the fire*. About the position of the limbers, first line wagons, and light ammunition column of the brigade in action you will find the necessary information in the *Artillery Training* book. The commander of the detachment may even at this stage place the ammunition column at the immediate disposal of the commander of the artillery brigade.

There is, of course, no occasion for the detachment to form up for action first, the troops being *unfolded* at once, *radiating* in the directions desired. The infantry will be led forward at first into *positions of readiness*, which should be covered from view and from fire, and be as *close* as possible to the enemy. From these positions the infantry then deploys for the actual attack (*E.F.S.R.*, Part I, sect. 102).

You have, therefore, first to ask yourself the question: Whence is the infantry to advance for the actual attack? Where is it therefore to *deploy?*

A glance at the map will show you that the infantry can deploy behind the long ridge extending from point 232·1 north of Failly by the southern border of Rupigny in the direction of Malroy, and being distant from the enemy's position roughly 1200 yards. Next arises the question: Is the infantry to be conducted into these positions all at once, or, according to paragraph 369 of (German) *Infantry Training*, from one section of the ground to another?

The advance must be carried out, above all, in a *uniform* manner, and in this case it will best be ensured if intermediate positions are selected, such as are afforded by the ground south-west of Chieulles and south of Vany.

The *approaches* to them must be carefully *reconnoitred* by the subordinate commanders riding forward.

The rifle battalion, covered by a weak skirmishing line, will leave the main road, gaining the cover under the southern slope of the high ground between Chieulles and the main road by traversing the meadows in the depression skirting the western edge of the Wald von Grimont. The vanguard will occupy with skirmishers the northern edge of the above high ground between Chieulles and the main road. Officer's patrols will reconnoitre in the direction of the western portion of the enemy's position (*G.F.S.R.*, paras. 119 and 148).[1] In this position the rifle battalion must remain (how long may that be?) until the other battalions have arrived at Vany. If we advanced the rifle battalion from the outset to the ridge west of Rupigny, it would have to remain *isolated* comparatively too long close to the enemy's front.

The IInd Battalion, followed by the IVth and IIIrd, turns on Schloss Grimont, leaves the Wald von Grimont at its north-east corner, and reaches the southern border of Vany by the meadow stretching from that corner north-east. The whole advance is perfectly covered from the enemy's artillery.

During this advance the battalions remain in column of route, pushing forward a weak skirmishing line as a point

[1] *E.F.S.R.*, Part I, sect. 94.—*Trans.*

as it were. As soon as the battalions have arrived at Vany they reconnoitre with officer's patrols the country west of Charly, Charly itself, and the country east of Charly.

You can measure for yourself that the IInd Battalion has to cover a little over 2 miles from the main road to the southern border of Vany as the crow flies. Considering that it has to march across country, it will take about an hour before it has arrived there.

From this *intermediate position* we have to gain the actual *position of readiness* on the meadows south of the long ridge of Rupigny. The rifle battalion will thereby come under the enemy's artillery fire, but the other battalions will reach their places under cover.

For the further deployment each battalion must be exactly pointed out the *space it is to deploy in* and the portion of the enemy's *position it is to attack*. To the rifle battalion will be apportioned for deployment the space between Rupigny and the main road, and for attack of the enemy's position the portion from the main road to Charly exclusively.

To the IInd Battalion will be given for deployment the slope south-east of Rupigny from about the cutting on the Vany–Rupigny road to 550 yards east of it, and for attack the southern edge of Charly. With due regard to what is laid down in paragraphs 394 and 437 of the (German) *Infantry Training*, the IIIrd Battalion will be launched obliquely to the front of the IInd Battalion, *i.e.* its front will run along the line traced from the right of the IInd Battalion to height marked 232·1 north-east. A gap must at first be left between the IIIrd and IInd Battalions that will be closed gradually afterwards, without, however, permitting the inner wings of both battalions to overlap. The space for deployment of the IIIrd Battalion will be about 450 yards, and the attack of the left of that battalion will be directed against the south-east corner of Charly.

This settles the *fighting areas* of the several battalions. *Touch in action* must be maintained with the battalion which is assigned the most important rôle in the main attack, *i.e.* with the IIIrd Battalion, to the movements of which the other battalions must conform.

The IVth Battalion follows, écheloned behind the right of the IIIrd Battalion, at a distance of at least 350 yards, as the *reserve* of the commander of the detachment, and accordingly will unfold south-west of height marked 232·1.

Having had in your mind paragraph 393 of the (German) *Infantry Training*, it may have struck you to turn off the enveloping battalion to Failly while you were advancing. I do not think such a wide sweep necessary in this case, as the country greatly facilitates the preliminary movements, especially so do the low-lying meadows stretching from north of Varny to the vineyards north-west of Failly.

The attack must not begin until every unit is carefully formed up in its appointed place. The whole deployment will take time which we can afford to spend, since, according to the reports received, we need not expect a counter-attack by the enemy. I would place under one commander the IInd and IIIrd Battalions, *i.e.* the two battalions detailed to carry out the main attack. If the conditions render it necessary, the battalion in reserve may be afterwards placed as well at the disposal of that commander.

As soon as the rifle battalion has reached the ridge west of Rupigny the artillery will change position and move by échelons to the height north-west of Chieulles. The artillery commander must be acquainted with the direction of the main attack, so as to prepare it by his fire and pave the way for the infantry.

Let me now take this opportunity of drawing your attention to the following point. In this case the troops had to unfold[1] for the main attack very early, leaving the road, and breaking off from the advanced guard. This

[1] The student will have become aware that the German Tactics distinguish between "unfolding" and "deploying" the troops for attack, the former implying that the troops relinquish the ordinary march formation, and are directed to certain portions of the battlefield, from which, when all are in position, they deploy for the attack.—*Trans.*

must be considered an exception to the usual procedure, peculiar to this case. In very many cases the main body will be able to continue advancing *in column of route, on the road by which it was marching, for some time* after the G.O.C. has decided on his plan of attack, *not unfolding for attack until compelled to do so for the sake of cover*. The longer its unfolding can be postponed, and the longer it can keep to the road, so much the easier and quicker can the attack be carried out, for as soon as the troops have to leave the roads their advance becomes *considerably* slower, owing to the obstacles met with in moving across country, though it frequently becomes necessary to move off to a flank in order, as in this case, to get cover from the enemy's view or fire. One will, therefore, endeavour to postpone, *to the last possible moment*, the branching off of the main from the secondary attack.

The officer commanding the *field company engineers* remains, as you know, with the staff of the officer commanding the troops till the time arrives to employ this company. If there be no special work for the engineers, such as forming bridges in rear of the attacking troops, they should be attached to the reserve. Although engineers can fight as infantry, yet their proper sphere is the execution of works which may be of material assistance to the course of the action. In this case it is desirable to have several temporary bridges thrown over the little stream (from the vineyard north-west of Failly, past north-east edge of Chieulles to the main road) to facilitate traffic by mounted men; and in case of assaulting Charly village the co-operation of the engineers in demolishing barricades, gates, etc., will be invaluable. The whole company may not be wanted for this work; the remainder will join the reserve by way of Chieulles.

The *reserve*, where large bodies of troops are engaged, is usually stationed at some point in rear until its intervention in the combat becomes necessary; but with detachments this is *seldom* advisable, for the action is so quickly decided that there would be a danger of the reserve not being at hand when wanted. It is generally better to have it following the main attack at a distance of about 350 to 550 yards, and whether écheloned and overlapping in rear of the right or of the left flank depends on circumstances, the country, etc. If the attack covers a very large extent of front, the best place for the reserve is *between* the main and secondary attacks. Thus placed, in rear of a likely gap between the two, it will guard against the danger of a counter-stroke penetrating between them ; but this position is exceptional. *As a rule*, the reserve follows the *outer* flank of the main attack, prepared to prolong the outflanking movement. Here we are concerned with the east side of Charly, but at the same time the main attack must be secured against any sudden counter-attack from out of the wood. It will be necessary to attack the east side of the village simultaneously with the assault on the southeast entrance thereto ; especially if, as is likely, the enemy holds the eastern border of the village with his reserves. You will see by this how difficult it is to get actually on an enemy's flank with a detachment, on account of the small number of troops available.

In an attack which is, in a general sense, an enveloping one, the troops actually engaged in attacking the flank have in reality to make a frontal attack, so far as they themselves are concerned, as soon as the enemy has succeeded in forming a new front towards the threatened side. This new front will, however, in many cases, be unduly *short and weak*, so that the attacker obtains *the fire-superiority*, and *therein lies the advantage of the enveloping attack*.

With regard to the *employment of the cavalry*, you must in attack, the same as in marches, observe the principle that, in order to have sufficient of this arm at hand to support the attack in case of need, no unnecessary bodies of cavalry should be detached. Where detachments are concerned we cannot count to any great extent on the effective intervention of cavalry in the fight. The proper sphere of cavalry is in providing for information and protection, and *continues such* despite the transition from march to combat. (The comparatively speaking numerous cavalry attacks that come off at our manœuvres are more for instructional purposes.) (*G.F.S.R.*, para. 131 (3).)[1]

It is a tactical axiom that *both* flanks of the attack should be covered by cavalry. To avoid, however, unduly disseminating the cavalry, the *bulk* of it must be employed *where it is most difficult to provide for protection*. It may be that the country affords so much cover from view at some part as to require a great deal of cavalry to reconnoitre there—it may be that the enemy has posted so much cavalry towards one of his flanks that mere patrols can make no way there, and that therefore a considerable formed body of cavalry must be employed in that quarter—or it may be that the general situation demands a special protection for the outer flank of the main attack, to protect it against being surprised just before the critical moment of the action by hostile bodies coming fresh into action. When, however, in the absence of any such considerations, you can employ your cavalry on whichever flank you like, choose that flank where the ground affords most facilities to cavalry for intervention in the action by means of a charge. In the present instance a clear view can be had of the country west of the main road as far as the Moselle, so on that side a few patrols are all that is wanted. On the other hand, it is more difficult to provide for the safety of the right flank of the main attack in the direction of the Wald von Failly, besides which the enemy has an entire squadron thereabouts, the presence of which will greatly embarrass that reconnaissance in the direction of Méchy which is so imperatively necessary. *It is here, therefore, that we must have the bulk of our cavalry;* a troop will do for the left flank. In any case, the orders must make it clear *to the cavalry commander* that he is responsible

[1] *E.F.S.R.*, Part I, sects. 65 (5) and 92.—*Trans.*

for there being sufficient cavalry on *both* flanks. In our case the orders must be so worded as to cause the cavalry to watch specially those roads by which reinforcements might reach the enemy during the attack, more particularly those passing through Méchy and Antilly.

Arrangements regarding the establishment of a *dressing station* by the section field ambulance, or as to the position of the reserve of ammunition, cannot always be made in the first orders, but here the situation is so simple that the course of the attack can be approximately foreseen. The field ambulance may therefore be sent at once to the exit from Vany to Rupigny, there to set up the dressing-station close to the houses and water supply, and covered from the enemy's fire, and to send forward the stretcher bearers and ambulance wagons to fetch the badly wounded men from the fighting-line, when the medical officers of the units and their assistants can no longer attend alone to the numerous wounded (*G.F.S.R.*, para. 478).[1] The position of the dressing station must be fixed by order of the officer commanding the detachment, for he alone can judge where the fighting is likely to be so severe that the services of the medical officers attached to units will require to be supplemented (*G.F.S.R.*, paras. 485–9).[1]

Four S.A.A. carts of the rifle battalion are with the battalion in front, the commander of the battalion dealing with them as laid down in (English) *Infantry Training*, sect. 168 ; each successive reinforcement of the rifles as it reaches the firing-line will take care that those already engaged in that line will be supplied with sufficient ammunition. If, in exceptional cases, fresh ammunition has to be brought up by single men, these are to be sent up from the troops in rear, which have not yet been under fire (*G.F.S.R.*, para. 507).[2] The other three battalions each take four of their six S.A.A. carts into action. *It is the duty of battalion commanders to see that empty carts are re-*

[1] *E.F.S.R.*, Part II, sect. 77.—*Trans.*
[2] *E. Inf. Tr.*, 1911, sect. 168.—*Trans.*

filled (*G.F.S.R.*, para. 508).[1] The eight S.A.A. carts of the four battalions form the brigade reserve of ammunition, which remains at the disposal of the commander of the detachment.[1] The light ammunition column is now placed under the orders of the artillery commander, who decides when, and by what route, it is to advance on to the battlefield. It takes post behind the batteries, availing itself of any cover, but not more than 660 yards distant from the firing-line (*G.F.S.R.*, para. 516 and *G.A.T.* 452).[2]

The orders should never lay down the line of retreat to be taken in the event of failure, as to do so would raise doubts as to the success of the attack (*G.F.S.R.*, para. 58).[3] This, of course, is not to debar the officer commanding the detachment from having an eye to the possibility of retreat, and making plans in his own mind in readiness for such an eventuality. As a rule the retreat is made in the direction of the 2nd line transport. No reference need be made to the latter in the orders on this occasion, as the orders for the advance have already stated where it is to remain, and *there is no reason for changing that arrangement.*

Lastly, we have to decide the *position of the officer commanding the detachment*. It must, above all things, be *easy to find*, so that reports may reach him without loss of time, and should be *in rear of the centre of the firing-line, if possible*, so that the G.O.C. can take in at a glance the course of the attack, and see not only his own firing-line, but that of the enemy as well, for even the best reports cannot keep him so well informed about the state of affairs as his own eyes can. The G.O.C. should not, however, be *too near* the firing-line, in order that he be not influenced by the ebb and flow of the combat ; and he must also keep an eye on the reserve, which, as the experience of recent warfare shows, has a tendency to get out of his control. Experience also shows that the G.O.C. can better watch the progress of the action by remaining stationary ; he

---

[1] *E. Inf. Tr.*, 1911, sect. 168.—*Trans.* [2] *E. Art. Tr.*, sect. 76.—*Trans.*
[3] *E.F.S.R.*, Part I, sect. 12 (14).

should, therefore, select his position so that, if possible, *it need not be changed*. To be continually riding about, prompted by a nervous anxiety to show himself everywhere, will make it impossible for him to supervise the general course of the action, or calmly consider his plans; if such a position as I have above described cannot be found, the G.O.C. should take up his stand where he can *personally supervise* the most important part of the battlefield, that is, *the main attack*. If the secondary attack has to work across country where it cannot be seen, the G.O.C. will send an officer of his staff—*intelligence officer*—who will keep him constantly informed as to its progress. This arrangement renders the G.O.C. independent of reports from his subordinate commanders, which are frequently far from being as complete as they should be; as the attention of these commanders is, commonly, wholly taken up with the conduct of the attack which they are leading, so that they forget to send reports to the G.O.C. (*G.F.S.R.*, para. 70).[1]

Beware of ordering: " Reports will find me with the artillery." Think of the situation. To be in the neighbourhood of artillery, firing and being fired at, is a very bad place for a superior commander with his staff, for there he has neither the quietness needed, nor will reports readily find him, because orderlies will be obliged, in most cases, to make wide détours. I select in our case here the northern corner of the Wald von Grimont. Communication will be established with the Rifle battalion by flag signalling, and with Lieut.-Colonel N., the officer commanding the main attack, by the infantry telephone detachment (*G.F.S.R.*, para. 555).

[1] *E.F.S.R.*, Part I, sect. 97.

THIRTEENTH LETTER

Copy No. 1.

OPERATION ORDER No. 4
BY
MAJOR-GENERAL A., COMMANDING DETACHED FORCE.

Reference: **CHATILLON-HÖHE,**
$\frac{1}{100.000}$ *Ordn.*   2.8.00.

1. *The Enemy*, strength about 2 battalions, 1 squadron, 1 battery, has taken up a position extending from point 204·8 on the main road to the south-east corner of **CHARLY**. His squadron is by the **WALD VON FAILLY**.

2. *The Detachment* will attack the enemy, enveloping his left flank, and will first take up a position of readiness south of the long spur of Rupigny.

3. *The* 1st *Field Artillery Brigade* will at once advance at a trot, passing to the left of the infantry, into a position on the **CHATILLON-HÖHE**, with the object of supporting in the first instance the advance of the Rifle Battalion. As soon as the Rifle Battalion has occupied with its firing line the ridge of the spur between the main road and **RUPIGNY**, the artillery brigade will change its position to the high ground south-west of **CHIEULLES**. Artillery officer's patrols on **CHARLY**.

4. *The Rifles* will first occupy a covered position at the southern foot of the high ground between **CHIEULLES** and the main road, wait there until the II/Battalion has reached the southern border of **VANY**, and then proceed to a position of readiness south of the spur between the main road and **RUPIGNY**. The battalion will send officer's patrols west of the main road towards height 204·8 north-west of **CHARLY**, and establish signalling communication with the north corner of the **WALD VON GRIMONT**.

5. *The* II/*Battalion* will at once turn on **SCHLOSS GRIMONT** and advance from the north-east corner of the **WALD VON GRIMONT** through the meadows to the southern border of **VANY**. *The* IV/ *and* III/*Battalions* will follow the II/Battalion. The battalions will next occupy a position of readiness south of the high ground between height marked 232·1 and **RUPIGNY**, that is to say, the II/Battalion with its left on the road **VANY–RUPIGNY**, the IV/ and III/Batta-

ORDERS FOR ATTACK

lions in the meadow north of the vineyards north-west of **FAILLY**. Officer's patrols will at once be pushed toward **CHARLY**. These battalions will establish telephone connection between the north corner of the **WALD VON GRIMONT** and **VANY**.

6. *After occupying the positions of readiness* the Rifle Battalion will deploy between the main road and **RUPIGNY** and fight a containing action against the enemy's position between the main road and **CHARLY** (the latter exclusive) in support of the main attack; the II/ and III/Battalions, under the orders of Lieut.-Colonel N., will deploy for the attack on **CHARLY**.

7. The IV/Battalion *and the* 1st *Field Co. R.F.* will follow in reserve écheloned and 550 yards in the right rear of the III/Battalion. The Field Co. R.E. will construct some bridges across the brook near the vineyards north-west of **FAILLY** and at the northern border of **CHIEULLES** up to the main road **METZ–ANTILLY**.

8. *The* 1st *Squadron and the* IInd *Squadron (less 1 troop)* 1st *Dragoons* will cover the right flank and reconnoitre towards the **WALD VON FAILLY** and **MÉCHY**, also sending patrols through **MALROY** to the **SCHLOSS BUY** and **ANTILLY**.

9. *The Section Field Ambulance* will at first follow the III/Battalion and then establish a dressing-station at the exit from **VANY** to **RUPIGNY**. *The detachment reserve S.A.A. carts* will remain at the same place. *The Light Ammunition Column* is placed under the orders of the artillery commander.

10. *Reports* will find me at the north corner of the **WALD VON GRIMONT**.

Verbally to the officers commanding Battalions in the Main Body, the Artillery, and the Field Co. R.E.	A., *Major-General.*
Copy sent to the Advanced Guard and the Cavalry by orderly officer at 5.45 a.m.	

You see that the issuing of this order, owing to its length, will take a good deal of time, though some of the movements may already be initiated while the order is being issued (trotting forward of the artillery; start of the II/, III/, and IV/Battalions). *Orders of such length are rarely issued in practice.* The moment the II/ and III/ Battalions have taken up their position of readiness, Lieut.-Colonel N. would have to issue the following order : " The II/ and III/Battalions will at once deploy for attack on Charly, the left of the II/Battalion being on the Vany-Rupigny road, its right 550 yards to the east of that road ; object, southern edge of Charly; the left of the III/Battalion being on the parish boundary of Rupigny (chain-dotted line), its right 450 yards east of that boundary line, with the direction on height 232·1 ; object, south-eastern corner of Charly. The III/Battalion will be the directing battalion."

We have, in conclusion, to show on the map the distribution of the attacking force just before the assault. This affords us an opportunity of following the course that the attack will probably take, in pursuance of the above orders. Details are not called for, but the object is to see whether you have a clear idea of the distribution of the troops, and a knowledge of the formation in which they are (very important especially for those who are not infantrymen !).

On the extreme right flank are two squadrons in squadron column, with patrols at the Wald von Failly and in the direction of Méchy. Each squadron is to be shown less one troop.

The firing line of the main attack is about 200 yards distant from Charly, its right wing embracing the south-east corner of that village.

Each battalion has *at least* six companies in firing line and supports ; the sketch must clearly show whether these companies have all their sections extended in the firing line, or some still retained in support. The other companies are in second line in extended order—those of the right battalion écheloned in rear of the right flank, those of

ORDERS FOR ATTACK

the left battalion in rear of the left flank. The battalion in reserve is deployed in one or two échelons, overlapping the main attack on the right and about 200 yards in rear, for the nearer the crisis is approaching the nearer the reserve must be at hand. The companies of that battalion are either in loose formation, or in fours, or in company column.

Between main and secondary attack there may be a gap, though not too large a one. The rifle battalion is about 350 yards from the enemy, the firing line being composed of six companies, the other two companies being in rear of the left flank, that is to say, in second line close to the main road. As this battalion is intended to support the assault with its fire, and not go nearer the enemy than it already is, the six companies are all in the firing line, the left flank of which is west of the main road, the frontage of it being at the most 550 yards.

A troop of cavalry throws out patrols to cover the left flank.

The batteries will be just west of Rupigny, *all three aligned*.

The limbers and teams, together with the line of wagons, you will show *overlapping on the right and left in rear*, the centre battery alone having its limbers and wagons directly behind it covered by the spur. The light ammunition column will stand in the valley just north of Chieulles.

Note that the following principles must be observed in marking such distributions as this on the map ; I mention them especially for those officers who do not belong to the infantry :—

Any body of troops which has *both flanks* protected (naturally or by other troops) is justified in showing as strong a front as possible. A unit which has only *one* flank protected will show its distribution in depth by placing the supports and local reserves in rear of the exposed flank.

The frontage of a *double company* (say 200 effective strength) in attack should not much exceed 110 yards, and rarely more than 160 yards, for a longer front cannot be kept at efficient strength throughout an action of any severity or duration.

The extreme frontage of a battalion in attack is that of the eight companies deployed side by side. This, however, would mean a surrender on the part of the battalion commander of nearly all that power of influencing the course of the battle which is his so long as he keeps a portion of his force in hand; so a battalion will, as a rule, keep at least a quarter of its strength in reserve. There cannot be any hard-and-fast rule as to whether a battalion is to put all eight companies in the front line, or six, or four. It depends entirely on circumstances.

One should in general avoid extending complete companies in the firing line, as they thereby become unmanageable. It is only at the last moment, just before the assault, as in this case, that whole companies—not necessarily all of them—may be extended in the firing line.

With regard to the intervals between men in the firing line, *i.e.* with regard to the number of men to be extended, you will do well to ask yourself the question, "Is the fire to be *decisive*, or only *preparatory* and *containing?*" If the former, the more rifles in the firing line the better, so enough men are extended to obtain the maximum possible fire effect, which must be kept up in spite of the heaviest losses. In the second case comparatively few men should be extended, as you have to reserve your force for the crisis of the action later on, and the greater extension of the men contributes to reduce casualties in the meantime.

The object in view and the nature of the country regulate the distance between firing line and the échelons in rear. In the present instance, immediately before the assault, the reserves must be as near the firing line as possible, that they may assist in winning the day; since the crisis of the action lasts but a few moments.

ORDERS FOR ATTACK

THIRTEENTH EXERCISE.
(See general map and Verny map.)

General Situation.

Blue forces, operating in their own country, are concentrating in the neighbourhood of the unfortified town of Metz. Red forces are advancing from Strassburg viâ Château Salins.

Special Situation
For the Detachment from the Blue Forces.

I. A detachment from the Blue forces, under the command of Colonel A., consisting of—

- 3 Battalions
- 1 Machine-Gun Detachment
- 2 Squadrons
- 3 Field Batteries
- 1 Field Co. R.E.
- 1 Light Ammunition Column

has gone into close billets at Sablon on the night 2/3 March, 1900, with outposts, 1 battalion, ½ squadron on the St. Peter brook, and has orders to occupy Verny and Pournoy-la-Grasse on the morning of the 3rd March to prevent the enemy advancing between the Seille and the Hospital Wald. Another strong detachment, under Colonel B., is to start from Grigy and occupy Orny and Haute-Grève on the 3rd March. Touch of the enemy has not yet been obtained, but, according to the report of a trustworthy frontier official at Solgne (general map), hostile cavalry occupied that village on the afternoon of the 1st March. The frontier official had to take to flight.

Required :—

The arrangements made by Colonel A. for the 3rd March, 1900, with reasons for the same.

II. Just as the advanced guard has set out, a reliable native of Pournoy-la-Grasse comes up to Colonel A. and reports that hostile infantry had moved into Liéhon last night.

At the same time an officer's patrol, sent out before daybreak, sends the following message :—

"Point 237·1 on the high ground east of the WALD VON AVIGY, 3.3.00, 6 a.m.—Small bodies of the enemy's cavalry are halting at CHÉRISEY, POURNOY-LA-GRASSE, and VERNY."

THIRTEENTH LETTER

Ten minutes later the following message arrives from the same patrol:—

"*Zgl.* (*Brick-kiln*) *at* **FLEURY**.
"3.3.00.   6.45 *a m*.

"A hostile squadron advancing from **POURNOY-LA-GRASSE** viâ **NOTRE DAME** to **FLEURY**. Is now at **NOTRE DAME**. In rear of it on the same road is infantry, strength unknown. A troop of hostile cavalry is advancing at the trot along the main road north of the **BOIS LAMENCÉ** in the direction of **FLEURY**, and two companies of infantry are on the march just east of the **BOIS LAMENCÉ**. I am retiring on **POUILLY**."

As the main guard of the advanced guard arrives at the St. Peter brook, Colonel A. hears there artillery fire towards the south-east, and at the same time the following report comes in from his cavalry at the southern outlet of Pouilly:—

"Have encountered hostile infantry on the main road south of **FLEURY** and near **NOTRE DAME**. Have been driven back on **POUILLY**. Some of the infantry of the enemy, whose total strength I estimate at 1 to 2 battalions, 1 squadron, and 1 battery, has just reached **FLEURY** and the brick-kiln on the main road. A hostile squadron remains halted where the road from **FLEURY** to **CHESNY** enters the **HOSPITAL WALD**."

Twenty minutes afterwards the cavalry commander reports from the southern outlet of Pouilly:—

"Enemy is occupying **FLEURY** and the group of buildings on the main road west of **FLEURY**. Hostile skirmishers on the height 218 north-east of **FLEURY**. Hostile battery has unlimbered between the main road and **FLEURY**."

At the same time Colonel B. sends word from Jury-le-Petit:—

"The enemy is taking up a position between the point marked 270·8, south-east of **PIERREJEUX**, and the **BOIS CAMA**. I am attacking through **PIERREJEUX**."

Required:—

Arrangements made by Colonel A. on the basis of these reports, with reasons for the same.

N.B.—The Hospital Wald has dense undergrowth, and troops in close order must keep to the roads for the purpose of passing through it.

FOURTEENTH LETTER

ORDERS FOR A MARCH AND ORDERS FOR ATTACK

THE state of affairs does not justify promulgating two orders, for at present the enemy is *so far off* that it is hardly likely that any fresh news arriving next morning will be of such a nature as to necessitate the whole of the orders for march being cancelled. Yet it is not incorrect to give two sets of orders, though I prefer one, in view of the absence of all complications in the situation, in connection with which I have but few prefatory remarks to make.

The object being to get touch of the enemy, who is distant, it would be a great mistake to put the bulk of the *cavalry* in the advanced guard. The work in hand calls for *independent* cavalry, operating in advance of the comparatively slow-moving *advanced guard*, and trotting on ahead in the direction of Solgne. Close connection between the advanced guard and the cavalry will consequently be soon dissolved. If, however, the cavalry were attached to the advanced guard, it would be doubtful whether we should get sufficient notice of the enemy's approach. The advanced guard must, of course, have sufficient cavalry to provide for close reconnaissance for the *immediate protection of its own march*. One troop I consider sufficient for that purpose; one troop will be given to the main body, thus leaving one squadron and a half for independent cavalry. It would be advisable to attach some cyclists to the cavalry.

I do not see any special reason for putting a *battery* in the advanced guard; and as to the *Field Company R.E.*

it is about the same whether it form part of the advanced guard or not, as there are good reasons for either course.

The principles for the employment of the machine-gun detachment are laid down in the (German) *Machine-Gun Training* of 1904.[1] It is absolutely necessary to have a knowledge of the second part of that training book. The machine-gun detachment, which must not be confounded with the machine-gun *companies*, whose employment I purposely do not touch upon, is, *as a rule*, directly under the command of the officer commanding the whole force; he *himself* therefore issues orders to these guns for the march as well as for action. It is an *exception* to attach them to any particular unit.

We have first to settle the question where the machine-gun detachment is to march in the column. According to one paragraph in the regulations, the three sections should remain together as much as possible, and according to another paragraph, you have the choice of either attaching the detachment to the cavalry or to the advanced guard.

The task of the independent cavalry being here merely distant reconnoitring, for which purpose it need not be particularly strong for fire-action, I decide to attach the machine-gun detachment to the advanced guard. Here it will best march with the vanguard, ready to come into action at once in case of a collision with the enemy. Later on, when the deployment of the infantry of the advanced guard is completed, the machine-gun detachment should be withdrawn from the firing line and held in readiness for employment elsewhere, as will be shown in subsequent exercises. Until the infantry of the advanced guard has all deployed for action the machine-guns will be invaluable for holding important points, and will have great and immediate effect on troops in column of route and hostile skirmishers advancing over open ground. Machine-guns are, however, incapable of sustained fire action.

[1] *E.F.S.R.*, Part I, sect. 7. *E. Inf. Tr.*, 1911, sects. 160–166.—*Trans.*

As to the direction in which Colonel B.'s detachment is marching, it need be referred to *merely in general terms* in the march orders ; so, too, Verny will be given as the immediate objective of the march of our detachment, although the special idea lays down that Pournoy-la-Grasse is to be occupied as well, for when, later on, we are in a position to occupy both the villages (and at present it appears far from certain that we shall be able to do so), it will be time enough to tell the subordinate commanders about it.

You can choose any point you like *in front of the outpost line* for the cavalry of the outposts to join the column of march, but you have to consider what time you will fix for its assembly there. I take for granted that the outpost cavalry reconnoitres along the roads leading to the south on the early morning. Soon after 7 a.m., or earlier, the independent cavalry trots through the outpost line and takes over the duties of distant reconnoitring. The outpost cavalry assembles at a point well out to the front, say the northern outlet of Pouilly, and joins the advanced guard and main body respectively. You can calculate when the advanced guard will arrive there, approximately (about 3 miles).

As we have not yet touch of the enemy, the 2nd line transport may follow as usual, as, in view of the information so far to hand, it is not impossible that we may reach and occupy Verny and Pournoy-la-Grasse at our leisure without anything being seen of the enemy. For the sake of convenience the transport may be formed up on the main road, late enough not to get in the way of the troops departing from Sablon.

The detachment must, to some extent, co-operate with that under Colonel B. to check the enemy's advance on Metz, and so cover the concentration of the Blue forces. The two detachments must therefore be in *close communication* with one another and keep each other acquainted of their respective intentions. A report must therefore be sent to Colonel B. at Grigy, or else a copy of the march orders. You will do well to make a note on the left of the fold of this.

Copy No. 1.

OPERATION ORDER No. 1

BY

COLONEL A., COMMANDING DETACHED FORCE.

Reference:
$\frac{1}{100.000}$ *Ordn.*

SABLON,
2.3.00.

1. *Independent Cavalry:*
   Major C.
   I/ and II/ (less 2 troops) 1st Dragoons.
   4 Cyclists from I/Battalion.

2. *Advanced Guard:*
   Lt.-Colonel D.
   1 Troop II/1st Dragoons.
   1st Field Co. R.E.
   I/Battalion.
   Machine-Gun Detachment.

3. *Main Body* (in order of march).
   1 Troop II/1st Dragoons.
   II/Battalion.
   1st Field Artillery Brigade.
   III/Battalion.
   Ammun. Col.

1. *The Enemy* is likely to be met with in the direction of **SOLGNE**.

2. *The Detachment* will march tomorrow on **VERNY**, and *another detachment* of our troops, under Colonel B., from **GRIGY** on **HAUTE-GRÈVE**.

3. *The Independent Cavalry* will march at 7 a.m. in the direction of **SOLGNE**, passing through **VERNY** and **CHÉRISEY**, and observing the **HOSPITAL WALD**.

4. *The Advanced Guard* will start at 7 a.m. and move by the main road to **VERNY**, keeping up communication with Colonel B.'s detachment.

5. *The Main Body* will be ready to start at 7.30 a.m., and follow the advanced guard at 1200 yards distance.

6. *The Infantry of the Outposts* will form up on the main road **SABLON–VERNY** as soon as the vanguard has passed the piquet line. *The Cavalry of the Outposts* will join the advanced guard and main body, respectively, at 8 a.m. at the northern outlet of **POUILLY.**

7. *The 2nd Line Transport* will form up at 7.40 a.m. in column of route on the main road south of **SABLON**, and follow the main body at 1¼ miles distance.

8. *Reports* will reach me at the head of the main guard.

Dictated to officers representing the several units and the outpost troops.

Copy sent to Colonel B. at Grigy by cyclist (or a message by same) at 10 p.m.

A.,
Colonel.

After the detachment has begun its march, Colonel A. receives several reports, *not by any means all of equal moment to him.*

The first intelligence informs him that touch is got of the enemy; that he has therefore got beyond Solgne already during the 2nd March. The report that the enemy has occupied Liéhon is probably correct: it shows that hostile infantry is following close on the heels of the cavalry, and Colonel A. must reckon on encountering the enemy in the course of the morning, as it is probable that the latter, having begun his advance on Metz, will continue it, having it open to him to move from Liéhon either through Haute-Grève or through Chérisey. It seems likely that the enemy's *main force* will keep to the main road, along which it has till now advanced, having only a weak detachment moving west of the Hospital Wald; as the two main roads are so separated by this wood, which has dense undergrowth and few cross-roads, that the enemy can hardly have two equally strong columns one on each side of it. At any rate, the first report of the patrol, which, by the way, has taken a very long time in reaching Colonel A., need not lead to any change in his present arrangements, which perfectly meet the situation.

The *second* report made by the officer's patrol shows that the enemy has pushed on as rapidly as unexpectedly, and is approaching Fleury. On receipt of this report, Colonel A. will have to *ride forward and make observations in person as soon as possible.* He has now to decide whether to take the offensive or the defensive. For the present he has no prospect of being able to attain his original object— the occupation of Verny and Pournoy-la-Grasse. He must be satisfied if he can *act up to the spirit of his orders* by preventing the enemy advancing too far northwards, consequently he must *continue his own forward movement,* which will entail assuming the offensive later on, in case the enemy prove not to be *so much stronger* as to make the success of such aggressive action *quite out of the question.* To decide *from the outset* to stand on *the defensive,* say at Haut-Guenot, or on the hill south of Magny, would be to fail in his duty; for he would be surrendering to the enemy all the country between the Seille and the Hospital Wald. The necessity for co-operating with Colonel B. also requires that Colonel A. continue advancing; for the further Colonel A. advances, the more of the enemy's attention will he draw upon himself, and the more will Colonel B.'s work be facilitated. Besides, as soon as the enemy can make use of the important cross-road from Fleury to Chesny, Colonel B.'s troops will be liable to be taken unexpectedly in flank from the Hospital Wald.

It therefore seems a case of an *encounter battle,* the detachment having to deploy from column of route against an enemy who is himself engaged in forming up. The second report, however, does not say *when* or *where* the enemy is forming up, so this report will not induce Colonel A. to alter his present arrangements. He will reckon on his cavalry having meanwhile got complete touch of the enemy, and on soon receiving such definite information as to give him plenty of time to issue orders for deployment from column of route, or for taking up a defensive position, *if such a course be absolutely necessary.* The only thing that has changed is *his own position*, as he should be well to the front when fighting seems imminent. Artillery officer's patrols will be sent ahead beyond Fleury. A summary of the information so far received and a notification of his decision to continue his advance must be sent by cyclists to Colonel B., so that this officer may not be left in the dark for a moment as to what is going on west of the Hospital Wald.

The *third report* is as complete as it can be under the circumstances given. The report *approximately* estimates the enemy's infantry at one to two battalions, so, even if we accept the higher estimate, Colonel A. is superior to the enemy both in infantry and artillery. Inactively to confront the enemy, or merely make a demonstration to delay him, would, besides being open to the objections I have already detailed, enable the enemy, under cover of his position at Fleury, to employ part of his reserve troops to participate in the fighting which has already begun east of the Hospital Wald, in which direction Colonel A. hears artillery fire, that is to say, supposing that the enemy has more troops coming up in rear, which, however, it is impossible for us to know. If Colonel A. succeeds, by a rapid assault, in capturing the position at Fleury, he will be in a favourable position to meet this latter contingency.

The officer commanding the detachment consequently decides to *attack vigorously*, employing his whole detachment for the purpose, even supposing that the enemy should advance beyond Fleury.

The enemy is at this moment himself not ready for action ; our object therefore should be *to get the start of him in deploying*, and not allow our unfolding for attack to delay it. We must arrange the main attack so that, if possible, no time may be lost over preparatory movements on the base line. The duty of the advanced-guard battalion, together with the machine-gun detachment, is to gain time and space for the infantry of the main body to deploy, and the artillery must therefore be immediately pushed forward in support of this object. The more the artillery succeeds in attaining this purpose without stronger bodies of infantry having to come into action the better. The artillery fire is intended to clear up the situation. By bringing the artillery into action at once we also wish to crush the enemy's artillery at the very beginning of the action, as soon as it opens fire.

First and foremost, Colonel A. must ride forward with his staff, which includes the officers commanding the artillery, the machine-gun detachment, and the Field Co. R.E., from the low-lying St. Peter's bridge to some point whence *a good view* can be obtained over the country that will be the scene of operations. (He will also take with him the officer commanding the advanced guard.) The Haut-Guenot will do, *and there he will issue the orders*. An encounter battle demands prompt action.

The infantry of the advanced guard will begin by occupying Pouilly, which is an important supporting-point, and *wait* there till the main body comes up and deploys for attack under cover of the advanced guard. The advanced guard should not, *for the present*, go beyond Pouilly; for the coming up of the main body must be secured, should the enemy be pushing on beyond Fleury.

The machine-gun detachment takes up its position at the south-east corner of Pouilly, which is about 1000 yards from the northern edge of Fleury; so its fire will be effective, should the enemy assume the offensive from Fleury.

The *artillery* can at once come into action on the Haut-Guenot. *Later on*, after some infantry has been pushed forward, the guns can move to more advanced positions. By holding Pouilly with infantry of the advanced guard, we satisfy the tactical *principle* that *artillery must be protected from hostile infantry fire by means of detachments of its own infantry pushed out in front of it;* for, contrary to our expectation, the enemy might push beyond Fleury.

The main body can be unfolded afterwards only east of Pouilly, as we cannot wish to advance along the Seille stream; we can therefore at once issue orders for the main body to turn off into the Bouillon Bottom and march on Tonneau. We need not yet order how and where it is to unfold. Under no circumstances must the 2nd line transport go beyond St. Peter's brook. To send it back at once, say to Metz, would be over-cautious.

Copy No. 1.

OPERATION ORDER No. 2

BY

COLONEL A., COMMANDING DETACHED FORCE.

Reference: **HAUT-GUENOT,**
$\frac{1}{100,000}$ *Ordn.*   3.3.00.

1. *The enemy*, strength 1 to 2 battalions, 1 squadron, 1 battery, has, with his foremost troops, reached **FLEURY** and **ZGL.** (brick-kiln) on the main road. His squadron is halted where the road from **FLEURY** to **CHESNY** enters the **HOSPITAL WALD.**—*Colonel B.'s Detachment* is engaged with the enemy west of **MÉCLEUVES.**

2. *Our Detachment* will unfold for action at **POUILLY.** Operation Order No. 1 of last night is cancelled.

3. *The 1st Field Artillery Brigade* will pass to the left of the infantry, unlimber on **HAUT-GUENOT,** and at once open fire on **FLEURY.** The ammunition column will be at the disposal of the artillery brigade.

4. *The 1st Battalion and the Machine-Gun Detachment* will occupy **POUILLY** and cover the deployment of our detachment for action.

5. *The Main Body* will turn into the valley of the **BOUILLON** brook and march on **TONNEAU.**

6. *The 1st Field Company R.E.* will throw some bridges across the **ST. PETER** brook between the **ST. PETER** bridge and a point 1600 yards east of it.

7. *I shall remain* on the **HAUT-GUENOT.**

Verbally to the commander   A.,
of the advanced guard   *Colonel.*
and leader of the main
body at 8 a.m.

FOURTEENTH LETTER

HAUT-GUENOT,
3.3.00.

To the officer commanding 2nd Line Transport.

The Detachment has met the enemy at **FLEURY**. The 2nd line transport will halt wherever this order will reach it.

In writing by cyclist   A.,
   at 8.5 a.m.   *Colonel.*

While the movements ordered are being carried out, Colonel A. receives the last report from his cavalry, making it absolutely plain that the enemy has, for the moment at least, no intention of advancing beyond Fleury, and is occupying that position. Colonel A. can now issue the orders for the attack on Fleury.

With regard to the enemy's position, the fact that there is a clear field of fire: from the houses north of the brick-kiln, from the road connecting the brick-kiln with Fleury, from the northern part of the western border of the village, and from the western part of the northern border of the village, is in the enemy's favour; but the ridge north-east of the village limits the field of fire to the north-east and east so much that he will probably have to take up a position outside the village in this quarter. The village is compact in form, and the outskirts admit of a strong exterior line of defence; it may, therefore, be considered a strong supporting point. There are suitable positions for the enemy's guns, either between the brick-kiln and Fleury, or on the high ground 218, east of the village. In the latter case, the enemy would have to adopt special precautions to protect them. The whole position has a frontage of about half a mile, and the west flank rests on the Seille, while the Hospital Wald to the east will prevent the attacker getting far round that flank. The position, therefore, is such a good one, that it is *highly probable* that the enemy will hold to it and await the attack. Although the field of action is narrowed by the Seille and the Hospital Wald, it is still possible to attack a flank, for the enemy cannot extend his flanks far enough to push them close up to the Seille and the Hospital Wald.

Colonel A. decides to make the *main attack on the north-east corner of Fleury*, for the following reasons : The ground gives no cover between Pouilly and the brick-kiln at Fleury ; an approach may be made, from the source of the Bouillon brook, sheltered by the copses east of Pouilly, to the hill 218 north-east of Fleury ; there is a good artillery position on the under-feature just east of Pouilly, for bringing fire to bear on the north-east angle of Fleury—the point selected for assault ; the enemy has not got a clear field of fire from the north-east of Fleury ; the proximity of the Seille to the enemy's west flank. *The secondary attack*, starting from Pouilly, will advance along the east side of the main road. Moreover, it is much better to drive the enemy back on the Seille, thereby separating him from his other forces, than in the direction of the Hospital Wald, where he would effect a junction with them.

The frontage of the attack, from the main road eastwards, should not be more than 1700 yards. The outer flank of the *secondary* attack can be easily secured against surprise, as the Seille valley is open to view ; but the outer flank of the *main* attack must be carefully protected against surprise from the Hospital Wald.

It would be quite incorrect to order the advanced guard battalion *to stop in Pouilly* during the attack on Fleury by the main body, with the idea of securing thereby a rallying position *in case of the attack failing*. This would be equivalent to dispensing with the services of one-third of the infantry at the decisive moment, and it is important to note that, in the great majority of cases, detachments, *if they attack at all*, do so with *every available man*.

The machine guns, as soon as the advanced-guard battalion is deployed, will, after being placed under cover in a position of readiness, form a mobile reserve in the hands of the commander of the detachment, and to be used by him especially for effective action against the portion to be assaulted and to prepare the assault. Their employment as well as any change in the position of the artillery, will be settled by orders issued afterwards.

Copy No. 1.

OPERATION ORDER No. 3

BY

COLONEL A., COMMANDING DETACHED FORCE.

Reference: **HAUT-GUENOT,**
$\frac{1}{100.000}$ *Ordn.*   3.3.00.

1. *The Enemy* has occupied **FLEURY** and the group of buildings on the main road west of **FLEURY**. A hostile battery is standing between **FLEURY** and the main road.

2. *The Detachment* will attack the enemy, enveloping his right flank.

3. *The* 1st *Field Artillery Brigade* will fire on the hostile battery.

4. *The* I/*Battalion* will remain for the present in **POUILLY** and then support the attack, which the II/Battalion, after deploying north of the long copse east of **POUILLY**, will carry out against the north-east corner of **FLEURY**. Infantry officer's patrols along the **SEILLE** viâ **POUILLY** and along the **HOSPITAL WALD** on **FLEURY**.

   The Machine-Gun Detachment will move under cover behind height 217·9 east of **POUILLY**, as soon as the I/Battalion is deployed.

5. *The* III/*Battalion* will follow in reserve écheloned to the left and 550 yards in rear of the II/Battalion.

6. *The Small Arms Ammunition Carts* will be at once emptied, and, after refilling, collect at the northern outlet of **POUILLY**.

7. *Reports* will find me on the high ground close east of **POUILLY**.

Verbally to II/ and III/Battalions and   A.,
1st F.A. Brigade.   *Colonel.*
In writing by orderly officer to I/Battalion and Machine-Gun Detachment at 8.25 a.m.

ORDERS FOR A MARCH AND FOR ATTACK

To the Officer Commanding the Cavalry.
         HAUT-GUENOT,
           3.3.00.

The Detachment is attacking the enemy at **FLEURY**. The I/ and II/1st Dragoons will cover the left flank of the attack, reconnoitre towards the **HOSPITAL WALD, POURNOY-LA-GRASSE,** and **ORNY**, and patrol along the **SEILLE** viâ **MOULIN-DE-FLEURY**. Communication must be kept up with Colonel B.'s Detachment. Reports will find me on the height close east of **POUILLY**.

In writing by orderly   A.,
 officer at 8.30 a.m.   *Colonel.*

To Colonel B. will be sent a message that the detachment is attacking the enemy ascertained to be at **FLEURY**.

As the main attack consists of only one battalion, it is unnecessary to specify the officer who is to command it.

In the order for the *cavalry* it is as well to refer to the necessity of keeping up communication with Colonel B.'s detachment, which might otherwise be easily forgotten in the excitement of battle. Patrols will be able to get through the Hospital Wald by the rides.

The contents of the S.A.A. carts will be issued to the men before the action begins. I assume at the same time that there is a chance of rapidly refilling the carts somewhere in the neighbourhood of Metz, thus enabling the commander of the detachment to dispense with retaining the contents of the S.A.A. carts of the battalion in reserve.

The commander of the detachment gives no directions for establishing a *dressing station*, as he has no field ambulance or part of it available. In our case *it is the business of the medical officers of the units* and their assistants to establish *collecting stations*.

As soon as the advanced guard occupies Pouilly, Colonel A. takes his stand on the hill just east of the village, as from there he can better watch the advance of the main attack, and is near the battalion hitherto in the advanced guard. The artillery will come into position on the same hill later on.

I do not consider it necessary, nor advisable, to work with the telephone detachments under the conditions prevailing here (*G.F.S.R.*, para. 47 (3)).[1]

FOURTEENTH EXERCISE.

By 2 p.m. Colonel A. has succeeded in dislodging the enemy (strength 2 battalions, 1 squadron, 1 field battery) from his position at Fleury. Colonel A.'s infantry have got into great disorder, but have ceased firing on the enemy, who has got out of range. The machine-gun detachment has reached the southern exit from the village, and has likewise ceased firing. Colonel A.'s batteries are in position on the road between Fleury and the brick-kiln, and are firing in the direction of the Bois Lamencé, towards which the enemy has retreated in confusion. The I/Battalion is at the brick-kiln and in the western part of the village; the II/Battalion, which has suffered heavily in the assault on Fleury, in the eastern part of the village; and the III/Battalion has re-formed on the eastern outskirts of the village, north of the vineyards. The Field Company R.E. and the refilled infantry S.A.A. carts are entering the northern outlet of the village. The ammunition column is standing on the main Metz road where the road coming from the northern outlet of Fleury joins it. Colonel A., standing by the brick-kiln, observes that the enemy is re-forming a firing line along the ridge about 550 yards north of the Bois Lamencé, and extending east and west of the main road, and that a battery is coming into action east of the main road on the same ridge, when the following report arrives from an officer's patrol:—

"*Southern border of the* **BOIS SEMBRONE,**
"3.3.co.   1.30 p.m.

"Three hostile battalions with two batteries on the road from **CHÉRISEY** via **POURNOY-LA-GRASSE** to **FLEURY**. Head of the column just passing the northern outlet of **POURNOY-LA-GRASSE**. None of the enemy in **ORNY**."

An officer arriving from the staff of Colonel B. reported to Colonel A. that Colonel B.'s detachment is maintaining its position on the line Hospital Wald–Pot-de-Vin–Mécleuves opposite a superior enemy.

Required:—

The arrangements made by Colonel A., with reasons for the same; marking on the map the distribution of the troops in the position selected.

[1] *E.F.S.R.*, Part I, sects. 17 and 18.—*Trans.*

Hints for orders dealing with the occupation of a defensive position.

Copy No........

OPERATION ORDER No.......

BY

.... COMMANDING..................

Reference map.   Place. Date.

(No distribution of troops.)

1. Information as to the *enemy* and *our other forces*.
2. *Intention of the O.C. Detachment.* (A brief statement, in general terms, as to the position which is to be defended. Sometimes cancelling previous march order.)
3. *Order for the Artillery.* (Position, target, opening of fire, artillery officer's patrols.)
4. *Order for Machine-Gun Detachments* if attached. (Position, target, opening of fire.)
5. *Order for the Infantry* of the first line. (Division into sections; allotment of troops into sections; whether field entrenchments are to be constructed. Exact limits of sections; infantry officer's patrols; laying infantry telephone lines.)
6. *Order for the General Reserve.* (Troops composing it, and its position.)
7. *Order for the Engineers.* (Steps to be taken to prepare the position for defence. Bridges to be constructed in rear of the position.)
8. *Order for the Cavalry.* (The bulk of it to protect one flank of the position. Patrols on the other flank.)
9. *Order for the Infantry Reserve S.A.A. Carts, Ammunition Columns,* and position of the *Dressing Station.*
10. *Order for the 2nd Line Transport.*
11. *Position of G.O.C.*

Manner of communicating the orders to the troops.
Hour of issue.

Signature.

FIFTEENTH LETTER

(In continuation of the preceding Letter.)

ORDERS FOR THE OCCUPATION OF A DEFENSIVE POSITION

AT 2 p.m. Colonel A.'s efforts are being directed towards restoring order among his troops, who have lost all formation in the course of the assault on Fleury. It is not enough to have captured the position, but the success must be rendered *permanent* and *assured* by reforming the troops who have been thrown into the confusion which inevitably accompanies a charge, fortifying the position against any attempt at recapture, and preparing as quickly as possible for any new duties that may present themselves (*E.F.S.R.*, Part I, sect. 106 (9)). Such a fresh task now lies before the detachment, for three fresh hostile battalions and two batteries are reported to be moving on Fleury viâ Notre Dame, and the G.O.C. himself observes how the hostile troops who have been driven back on the Bois Lamencé are endeavouring to prepare for a fresh stand. It is quite impossible to continue the offensive under such circumstances; on the contrary, the G.O.C. will be satisfied if he can hold to the position that he has won. To do so is necessary not only in pursuance of the duty incumbent on him of preventing the enemy's advance on Metz, but also to co-operate with Colonel B.'s detachment, which is apparently engaged along the line Hospital Wald–Mécleuve in a stationary action.

Colonel A.'s own observations and the very complete report made by the officer's patrol leave no room for doubt as to the mode of the enemy's attack. Three bat-

OCCUPATION OF A DEFENSIVE POSITION

talions are moving on Fleury direct, by the Notre Dame road ; while it seems probable *that at any rate some* of the recently defeated troops will face about again and simultaneously advance along the main road against the brick-kiln. The situation being thus clear, Colonel A. is *at once* able to issue orders *for the occupation* of a position for defence.

For the purposes of future exercises, you must thoroughly understand that it is impossible *to occupy* a regular position for defence until *the way in which the enemy is advancing is apparent*, as here ; that is to say, until we can form an approximate idea as to *the way in which his forces are distributed*, should he be advancing in several columns. If, however, either we have as yet *no notification* of the enemy's advance, or are *in doubt as to how he intends to attack*, the practice is first to take up a *position of readiness*, from which later on, after the receipt of more precise information, is evolved the occupation of the position for defence proper. Beginners, both in theory and practice, are apt to slur over this distinction, and to commit the mistake of taking up a defensive position *too soon*. But how extremely detrimental to a commander's prestige and authority with his subordinates if his measures for defence have to be completely changed all of a sudden ! It is one of the *most serious disadvantages* in connection with the defence, that one is frequently kept in uncertainty as to the way in which the enemy is advancing ; and (especially if the cavalry fails to send in serviceable reports) cannot proceed to select and occupy the appropriate points until comparatively late in the day—*frequently not until it is too late*. In this case there is no doubt whatever that the enemy means attacking ; otherwise why should he have pushed forward fresh troops west of the Hospital Wald ? The Seille and the Hospital Wald limit the ground in such a manner that the enemy cannot pass by Fleury in his advance on Metz ; he cannot turn the position, but *must* attack it. This *important* condition in a defensive position is therefore satisfied (*E.F.S.R.*, Part I, sect. 107 (1)).

This being so, let us see whether the position possesses that which may be considered *the principal point in favour of the defence*, the power of turning to account to the utmost the range and accuracy of modern fire-arms. It is just such a position as would be chosen for defence nowadays, *being a commanding position with a clear field of fire for artillery and infantry, and with supporting points well adapted for defence.*

The machine-gun detachment co-operated in establishing a superiority of fire at the point selected for assault, by directing its fire on hill 218. Finally, when the village had been taken, it hurried forward to the southern outlet of Fleury, in order to fire vigorously on the enemy as he was retiring on the Bois Lamencé. To assist in the defence which is now to be undertaken, the machine-guns will continue in their present position, whence they can sweep with their fire the important road which passes through Notre Dame (*E. Inf. Tr.*, 1911, sect. 162 (9), etc.).

As we are already told in the data that the batteries are in position on the road between the village and the brick-kiln (where they are, it is true, somewhat confined), and as there is at present no reason for removing them from there, the guns will be sufficiently protected if the brick-kiln and the southern border of Fleury are occupied by infantry. In this respect, therefore, the situation is pretty favourable, but I may as well tell you that you will often, in defensive positions, be unable to protect the artillery by infantry as it ought to be, as the ground often necessitates artillery and infantry being on the same line, and it is, therefore, *difficult to protect artillery against hostile infantry*, as the artillery regulations lay down, by throwing out infantry some 650 yards in advance of the guns. Considering the importance of artillery in deciding the infantry action, *this is another great disadvantage of the defence.* Officer's patrols and scouts must of course be active at this moment in compliance with the regulations of Artillery Training.

OCCUPATION OF A DEFENSIVE POSITION

When selecting infantry positions in practice, as, for instance, in staff rides, etc., I should like to draw your attention especially to the advisability of dismounting at some points of the position when you are on horseback, and then to lie down and to convince yourself of *how the field of fire is constituted*. On horseback or standing dismounted you are apt to commit great errors in judging the field of fire; and the reports of others will never give you a more correct idea of what it looks like than *when you judge for yourself*. (A field of fire extending to 1400 yards is desirable, but 900 yards is sufficient.)

From the high ground about the brick-kiln there is a clear field of fire towards the Seille, to the south and to the south-east, as also there is from the gardens between the brick-kiln and the village. It is not so, however, in Fleury itself. The vineyards in front of the south border of the village would not materially obstruct the fire, for in March the vines have not yet got their numerous tendrils and foliage. (Were it August, the vineyards would be a great disadvantage, unless there were time to remove the vines.) The spur itself, however, on which the vineyards stand, almost immediately in front of the eastern part of the south border of the village, obstructs the fire from the edge of the village, so that the defenders *will here have, in places, to move up into the vineyards*. There is, besides this, another spur, about half-way between Notre Dame and Fleury, which will cover the enemy's infantry, and enable it to get within about 450 yards of the village. *This constitutes the weakness of the position.* As, however, there is no other position available, we must take the country as we find it. *It is very difficult to find a position without any defects.*

There is no obstacle in front of the position, for the insignificant brooks are of no tactical importance. I will take this opportunity of saying a word or two on the subject of *obstacles in front of positions*. Beginners are apt to overestimate the importance of such obstacles, and, in selecting a position, to think more of an obstacle in front of it than of commanding ground with a clear field of fire. It is *seldom* that there is any advantage in having an obstacle along the *whole* front. Such an obstacle would limit one to a purely *passive* defence, as in the case of rear guards, flank guards, and outposts, where the object is to gain time; or in the defence of bridges, villages, and railway stations; or in holding some particular bit of ground. In such cases, of course, an obstacle in front is a great advantage, especially when it also covers both flanks, or at any rate the most threatened flank. The attacker's infantry has difficulty in getting over it; his artillery still more so; it renders mutual support and communication difficult; and the attacker may be placed in a critical position if, after passing it, he is driven back again on it. In such cases, however, it is a matter of doubt whether the enemy who finds you occupying a position difficult to attack will not prefer to profit by the circumstance that you, yourself shut in by the obstacle, will have great difficulty in getting out of your position, and endeavour to attain his object *without fighting*, by *marching past you* and so *outmanœuvring you*. To attain *decisive results* in defence, you must, above all things, so place yourself as to *entice the enemy into attacking you*. Having done so, however, do not confine yourself to a mere defensive, for that never can lead to the *annihilation* of the enemy, but let your general reserve take the offensive and drive back the enemy, who has already been shaken by the fire of your other troops, so that he will "forget to return" to the attack. In such case, however, an obstacle in front of your position, at any rate in front of the flank from which your reserve has to sally out to deliver the counter-stroke, would be an obstacle to you yourself. So beware of obstacles. The best obstacle to oppose to the enemy in the majority of cases is the *grazing mass fire*[1] of modern weapons.

---

[1] Means that each man fires in his own time a given number of rounds at a given objective, which should be large, the object being to pour a continuous rain of concentrated fire on the enemy at a certain point.—*Trans.*

OCCUPATION OF A DEFENSIVE POSITION

Let us now collate what I have just said with the cavalry reports as to the way in which the enemy is advancing. The bulk of his force is moving against the very flank which we ourselves recognise to be the weaker (the vineyards), so we may count upon the enemy making his main attack there, for he is *pretty sure to do the very thing that is most awkward for you.* But although everything points to the probability of the assault being made on this flank, it is none the less always desirable to take such precautions on *both* flanks as to obviate the possibility of being taken by surprise, and to give us *plenty of time to adopt counter measures.* Infantry officer's patrols must be used for close reconnaissance (*G.F.S.R.*, paras. 119 and 148).[1] As to the country towards the Seille, there is no cause for anxiety, for we have a clear view over it, and, irrespective of the reasons above detailed, the enemy is unlikely to attack in any strength in this quarter, on account of the river— but there is no clear view in front of the threatened left flank, owing to the folds in the ground south of Fleury The *cavalry* must be active in this quarter, as well as infantry patrols with signallers, to keep us continually informed as to how far the enemy has got. In other respects the flanks of the position require no special attention; Fleury is a sufficiently strong supporting point for the left flank, and the brick-kiln for the right flank. Admitting that the ground favours the enemy's advance against our left flank, the reserve must be posted so as to protect it, as I shall show later on.

Let us finally take a glance at the country *behind* the position. It can be traversed in all directions; the line of retreat runs straight back from the front; bridges have by this time been made over the St. Peter brook; and in case of our being driven from the position, Pouilly would be a good rallying position.

The extent of frontage of the position has next to be considered. In the attack 1600 yards is a suitable maximum

[1] *E.F.S.R.*, Part I, sects. 90 (5), 94, 97.—*Trans.*

frontage of a detachment of the size of ours. The frontage of a similar force for an obstinate defence should not exceed 1100 yards, or, under extremely favourable conditions, 1300 yards, as in defence much greater depth of formation is necessary, and the reserve bears a larger proportion to the whole force, and consequently the frontage has to be less than in attack. The *narrower* the frontage held at the beginning of an action *the better*, for the act of bringing up the reserves is bound to increase the frontage during the course of the action. There is no objection to the position on the score of frontage, it being about 880 yards in a direct line between the brick-kiln and the eastern side of the village.

As to the distribution of the infantry, the position is divided into *sections*, for the defence of each of which a battalion is detailed. Hard-and-fast rules cannot be laid down as to the number and frontage of these sections. Note for general guidance that when the position is on ground affording a bad field of fire, allowing the enemy to approach it under cover to within close range and thus rendering defence very difficult, the sections must have less frontage, and consequently be more numerous ($E.F.S.R.$, Part I, sect. 108 (6)). In the present instance that portion of the position between the brick-kiln and the western border of the village lends itself easily to defence and can be defended by few troops. The village itself is not so well adapted to defence, so requires a larger garrison. Thus the position is not only held in varying strength in different parts, but the defenders are not evenly distributed even inside the sections—*only the important points, e.g.* the brick-kiln and the gardens between it and the village, being strongly held; the ground between these points being either *very lightly occupied* or even *merely watched*, and defended by fire from the points that are occupied. Moreover, the artillery has to be considered, for this arm cannot always fire over the heads of the infantry, and therefore will occupy a portion of the front line, thus materially co-operating in the defence of

OCCUPATION OF A DEFENSIVE POSITION

the section to which it belongs. A section, therefore, which comprises some artillery may have a *correspondingly increased frontage*. The machine-guns being unsuited for long-sustained fire action, they will get special tasks to perform, but a distinct section of the line will not be apportioned to them for defence (*E.I.T.*, 1911, sect. 161 (1-4)).

Each section in defence must provide its own " section reserve," whose strength will vary according to circumstances and affect the frontage of the section.

A battalion can defend a frontage up to about 550 yards, and under favourable conditions more than 550 yards, provided there is some artillery in the section. If we in this case detail a battalion to the section from the brick-kiln inclusive to the western border of the village exclusive, the frontage will be about 550 yards. The line to be occupied along the south border of Fleury is about 440 yards in a straight line, *rather too much*, considering that the enemy will probably make his main attack on the village, and that the field of fire in some places in front of the village is rather poor. It is not, however, advisable, considering the troops available, to cut up the village into two sections. It is better to be satisfied with holding the first line weakly, *i.e.* a battalion to the village, and keep an entire battalion as general reserve, which must, however, be so placed as to be able to lend a hand in the defence of the village if necessary. Supposing even we had four instead of three battalions in the present instance, it would be better to have two complete battalions in the general reserve than to hold the village with two battalions, for it is, as a rule, preferable to have *rather a weak first line and a strong general reserve*.

In framing the orders we must be very careful accurately to define the dividing lines between sections. With a view to this I recommend you to employ to the full the words " inclusive " and " exclusive."

The best place for the general reserve is, as a rule, *in échelon behind the threatened flank*, where it will guard against enveloping movements, which are what the defence has most to fear. It must at the same time be so placed that it can easily come out from behind cover to deliver a counter-stroke, and should be well off to the exposed side of the flank, so that by *a direct advance to its own front* it will fall on the flank of the enemy's flank attack. From the above we see that *it is impossible to fix a suitable place for the general reserve so long as we are in doubt what point the enemy intends to assault.* Highly desirable as it is to be able to convert the defensive attitude into an offensive one, yet it is in practice very difficult to do so. *The fire from the position must co-operate with the counter-stroke.* But such action is difficult of performance, because the numbers usually at our disposal do not allow of making the reserve sufficiently strong. *He who resolves to act on the defensive is, as a rule, the weaker party, or at least considers himself the weaker party;* he is apt to use his reserve for the passive defence of the position.

In the case now before us there are two possible places for the general reserve, either just east of the north-east corner of the village, or under cover behind the western portion of the under-feature marked 218 east of Fleury. From either of these positions a counter-stroke can be made against the enemy's enveloping movement, but from the latter there is more prospect of falling on the enemy's flank; the first position is in so far preferable, as from it it is easier to support *directly* the defence of the village. I select the position behind the under-feature marked 218.

The II/Battalion has suffered heavily in the assault on Fleury; it would not be advisable therefore to entrust this battalion with the important and arduous task of defending the village, but make it the general reserve, thus giving it time *to restore its formation.* It will be simplest for the I/Battalion to remain in its present position, reforming as quickly as possible. The III/Battalion, which was the reserve during the attack, has already reassembled on the eastern outskirts of the village, and consequently

OCCUPATION OF A DEFENSIVE POSITION

is in a more fit state to occupy Fleury than would be the jumbled-up companies of the II/Battalion. There is ample time to carry out this arrangement, as the enemy is yet at some distance. There will not, of course, be *very much* time to spare after the III/Battalion has occupied the village, but it must be utilised to the full. The least that should be done is to take the ranges of any prominent objects in front of the position, and clear the field of fire by removing the vine-stakes—an easy task, which need not take long. Fire-trenches may also be commenced, as work can go on up to the moment of opening fire; even the simplest artificial cover is of great value.

Colonel A. will see that both sections are at once placed in a state of defence, so as to be sure that the work is performed in the most efficient manner.

The engineers will lend their assistance with the most difficult tasks, and wherever the services of skilled workmen will be most valuable, *i.e.* in the village, and in the buildings round the brick-kiln; but the officer commanding the field company will distribute his men between these two localities as he thinks best. If it comes to severe fighting, the engineers can act as infantry, and join in the defence of the position.

The artillery are sufficiently covered by their *shields*. If there is time they can make epaulments or gun-pits.

Colonel A. has finally to see that his infantry make up their ammunition, which will have been almost expended during the attack on Fleury, from the refilled small-arm ammunition carts. Two S.A.A. carts from each battalion form Colonel A.'s reserve of ammunition. As soon as three of these carts are empty they must return to Metz to refill.[1]

The artillery brigade commander will see that the batteries refill from the light ammunition column as soon as it has come up from Metz refilled.

Colonel A. may, for the present, remain where he is, by the brick-kiln, as from this point he can overlook the

[1] This is as much as possible in accordance with English Regulations.

whole field of action. It is now the moment for telephone connection being established with all portions of the defensive line, especially with the general reserve and with the battalion commander in Fleury. As soon, however, as the enemy develops his attack against the eastern side of the village he will move to the under-feature 218, east of Fleury, *to be near his general reserve* and machine-gun detachment, which in the course of action is withdrawn to the general reserve, and be able to take steps for bringing about the decision of the fight.

Copy No. 1.

OPERATION ORDER No. 3

BY

COLONEL A., COMMANDING DETACHED FORCE.

Reference: **BRICK-KILN** *of* **FLEURY,**
$\frac{1}{100,000}$ *Ordn.*   3.3.04.

1. *The Enemy*, who has just been *defeated* by us, has retired in disorder on the **BOIS LAMENCÉ**, but his battery is just coming into action again on the ridge north-west of the **BOIS LAMENCÉ**, and three fresh hostile battalions with two batteries are advancing on **FLEURY** from **POURNOY-LA-GRASSE** viâ **NOTRE DAME.**

    Colonel B.'s Detachment is holding its ground on the line **HOSPITAL WALD—MÉCLEUVES.**

2. *Our Detachment* will hold the brick-kiln and the village of **FLEURY** as a defensive position.

3. *The Artillery* will remain in its present position, and fire on the enemy's battery north of the **BOIS LAMENCÉ.**

4. *The Machine-Gun Detachment* will remain for the present where it is.

5. *The I/Battalion* will occupy the section brick-kiln inclusive to western border of **FLEURY** exclusive. *The III/Battalion* will defend **FLEURY.** The position will at once be placed in a state of defence. Infantry officer's patrols are to be pushed towards the **BOIS LAMENCÉ** by **MOULIN-DE-FLEURY**, and from **FLEURY** on **NOTRE DAME** and along the **HOSPITAL WALD.** The infantry will establish telephone connection between brick-kiln, **FLEURY**, and hill 218.

OCCUPATION OF A DEFENSIVE POSITION

6. *The* II/*Battalion* will form up as general reserve north of hill 218.
7. *The* 1st *Field Co. R.E.* will assist the I/ and III/Battalions in preparing their sections for defence.
8. *The* I/ *and* II/*Squadrons* 1st *Dragoons* will cover the left flank by reconnoitring the **HOSPITAL WALD**, and in the direction of **POURNOY-LA-GRASSE**. Patrols are also to be sent along the **SEILLE** towards the **WALD VON AVIGY**, and communication is to be kept up with Colonel B.'s detachment.
9. *The refilled S.A.A. carts*, halting at the northern exit of **FLEURY**, are to be emptied at once.
10. *Reports* to the brick-kiln, where I shall be.

Copy sent to the Cavalry by orderly officer; verbally to the other assembled commanding officers.

A.,
Colonel.

Copy sent to Colonel B. by cyclist orderly.

At 2.10 p.m.

The situation demands as prompt execution as possible of the orders, on which account it is better to assemble the commanding officers, and give them *one* set of orders by word of mouth. This order is taken down in writing by officers of the staff, and then transmitted to the cavalry by an orderly officer. If in this case several "separate" orders were issued, more time would be taken in promulgating the orders. We see thus that, provided the troops are *not unduly scattered* over the country, it is better to issue *combined* orders for taking up a defensive position. Remember also that, when taking up a defensive position, *even more than under any other circumstances*, each subordinate commander must become acquainted with the various measures to be adopted, *in their mutual connection with one another as a whole*, and clearly understand the significance, in relation to the action of other commanders, of that particular measure which applies to him. It may frequently happen, especially in making arrangements for defence on a large scale, that the orders will have to go much more into *details* than orders usually do, because the least friction may interfere with the *efficient joint action of the various portions* of the force. In such a case the independent action of subordinate commanders has often to be considerably limited, as there are certain details which it would be unadvisable to leave to their discretion. We have here an example of the necessity for being on one's guard against *applying cast-iron rules and forms to all sorts of tactical situations.* In tactics one must carefully distinguish between different situations ; *there are no models capable of universal application.* For instance, I should be far from calling it a mistake if, in the present case, you gave more detailed instructions under No. 5 of the above orders as to *the manner* in which the two battalions are to occupy the sections allotted to them.

In conclusion a few words about the distribution of the troops which has to be shown on the map. This must, above all things, accurately show how many troops hold the first line, and how many are detailed as Section reserves and General reserve respectively.

Beginning from the right flank, you must show a few cavalry patrols along the banks of the Seille. In the section held by the I/Battalion there are four companies in the *first line*, two of them holding the brick-kiln, the other two the gardens west of the village ; the other half-battalion forming the *section reserve*, under cover of the buildings round the brick-kiln, *i.e.* in rear of the outer flank. At the beginning of the action each company in the front line will have only one or two sections in the firing line, the other three or two sections of each company being in *support*, under cover close behind the firing line. Thus at the beginning of a defensive action the firing line is comparatively weak. The firing line should be made as strong as possible *as soon as the manner of the attacker's advance becomes apparent,* for he often offers large targets on which our fire may be effective even at long ranges,

OCCUPATION OF A DEFENSIVE POSITION

so that every available rifle should then be brought to bear, especially when the target is exposed to view for a short time only. If the supports were far behind the firing line, they would incur heavy losses in reinforcing the firing line if the ground over which they had to move were exposed to the effective fire of the enemy, *and the effect produced by the reinforcement would be considerably impaired*. In cases where it is impossible to bring up the supports under cover, it is better to place them either in, or close behind, the firing line.

Between the brick-kiln and the village are to be shown the three batteries in line. The first line wagons near the main road, about half-way between Pouilly and Fleury, but not more than half a mile from the firing battery (see Fig. 24, and Chap. VII, sects. 65 and 67, *English Field Artillery Training*, 1908). The light ammunition column under cover of Pouilly.

The battalion in Fleury has likewise four companies in the firing line and supports. The two companies on the right have their firing line (one or two sections of each company) along the crest of the spur in front of the south border of the village, and astride the Notre Dame road, the supports being by the road at its entrance into the village. The firing line of the other two companies is in the vineyards, south of the eastern outlet from the village, the supports being at the south-east corner of the village. The other half-battalion is the section reserve in the village itself, at the open space north of the south-eastern exit of the village, where it can either support the firing line or defend the entrances to the village, as may be required. Let me remind you to decide, in occupying the village, whether you intend to confine yourself to holding the border, or whether some of the houses inside the village are to be defended as well. If the object be merely to fight a delaying action, *i.e. if you intend leaving the village sooner or later*, do not occupy the houses, because the men defending the houses are liable to be cut off when the retirement begins. In the present instance the village has to be *obstinately defended*, in order to act up to the instructions given to Colonel A. If we are driven from the outskirts, we must offer a determined resistance in the *interior* of the village, and drive the assailants out again, with the assistance of the general reserve. Any buildings, therefore, which command the streets, or which offer special advantages owing to their position at angles or at open spaces, or through being solidly built, should be placed in a state of defence. When the necessity arises these buildings should be garrisoned by portions of the section reserve. The allotment cannot be decided by looking at the map. I refrain, therefore, from giving any distribution, and merely wished to call your attention to this point. It would be as well if you studied once more at this occasion the chapter on attack and defence of villages given in text-books on minor tactics. It is unnecessary, I think, in this case, to define the limits of foreground to be watched by the two sections of defence, to prevent portions being kept unguarded or not swept by fire.

The machine-gun detachment is posted at the southern outlet of the village, in the gardens on both sides of the road. The six guns are placed at twenty yards interval, the ammunition close behind them, the S.A.A. carts under cover behind the nearest houses (*E. Inf.Tr.*, sect.162 (11–15)).

The battalion forming the general reserve will be formed in quarter-column, or quarter-column of half-battalions, at the north-east corner of the village, or in any other formation suitable to deploy for attack.

The cavalry should be shown in squadron columns, under cover, about level with Fleury, and near the Hospital Wald.

There is, therefore, at the most, the strength of four companies (eight half-companies), *i.e.* one-sixth of the whole amount of infantry available, in the firing line at the outset, occupying the most important points; the remainder being kept in hand until the enemy comes nearer; *thus not a single man is unnecessarily deployed until the enemy's movements render it necessary.*

OCCUPATION OF A DEFENSIVE POSITION

So long as infantry maintains a steady fire, its only vulnerable points are its *unsupported flanks;* these must, therefore, be specially protected by *reserves*, either section reserves or the general reserve, on which account the reserve of the right section is placed in rear of the *right* flank, and the general reserve in rear of the *left* flank. *The supports* are under cover, *as near the firing line as possible;* the reserves, too, should be *as near the firing line as possible*, being only far enough back to escape the enemy's fire, *but not so far as to interfere with their promptly reinforcing the front line.*

The artillery will remain in its present position until the gardens west of the village obstruct its firing on the enemy's main attack. It will then change position, in échelon of batteries, to the hill 218, east of the village, to be able to support the infantry at the decisive moment of the action. It would be a mistake for the guns to remain between the brick-kiln and the village, and continue firing on the enemy's artillery; for as soon as the enemy has committed the bulk of his infantry to the main attack, *our whole available strength must be massed against it, with a view to repulsing the assault.* It is hardly necessary to mention that it is very difficult to seize the right moment for this change of position, or to remind you that our infantry will form the sole target of the enemy's artillery fire, while our guns are changing position. Bear in mind for future occasions, whenever planning how to prepare a position for defence, that though it is sufficient, at the beginning of the action, if the artillery can command the enemy's lines of approach and the country in front of the position; yet, at the critical moment of the assault, the most effective artillery fire possible must be brought to bear on the enemy's infantry who are delivering the main attack, and if this can be done without our guns having to change position, so much the better. *The defeat of the infantry assault is unquestionably the main thing.*

The following are the considerations which will regulate the position of the cavalry: In defence, as in attack, the cavalry must, throughout the whole course of the action, continue to provide for protection and information; in defence, again, cavalry will be able to intervene in the actual fighting *to a somewhat greater extent than in attack*. Its action will consist either in suddenly falling on *the enemy's flank* just before the moment of assault, to make him offer a target for our most effective infantry fire—in which case, however, the cavalry must be prepared for heavy losses—or in charging the enemy's infantry at the moment when it is beginning to give way before the counter-stroke made by the general reserve, to convert the retreat into a disorderly flight. The cavalry must, therefore, not be too far from the infantry, and is best placed either *in prolongation of*, or *écheloned in rear of the threatened flank;* in the present case under cover of hill 218, east of Fleury. The officer commanding the detachment must, in any case, frame his orders in such unmistakable terms as will ensure his *retaining perfect control of his cavalry*.

Any entrenchments are to be shown by the conventional signs and by giving any necessary explanations.

FIFTEENTH EXERCISE.
(See general map and Gravelotte map.)

News having been received that hostile troops were advancing from Verdun on the fortress of Metz, a detached force under General A. was thrown out from Metz, on the 1.12.00, to the Yron brook, with orders to destroy the railway viaduct over the Orne at Conflans-en-Jarnisy (general map), and observe the roads leading to Verdun and Etain, but, should the enemy advance, to fall back slowly, viâ Rozérieulles, on Metz, without engaging the enemy. The detachment had succeeded in destroying the viaduct in the afternoon, and the cavalry had encountered, firstly, hostile cavalry in inferior numbers in the Orne valley, and subsequently hostile infantry 3 miles west of Conflans-en-Jarnisy, and could make no further progress in that direction.

OCCUPATION OF A DEFENSIVE POSITION

General A.'s detachment occupies both the roads, and, on account of the extreme coldness of the weather, is billeted for the night as follows:—

General A. and staff	Vionville.
IV/K.R. Rifles and II/15th Hussars	Doncourt-en-Jarnisy, with outposts on the line Moulinelle–Droitaumont–La Grange west of Bruville.
III/Northumberland Fusiliers and I/15th Hussars	On outposts on the line Ville-sur-Yron–Puxieux.
Reserve of outposts	In Mars-la-Tour.
I/Essex Regiment	Tronville.
II/Suffolk Regiment and 21st Field Battery (with O.C. Artillery) Machine-Gun Detachment	Vionville.
22nd Field Battery and 1st Field Co. R.E.	Flavigny.
23rd Field Battery, Section Field Ambulance, and Light Ammunition Column	Rezonville.

There is a line of telegraph from Metz to Gravelotte, viâ Ste. Ruffine and Rozérieulles. Telephone connection has been established between Vionville and Doncourt-en-Jarnisy.

At 10 p.m. the following report arrives from an officer's patrol which had been sent through Hannonville-au-Passage: "Hostile infantry posts 1¼ miles west of Hannonville; numerous bivouac fires about 2½ miles west of these posts; estimate enemy about four battalions strong."

At the same time the IV/K.R. Rifles report by telephone: "Enemy has pushed infantry posts to within 1¼ miles west of Conflans-en-Jarnisy. An infantry prisoner says his battalion had arrived by rail from Etain, and that the other battalions of his regiment would arrive during the night."

Required:—

The arrangements made by General A. for the 2nd December, and his reasons for them.

SIXTEENTH LETTER

RETREAT

ON the 1st December General A. has performed the chief part of the commission laid on him; he has destroyed the viaduct, and established the fact that the enemy is advancing on Metz. The statement of the prisoner bears the stamp of credibility, and his assertion that the other battalions of the regiment to which he belongs were coming by rail from Etain is of special importance. If this information be correct, the enemy now west of Conflans-en-Jarnisy will probably next morning continue his advance on Metz either viâ Doncourt-en-Jarnisy, or on a more northerly line viâ Jouaville, and thence viâ Vernéville or Amanweiler. The rifle battalion at present in Doncourt, to which the II/15th Hussars is attached, will have no difficulty in gaining information on this point. As, moreover, the officer's patrol sent through Hannonville-au-Passage has seen, on the evening of the 1st, a bivouac of several hostile battalions, about 4 miles west of Mars-la-Tour, it may be assumed that this force will move on Metz next morning on the main road through Mars-la-Tour. It is, therefore, more than likely that next morning General A. will have to deal with an enemy in greatly superior force on both roads.

The information to hand up to the present (*i.e.* up to 10 p.m. on the 1st December) is, of course, far from reliable. The only thing that is certain is that we have got a general *touch* of the enemy, for the prisoner's statement may be incorrect, and the officer may have made a mistake as to the strength of the troops in the bivouac, for it is very difficult to get any sort of correct idea of the strength of a force, merely judging by the extent of the bivouac fires at night. It is, therefore, desirable to get *more precise* information next morning as to the enemy's strength and intentions, especially as to the mode of his advance on Metz. In all probability the cavalry will not find out anything more until the enemy begins to *move*. If his cavalry receives no reinforcement next morning, ours will be able to get a closer view from the position *on the flanks* of his columns; since up to the present the enemy appears to be weaker than us in cavalry, for the patrols of that arm encountered in the Orne valley fell back on their own infantry, nor has it been seen in any numbers on either side of the Verdun main road passing through Mars-la-Tour.

General A. would be going against his orders were he to make a reconnaissance in force with the whole of his detachment, to ascertain the strength and intentions of the enemy, for he has express instructions to avoid fighting. Still he should not begin to fall back *until* he has ascertained for certain (1) that the enemy *is* advancing on Metz, (2) *in what manner* he is doing so. The cavalry will play the principal part in obtaining this information, being *supported* by the rest of the detachment, *should the enemy prove to be stronger in cavalry*. Hence he arrives at the following decision :—

If, contrary to expectations, the enemy remains in his present positions, General A. will likewise stand fast, and reconnoitre to the best of his ability. If, on the other hand, the enemy resumes his advance on Metz, General A. will at once fall back on that town, *without, if possible, exchanging a shot*.

In the second case, however, the retreat must be commenced *soon* enough to prevent our being involved in an action by an *unexpectedly rapid* advance of the enemy in superior force, especially in view of the fact that the valley west of Gravelotte, and the deep and precipitous Mance valley, which forms an inconvenient obstacle, will have to be crossed in retreat. Hence it follows that the detachment must be *held in readiness to start* betimes, and be formed up so as to be able to begin the retreat *at a moment's notice*. It would not do, therefore, to let the troops wait in their billets for the order to withdraw; *they must be brought up to the road they are to march by; the column must, therefore, be formed on the route to be followed* (*G.F.S.R.*, para. 336 (3)). I should be opposed to assembling the troops in mass in rendezvous formations by the roadside, as time would be wasted in forming column of route. The places of assembly should be so chosen that no unit need make a détour to reach them—say the eastern outlet of Rezonville for the tail of the main body, and the eastern outlet of Vionville for the tail of the main guard of the rear guard (*G.F.S.R.*, para. 98). The distribution of troops must in that case be promulgated with the first orders issued.

As in the present instance there is no intention of delaying the enemy's advance—on the contrary, an engagement is to be avoided—the *infantry* of the outposts must be *withdrawn* early. Suppose General A., with a view to deceiving the enemy as to his intentions, caused the infantry of the outposts to stand fast provisionally, it is doubtful whether the flank piquets and supports could regain the main road in time, if the enemy were to press his advance. In such event the rear guard might have to fight, against its will, to prevent their being cut off. If, however, the rear guard be involved in an action, it is impossible to say how it may eventually affect the main body. The *cavalry* of the outposts, on the contrary, must not only keep touch with the enemy as hitherto, but reconnoitre the country on both sides of the main road as soon as day breaks, not only *to discover any change in the enemy's dispositions*, but further *to screen* as far as possible from his observation the withdrawal of our outposts.

In December the sun rises about 8 a.m., and the enemy is not likely to start earlier than this, so it will do if the detachment is assembled by this hour, as between the troops of the opposing parties there intervenes a distance of somewhat under 4 miles.

The IV/K.R. Rifles and the II/15th Hussars will receive a special order. The existing situation authorises the employment of these troops as a right flank guard in retreat, although at the outset they are about 4 miles from the main body. The telephone connection cannot be relied upon; it will, moreover, come to an end as soon as the detachment starts.

The 2nd line transport of the whole detachment must be sent on at least two hours in advance, being assembled at some point where the wagons from the various villages in which the troops have been billeted can conveniently unite—say at the eastern outlet of Rezonville—the transport of the IV/K.R. Rifles and the II/15th Hussars joining it at Gravelotte. It is not advisable, at this stage, to send the 2nd line transport right back to Metz, General A. being as yet unable to tell where it may be wanted on the evening of the 2nd. It will also be as well for the engineers to accompany the transport until the latter has got across the awkwardest part of the road—the Mance valley—and, should any accident happen to the wagons there, the engineers can see to keeping the road open. They can also prepare the bridge in the Mance valley for destruction, in case it may become necessary to check a too rapid advance on the part of the enemy. They had best wait somewhere near the Mance valley for the main body, in order to be at the disposal of the G.O.C., should their services be again required outside Metz.

With the object of expediting deployment if forced to fight, you may *reduce the length of the column of route* by having the infantry formed up on the main road in columns of half-sections and the artillery in column of sections, as both main roads are broad enough; and when making a retreat in such proximity to the enemy, it is always desirable to be able to deploy for action as quickly as

SIXTEENTH LETTER

possible (*G.F.S.R.*, para. 355; *E.F.S.R.*, Part I, sect. 25). It is, of course, impossible to see by the map whether the main road is broad enough, or whether its breadth may not be considerably contracted where it passes through villages, for instance, which would interrupt regular forward movement. Whenever a column of route is shortened it is desirable that part of the road should always be left clear enough for mounted officers and cyclists to pass backwards and forwards at a rapid pace without being checked or interfering with the troops; as otherwise a regular transmission of orders and messages is almost impossible. It is not safe to order a broader march formation solely on the authority of the map when one is not certain of the breadth of the roads or *of that of the village streets*. Some previous reconnaissance is often necessary. *In the present case, however*, these remarks do not apply, as General A. is familiar with the road, having recently marched over it.

Copy No. 1.

OPERATION ORDER No. 4

BY

MAJOR-GENERAL A., COMMANDING DETACHED FORCE.

Reference: **VIONVILLE,**
$\frac{1}{100,000}$ *Ordn.*   1.12.00.

1. *Advanced Party:*
    Major D.
    1st Field Co. R.E.

2. *Main Body* (in order of march).
    Sect. Field Ambul.
    Light Ammun. Col.
    II/Suffolk Regt.
    22nd and 23rd Field Batteries R.A.
    I/Essex Regt.
    1 N.C.O., 8 men I/15th Hussars.

1. *The Rear Guard* will be formed up in reduced column of route (Infantry in column of half-sections, Machine-Gun Detachment and R.A. in column of sections), prepared to march off, on the main road to **METZ**, at 8 a.m. tomorrow, with the tail[1] of the main guard at the east end of **VIONVILLE**, and the *Main Body* in similar formation on the same road and at the same hour with its tail[1] at the east end of **REZON-**

---

[1] Portion nearest the enemy.—*Trans.*

RETREAT

3. *Rear Guard:*
    Lieut.-Colonel B.
    I/15th Hussars.
    21st Field Battery R.A.
    III/Northumberland Fusiliers.
    Machine-Gun Detachment.

4. *Right Flank Guard:*
    Lieut.-Colonel C.
    II/15th Hussars.
    IV/K R. Rifles.

VILLE. Flag-signalling communication between the east end of **VIONVILLE** and the east end of **REZONVILLE** is to be established by the infantry. Special orders are being sent to the right flank guard.

2. *The I/15th Hussars* will continue the reconnaissance of the **VERDUN** main road at 6.30 a.m., and maintain communication with the right flank guard.

3. *The 1st Field Co. R.E.* will march off from **REZONVILLE** at 6 a.m., escort the 2nd line transport as far as the **MANCE** valley, prepare the bridge on which the main road crosses the **MANCE** valley for destruction, and there await the arrival of the main body.

4. *The 2nd Line Transport* of the rear guard and of the main body will be formed up in column of route, with its tail at the east end of **REZONVILLE**, at 6 a.m., ready to start; will retire on Metz by the main road, joining the 2nd line transport of the right flank guard at **GRAVELOTTE**, and await further orders at the east end of **LONGEVILLE-BEI-METZ**.

5. Officers commanding rear guard, right flank guard, and units in the main body will attend to *receive orders* at 8 a.m. at the east end of **VIONVILLE**.

Dictated to officers representing the several units.
11 p.m.

A.,
Major-General.

SIXTEENTH LETTER

To Lieut.-Colonel C., commanding Right Flank Guard at
DONCOURT-EN-JARNISY.

VIONVILLE,
1.12.00.

1. *Enemy's* infantry outposts 1¼ miles west of **HANNONVILLE-AU-PASSAGE**. A bivouac of the enemy, estimated by the officer who reconnoitred it to be occupied by about 4 battalions, is 3¾ miles west of **MARS-LA-TOUR**.

2. *Should the Enemy advance to-morrow morning*, I shall withdraw on **METZ** with the detachment, avoiding any engagement with the enemy. If the enemy does not advance, I shall for the present stop here. The detachment will be formed up on the main road at 8 a.m. to-morrow, ready to move off.

3. Ascertain early to-morrow morning whether the enemy is advancing in the **ORNE** valley. Should he do so, you will at once withdraw on **GRAVELOTTE**. Be ready to move off to-morrow at 8 a.m., and call in your outpost companies in time to prevent their getting in contact with the enemy. I expect an early report from you, whether the enemy is following you on **GRAVELOTTE** or is advancing on **JOUAVILLE**.

4. *Your 2nd Line Transport* will join that of the detachment at **GRAVELOTTE** at 6.35 a.m. to-morrow.

5. One of your officers to be at the east end of **VIONVILLE** to-morrow at 8 a.m., where *orders will be issued*.

In writing by orderly officer   A.,
at 11.40 p.m.   *Major-General.*

It is necessary for the officer carrying the orders to Lieut.-Colonel C. to give verbally further explanations to him with regard to the views held by General A. on the situation; it would, therefore, not be sufficient to transmit the orders by telephone.

The orders to the officer commanding the rifle battalion are, as you see, somewhat different in form from those you have been made acquainted with till now. We are not tied to a definite form. The departure from the usual form is caused here by the distance the battalion is away, which prevents more than a general supervision of it by the commander of the detachment. So Lieut.-Colonel C. must, on the one hand, be made more independent, but, on the other, details must be prescribed for him by the commander of the detachment, which he would otherwise not lay down—as, *e.g.*, the withdrawal of the outpost companies or the mode of reconnaissance—so as to make quite sure of Lieut.-Colonel C. acting according to the intentions of the officer commanding the detachment. Though there is telephone connection, an officer is ordered to attend the issue of orders next morning, as it is better to be on the safe side.

SIXTEENTH EXERCISE.

At 10 a.m. on the 2nd December General A. receives by telephone the following message from the O.C. IV/K.R. Rifles:—

DONCOURT-EN-JARNISY.
2.12.00.   9.25 *a.m.*

II/15th Hussars reports this moment:—

"Hostile column of several battalions with one battery advancing in the **ORNE** valley; will reach **CONFLANS-EN-JARNISY** about 10 a.m."

I start at once retreating on **GRAVELOTTE**.

At the same time the I/15th Hussars reports from **HANNONVILLE-AU-PASSAGE** at 9.45 a.m.:—

"Large hostile column, strength unable to discover, advancing by main road; will reach **HANNONVILLE-AU-PASSAGE** about 10 a.m."

Required:—

Major-General A.'s arrangements and reasons for them.

SEVENTEENTH LETTER
(In continuation of the preceding Letter.)

RETREAT

THE order for the retreat can be issued at once, *as there is no need for special deliberation.* The officer commanding the right flank also knows what he has to do, and is already retreating. As the head of the main body is about 2 miles from Gravelotte, it should arrive there a little before 11 a.m., and should there join the right flank guard, for the latter should leave Doncourt-en-Jarnisy at 9.25 a.m., reaching Caulre, *if all goes well*, at 10 a.m., and Gravelotte about 11 a.m.

The main guard of the rear guard will start at once, the rear party gaining its proper distance by waiting.

In the orders to be issued now you must not omit promulgating the order for the right flank guard too, so that the main body and rear guard may clearly see *the measures adopted for the protection of their right flank.*

A comparison of this exercise with similar previous ones for a retreat will show the necessity of avoiding working out tactical exercises according to one set form, an error into which beginners easily fall, and to which the models given by me may to some extent conduce. The different way in which this exercise is worked out should impress upon you that *there is no greater mistake in tactics than striving after set forms.* Each case is different; each case must be appreciated and solved *apart from all others.*

OPERATION ORDER No. 5

Copy No. 1.

BY

MAJOR-GENERAL A., COMMANDING DETACHED FORCE.

Reference:
$\frac{1}{100,000}$ *Ordn.*

Hill 550 yards west of
VIONVILLE,
2.12.00.

1. *The Enemy* is advancing in the **ORNE** valley on **CONFLANS-EN-JARNISY**, and by the **VERDUN** road on **HANNONVILLE-AU-PASSAGE**.

2. *The Detachment* will fall back at once on **METZ**.

3. *The Main Body* will start at once by the main road, and move viâ **ROZÉRIEULLES** on **METZ**.

4. *The Rear Guard* will at once follow, at $1\frac{1}{4}$ miles distance, keeping touch of the enemy with patrols, and reconnoitring through **VILLE-SUR-YRON** and **PUXIEUX**.

5. *The Right Flank Guard* will join the detachment at **GRAVELOTTE**, keeping touch of the enemy with patrols, and reconnoitring through **DROITAUMONT** and **JOUAVILLE**.

6. *Reports* will find me with the rear guard.

Verbally to officers commanding units in the rear guard and main body.

Copy sent to the right flank guard by orderly officer at 10.5 a.m.

A.,
Major-General.

SEVENTEENTH EXERCISE.

The head of the main body[1] has reached the Mance valley at 11.15 a.m., where the Field Co. R.E. is just finishing its task. The IV/K.R. Rifles was delayed in leaving Doncourt-en-Jarnisy, so that it has only just reached Malmaison.

Several reports concerning the enemy have reached General A., from which it appears that the southern hostile column, which has

---

[1] *i.e.* the portion furthest from the enemy.—*Trans.*

apparently received a reinforcement in cavalry, is at this moment passing through Mars-la-Tour, while the northern hostile column, estimated at about 4 battalions, 1 squadron, and 1 battery, had not long passed Doncourt-en-Jarnisy. It has not been possible to determine accurately the enemy's strength.

At the same hour General A. receives at Gravelotte the following telegram from the Governor of Metz:—

"Your message, despatched from Vionville at 10.10 a.m., just received by telegram. Preparations for defence on the heights of St. Quentin not yet completed. Endeavour to check the enemy to-day west of the Montveau valley."

Required:—

The arrangements made by General A., and show on the map any positions that may be taken up.

Hints for Ordering the Occupation of a Position of Readiness.

Copy No.......

OPERATION ORDER No.......

BY

.... COMMANDING ....

Reference   *Place.*
map.   *Date.*

(No distribution of troops.)

1. Information about the *enemy* and other bodies of *one's own troops*, as may affect the recipient of the order.

2. *Intention* of the officer issuing the order. (Indicating the place where the bulk of the detachment is to form up in assembly formation. Cancelling previous march order.)

3. *Order for the Cavalry.* (*Frequently detailing squadrons* to proceed along the main approaches of the enemy, or keeping the advanced cavalry *concentrated* with patrols for distant reconnoitring and standing patrols for close reconnaissance.)

4. *Order for the Artillery.* (Either in a *position of readiness* or unlimbered behind a position, whence the various approaches of the enemy can be taken under fire, or simply *waiting* together with the bulk of the infantry.)

RETREAT

5. *Order for any Machine-Gun Detachments* that may be with the force. (Where to place them. Entrenchments or cover.)

6. *Order for the Infantry.* (Occupation of the main points, the bulk being concentrated under cover, as indicated in paragraph 2 of this order.)

7. *Order for any Entrenchments* to be carried out in the positions. (Distribution of the works to be carried out by the troops who will have to defend them. The most difficult work allotted to the engineers. Establishing telephone connection.)

8. *Order for the S.A.A. Carts of the Infantry, Light Ammunition Column,* and establishment of *Main Dressing Station.* (The latter, as a rule, cannot yet be fixed.)

9. *Order for the 2nd Line Transport.*

10. *Place to which reports are to be sent, and, when necessary, Position of the officer commanding.*

The mode of issue, the individuals to whom issued, and the hour of issue.	Signature. Rank.

EIGHTEENTH LETTER

(In continuation of the preceding Letter.)

A POSITION OF READINESS

THE telegram from the Governor of Metz orders General A. to check the enemy west of the Montveau valley. General A. must therefore choose a defensive position suitable for this purpose, and has now *a totally different duty to perform—that of engaging the enemy*. It is purely a case of delaying the enemy; that is, of *gaining time*; for a decisive result is out of the question in view of the apparently *great numerical* superiority which the enemy possesses.

We have, in the first place, to calculate the position of the various portions of the column on the march at 11.15 a.m. You will then see that General A. has the choice between (1) a position near to and north of Gravelotte, (2) a position on the ridge east of the Mance valley, say, from Moskau to Le Point-du-Jour, or (3) may endeavour to defend *both in succession*.

There is no question that the enemy will have to attack both the above-mentioned positions in advancing on Metz. It is also very unlikely that his northern column will try to turn the position from the north, say, by way of Vernéville; for it is more to his advantage that his two columns should join hands and attack in one body than that they should still further diverge, and so leave *all unity of action wholly to chance*.

The next thing to do is to weigh the advantages and disadvantages of the *two* positions; the points to be considered in which process are detailed in my fifteenth letter.

Omitting what is less important, I have only to deal with the following :—

In the first position there is a good *field of fire for artillery* from the high ground by Mogador, in a westerly and south-westerly direction ; and the road Gravelotte–Rezonville, by which the southern column is advancing, can be well swept by fire ; but it is otherwise as regards the road from Malmaison to Doncourt-en-Jarnisy. The only good artillery positions for the enemy are on each side of the road Gravelotte–Rezonville. The maximum frontage that General A. with the troops at his disposal can occupy is from Gravelotte to Mogador—both points inclusive ; and even then the enemy's northern column can easily take the position in flank by merely continuing its advance on the Malmaison road. The village of Gravelotte is not very well adapted for defence, the western border not being sharply defined, owing to the farm-buildings in front of it, which would render supervision of the defenders difficult, and tend to their dissemination.

The principal disadvantage of the position, however, is that *close behind* it is the deep and precipitous Mance valley, clothed with dense woods on both sides, which can be traversed *by means of the road only*, unless time be no object. If driven from the position, the detachment would find retreat difficult, the more so as, after crossing the valley, the ascent of the hill-side to Le Point-du-Jour would have to be made under the enemy's fire. *The knowledge that retreat is difficult paralyses the energies of the commander, and is prejudicial to the moral of the troops ; and a premature retreat is likely to lead to heavy losses.*

The second position gives a clear *field for artillery fire* from about Moskau against the enemy's line of advance through Gravelotte, especially on the cutting through which the main road runs just east of Gravelotte, and the bridge in the Mance valley. In that direction the machine-gun detachment must bring its fire to bear. The fire of artillery would not be quite so good because of the wood, but still good enough in the direction of Malmaison. In attacking the position the enemy will have to pass through the dense woods on both sides of the Mance valley, which are certain to dissolve tactical formations; and on emerging from the woods he will soon come under our effective infantry fire, almost the whole slope being swept by fire from the summit. He will find it far from easy to envelop a flank, as from Moskau there is an excellent field of fire in all directions, and there is good cover for defenders in the quarries of[1] Point-du-Jour. In this case it is a good thing to have the Mance valley as an *obstacle along the whole front* of the position, as our object is only to delay the enemy, *with no idea of taking the offensive.*

The enemy will find suitable artillery positions east and south of Gravelotte, and, still better, near Mogador. The quarries west of St. Hubert will favour the advance of the enemy's *infantry*, which, however, our infantry and machine-gun fire at point-blank range will be able to prevent getting beyond those quarries.

The farm of St. Hubert must be strongly held as a part of the line of defence, for such points as farms, copses, ditches, hollow roads, etc., which lie *within effective infantry range* in front of a position, and would, if left to the attacker, assist him in his advance, *should be considered* as *parts of the main position*. It is generally inconvenient for the defender to have to split up his forces through occupying such points in advance of the general front; here, however, the disadvantage is compensated for by the fact that from St. Hubert effective rifle-fire can be brought to bear on the greater part of the road, which here partakes of the nature of a defile. On the other hand, do not overestimate the importance of St. Hubert, for such isolated farms, especially when exposed to the enemy's artillery fire, are soon *rendered almost untenable by artillery fire alone*, and then exposed to the first *enveloping* infantry attack. A *protracted* defence of St. Hubert is impossible; as it is,

[1] Steinbrüche von . . .—*Trans.*

the troops holding it must partly be sacrificed; but the defence of this farm will *gain time*, as the enemy must capture St. Hubert before proceeding to the attack of the main position, besides which his tactical formations will be thrown into such disorder in the attack on the farm that he will have some trouble in restoring order before continuing his advance on the main position.

In rear of this position also there is an obstacle—the Montveau valley—*but not so near at hand* as the Mance valley is behind the first position; yet the retreat from Moskau on Chatel St. Germain is rendered difficult by the steep descent into the valley with its dense undergrowth and paucity of paths. The conditions are more favourable for retreat in rear of the left flank of the position, in the direction of Rozérieulles.

A comparison of the two positions is all in favour of the second.

We have now to consider whether General A. should not defend *both* positions *one after the other*. As his object is solely to gain time, there can be no doubt that this object will be better attained if the enemy has first to deploy in front of Gravelotte, and then, after taking it, again deploy for the attack on Le Point-du-Jour. The retreat across the Mance valley, however, is so difficult that, to avoid heavy losses and complete disorganisation, it will have to be carried out under cover of a rallying position already held at Le Point-du-Jour. General A. might either (1) occupy a main position at Gravelotte, and very shortly afterwards a rallying position at Le Point-du-Jour, or (2) make his main position at Le Point-du-Jour, and hold the Gravelotte position lightly, *as an advanced position*. Either plan, however, would lead to **splitting up the force,** and be at variance with the general principle that *one's whole force should, if possible, be massed in one main position*. The former arrangement would necessitate a very early withdrawal of the troops to hold the rallying position, if they are to occupy it in good time—which would deprive us of their assistance in the main action.

If, on the other hand, Gravelotte be held as an advanced position—by the rear guard, for example—there would be some difficulty in leaving the front of the main position clear—for the difficulty of retreating through the dense wood is such, whether on Moskau or on the quarries of Le Point-du-Jour, that *nearly the whole of the rear guard would fall back by the main road*. Owing to the difficulties of retreat I am also against constructing sham-entrenchments at, and north of, Gravelotte in compliance with *Infantry Training*, so as to gain time, and to occupy these entrenchments with but weak forces, which are to retire without engaging in action.

General A. decides to give up all idea of defending Gravelotte, and to concentrate his detachment at the position of Le Point-du-Jour.

Let me beg of you to bear this case in mind as an illustration of the difference between advanced *posts* in front of a position and *advanced* positions. St. Hubert is an *advanced post*; the Gravelotte position is an *advanced position*, for it is *a long way beyond* the reach of infantry fire, and almost out of artillery range. *As a rule* there is no reason why advanced *posts* or *points* should not be defended, as one cannot afford to abandon them to the enemy. *Advanced positions*, on the contrary, *should never*, when possible, be defended; as, irrespective of the difficulty of retreating from them, and the danger of the enemy following so closely on the heels of our retreating troops that we cannot fire upon him, it is as likely as not that the main action may take place *in front of* the position proper, should the troops in the main position be induced to come to the assistance of the advanced position which is imperilled. You will doubtless have noticed that I have intentionally laid the scene of the present exercise in this part of the country in order that you may consider these questions in the light of military history.

In the fifteenth letter I told you that it is not possible to occupy a defensive position until we know with some degree of certainty in what manner the enemy will attack, and especially *how his troops are distributed*. In the present instance we are not in possession of information on these points, owing to the unfortunate circumstance that the enemy's cavalry has been reinforced. General A.'s cavalry has therefore been unable to get near enough to the enemy to obtain reliable information as to the strength of the two columns. Of the two, we know more about the northern column; but we have no definite information about the southern column either—a deficiency the more regrettable as the report sent in yesterday evening by the officer's patrol as to the strength of the troops in the bivouac seen by him requires confirmation. Up to the present, all that General A. knows is that *probably* several hostile battalions are advancing on each road, and that a battery has been observed in the northern column. The only course open to him, therefore, is provisionally to take up a " position of readiness," until the situation clears up more.

A *Position of Readiness* is, as the name implies, a position in which the troops are merely drawn up at some suitable point *in readiness* for contingencies, with a view to subsequently either *occupying* a regular defensive position, or *attacking* the enemy, or *marching* in any required direction. *In the majority of cases the occupation of a position of readiness is merely a preliminary step to occupying a defensive position*, and, in such case, before selecting the place where the troops are to be assembled in readiness, the line to be subsequently defended must be *at any rate approximately* fixed.

General A. intends to extend the position that he will occupy at the outset from Moskau to Le Point-du-Jour, a frontage of about 1100 yards, which he can comfortably defend with his detachment. At the present stage of the operations it is impossible to say whether he may not be obliged to increase his front later on, to meet attacks on his flank; but in any case the first line should be *as short as possible*.

The enemy can either make a direct frontal attack, by St. Hubert, or can, simultaneously with a frontal attack on St. Hubert, attack Moskau, or the left flank of the position near Le Point-du-Jour. Should he attack the right flank, the northern column need only continue in its present line of advance by Malmaison through La Haye-aux-Mures, where several roads and the shallow depression north of Moskau somewhat favour the attack, though the farm at Moskau will stand the defenders in good stead as a supporting point for their flank. Should, on the contrary, the left flank be attacked, General A. will be obliged to prolong the line in that direction by occupying the quarries of Le Point-du-Jour, while the enemy will first have to traverse the Bois-des-Trois-Têtes, where there are only unimportant footpaths, and then carry out an attack *under great difficulties*—the defender being well under cover. An attack on the left flank carries with it, of course, the special advantage that it will *seriously threaten the defender's main line of retreat*, which runs from behind the left flank of the position to Rozérieulles.

The above considerations do not enable us to arrive at any definite conclusion as to in what manner the enemy will attack. General A. will accordingly do best to fix the place for the assembly of his troops under cover in rear of the centre of his position, so as to utilise existing roads for ready access to all parts of the position; that is to say in rear of (*i.e.* east of) the hill 345·2. Here the bulk of his infantry will be drawn up in assembly formation, the battalions in line of quarter-columns.

At the outset the infantry should occupy only such *supporting points* as, no matter how the enemy attacks, will *under any circumstances* play an important part; this is termed "*the occupation of the framework of the position.*" Such supporting points receive sufficiently strong garrisons, which utilise the time at their disposal in putting these points in a state of defence—*not too strong*, however, in order that as large a proportion of the troops as possible may be kept in hand at this early stage of the operations. Moskau and St. Hubert are such points in the present instance. Two companies are enough for each. The machine-gun detachment also will be allotted to St. Hubert. There can be no possibility of doubt on this point. Telephone connection will be established at once with these two supporting points.

With a view to avoiding an admixture of different battalions when the position proper is subsequently occupied, *the infantry for these two points are drawn from those battalions which will later on have to garrison the sections to which Moskau and St. Hubert will belong.* General A. must therefore decide *from the very first* how he intends (approximately) to divide the position into sections, and what battalions are to hold the first line. The battalion which is to hold the section to which Moskau will belong can extend to 440 yards south of Moskau, and the battalion for the section to which St. Hubert will belong can carry on the line from that point to beyond the turn of the main road, east of St. Hubert ; a third battalion possibly continuing the line further south ; though it will depend on circumstances how far south the line will go. The *final* decision as to the sections will be arrived at when the position is being occupied.

The entrenchments must be started as soon as possible. For this reason General A. will detail the II/Suffolk and the I/Essex, *who will be first to arrive*, to occupy the most important points—the II/Suffolk garrisoning St. Hubert.

The *cavalry* will, as hitherto, reconnoitre.

When a position of readiness has to be taken up, it will often be necessary to send *separate and complete squadrons* of cavalry in the various directions in which the enemy has been last reported, or where he is probably advancing. This will entail an unavoidable *splitting up* of the cavalry. The employment of the cavalry is in this case, therefore, *very different* from its employment in the attack and defence of positions, in which cases the bulk of it should be *massed* on that flank where there is most scope for its action, while only patrols watch the less important flank. In the case of a position of readiness *one flank is about as important as the other*, and there must be careful reconnaissance in all directions. If circumstances admit of your keeping your advanced cavalry more concentrated, for instance, on some eminence *between* the main approaches, and thus avoiding dissemination of this arm, so much the better! *Standing* patrols placed on commanding points can then keep the enemy's lines of approach *constantly* under observation, while at the same time *moving* distant patrols endeavour actively to seek him out.

The artillery should be placed at points whence it will have as wide a range as possible, and will command all the avenues of approach open to the enemy. In the present case we are concerned with the roads through Gravelotte and Malmaison, which can both be commanded from Moskau. General A. will, however, only indicate the position in general terms, viz. "near Moskau," leaving the officer commanding the artillery to arrange details on the spot.

The artillery position must also be so situated as to command any points which may serve as positions for the enemy's guns; such points here are Mogador and the hill north of it. It is an excellent thing when *one* position will meet all these requirements.

When time permits, additional cover to that afforded by the protective shields of the guns should be made. Bear in mind: blinds, dummy-trenches, clearing the field of fire.

Every preparation should be made, so that, if possible, our guns may rapidly open fire *before the enemy's batteries can come into position*. Officer's patrols are left behind.

If artillery positions suiting every contingency cannot be found at the outset, the batteries will await the development of events beside or behind the bulk of the infantry, in any convenient assembly formation.

The battalions to occupy sections in the first line prepare them for defence, as a matter of principle, themselves.

Though General A. does not yet know how far his line must extend to the south, he can, *at all events provisionally*, have the position prepared for defence as far as the quarries, *without necessarily having subsequently on that account to occupy it as far as that.* There is not much to be done in the southern section, so the III/Northumberland Fusiliers, hitherto in the rear guard, which will be the last to arrive, may be detailed for this section. With positions of readiness it is, as a general rule, not such a simple matter as it is in this case to decide the right moment for beginning to place the intended position in a state of defence. If one has to await the arrival of more definite information as to the enemy's deployment, or if there be several positions suitable for defence and one cannot decide which to defend until later on, it will often happen that there will then be *no time* available *for thorough-going* preparations for defence. Sometimes we have also to put up with the disadvantage of having *our entrenchments prematurely discovered by the enemy's reconnoitring cavalry, our position being thus betrayed.*

The *position of the dressing station* cannot be fixed until the direction of the enemy's main attack is certain. No change need be made in the existing arrangements for the *2nd line transport*, so *no reference is necessary to it in the orders.*

In these orders, too, it must be clearly stated that the hitherto-existing rôles of the various portions of the column of march are to be considered terminated. For the same reasons as in orders for attack I would make this clear in the orders.

Under paragraph 2 of the orders it will be as well for General A. to explain to his subordinates *why, contrary to his arrangements for retreat, he is about to take up a position of readiness.*

Telegraphic communication may be kept up between Rozérieulles and Metz, but the section between Gravelotte and Rozérieulles must be destroyed by the engineers.

The following are the orders:—

EIGHTEENTH LETTER

OPERATION ORDER No. 6   *Copy No. 1.*

BY

MAJOR-GENERAL A., COMMANDING DETACHED FORCE.

Reference: **GRAVELOTTE,**
$\frac{1}{100,000}$ *Ordn.*   2.12.00.

1. *The Enemy's northern column* is in pursuit through **DONCOURT-EN-JARNISY**, his *southern column* through **MARS-LA-TOUR**.

2. *The Detached Force* will, in accordance with an order just received from **METZ** to check the enemy, take up a position of readiness north-east of **LE POINT-DU-JOUR**. To-day's march orders are cancelled.

3. *The* II/15th *Hussars* will continue to reconnoitre in the direction of **JOUAVILLE** and **DONCOURT-EN-JARNISY**, and through **ST. MARCEL**; *the* I/15th *Hussars* in the direction of **MARS-LA-TOUR**, **FLAVIGNY**, **BOIS-DE-VIONVILLE**, and **BOIS-DES-OGNONS**.

4. *The Field Artillery Brigade* will take up a position of readiness near **MOSKAU**.

5. *The* I/*Essex Regiment* will occupy **MOSKAU** with two companies, and *the* II/*Suffolk Regiment* **ST. HUBERT** with two companies; *the rest of the infantry* and *the section field ambulance* will take up a position in assembly formation east of the hill 345·2, north-east of **LE POINT-DU-JOUR**.

6. *The Machine-Gun Detachment* will at once occupy **ST. HUBERT**.

7. *The* I/*Essex* will put in a state of defence the line from **MOSKAU** inclusive to 440 yards south of **MOSKAU**; *the* II/*Suffolk* thence to the bend in the high road east of **ST. HUBERT**, inclusive; and *the* III/*Northumberland Fusiliers* thence to the quarries of **LE POINT-DU-JOUR** exclusive. These three infantry battalions will establish telephone connection between the bend of the high road east of **ST. HUBERT** and **ST. HUBERT, MOSKAU,** and the hill 345·2 north-east of **LE POINT-DU-JOUR**. *The* 1st *Field Co. R.E.* will assist in preparing **MOSKAU** and **ST. HUBERT** for defence, obstruct the road where it crosses the **MANCE** valley, and destroy the line of telegraph from **GRAVELOTTE** to **ROZÉRIEULLES**, exclusive.

A POSITION OF READINESS

8. *The S.A.A. Carts* per battalion with the I/Essex, II/Suffolk, and III/Northumberland Fusiliers, will be emptied; the detachment reserve S.A.A. carts will remain at my disposal. The light ammunition column is placed at the disposal of the officer commanding the artillery.

9. *Reports* to the bend in the main road, east of **ST. HUBERT**, where I will be.

Verbally to officers commanding units in the main body.

In writing to the rear guard by cyclist, and to the right flank guard by Lieutenant N.

11.20 a.m.

A.,
Major-General.

EIGHTEENTH EXERCISE.

At 1.15 p.m. the situation has been so far cleared up that General A., who has assembled by him his subordinate commanders, with the exception of the officers commanding the squadrons of cavalry, is aware that 2 hostile battalions and 2 batteries are deploying at Gravelotte, and 4 battalions and 1 battery are deploying at Malmaison; while the enemy's cavalry is making vain efforts to reconnoitre in the direction of the high ground of Le Point-du-Jour, by way of the Bois-des-Trois-Têtes and La Haye-aux-Mures. General A. can also see that a hostile firing line, deployed on both sides of the high road, is gaining ground from Gravelotte in the direction of St. Hubert, and that another hostile firing line is advancing from the high ground north of Mogador in an easterly direction, towards the Mance valley; while at the same time three hostile batteries are coming into position south-east of Mogador. There is nothing visible of the enemy south of Gravelotte, except cavalry.

Required :—

The arrangements made by General A., giving reasons for the measures adopted, and show on the map in detail the position occupied.

NINETEENTH LETTER

(In continuation of the preceding Letter.)

POSITION FOR DEFENCE

THERE is now no doubt that the enemy will make his main attack on Moskau, simultaneously with a weaker secondary attack deployed on both sides of the Gravelotte road, so General A. can now *occupy* his defensive position; his batteries at the same time opening fire on those of the enemy, which have come into position near Mogador, thereby diverting the fire of the latter from St. Hubert by drawing it upon themselves. The data assume that the enemy's advance has been so skilfully made that our batteries had no opportunity of firing on his columns of route. Thus the first shot is by order of the G.O.C., *as it always should be*, for a premature opening of fire, possibly on small bodies of the enemy, assists the enemy in reconnoitring the position. Our artillery will not fire on the enemy's infantry until it advances to attack. The main object, however, of the defence is to repulse the attacking infantry, and to this end the defender's guns must be prepared to leave any cover and see the infantry. If at that time the attacking artillery is not fought down yet, it must at least be kept engaged by some guns at the same time. I have called your attention once more to this task of the artillery, so that you may examine the position you have chosen to see whether the artillery can act with this view.

The machine-gun detachment will open fire on the skirmishers advancing from Gravelotte as soon as they come within range—the range of the machine-gun being the same as that of the infantry rifle. The effect of this fire should be deadly, as the attackers will be compelled by the nature of the ground to crowd together at the main road. If we have to retreat from St. Hubert, the machine-guns must be withdrawn in good time behind the high ground of Moskau, when they can again come into action later on against the enemy's main attack. In view of the great mobility of the machine-guns there will be no difficulty in thus moving them.

In order to keep a strong general reserve in hand, General A. intends having only two battalions in the first line, in the hope that the I/Suffolk will be able to hold its ground against the two hostile battalions advancing through Gravelotte. This battalion has, in addition to St. Hubert, a frontage of about 440 yards to defend, which is the utmost possible. Should the line have to be prolonged to the south, it will have to be done at a later period by the general reserve. The latter may be disposed in two different ways. *Both* battalions may be placed in rear of the threatened *right* flank, with a view to their employment defensively or offensively. If in this case the left flank has to be prolonged, the order must be given in good time to the battalion required for the purpose, as it will have a long way to go. Or, if you are apprehensive for your left flank, the general reserve will have to be divided, and the III/Northumberland Fusiliers posted under cover by the side of the road from Le Point-du-Jour to Rozérieulles. The latter arrangement is justified by the consideration that the detachment has to confine itself to the defensive, and so will probably have to abandon all idea of making *an offensive counterstroke*.

It is as yet a somewhat doubtful question what the enemy's strength in the neighbourhood of Gravelotte really is. According to the data General A. has ascertained by 1.15 p.m. that *two* hostile battalions are deploying at Gravelotte, whereas the evening before the officer's patrol reported the presence of *four* hostile battalions in a bivouac on the southern road. It seems probable, therefore, that the officer in question made a mistake, though there is still room for uncertainty. This shows *how long, under certain circumstances, the effect of uncertain information lasts.* I wished to impress this upon you in the present example. The chance of the enemy being in greater strength than two battalions at Gravelotte is an inducement to divide the general reserve, as well as the circumstance that the line of retreat requires some special protection, owing to its disadvantageous position with regard to the position. In the present case, therefore, I consider that, *as an exceptional measure*, the reserve ought to be divided. There is no hard-and-fast rule !

The cavalry can now be *gradually* so distributed as to have the bulk of it in readiness on the threatened flank, protecting it by reconnaissance—only patrols remaining in observation of the southern border of Gravelotte, with orders to report should any considerable body of the enemy advance south of Gravelotte (*G.F.S.R.*, para. 132).[1]

It will not be easy to find a good position for a *dressing station*. The heaviest losses are to be expected on the right flank, but if the dressing station were in rear of it, near Châtel St. Germain, it would be too difficult to transport the severely wounded down the steep valley slopes, and along the rough woodland tracks. Rozérieulles, again, is too far from Moskau ; so the dressing station might be formed in the old quarries,[2] east of Le Point-du-Jour, where it would be completely sheltered from fire, and could be easily got at by road ; though this position would have the disadvantage of total *absence of water and distance from any village* (*G.F.S.R.*, para. 487).[3]

With regard to the detachment reserve S.A.A. carts, which the previous orders retained at the disposal of the

---

[1] *E.F.S.R.*, Part I, sects. 92 and 94.—*Trans.*
[2] Alter St. Br. = "Alter Steinbruch" on map.—*Trans.*
[3] *E.F.S.R.*, Part II, sect. 77.—*Trans.*

POSITION FOR DEFENCE

G.O.C., their position must now be settled. There is more than one suitable place; either behind the hill 345·2, *i.e.* in rear of the centre of the position; or at the junction of roads, 550 yards north-east of Moskau, *i.e.* in rear of the threatened flank. Good reasons can be adduced for both.

General A.'s position will be in the vicinity of the threatened flank.

Copy No. 1.

OPERATION ORDER No. 7
BY
MAJOR-GENERAL A., COMMANDING DETACHED FORCE.

Reference:
$\frac{1}{100,000}$ *Ordn.*

Bend of road east of
ST. HUBERT,
2.12.00.

1. Two battalions of *the enemy* are advancing through **GRAVELOTTE** on **ST. HUBERT**, and four battalions through **MALMAISON** on **MOSKAU**. He has three batteries in position south-east of **MOGADOR**.

2. *The Detached Force* will defend a position extending from Moskau to 220 yards south of the bend in the main road east of **ST. HUBERT**.

3. *The Artillery Brigade* will at once open fire on the enemy's artillery.

4. *The Machine-Gun Detachment* will open fire on any hostile infantry advancing from **GRAVELOTTE**.

5. *The I/Essex* will at once occupy the section from **MOSKAU** to the pit 440 yards south of **MOSKAU**, both inclusive.

   The II/Suffolk the section thence to 220 yards south of the bend in the main road east of **ST. HUBERT**. The farm **ST. HUBERT** is to be held to the last.

6. *The IV/K.R. Rifles, the III/Northumberland Fusiliers*, and *the 1st Field Co. R.E.* will form the general reserve. The first-mentioned battalion will move to the junction of roads 550 yards north-east of **MOSKAU**, and the Fusiliers and the R.E. to the quarry (St. Br.) south-east of **LE POINT-DU-JOUR**.

7. *The* II/15th *Hussars* will remain near **LEIPZIG**, to cover the right flank by reconnoitring towards **MALMAISON**. The I/15th Hussars will continue reconnoitring with patrols the country south of **GRAVELOTTE**, the remainder of this squadron joining the II/.

8. *The Section Field Ambulance* will establish its dressing station at the old quarry east of **LE POINT-DU-JOUR**. *The Detachment Reserve S.A.A. Carts* will remain behind the hill 345·2.

9. *Reports* to **MOSKAU**, where I will be.

Verbally to the assembled commanding officers.

A.,
Major-General.

Copies sent to both squadrons by Lieutenants M. and N.

1.20 p.m.

NINETEENTH EXERCISE.

(See general map and Gravelotte map.)

A Blue Division, operating in its own country, has thrown a bridge across the Moselle between Ay and Hagendingen (general map), by which it has crossed on the 1.9.00, and is advancing towards the Orne, viâ Pierrevillers and Malancourt, to anticipate, if possible, the enemy in that quarter, who is reported advancing on Briey. On the report received from natives that hostile infantry had arrived in Hatrize (on the railway south-west of Briey), a left-flank guard, under General A., consisting of 3 battalions, 1 machine-gun detachment, 1 squadron, 3 field batteries, ½ of a field company R.E., 1 light ammunition column, and 1 section field ambulance, was detached to Maizières with orders to march, viâ Bronvaux and St. Privat, on Auboué, to protect the flank of the Division and to reconnoitre towards the railway between Moineville and Jarny.

As, at 9 a.m., the head of the vanguard of the detachment strikes, at Marengo, the high road from Saulny to St. Privat, General A., who has ridden up to this point, hears heavy artillery and musketry fire to the northwards, and at the same time the following reports arrive in quick succession:—

1. From the squadron which has trotted on ahead on St. Privat, to the effect that hostile infantry has fired on it from St. Privat, but that Roncourt was found to be unoccupied by the enemy.

POSITION FOR DEFENCE

2. An officer's patrol, which had pushed forward by way of St. Ail in the direction of Auboué, saw a column of hostile infantry, with a battery, on the march from Auboué to Ste. Marie-aux-Chênes, and estimated that the head of the column would arrive at the latter place about 9.30 a.m.

3. A N.C.O.'s patrol pushed out in the direction of Montois-la-Montagne reports this place occupied by hostile infantry, which was apparently keeping up a heavy fire in the direction of Malancourt.

4 An officer's patrol, which had been sent by way of Batilly, reports :—

"Moineville, Hatrize, and Giraumont-en-Jarnisy unoccupied by the enemy."

Required :—
1. An appreciation of the situation by General A.
2. His orders.

N.B.—The Wald von Jaumont has dense undergrowth.

TWENTIETH LETTER

ATTACK MADE BY A FLANKING DETACHMENT

(Encounter of two forces, being both in motion.)

THE Blue Division purposes to anticipate the enemy on the Orne, with a view to crossing this river, and advancing further, viâ Briey. The rôle of the Division is therefore an *offensive* one. The information concerning the enemy was extremely vague at the outset, for all that was known was that he was advancing on Briey, but whether or not he had yet reached that town it was impossible to say definitely. The information supplied by the natives about Hatrize was doubtful too.

While the detachment is still occupied in traversing the hilly country west of the Moselle, it comes *all of a sudden and unexpectedly* on the enemy, and the heavy firing heard at the same moment towards the north shows that the main body is already hotly engaged with the enemy. It seems probable that the enemy is in a defensive position, judging from the report furnished by the N.C.O.'s patrol that the enemy was holding Montois-la-Montagne, and was firing in an easterly direction. At the same time General A. is aware that the Blue Division is still for the most part entangled in the hilly and wooded country, from which it has to debouch before anything else can be done. *If the enemy were on the offensive, and trying to prevent the Blue Division from issuing from the defile, the non-commissioned officer could not have failed to notice it. The defensive attitude of the enemy at the moment when seen by the N.C.O.'s patrol is a favourable sign.* We cannot, of course, know for certain whence this enemy has sprung who is now opposing the advance of the Blue Division, but an inspection of the network of roads leading to Briey makes it probable that he crossed the Orne at Homécourt.

So far the flanking detachment has only been able to establish the presence of the enemy at St. Privat. As, however, the village of Roncourt, north of St. Privat, is unoccupied by hostile troops, and as some of our cavalry have ridden round by Amanweiler and encountered no enemy until arriving in front of St. Privat, we may conclude with some degree of certainty that the enemy in front of the flanking detachment has, for the present, only occupied St. Privat, having probably crossed the Orne at Auboué and advanced viâ Ste. Marie-aux-Chênes. He is probably in connection with the column which the officer's patrol reported to be advancing from Auboué on Ste. Marie-aux-Chênes, that is to say, is its advanced guard, *pushed well to the front*. This hypothesis is, at any rate, more probable than that the troops in St. Privat are a detachment from those in Montois-la-Montagne, because in the latter case we should have found Roncourt occupied. No artillery has, up to the present, been seen at St. Privat, but may at any moment be expected to come into action. *In any case we must be prepared to find some artillery at St. Privat.* Our cavalry has, however, stated definitely that St. Privat is occupied *by infantry*, which is more than saying that they were *fired upon* from St. Privat. I draw the distinction, because the cavalry should not say they were fired on by infantry unless quite sure that it was not dismounted cavalry.

Nowadays, however, it is a matter of great importance to the officer commanding the troops that his reconnoitring cavalry succeed in establishing as a fact the presence (or otherwise) of hostile *infantry*, for until this point be cleared up he cannot draw any reliable conclusion as to the enemy's arrangements. *You can now continue drawing further conclusions.* In the first place, it is noteworthy that the officer's patrol expressly states that the column on the march from Aboué to Ste. Marie-aux-Chênes comprises only *one* battery. The statement is probably correct, for the officer was able to watch the column *from a position on its flank* (G.F.S.R., para. 127). We may further infer that we have to deal with either the *main body* of a flanking detachment or the *advanced guard* of some stronger body in rear—not, in all probability, with the enemy's main body, as in that case there would be more artillery present. As, however, St. Privat is held by infantry, it seems probable that the column reported by the officer's patrol is the main body of a detachment which has been delayed in the Orne valley by some accident; while its advanced guard, say a battalion with a few cavalry, is holding St. Privat. But if it is a detachment which is moving on Ste. Marie-aux-Chênes, the main body of the enemy's forces, or at least the largest portion of it, is probably at Montois-la-Montagne; and this theory accounts for the heavy artillery firing north of Roncourt. There are other possible interpretations of the information to hand, but none likely to be so correct as this. It is of great importance to the commander of the detachment to know the fact also that there is no enemy in the country west and south-west of Ste. Marie-aux-Chênes.

As General A. now knows that the northern column is standing on the *defensive*, it is open to him to make further inferences. That is to say, the fact of the enemy's northern column being so near the river, which means *having a defile immediately in its rear*, points to the probability of it having been *forced* into this position through encountering the Blue Division on the march, the latter being the *stronger*. Were the *enemy* the stronger, he would endeavour to drive back the Blue Division on the defile behind *it*. If this assumption be correct, we have apparently the somewhat peculiar case of an encounter battle in which *both* opponents seek to gain elbow-room for debouching. The bulk of the enemy's forces is apparently still engaged in crossing the Orne; the Blue Division, too, has yet to finish debouching from the wooded defile, and must then at once assume a most vigorous offensive to drive back the enemy, who *every moment* is receiving accessions of strength, as quickly as possible on the Orne, and secure the passages over the river.

We thus, in spite of the scantiness of the data, can form an approximate idea of the general situation, though, of course, we cannot aspire to *absolute certainty*.

It will be awkward for General A. if there should, after all, prove to be *only a handful of men* holding St. Privat, while he, on the contrary, has had to deploy his whole force before trying conclusions with the village; for such would involve a grievous waste of time. Ill-luck of this kind is the more difficult to escape, the less efficiently cavalry is carrying out its reconnoitring duties. Its reconnaissance will often have to be supplemented by *deploying artillery* and advanced-guard *infantry* in front of a locality that has to be attacked, to induce the enemy to show himself.

The offensive intentions of the Division must determine the action of the flank detachment, *for such small bodies should never fight on their own account*. Their *raison d'être* is to serve the main body, and *assist* it to attain the object *it* has in view. *By drawing the enemy on itself the detachment will facilitate the task of the main body.* A defensive rôle is wholly out of place here, for that would be leaving the enemy perfect freedom of action. *To stand on the defensive in the present instance would be tantamount to doing nothing.* St. Privat must be attacked with the utmost vigour; the more so as in all probability St. Privat is, as we have seen above, only occupied by one battalion.

Suppose it turns out that much stronger forces than General A. thinks are holding St. Privat. There would be no great harm done, *provided we entangle the column advancing on Ste. Marie in an action*. We should, however, have to abandon all idea of carrying out our attack to the extent of assaulting the enemy's position, unless we wish to run the risk of being annihilated.

It would in any event be desirable that the attack on

St. Privat be got over *before the column advancing from Auboué on Ste. Marie can join in*. To attain this end the attack must be *prompt and energetic*. General A. must anticipate the enemy in deployment, and will be fully justified in so acting, for there can be no doubt in his mind that such a line of action *will be in accordance with the intentions of his superior*. To *wait* for orders what to do would be a useless waste of time.

The officer's patrol reports that the head of the enemy's column will reach Ste. Marie-aux-Chênes about 9.30 a.m.; it will therefore be at St. Privat by 10.15 easily, though, of course, the battery can trot on ahead. Our detachment will take at least thirty minutes before the infantry can be deployed at Marengo to begin the attack, which therefore cannot be earlier than 9.30 a.m., and we shall be uncommonly lucky if the village is in our hands by 10.15 a.m.

A direct line of advance, provided it offers reasonable hopes of success, is preferable in attack, where time is an object. The shortest line here would mean *a direct frontal attack* on the east side of the village; this, however, is hardly practicable; for, even supposing that there were only half a battalion holding St. Privat, the defender's fire from behind cover would inflict *such severe losses* that the attacker would never be able to get near such a strong position. General A. must not therefore be tempted, *for the sake of gaining time, to imperil the success* of the attack. There must be only a vigorous demonstration against the east side of the village, and the G.O.C. has the usual alternative of making his main attack on either the right or the left flank of the enemy.

The exact position of the various portions of the column does not matter, as movement is confined to the road. The whole detachment must debouch from the wood rapidly, and the sure and quickest way of doing so is to keep to the main road.

The *demonstration* against the east side of the village will advance north of and parallel to the main road, but to decide on which flank the *main attack* is to be made some little reflection is necessary.

You see that the attack on the right flank would be attended with *great difficulties*, nor would there be much advantage in threatening the enemy's line of retreat on Ste. Marie, for there is nothing to prevent the defenders of the village retiring on Homécourt. An attack on the right flank would also run a risk, especially if anything unforeseen occurred to delay it, of being itself taken in flank by the column from Ste. Marie, if the latter reached the high ground S.S.W. of St. Privat, while the flank attack was being made. It is very likely that the enemy would attempt this manœuvre, as the flank attack is bound to be seen, the moment it sets out from Marengo. Neither should the consideration that the extreme right flank of the *whole* of the hostile forces rests on Jerusalem have any weight in inducing General A. to make his main attack in this quarter, for his great object is to gain possession of St. Privat with as little delay as possible. *All else is of secondary importance.*

There is far more prospect of success with the *left* flank, viz. in attacking the eastern half of the north border of the village or the whole of the northern border, should the enemy have occupied it notwithstanding the vigorous demonstration against his front. From in front of the north-east angle of the village there runs a long ridge in a northerly direction, which limits the fire from the north side of the village in a north-easterly direction to about 400 yards. A spur runs from this ridge towards Marengo, under cover of which the attacker can get within 400 yards of the north side of St. Privat without coming under fire. He need only move north along the edge of the wood, till he strikes the road from the Marengo quarries (St. Br. on map), and then attack straight on St. Privat. Supposing that the hostile column were to move on Roncourt to take the main attack in flank, it would have to proceed with caution, on account of the proximity of the main body of the Blue Division. Again by so doing it would play into General A.'s hands, as *his object is to draw the column on himself*. So, too, it would be with unmixed satisfaction that General A. would view any movement of hostile troops from Montois-la-Montagne towards St. Privat.

It remains now for you to have a glance back on the ground *in rear* of your attack. The Wald von Jaumont having dense undergrowth, it is not altogether pleasant to know this. In case of having to retreat through it, movement will be confined to the *roads*. The advanced-guard battalion could retire on Marengo, and thence on Bronvaux, or Fêves, or Norroy-le-Veneur. The main attack and reserve would have to fall back first on the Jaumont quarries, and thence on Pierrevillers, and so probably effect a junction with its Division. The whole of the west border of the Wald von Jaumont is favourable for defence as a rallying position in case of need.

General A.'s decision, accordingly, is as follows: A demonstration against the east side of the village, combined with a *prompt and vigorous* main attack on the north-east angle of St. Privat, taking the chance of finding the enemy in superior numbers to us.

The orders for the *deployment* of the main body must in this case be combined with the orders for the *attack*.

The artillery must be at once brought to the front; for by this means we shall ascertain whether the enemy has artillery at St. Privat or not. Should his guns have been up to the present concealed in the neighbourhood of the village, they will show themselves as soon as our artillery opens fire on any part of the village. If, however, the enemy has artillery at St. Privat, our batteries must endeavour to silence it *as a preliminary measure*, although it is to the infantry that we look for a speedy decision of the action. Until the enemy's guns are silenced, our artillery will not fire on the point to be assaulted by the infantry.

If it turns out that the enemy has *no artillery* at St. Privat, it will simplify matters for the detachment. Our artillery can, *from the first*, fire on the north-east corner of the village. None the less, however, the artillery must be on the look out for the enemy's guns suddenly and unexpectedly opening fire; for, as we know, the approaching column will probably push its artillery on ahead. *Artillery officer's patrols* must be most active.

In any case the north-east corner of the village may be indicated as the first target for the guns; later they would, at any rate, have the advantage of *knowing exactly the range* of the point to be assaulted. They will come into action at Marengo.

There is nothing particular to be said about the order for the infantry making the secondary attack. The officer commanding it will decide *when* it should quit cover at Marengo and move on to St. Privat. *The officer commanding the main attack* must likewise have a free hand in deciding *how far* he will go in a northerly direction, and in selecting *the moment* for the beginning of the attack proper. It is impossible under these circumstances to make use of the telephone.

The battalion in reserve had best be écheloned in rear of the outer flank of the main attack, and close up, as a crisis is expected soon. The machine-gun detachment has for the present no special task given; it will for the moment remain with the reserve.

The squadron has three distinct duties during the attack. Firstly, it has to keep up communication with the Blue Division, and report the progress of the action in that quarter; secondly, it must instantly acquaint General A. should any movement on the part of the enemy from the direction of Montois-la-Montagne affect the main attack; and thirdly, it must keep a look out towards Roncourt, and the country south of St. Privat—that is to say, towards both flanks—to ascertain the direction in which the approaching hostile column is moving after passing through Ste. Marie-aux-Chênes. To watch the country south of St. Privat a few strong patrols will be sufficient, which should be able to hold their own against the enemy's cavalry on the high ground south of St. Privat, whence they can overlook the whole country to beyond Ste. Marie. The bulk of the squadron should be on the right flank of the main attack, and fill the gap between the latter and the Blue Division.

There is no time for issuing extra ammunition.—The 2nd line transport need not be mentioned. Why not?

I may here introduce an observation of a general nature. In the attack of a flanking detachment the following question frequently arises: Should we attack the *outermost* flank of the enemy, thus, in case of success, driving him back on his other troops, and placing ourselves on the flank of the *whole* line held by the enemy; or should we turn to account any gap (should such be ascertained to exist) in the enemy's general line, and attack, as in the present instance, the *inner* flank of the troops directly opposed to our flanking detachment? *No rule of universal application can be laid down on this subject.* The main thing is to observe the principle that the point of most importance is to defeat the enemy *by any means open to us,* and that therefore we must attack *in whatever direction is most favourable.* If we have an *equally* good chance of success with *either* flank, then ask yourself the question: How will the flanking detachment best attain that which must ever be its object, viz. to assist the main body in performing the task imposed upon it?

Copy No. 1.

OPERATION ORDER No. 2

BY

MAJOR-GENERAL A., COMMANDING LEFT FLANKING FORCE.

Reference: **MARENGO,**
$\frac{1}{100,000}$ *Ordn.*   1.9.00.

1. *The Enemy* has occupied **ST. PRIVAT** with infantry, and a column of hostile infantry, with a battery, is on the march from **AUBOUÉ** to **ST. MARIE-AUX-CHÊNES.** *Our Division* is attacking **MONTOIS-LA-MONTAGNE.**

ATTACK BY A FLANKING DETACHMENT

2. *The Detachment* will attack **ST. PRIVAT,** enveloping the enemy's left flank. This morning's march orders are cancelled.

3. *The Batteries R.A.* will pass the infantry on the left and at once move into position near **MARENGO,** and fire on the north-east corner of **ST. PRIVAT.** The light ammunition column is placed at the disposal of the O.C. artillery brigade.

4. *The* I/*Battalion* will advance, north of the main road, in support of the attack, which *the* II/*Battalion,* advancing along the west edge of the **WALD VON JAUMONT,** will make on the north-east corner of **ST. PRIVAT.**

5. *The* III/*Battalion, the Machine-Gun Detachment, and the R.E.* will form the reserve, which will move 350 yards in rear of the right flank of the II/Battalion.

6. *The* I/1st *Dragoons* will keep up communication with the Division,—cover the right flank of the attack by observation through **RONCOURT** towards **MONTOIS-LA-MONTAGNE** and **ST. MARIE-AUX-CHÊNES,**—and reconnoitre by way of the high ground south of **ST. PRIVAT** towards **ST. MARIE-AUX-CHÊNES.**

7. *The Section Field Ambulance* will establish a dressing station at **MARENGO.**

8. *Reports* to **MARENGO.**

Verbally to the advanced guard and artillery.

In writing to the squadron by N.C.O. and to main body by Lieutenant A.

Verbal report to G.O.C. Blue Division by Lieutenant B.

9.10 a.m.

A.,
Major-General.

TWENTIETH EXERCISE.
(I recommend working with the general map only.)

The 1st Division is engaged on the 1.9.00 in crossing the Moselle between Ennery and Hauconcourt, with a view to effecting a junction on the following day, at Mars-la-Tour, with the 2nd Division, which is advancing viâ the unfortified town of Metz. These troops

TWENTIETH LETTER

are operating in an enemy's country. The enemy is known to be advancing with an army corps (2 divisions) from Verdun towards the Moselle. The advanced guard of the 1st Division, composed of—

I/Battalion	1st Field Artillery Brigade
II/Battalion	1st Field Co. R.E.
III/Battalion	2 Sections Field Ambulance
Machine-Gun Detachment	1 Light Ammunition Column
1st Dragoons	

commanded by General A., is advancing viâ Fèves. General A. has received a notification to the effect that the main body would be delayed about two hours in starting, but that the advanced guard is to continue its advance till further orders, and cover the main body as it debouches from the woods. The general officer in command of the 1st Division is at present at Hauconcourt, and the General commanding both divisions is with the 2nd Division, which will not arrive at Moulins-bei-Metz till 1 p.m.

General A., who has ridden up to the head of the vanguard, is about to cross the Metz–St. Privat road near the Amanweiler quarries, when he receives, at 10 a.m., the following report from his cavalry, which with the machine-gun detachment had advanced to west of Vernéville :—

"Column on the march through **ST. MARCEL**, strength estimated at 4 or 5 battalions and 2 batteries, but only 1 squadron. Its vanguard reached **CAULRE** at 9.35 a.m., and is moving on **VERNÉVILLE**. The tail of the column was then at **GREYÈRES**. Another, apparently stronger, column moving through **MARS-LA-TOUR** on **VIONVILLE**. No enemy on main road between **DONCOURT-EN-JARNISY** and **JARNY**."

At 10.35 a.m. a report is received from the cavalry at the west edge of Vernéville that the enemy had advanced very slowly on that village, and that at 10.25 a.m. a weak firing line had occupied the copse about half-way between Caulre and Vernéville.

Required :—
1. State what General A. should do to carry out his orders.
2. Give the reports, the despatches, and the orders he issues.
3. Give reasons for the above.

N.B.—All the woods on the left bank of the Moselle have dense undergrowth. Infantry in extended order would have great difficulty in working through them.

TWENTY-FIRST LETTER

ADVANCED-GUARD ACTION
(Collision of two forces in movement.)

ON receipt of the first report from his cavalry, the officer commanding the advanced guard will at once see that he must act on his own responsibility. Neither can the advanced guard look for immediate support from the main body, the latter having been delayed (the data do not state from what cause) for two hours in starting from Hauconcourt. *For two hours, therefore, General A. may be left without support.* His duty is to cover the main body while it debouches from the defile formed by the dense woods on each side the Hauconcourt–Amanweiler road. This duty was assigned to him at a time when hardly anything was known of the enemy's whereabouts.

The enemy's approach having been reported, it might, of course, be possible to cover the debouching from the defile by *offensive* action, viz. by the advanced guard attacking and pushing the enemy on Vernéville. To be justified in such action, however, it must be first established *beyond the shadow of a doubt* that the enemy is *inferior* to the advanced guard in numbers. *This, though, is far from being the case.*

If you measure the distance between Caulre and Greyères, you will find it is $3\frac{1}{4}$ miles, which is the road space occupied by the enemy's column, from the head of the vanguard to the tail of the main body. We may therefore deduce from this length that the enemy has from four to five battalions and two batteries (leaving engineers, etc., apart) approaching Caulre, which agrees with the estimate made by the cavalry. It thus appears that in all probability the enemy is *about the same strength* as General A.'s advanced guard, so that, to say the least, it is doubtful whether he can be repulsed. The advanced guard, however, cannot afford to commit itself to any undertaking the success of which is doubtful; for in the event of a reverse the whole main body of the 1st Division would be affected; for it would have great difficulty in debouching from the wood in face of an enemy flushed by a recent success, *and would in any case suffer heavy losses in making the attempt.* It is therefore safer for the advanced guard to await the enemy in a suitable position, taking care to go no further in advance of the main body than is *absolutely necessary*, so as to be within reinforcing distance in case of need. Considering the general situation, therefore, the advanced guard must act on the *defensive*.

The following are the only positions for defence that need be considered:—

(1) A position immediately in front of the Amanweiler quarries, extending either to Marengo or the Wald von Saulny.

(2) A position near Amanweiler, extending either towards St. Privat or up to Montigny-la-Grange.

(3) A position approximately on the line Envie–Champenois, supplemented by the spurs north and south of these two farms.

The following calculation will show that time will not admit of the advanced guard reaching a position at Vernéville—irrespective of the consideration that such a position would be too far in advance of the main body—and that it is open to doubt whether even Champenois can be reached in the time available.

The head of the enemy's vanguard can, *if nothing occurs to delay his advance*, reach the east side of Vernéville 45 minutes after 9.35 a.m., *i.e.* at 10.20 a.m., as the distance thither from Caulre is about $2\frac{1}{4}$ miles. By 10.20

ADVANCED-GUARD ACTION

a.m. General A.'s vanguard will have got 1 mile further—not quite in Amanweiler—and is still 3 miles from Vernéville, where it could not arrive till 11.20 a.m., so the enemy has a considerable start if he wish to occupy Vernéville.

Supposing, as before, that nothing delays the enemy, it is 72 minutes marching from Caulre to Champenois, so the head of the enemy's vanguard can be at Champenois by 10.47 a.m. The head of General A.'s vanguard has about 3 miles to go, so would be there about 11 a.m. Now let us assume that the advanced guard will be prepared to receive the enemy at Champenois as soon as two battalions and a battery are in position there. This would occupy at least half an hour more. I leave the calculation to you.

At the time the first report was sent off, the three squadrons with the machine-gun detachment were, of course, still west of Vernéville, and we may assume that they will have compelled the enemy, who has only one squadron, to advance slowly, *as his reconnaissance will be crippled by our superiority in cavalry*, and he will have to advance with great caution. If ably led, it is *possible* that our cavalry may succeed in holding the west side of Vernéville for a time, but we cannot *depend* on the time above mentioned being gained. If, however, our cavalry fail to check the enemy's advance, the two opposing vanguards will come into conflict about Champenois—thus bringing about an encounter action, in entering on which it is doubtful whether the Champenois position can be maintained, as the woods close to and east of Chantrenne and the scattered copses north-east of Vernéville run so close to the two farms that they would *greatly facilitate an outflanking movement on the part of the enemy*. Another great disadvantage of the Champenois position is that its distance from the quarries of Amanweiler is such as to render questionable whether the main body of the 1st Division could lend the necessary support. From this it appears that *you had better abandon any idea of trying to occupy the Champenois position*.

We have, therefore, to choose between the position at the *Amanweiler quarries* and *that west of Amanweiler*.

An examination of the former shows, without going into details, that the position is not a bad one in itself. The position, however, is *too near the mouth of the defile*. Imagine the advanced guard engaged on a line extending from the quarries to a point west of Marengo. In such case the main body of the 1st Division would have to deploy in the narrow space between the quarries and the main road running to St. Privat—for the quarries themselves, though they would favour a passive defence, would impede the deployment of a large force, and especially its forward movement. All the columns would have to debouch from this one gap between the quarries and Marengo, under very insufficient cover (as an inspection of the hachures in the $\frac{1}{100,000}$ map, or, more clearly, of the contours in the $\frac{1}{25,000}$ map will show) of the insignificant ridge, which in reality is hardly perceptible, running from in front of the quarries towards St. Privat. Should the enemy succeed in placing artillery near Amanweiler, *an undisturbed deployment* of our main body would be out of the question. *On this account, I do not consider the position at the quarries a suitable one.*

In addition to the above considerations, it is desirable, with regard to the 2nd Division, that General A. take up a position *rather further to the west*. We are told that the 2nd Division will reach Moulins-bei-Metz about 1 p.m., so it will be 2 p.m. (3 miles) before it arrives on the high ground at Le Point-du-Jour. Our cavalry, however, has reported that what appears to be a strong column of the enemy is advancing through Mars-la-Tour and Vionville. How far this column had got was unknown, but, even assuming that the head of the column did not leave Mars-la-Tour till 9.35 a.m., it can (if it intends marching on Metz—and beyond a doubt it will) be at Le Point-du-Jour (a distance of $8\frac{1}{2}$ miles) about 12.20 p.m. At any rate this column, if it occupies the heights of Point-du-Jour, would very seriously embarrass the advance of the 2nd Division up the steep ascent from the Moselle valley (and doubtless the enemy has already been acquainted by his cavalry of the approach of the 2nd Division, irrespective of the fact that the inhabitants of the country are friendly to him, and will render him ample and reliable information). When, however, the officer commanding this hostile column learns that the column marching parallel with his is engaged with a strong body of the enemy between Vernéville and Amanweiler, he will probably feel disposed *to wait the development of the situation awhile* before crossing the Mance valley and taking up a position at Point-du-Jour, while matters wear such an uncertain aspect in the direction of his left flank. Should—though it is not likely—the enemy's southern column support the northern, if only by sending a detachment to assist it, so much the better for our 2nd Division. General A. will doubtless further the common cause by trying to hold a position west of Amanweiler, *where he will be on the flank of the Point-du-Jour position.*

So far we have no positive information as to how the enemy is advancing after passing Caulre, so General A. must for the present wait near Amanweiler before committing himself to the occupation of a definite position; that is to say, he must take up *a position of readiness* west of Amanweiler.

It is unlikely that the enemy, on ascertaining the presence of considerable bodies of troops in the neighbourhood of Amanweiler, will make a direct frontal attack on each side of the Vernéville–Amanweiler road; for this road is completely visible from height 331 south-west of Amanweiler (height marked 330·9 in the $\frac{1}{75,000}$ map), and from its easterly prolongation. He will probably combine his attack with an enveloping attack from the *north* or from the *south*.

The spinneys north-east of Vernéville and south of the Verdun railway will favour an attack from the north, but the spaces of open ground between them can be swept by fire from the high ground about 700 yards west of Amanweiler. *If the enemy move in this direction, General A.'s best position would be on both sides of the road from Amanweiler to Habonville, on the high ground referred to.*

If the enemy attack from *the south*, he would not find it enough to go round by Envie, as he would suffer heavy losses after passing that farm, but he would probably make a wider détour, through Chantrenne, and thence up the valley to La Folie, with a view to gaining the hill 340 north-west of La Folie. *In that case, General A. should take up a position for defence from the above-mentioned hill 331 to Montigny-la-Grange Castle inclusive, a building well adapted for defence.* It is more likely that the enemy *will* attack from the south, as he will thereby keep better touch with his own main column moving by the main road through Vionville. An attack from the south would likewise be less inconvenient to General A. than would one from the north, because Montigny castle makes an excellent supporting point for his left flank. Were he, on the contrary, compelled to occupy the northern position, he might have no option but to extend his line unduly, which is always dangerous.

The position of readiness must be so situated that the troops can rapidly occupy either the northern or the southern position. I should select *the west side of Amanweiler*, which is well covered from view by the high ground in front. Here, then, the bulk of the infantry will assemble. The entire length of the advanced guard being $2\frac{1}{2}$ miles, and the distance to be covered to the position about $1\frac{3}{4}$ miles, the whole force can be formed up on the west of Amanweiler, 85 minutes after 10 a.m.=11.25 a.m.

It is not advisable that General A. should issue the orders for taking up the position of readiness while he is at *the quarries*. Far better that these orders be issued *after making investigations on the spot*. For the present the whole force must anyhow continue marching as before, so there is no urgent need for orders to be issued.

ADVANCED-GUARD ACTION

Not so, however, as regards the *orders for the cavalry*, to whose action there now attaches the utmost importance. The three squadrons have a twofold duty to perform, to delay the enemy's advance and render such prompt information as to the manner in which he is deploying as to enable General A. to decide quickly which of the abovementioned positions he will defend.

The best means of checking the enemy's advance is by the fire of dismounted men from the west side of Vernéville. This will compel him to deploy some infantry, as for cavalry to seek to *gain time* by *charging* infantry would lead to *losses out of all proportion to the effect produced. Neither would much time be gained*, even by a successful charge, as its effect lasts but a few moments. The machine-gun detachment forms a most valuable accessory.

It may or may not be possible to deceive the enemy as to the number of the troops barring his advance and as to what arm they belong, but we must, at any rate, endeavour to do so. We may, of course, safely assume that the officer commanding the cavalry has already, of his own motion, thought of checking the enemy at Vernéville; still it will be as well not to depend on it, but send him an *express order* to the effect that you expect him to make a brief stand at Vernéville. If he has already thought of doing so, your order will show him that such action will be in conformity with your view of the general situation, which will be satisfactory to him.

While on this subject I recommend you to read once more in (Engl.) *Cavalry Training* (sects. 141 and 152) *the principles* laid down there *for dismounted action of cavalry*. In the present case one of the squadrons must be told off for a "*mounted reserve*," to watch the enemy's advance, especially *from a position on the flanks;* for the copses north-west and south-west of Vernéville, from which a sudden assault might be made on the village, call for special precautionary measures on our part. Active patrolling is not enough, but whole troops must be employed to drive back the enemy's cavalry *on its own infantry*. This leaves two squadrons for dismounted action; the led horses being kept under cover *as near as possible to the firing line*, and well out of view from *any* part of the country in front. If the *usual* procedure in the dismounted action of a squadron is followed, *i.e.* with the led horses *mobile and not in a fixed position*, each squadron can bring into action half its strength, say 60 men dismounted, so there are 120 men available for fire action, no supports being necessary. *If the led horses can be left permanently in one place*, we shall be able to hold the border of the village in much greater strength. *The task in hand each time* determines whether the led horses should be *mobile* or *remain permanently in one place*. In the present case there are good reasons for *either* procedure; but I prefer here *the latter*, because the led horses can be kept under perfect cover quite close to the firing line.

You will find details for attaching *machine-gun detachments* to the independent cavalry in the (English) *Infantry Training*, 1911, paras. 160-166.

The officer commanding the cavalry is responsible for Vernéville being evacuated in good time, after which his duty is to find out in what manner the enemy is deploying for attack. *How* he will proceed depends on the enemy's movements. In any case patrols must watch the ground between Champenois and Anoux-la-Grange, and between Champenois and Malmaison, to notice the first signs of the enemy diverging to north or south of the main road. It is also of importance to General A. to learn what is going on on the Gravelotte-Vionville road. An officer's patrol can furnish this information.

Above all things the orders must reach the cavalry *as quickly as possible; every moment is precious; and the orders should find the cavalry still in Vernéville*. They should, therefore, be despatched immediately on receipt of the first report. You might first despatch a cyclist (better two) with the written order, and then an orderly officer; the cyclist will no doubt arrive before the officer; the danger of the cavalry having left Vernéville before the arrival of the order is thus lessened (*G.F.S.R.*, para. 84).[1] The orderly officer is meant to inform the cavalry commander on the general situation (*G.F.S.R.*, para. 71).

We will assume that the process of arriving at a decision and dictating the orders occupies five minutes. The cavalry are still west of Vernéville, *i.e.* about 4½ miles from the Amanweiler quarries, and should receive the orders in 14 minutes, *i.e.* at 10.19; for a cyclist can cover a mile on a good road in about 3 minutes; a well-mounted orderly officer in 4 minutes. The use of the cavalry-telegraph between Vernéville and Amanweiler is not admissible here. Why not?

The orders to the cavalry are as follows:—

To Lieut.-Colonel ——, *commanding advanced cavalry west of* **VERNÉVILLE.**

AMANWEILER *Quarries*,
1.9.00.

No. 1.

1. *The Advanced Guard* will take up a position of readiness immediately west of **AMANWEILER**, where the head of the vanguard will arrive at 10.35 a.m.

2. *The* 1st *Dragoons* will endeavour to check the enemy by holding **VERNÉVILLE** with dismounted men, and will keep a look-out towards **ANOUX-LA-GRANGE, BAGNEUX,** and **MALMAISON.** An officer's patrol to be detached to reconnoitre the **GRAVELOTTE–VIONVILLE** road

3. *Reports* to the high ground marked 331 south-west of **AMANWEILER.**

In writing to O.C. cavalry by cyclists and by orderly officer, 10.5 a.m.

A.,
Major-General, Commanding Advanced Guard 1st Division.

[1] *E.F.S.R.*, Part I, sect. 20.—*Trans.*

It must not be supposed that, having despatched these orders to his cavalry, the advanced-guard commander has nothing more to do.

General A. must now *report*, not only to his own main body, but also to the general officer commanding the two divisions, that he has encountered the enemy. Were the news far less important than it is, it would be General A.'s duty to report it in detail, because it is the *first encounter* with a hostile force, concerning which up to the present next to nothing was known, and *information of this nature is of the utmost value to the various headquarters of the higher units*.

General A.'s report must contain, to begin with, *a repetition, word for word, of the cavalry report*. Next will come a statement that he *intends* taking up a position of readiness, together with a brief exposition of the *reasons* which have induced him to select the position west of Amanweiler, and the substance of *the orders just sent to the cavalry*, as it is necessary that the officer commanding the main body should have a general idea what measures have already been adopted with a view to reconnaissance before he arrives at Amanweiler and takes over the command. A statement should also be made that a *report was sent at the same time* to the commander of the *whole* force.

It now becomes necessary to establish close connection with the main body of the 1st Division, as well as with the headquarters of the 2nd Division, and with General Headquarters. As the roads are good cyclists will be used. Of course it would be desirable to have telephone connection now with the main body of the Division; it would have been the duty of the Division to establish such connection, but for some reason or other this has not been done. The infantry telephone detachments are not available for that purpose, as they are needed to establish connection between the various portions of the advanced guard itself.

ADVANCED-GUARD ACTION

To Lieut.-General B., commanding 1st Division,
on the road to **HAUCONCOURT**.

AMANWEILER *Quarries*,
1.9.00.

REPORT NO. 1.

O.C. 1st Dragoons reports: "Column on the march through **ST. MARCEL**, strength estimated at 4 or 5 battalions and 2 batteries, but only 1 squadron. Its vanguard reached **CAULRE** at 9.35 a.m., and is moving on **VERNÉVILLE**. Tail of the column was then at **GREYÈRES**. Another strong column moving through **MARS-LA-TOUR** on **VIONVILLE**. No enemy on main road between **DONCOURT-EN-JARNISY** and **JARNY**."

Have sent orders to O.C. 1st Dragoons to check the enemy at **VERNÉVILLE** with dismounted men. The advanced guard is about to take up a position of readiness just west of **AMANWEILER**, where my vanguard will arrive at 10.35 a.m. I shall defend the ground west of **AMANWEILER** with the object of covering the deployment of the Division. I am observing in the direction of **ANOUX-LA-GRANGE, BAGNEUX, MALMAISON,** and through **GRAVELOTTE** towards **VIONVILLE**. I am reporting to General Headquarters.

By cyclist,
10.5 a.m.

A.,
Major-General, Commanding
Advanced Guard, 1st Division.

The report sent to General Headquarters comprises firstly a literal repetition of the report received from the cavalry, as above; after which comes the following:—

"I am about to take up a position with the Advanced Guard west of Amanweiler. Am observing in the direction of Anoux-la-Grange, Bagneux, Malmaison, and Vionville. The main body of the 1st Division, to which I am sending a report, has been delayed two hours in leaving Hauconcourt."

After the despatch of these reports General A. and his staff will ride at a rapid pace to hill 331 south-west of Amanweiler, to look round before issuing the orders for occupying a position of readiness. Officers commanding units will likewise assemble at the above-mentioned hill, in order to receive the orders verbally.

Meanwhile, General A. receives the second report from his cavalry.

This will *in no wise* affect his plans, for it merely shows that his superiority in cavalry has produced the expected result of delaying the enemy's advance, so that the advanced guard will not be interfered with while marching to its position of readiness. The situation, however, is in other respects much the same as before, so it is *too soon* to think about *taking up* a position for defence.

It is *not* absolutely essential to forward the second report received from the cavalry to the officer commanding 1st Division, for it would tell him nothing new; but it would be advisable to do so, as it will show him that the advanced-guard commander will be able to *carry out* his intention, as announced before, of occupying a position of readiness west of Amanweiler, *without being interfered with by the enemy*. On the other hand, a report to General Headquarters is quite unnecessary.

The report to General B. will be as follows:—

*To Lieut.-General B., commanding 1st Division
on the road to* **HAUCONCOURT**.

Hill 331, S.W. of
AMANWEILER,
1.9.00.

REPORT No. 2.

O.C. 1st Dragoons reports that "the enemy is advancing very slowly on **VERNÉVILLE**, and that at 10.25 a.m. a weak firing line had occupied small copse half-way between **CAULRE** and **VERNÉVILLE**." My vanguard has just passed through **AMANWEILER**.

By cyclist,
10.40 a.m.

A.,
*Major-General, commanding
Advanced Guard 1st Division.*

In the meantime the subordinate commanders join the officer commanding the advanced guard, and now learn for the first time, through the medium of the orders, that the cavalry has encountered the enemy, whose strength, by the way, need be only approximately indicated in the orders.

The march orders for the 1st Division will have already informed the subordinate commanders that the 2nd Division is moving through Metz, so no further reference need be made to this. It must be notified, however, that the main body of the 1st Division has suffered a delay, although such information partakes of the nature of *unfavourable news;* still it is necessary that all should know that the advanced guard is temporarily *thrown on its own resources*, as this circumstance must influence the action of every subordinate commander, more particularly with reference to *economising reserves*. It would be a *mistake to follow without consideration the general rule*, previously mentioned, *that unfavourable news should be concealed as far as possible. To do so in the present instance might lead to serious errors on the part of subordinate commanders.*

The cavalry have already been informed what they have to do; still I would include among the orders the reconnaissance that is required of them, so that the other subordinate commanders may clearly comprehend the arrangements made.

As soon as it comes to fighting, *artillery* will play the principal part, as the object is to *gain time*. For this purpose the guns had better take up a *position of readiness*, under cover of the so-often-mentioned hill 331. At present it is hardly possible to decide the exact position for the batteries. For all we know, we may even have to defend a position altogether different from the one we have in view. The only thing for the artillery to do is to watch the enemy's advance and wait.

Whatever turn the action may take, however, the hill 331 is *sure* to play an important part; it should therefore be at once occupied by the first infantry to arrive. Four companies may be detailed for the purpose, which will ensure an effective infantry fire from the outset, and prevent the artillery, when it comes into position on the hill, being exposed too soon to the enemy's infantry fire. For this latter purpose the infantry can be pushed out some 600 yards in front of the guns, a detail to which the orders need not refer, but which can be arranged on the spot.

The village of Amanweiler itself is not very well suited for defence, as it has a *limited field of fire ;* it could only be utilised as a *rallying position* should we have to retreat from a position in front. In such event the edge of the village must be *obstinately held*, so it will be as well for the engineers at once to *prepare the western outskirts for defence ;* especially as, in view of the uncertainty that exists as to where and how we shall have to stand on the defensive later on, it is impossible to make preparations for defence, except as regards hill 331. This will leave the engineers free to strengthen the village. The *Dressing Station* will probably have to be established in Amanweiler, but I would say nothing about it in the orders, as it will be time enough to do so later on, when we know something definite as to how the enemy is going to attack. On the other hand, it will be as well for the orders to lay down that the extra ammunition is to be issued from the S.A.A. carts with the battalions, as it is doubtful whether there will be time for this later on. No order can be given about the *2nd Line Transport*, as it is far behind with the rest of the transport of the 1st Division, and under the orders of General B.

Copy No. 1.

OPERATION ORDER No. 2
BY
MAJOR-GENERAL A., COMMANDING ADVANCED GUARD.

Reference:
$\frac{1}{100,000}$ *Ordn.*

Height 331, S.W. of
AMANWEILER,
1.9.00.

1. *A Hostile Column* consisting of several battalions and two batteries is advancing from **CAULRE** on **VERNÉVILLE**.

2. *The Advanced Guard*, which can expect no reinforcements for two hours, will take up a position of readiness west of **AMANWEILER**. To-day's march orders are cancelled.

3. *The 1st Dragoons* are watching the enemy in the direction of **ANOUX - LA - GRANGE, BAGNEUX, MALMAISON,** and **VIONVILLE**.

ADVANCED-GUARD ACTION

4. *The Artillery* will move forward at the trot, passing the infantry to the right, and take up a position of readiness immediately east of the hill 331, south-west of **AMANWEILER**. The light ammunition column is placed at the disposal of the O.C. Artillery.

5. *Four Companies of I/Battalion* will at once occupy the above-mentioned hill. *The remainder of the infantry and the sections Field Ambulance* will be formed up immediately west of **AMANWEILER**. The battalions to be in line of quarter-columns.

6. *The 1st Field Co. R.E.* will at once put the west side of **AMANWEILER** in a state of defence, and the I/Battalion will construct shelter trenches on the hill 331, south-west of **AMANWEILER**.

7. *The ammunition of the 4 S.A.A. carts of each battalion* will at once be issued; the two other carts of each battalion will remain at my disposal.

8. *Reports* to the high ground 331, south-west of **AMANWEILER**.

Verbally to the assembled
commanding officers.

In writing to O.C. 1st
Dragoons by N.C.O.
10.45 a.m.

A.,
Major-General.

I do not approve of a suggestion which has been made to the effect that the cavalry should fall back on Champenois, or to a point west of Amanweiler, to cover the artillery, who are to move into position while the rest of the advanced guard is forming up. Such an arrangement would not ensure adequate protection to the guns against surprise, as three squadrons and the machine-gun detachment are not sufficient escort. Though the presence of only *one* hostile squadron is reported so far, it is impossible to say whether the enemy's cavalry might not, *contrary to all expectations*, suddenly be reinforced, and if so, it would be *doubtful* whether our three squadrons could gain the necessary time for the guns to limber up.

The only preparation for defence that can be made is to throw up trenches on hill 331, which is the only point which is tolerably *certain* to be attacked, no matter what turn the action may take. Any other points outlining a possible future position, such as Montigny-la-Grange, cannot be occupied until it has become evident that the enemy will attack them. It will, for instance, be useless to have occupied Montigny at the outset, if the enemy eventually attacks the northern flank. *At the moment of issuing the orders there is absolutely nothing to show whether it will be to the north or to the south of the hill 331 that we shall subsequently have to deploy.* Under such circumstances the G.O.C. cannot commit himself to any position in particular, but must reserve to himself the fullest *freedom of decision*.

The preparation of Amanweiler for defence may be of use to us, no matter which of the two positions is occupied. It may be as well to say that *at the outset no garrison need be detailed for Amanweiler*, as it would be wrong to tell off a reserve to cover the line of retreat instead of employing it in the main action.

In conclusion, let me advise you to work out a continuation of the problem on the following data :—

At 11.15 a.m. the officer commanding the cavalry reports from the east side of Vernéville : " Have just been compelled to retire from VERNÉVILLE, which is occupied by a battalion of the enemy. During my retreat have been fired on by batteries in position about a mile west of VERNÉVILLE. A long column of the enemy, estimated at 3 battalions, on the road from CAULRE to LA HAYE-AUX-MURES ; its head just reached the VERNÉVILLE–GRAVELOTTE road. I am falling back on ENVIE."

I intentionally omit the solution to this problem, as you can hardly go wrong.

ADVANCED-GUARD ACTION

TWENTY-FIRST EXERCISE.

(See general map and the maps Verny and Ars-a.d.-Mosel.)

An Army Corps (two divisions), operating in an enemy's country, is advancing viâ Remilly and Delme (general map, the former on the Strassburg railway, the latter on the Strassburg main road) on the unfortified town of Metz. On the 1.7.00 it detaches a force consisting of 6 battalions infantry, 2 squadrons, and 3 field batteries, through Vigny (general map), on Verny, with orders to advance west of the Hospital Wald on Metz. The advanced guard of this detached force consists of 2 battalions, 2 squadrons, 1 battery, and $\frac{1}{3}$ light ammunition column, and is commanded by Colonel B. The head of its vanguard has reached Pouilly at 2 p.m., when Colonel B. receives the following order from General N., commanding detached force :—

Copy No. 2.

OPERATION ORDER No. 4[1]
BY
MAJOR-GENERAL N., COMMANDING DETACHED FORCE.

Reference: *Brick-kiln west of* **FLEURY**,
$\frac{1}{100,000}$ *Ordn.* 1.7.00.

1. *The Enemy*, having advanced from Diedenhofen through Metz, is said by inhabitants to have occupied **SABLON** with infantry. Hostile cavalry patrols are reported at **GRIGY, HAUTE-BÉVOYE, HORGNE-AU-SABLON, GRANGE-AUX-ORMES**, and south of **AUGNY**.

2. *The Main Body* will billet to-night in **VERNY, POURNOY-LA-GRASSE**, and **CHÉRISEY**.

3. *The Advanced Guard* will billet its main guard in **FLEURY**, and place outposts as far as the **SEILLE** in prolongation of the outposts established by the remainder of the Army Corps, which are on the line **ARS-LAQUENEXY–GROSSER WALD VON CHAMPEL**—northern point of the **WALD VON CRÉPY** inclusive. Reconnoitring on both sides of the **SEILLE** towards **MONTIGNY, SABLON**, and **QUEULEU**.

4. *Should the Enemy attack*, the advanced guard will hold the ground at **POUILLY**.

---

[1] *G.F.S.R.*, para. 220; *E.F.S.R.*, Part I, sects. 76 (1), 78 (1).—*Trans.*

5. The Advanced Guard may order *its 2nd Line Transport* to join it.

6. *Headquarters of the Detached Force* will billet in **VERNY**.

In writing by orderly officer.

1.45 p.m.

N.,
Major-General.

Required :—
1. The orders of Colonel B.
2. A rough sketch showing the way in which the main guard is billeted in Fleury, the positions of guards and sentries, and the alarm posts.

MODEL FOR

ORDERS FOR AN ADVANCED GUARD TO TAKE UP AN OUTPOST LINE AND OCCUPY BILLETS

(*G.F.S.R.*, para. 221 ; *E.F.S.R.*, Part I, sect. 78 (2).)

Copy No......

OPERATION ORDER No......

BY

..........COMMANDING ADVANCED GUARD.

Reference :
map used.

Place.
Date.

Distribution of troops.

1. *Main Guard*, etc.
2. *Outposts :* Outpost Commander, etc.

(This distribution can be omitted where small bodies are dealt with ; the body of the order will then contain what is necessary to mention.)

1. Information as to *the enemy* and *our other forces.* (Position of the main body, touch with neighbouring troops.)

2. Arrangements *for the troops not detailed for outpost duty.* (Billets of main guard, appointment of a cantonment commandant—any special measures for reconnaissance by cavalry not detailed for outpost duty ; statement how far in front the outpost cavalry has to watch the country ; any special measures for security to be taken by the main guard direct ; touch with neighbouring units ; alarm post for the main guard when necessary.)

ADVANCED-GUARD ACTION

3. Order detailing the *outpost commander* and the *troops* under his command. General statement as to the line to be occupied or roads to be watched. (In the case of a detachment, seldom necessary to divide the line into sections, each under a separate outpost commander.) Reconnaissance. Special missions.

4. Dispositions in case of being attacked. (Retiring or holding fast; localities which require to be specially held.)

5. Under certain circumstances special arrangements for the *2nd Line Transport* (especially whether to accompany the outpost troops or not).

6. *Position of officer commanding advanced guard.*

Manner of communicating
the orders to the troops.
Hour of issue.

Signature.

TWENTY-SECOND LETTER

ORDERS FOR AN ADVANCED GUARD TO TAKE UP AN OUTPOST LINE AND OCCUPY BILLETS

EXPERIENCE has shown me that outpost orders are the most difficult of all, until you have had some practice in framing them, so I cannot do better than repeat the advice I have so often given you, viz. to imagine yourself in the actual situation with which you are dealing, and then you will be able to adopt the proper measures in conformity with the instructions contained in the *Field Service Regulations*. There is more than one way of solving all outpost problems, more so than is the case with all other exercises in applied tactics, so there need be no occasion for surprise if in places your conclusions are totally different to mine. The great point is not to violate any of the principles laid down in the *Field Service Regulations*, which, however, permit *the utmost latitude* in all matters of secondary importance, more especially in connection with outposts, *for nothing in tactics is so impatient of the fetters of hard-and-fast rules under ever-varying circumstances as the service of outposts* (G.F.S.R., para. 200).[1]

My object in premising in the data so large a detachment as six battalions, the advanced guard being of corresponding strength, was to have an opportunity of discussing the subject of "advanced-guard orders directing the occupation of an outpost line." The advanced guard of a small detachment seldom exceeds a battalion with some cavalry—the whole of which would generally be required for outposts.

[1] *E.F.S.R.*, Part I, sect. 75.—*Trans.*

ADVANCED-GUARD ORDERS

In such case the advanced-guard commander becomes the outpost commander, causing advanced guard and outpost orders to be one and the same.

At the moment when the detachment halts, the cavalry is actively engaged in reconnaissance, its patrols providing for security while the outpost line is being taken up (*G.F.S.R.*, para. 207). What has hitherto been the vanguard *ceases to act that part*, and the advanced guard now falls into *outposts* and *main guard* (*G.F.S.R.*, para. 204).

The officer commanding the advanced guard will be somewhere on the main road, south of Pouilly, and will give his orders *as quickly as possible, trusting entirely to the map* (*G.F.S.R.*, para. 221).[1] Any delay will deprive the troops of some of their rest. It is therefore best to make arrangements *promptly*, even if it becomes necessary later on to make changes. It may be here noticed, although it is anticipating events to do so, that the same considerations affect the outpost commander, though he, being *more concerned with details*, will rapidly survey the actual ground from some suitable point before issuing his orders.

As the officer commanding the advanced guard knows that the rest of the outposts of the Army Corps extend to the northern point of the Wald von Crépy, the map will show him that his outposts must carry on the line to the Seille, which will protect the left flank (*G.F.S.R.*, para. 203).[2] That is all that need be told the outpost commander, whose business it is to see to everything else. As the enemy is apparently so near that he could without much difficulty reach and surprise Fleury, it will be necessary, not only to block the roads, but also to watch the country between them, to prevent the enemy penetrating unnoticed either with patrols or in greater strength. A battalion and half a squadron are sufficient; for, under ordinary circumstances, as here, they can watch a front of about 3 miles.

The duty of the cavalry attached to the outposts is to

---

[1] *E.F.S.R.*, Part I, sect. 78.—*Trans.*
[2] *Ibid.*, sect. 76.—*Trans.*

reconnoitre only far enough to ensure *protection, distant reconnoitring* being the duty of the cavalry not belonging to the outposts.

Artillery and machine-guns are *very seldom* required in outposts, such as when one wishes to hold extremely important defiles. They would be placed in position at some suitable point *during the day only*, and be brought into a place of the main guard at night.

In connection with the *strength* of outposts, remember that every horse and every man on outposts at night loses his rest, and *therefore cannot be fit for much next day*. As few troops as possible should consequently be employed. You should always ask yourself the question, " What arrangement will enable me to do with *as few troops as possible?* "

If you have in front of you some *obstacle* with few points of passage across it (river, swampy meadows, etc.)—if there is a *range of heights* affording a *good view* over the whole country in front—if the *flanks* of the outpost line *rest on natural obstacles or on other troops*, thus rendering it unnecessary to double them back, you can do with fewer troops. These three points should be specially attended to.

There is another subject of some importance on which I should like to say a few words. It frequently happens that when an obstacle, such as the St. Peter brook in the present instance, is in the front, and the troops have to continue their advance next day, either the whole advanced guard or only the outposts are placed *on the side of the obstacle nearer the enemy*, with a view to *securing the passage of the main body*. In the present instance the advanced guard is not intended to secure the latter, as the main guard is under orders to stop in Fleury; neither is it necessary to push the outposts so far out, as the St. Peter brook is too insignificant to be worth securing in itself; and, once across it, we should have to advance the outpost line right up to the Seille, north of Magny—which is too far. It may be asked whether, by holding the line of the

ADVANCED-GUARD ORDERS

brook, we cannot do with fewer troops for outposts; but it is too insignificant as an obstacle. Infantry could cross it nearly anywhere, even at night, without much difficulty. Though this is not likely, it would nevertheless be necessary to double back to the Seille, the left flank thus annulling any seeming advantage of sparing men. *The best position is on the high ground between the Hospital Wald and the Seille*, which affords such a good view, and has its left flank so secured, that it can be held by comparatively few troops.

There are bridges over the Seille at Marly and Moulin-de-Fleury. That at Marly ought not to be destroyed (though such a measure might make the flank additionally secure), as we shall require to make use of it *for reconnoitring* west of the Seille during the night and next morning. As to the bridge at Moulin-de-Fleury, it may be either destroyed or kept for the passage of reconnoitring patrols; in the latter case special measures must be taken *by the main guard* for holding it, as it is beyond the sphere of the outposts. A piquet commanded by an officer must, therefore, be sent thither *from Fleury*.

In case of the enemy attacking, the outposts, supported if necessary by the rest of the advanced guard, must check his advance until the main body of the detachment is ready for action, or for marching, as the case may be. The detachment orders distinctly state that the Pouilly position is to be held. If they had not expressly said so, the advanced-guard orders would have to make it clear, whether the outposts should hold on until the main guard arrives in support, or whether the outposts should withdraw on the main guard (in this case on Fleury). If Pouilly, from which there is a good field of fire to north and west, is to be held as long as possible, the country between Pouilly and the Hospital Wald must not be left open to the enemy, so the defence must extend up to the wood (hill marked 217·9).

The portion of the advanced guard which is not detailed for outpost duty go to Fleury, and the question has now to be considered whether these troops are to be sheltered in *ordinary billets, close billets,* or *alarm quarters* (G.F.S.R., paras. 375, 386).[1]

As an additional measure of security I would order four companies to occupy alarm quarters, and the remainder ordinary billets.

Colonel B., as the senior officer in Fleury, would be *cantonment commandant,* but can appoint a field officer for this duty (G.F.S.R., para. 382). It is the duty of the cantonment commandant, as different units will jointly occupy Fleury, to see to the distribution of quarters, and to take all necessary measures with regard to *interior economy, external measures of protection,* and the *readiness of the troops for action.*

Time will not, in the present instance, admit of making *elaborate preparations* for distributing the various units in the village; the *more summary method* described in paragraph 380 of (German)[2] *Field Service Regulations* must be adopted. Colonel B. will, therefore, appoint the officer commanding II/Battalion *cantonment commandant,* and direct him to *proceed in advance* to Fleury, accompanied by the quartermasters, etc., from each unit. The cantonment commandant will be assisted in his duties by an *officer for cantonment duty,* who accompanies him.

With regard to the *2nd line transport,* the advanced-guard commander must arrange whether it be placed at the disposal of the outposts and main guard or not, unless orders have already been issued on this subject by superior authority. If he thinks it very likely that the enemy will attack, he will leave the transport south of Fleury, or only allow the troops in Fleury to have access to it, and not encumber the outpost troops with unwieldy baggage-wagons, or run the risk of the latter being captured. On the other hand, it should be remembered that it is of importance to the troops to have access to their baggage,

[1] *E.F.S.R.,* Part 1, sects. 45 and 54.—*Trans.*
[2] *Ibid.,* sect. 51.—*Trans.*

every day, if possible, if only for a few hours; it is a convenience to all ranks of which they should not be deprived unless absolutely necessary. Neither is there any occasion for anxiety concerning the safety of the transport at night, as it is *seldom* that attacks are made on outposts by night, although there is always the possibility of them. In spite of the comparative proximity of the enemy, therefore, I would allow the 2nd line regimental transport to join both the main guard and the outposts—*the latter for a few hours*. The outpost commander will be responsible for promptly sending back the transport in case the enemy attacks. In cases where the country is less favourable than here, or where the enemy is even nearer than in the present instance, not only outposts and main guard, but even the main body may have to do without their baggage for days together, *though it is a great hardship to all ranks*. The advanced-guard commander will, therefore, order the 2nd line regimental transport to be brought up on the main road as far as the Fleury brick-kiln (" Zgl." on map), where instructions will await it from Fleury and from the outpost commander.

Copy No. 1.

OPERATION ORDER No. 2
BY
COLONEL B., COMMANDING ADVANCED GUARD.

Reference: *Main road south of* **POUILLY**,
$\frac{1}{100.000}$ *Ordn.*   1.7.00.

1. *The Enemy's infantry* is said to have reached **SABLON**, and his patrols have been seen near **HAUTE-BÉVOYE, HORGNE-AU-SABLON, GRANGE-AUX-ORMES,** and south of **AUGNY**.—*Our Army Corps* has occupied an outpost line from **ARS-LAQUENEXY** to the north corner of the **WALD VON CRÉPY** inclusive. *The main body of our detached force* is billeted in **VERNY, CHÉRISEY,** and **POURNOY-LA-GRASSE.**

2. *The Main Guard*, that is to say the II/Battalion (which will place two companies in alarm quarters on the north side of **FLEURY** and two companies in alarm quarters at the brick-

kiln on the main road), half 1ˢᵗ and the II/1ˢᵗ Dragoons, the 1ˢᵗ Field Artillery Battery, and ½ Light Ammunition Column will occupy billets in **FLEURY**. The cavalry will constantly reconnoitre west of the **SEILLE** towards **MONTIGNY** and **AUGNY**. Lieut.-Colonel C. is appointed Cantonment Commandant, and will place an officer's picquet on the **SEILLE** crossing at **MOULIN-DE-FLEURY**.

3. *Lieut.-Colonel D.* will take up a line of outposts with the I/Battalion and half I/1ˢᵗ Dragoons in continuation of the outposts of the Army Corps, and will be responsible from the north corner of the **WALD VON CRÉPY** exclusive to the **SEILLE**. Reconnoitring east of the **SEILLE** towards **SABLON** and **QUEULEU**.

4. *If the Enemy attacks,* the advanced guard will hold the position from hill 217·9, east of **POUILLY**, to **POUILLY**, both inclusive.

5. *The 2nd Line Regimental Transport* will move up to the brick-kiln of **FLEURY**, and can then join the main guard and the outposts.

6. *Reports* will reach me at the Mayor's house in **FLEURY**.

               B.,
In writing to the O.C. Cavalry   *Colonel.*
 by orderly officer.
Verbally to the other commanding officers.
   2.5 p.m

Lieut.-Colonel C., by the summary method, marks off the village of Fleury by the main streets into three districts. That on the north-west and north side, which is most exposed to danger, will be occupied by infantry only; that on the south side, which is safest, by artillery and ½ light ammunition column only (*G.F.S.R.*, paras. 380, 381);[1] and the central district, which is of circular shape, can be jointly occupied by cavalry and infantry—the former using the stables which are there. Lieut.-Colonel C. will select one of the big farm-buildings near the road on the north side of the village as alarm quarters for two companies; and all further details will be arranged by the quarter-

[1] *E.F.S.R.*, Part I, sects. 45 and 51.—*Trans.*

masters. The troops can now march in. The officer for cantonment duty will first decide the position of the inlying guard and its sentries. It should consist of as few men as possible. The battalion will furnish a N.C.O. to command this guard, and the bugler ; also a sentry over the colours, and one over the transport of the battalion, which will be parked somewhere in the village. The squadron posts a sentry over its transport, the battery a sentry on its gun-park and the light ammunition column, which are stationed near the southern exit of Fleury. With a small force like this it is not necessary to have a piquet for police purposes, otherwise the infantry would furnish it. The position of the inlying guard is communicated to the *battalion officer of the day*, and *the squadron* and *battery N.C.O. of the day* on their reporting themselves to the officer on cantonment duty (*G.F.S.R.*, para. 384). The latter will, *at the same time*, inform them of *the arrangements made with regard to outlying guards* and *alarm posts*, and any *other special arrangements*. The officer for cantonment duty ought to get this finished in good time, so that all orders may be communicated to the men before they disperse to their quarters.

For the close protection of Fleury, with the outposts so close at hand, a few N.C.O.'s posts, which will be furnished by the two companies in alarm quarters at the northern exit, will be sufficient (*G.F.S.R.*, para. 385). There is no need for a particular outlying guard (*E.F.S.R.*, Part I, sects. 47–49).

A *N.C.O.'s Post* (No. 1) holds the road-fork (218) east of Fleury, to watch in the direction of the Hospital Wald.

A *N.C.O.'s Post* (No. 2) stands on the northern *road joining the village with the main road*, at a point due north of the north-west angle of the village.

The two companies in alarm quarters at the brick-kiln push a post (1 N.C.O., 9 men) to the house at the junction of the road from Moulin-de-Fleury with the main road. These two companies furnish a piquet (1 officer, 12 men) in Moulin-de-Fleury.

The cantonment commandant will fix the various *alarm posts* (G.F.S.R., para. 389) (E.F.S.R., Part I, sect. 47 (3)). The brick-kiln would be held by the two companies already there, who can thence flank with their fire the west side of the village. The best place for the alarm post for the other six companies is at the main entrance to the village in the middle of the north side.

The best place for the alarm post of the squadron is *outside the village*, not in the narrow streets where there is no room to move. You have the choice between the outlet facing the brick-kiln and the outlet of the path to the Hospital Wald; for the outlet facing Notre Dame must be reserved for the battery and ammunition column, otherwise the cavalry and the artillery would get into each other's way in reaching their alarm post. The outlet of the footpath is, however, *unsuitable*, as it is too narrow, so the alarm post of the squadron will be fixed at the outlet facing the brick-kiln.

The alarm post of the battery and of the light ammunition column is at the outlet facing Notre Dame.

A distinction must be made between the alarm posts of the various units here referred to, and an *alarm rendezvous* of large bodies of troops. In the present instance the officer commanding the advanced guard has not, in his advanced-guard orders, fixed any alarm rendezvous for the whole main guard, but desires that the various units, after falling in at their various alarm posts, await further orders. Should it, however, be desired that the main guard *assemble* somewhere *with as little delay as possible*, the advanced-guard orders must contain the following: " Alarm rendezvous for the main guard at the southern outlet of Pouilly." In that case the various units would first of all fall in at their various alarm posts, and then march to the southern outlet at Pouilly. An alarm rendezvous, however, is, as a rule, only resorted to when the commander can see from the very outset that his whole force will have to come into action from one fixed point.

ADVANCED-GUARD ORDERS

Finally, Lieut.-Colonel C. would have to draw up a set of rules in compliance with paragraphs 395, 397–403 of the (German) *Field Service Regulations* (E.F.S.R., Part I, sects. 47–49, and 52).

TWENTY-SECOND EXERCISE

(N.B.—Use the $\frac{1}{25,000}$ map.)

Give the outpost orders issued by Lieut.-Colonel D. in pursuance of the advanced-guard orders in the previous exercise, showing on the map the position of the outposts, including sentry and vedette posts, and state the strength of the various fractions of the outpost line. (Explanations are required.)

At 4 p.m. the following report is received from the cavalry:—

"Small bodies of hostile cavalry (6 to 8 troopers each) are posted just south of **ST. PRIVAT** (south of **MONTIGNY**), at the bridge by which the main road crosses the **SEILLE**, south of **SABLON**, and on the hill west of **HAUTE-BÉVOYE**. An infantry post is stationed on the main road at the southern exit of **SABLON** to **MAGNY**."

MODEL FOR

OUTPOST ORDERS FOR MIXED OUTPOSTS.

Copy No......

OPERATION ORDER No......

BY

Lieut.-Colonel........., Commanding Outposts.

Reference: *Place.*
Map used.   *Date.*

1. Information as to the *enemy* and *our other forces*. (Places where the main body and the main guard are billeted. Mention of any neighbouring outposts furnished by our other forces.)

2. *Task of the Outpost Troops.* (Troops composing the outposts, and a very general statement as to the line to be occupied.)

3. *Order for the Outpost Mounted Troops.* (Either charging officer commanding outpost mounted troops with reconnoitring and securing the whole outpost line, or distributing the mounted troops among the outpost companies in small parties. Where to place the mounted troops, detailing orderlies, feeding, off-saddling, shifting saddles.)

4. *Order for the Outpost Companies.* (Begin from the right flank, assigning a definite part of the outpost line to the outpost companies, their approximate positions. Reconnoitring.)

5. *Order for the Reserve of Outposts.* (Troops, position, officer for cantonment or bivouac duty. Any measures to be adopted for security by the reserve.)

6. *Dispositions in case enemy attacks.* (Line or localities to be held.)

7. *Arrangements for supplies.* (*G.F.S.R.*, para. 276; *E.F.S.R.*, Part I, sect. 78 (2) (vi.)).

8. *Position of Outpost Commander.* (With the reserve as a rule.)

How issued; to whom; at what time.   Signature.

NOTE.—The outpost commander has, as a rule, two sets of orders to give. The first contains the most urgent measures to set the service of outposts quickly in operation; the second is not issued till later on, after an examination of the situation on the actual ground, and comprises the requisite supplementary orders, such as degree of readiness for action, position of the outpost mounted troops during night, entrenchments and obstacles, readiness to fight or march next morning, concentration of outpost cavalry next morning. This will ensure unity of action within the outpost line.

TWENTY-THIRD LETTER

(In continuation of the preceding Letter.)

OUTPOST ORDERS

IN the present instance Lieut.-Colonel D., with the senior major and his adjutant, will not be long in reaching the hill north of Pouilly at a gallop, where, after a rapid survey of the ground, he can, with the help of the map, frame his orders. There is no doubt that a *more thorough* examination of the ground would ensure a *more perfect* arrangement of outposts. Such, however, would take a long time, and the main thing is to post *quickly* troops to provide for immediate security against surprise, and let the remaining troops *quickly* come to rest (*G.F.S.R.*, para. 225). The outpost commander will in any case have to ride round the outposts later on, and can then make any *slight* modifications and additions that may be necessary, bearing in mind the principle laid down in paragraph 412 of (German) *Field Service Regulations*.

Boiscarré immediately adjoins the north corner of the Wald von Crépy, and next to it is the Haut-Guenot, an important point, whence, as the map shows, there is a commanding view of the whole St. Peter brook valley, though the hill 194·7, south-east of Magny, hides some of the ground north of the brook. This latter hill commands an extensive view towards the high ground about Haute-Bévoye and of the Seille valley beyond Magny. The Seille valley west of Magny can be seen from Haut-Boutan. Lieut.-Colonel D. will at once recognise that these three hills are suitable positions for *his outpost cavalry* (*G.F.S.R.*, para. 266). If the cavalry be pushed further out than this, it would probably result in useless skirmishes, causing unnecessary disturbance to all troops (*G.F.S.R.*, para. 210).[1]

The outpost cavalry will only be pushed forward as an *independent* protective force in exceptional cases (*G.F.S.R.*, para. 212). It is mostly employed in close connection with the outpost companies, and its duties are :—

1. To watch the ground beyond the infantry outpost line by pushing forward piquets and vedettes to points affording an extensive view, or to important road junctions.

2. To reconnoitre within prescribed limits ; if these extend to the enemy's outpost line, patrols must maintain constant touch.

3. To furnish mounted orderlies to the outpost companies and to the outpost reserve. Their numbers must be reduced as far as possible by the use of cyclists, flag-signallers, and infantry telephone.

The commander of the outposts decides whether small detachments of mounted men are to be detailed to the outpost companies, and to be employed under the orders of their commanders within the sections allotted to them, or whether the duties of protection and reconnaissance, as affecting the cavalry, are to be vested in the officer commanding the outpost cavalry (*G.F.S.R.*, paras. 267 and 268).[2] Which of the two methods is to be adopted depends on circumstances ; no fixed rules can be laid down, and both methods may be used even side by side in one and the same outpost line ; there is no restriction.

The remainder of the outpost cavalry will join the outpost reserve.

How in the present case the commander of the outpost cavalry will post his piquets and vedettes, or what patrols he will send out, is left to him. He is responsible for that. The enemy is so near that touch of him must not be lost.

In the advanced-guard orders it was laid down that,

---

[1] *F.S.R.*, Part I, sect. 75 (10).—*Trans.*
[2] *Ibid.*, sect. 77 (2) and (3).—*Trans.*

OUTPOST ORDERS

in case of the enemy attacking, a position was to be held extending from hill 217·9 east of Pouilly to Pouilly inclusive. The outpost companies should, therefore, be posted on this line, for it is *their* resistance which affords the troops in rear of them time to prepare for action. The duty of protection is fulfilled chiefly by the outpost companies (*G.F.S.R.*, para. 231). The outpost reserve serves as a support to them.

It is *seldom* that the reserve of the outposts occupies the line to be held; in such a case the reserve is placed, as a rule, *immediately behind* it, and the outpost orders must then distinctively say that the outpost companies are to fall back on the reserve.

It might therefore be suggested that the outpost companies be posted on the line Haut-Guenot–St. Thiébault (the left flank being doubled back to the Seille west of Pouilly), and the piquets advanced far enough for their sentries to be along the St. Peter brook. Now, irrespective of the fact that this line would involve a very considerable frontage, requiring large numbers to hold it—the Haut-Guenot is 900 yards and St. Thiébault about 1200 yards from the line to be held in case of attack, and the retirement of the companies on the reserve *by night* would be attended with such difficulties that the Pouilly position would run a great risk of being lost.

With regard to the depth of outpost systems, beginners often make the mistake of *not* giving *sufficient depth*. But the safety of the troops in rear depends on the outpost system having sufficient depth. Taking the distance of the reserve from the companies as 1100 yards,—the distance of the companies from their piquets as about the same,—and the distance of the sentries from the piquets as not exceeding 400 yards,—then the whole depth, from reserve to the sentry line, is 2600 yards. *The enemy will have to* **fight** *his way over the above distance, plus the distance from the reserve to the troops covered, before he can endanger the main body of the force.*

The line to be occupied by the outpost companies must now be divided into sections of the outpost line. *In doing this we have to be guided by the roads.* As far as possible there should be an outpost company on each main road leading in the enemy's direction. By night, in particular, the movements of large bodies of the enemy are confined to the roads, so any night attack is bound to encounter an outpost company, if the above arrangement be carried out. Small bodies of the enemy moving across country may, of course, harass the outposts, but cannot be a danger to the main body (*G.F.S.R.*, para. 203).[1]

The main road here is the Pouilly–Metz chaussée, on which there must, *as a matter of course*, be an outpost company, viz. on the north side of Pouilly, which it will hold in case of the enemy attacking, and where it forms a species of bivouac. The exact position of the company will be fixed by the officer commanding it on arrival there. *The position of this company is the basis on which we shall found our other arrangements.*

In average country two companies furnishing piquets can guard a front of about $1\frac{1}{4}$ miles, so the left section of the outpost line may extend from the bend of the Seille to the Bouillon brook, which forms a natural and suitable line of demarcation. The remaining frontage, as far as the Wald von Crépy—about a mile—will form the right section of the outpost line, held by another two companies, furnishing piquets; the position of the companies will be somewhere near hill 217·9, which forms part of the line of resistance. Here again it is left to the officers commanding the outpost companies to find the best position for them on arriving on the ground.

Officers who do not belong to the infantry may find some difficulty in grasping the arrangements as to the positions of the outpost companies. To them I give the following hints.

First of all, consider which is the *most important* road

[1] *E.F.S.R.*, Part I, sects. 75 (5), 76 (4) and (5).

passing through a position, and place an outpost company on it. The remainder of the outpost line is then allotted to the other companies in portions of, roughly, ¾ mile for a single company, or 1¼ miles for a double company. As lines of demarcation between outpost companies look out for rivulets, brooks, swampy meadows, marshes, etc., but not roads. The outpost companies not on the main road should be placed as far as possible on roads. If *several* roads, all about *equally important*, run through the position, consider whether one or the other might not be sufficiently guarded by a piquet.

One question we need solve still is, What is to be done with the Marly bridge? It is situated quite beyond the sphere of the outpost companies, but some very disagreeable disturbance of the outposts might arise from it, especially at night, and yet we want it intact for our reconnoitring. It will be best secured by a detached post furnished by the company on the left, under an officer (*G.F.S.R.*, para. 235).[1] It is advisable to detail to this detached post one or two cavalry patrols. Communication must be maintained with the company by cyclists.

The *outpost reserve* should be on the main road, covered from view, and so placed in rear of the position to be held as to be able to move rapidly to the support of any part of it. Whether the reserve should be in alarm quarters or bivouac will depend on the degree of readiness for action necessary in each individual case. In this case I would have the reserve bivouac at the western part of the south border of Pouilly, as in that position it cannot be seen from the high ground about Haute-Bévoye and Mercy-bei-Metz, and is close to the main road immediately behind that part of the position which is most exposed to attack. In view of the proximity of the enemy it would not do to let the reserve occupy alarm quarters in Pouilly, as when bivouacked it can afford readier support to the right section of the outpost line in particular than it could if it

[1] *E.F.S.R.*, Part I, sect. 83.—*Trans.*

had first to get out of the buildings and assemble in the village street.

It might be otherwise if the weather were very wintry or wet. In such case we might, *to spare the troops*, put up with any slight disadvantage from a tactical point of view, and put the reserve in alarm quarters in Pouilly.

There is here no occasion for any detached party to provide for security being sent out from the reserve *direct*, as the west flank rests on the Seille, and the right section of the outpost line provides sufficiently for security on the east. Neither is it necessary, the force being such a small one, for the reserve to secure itself with *special* outlying guards, but inlying and outlying guards may be all in one. All that is wanted is a colour-guard with a sentry over the colours, which will also furnish two double sentries, one on each entrance to the village, *to prevent anyone going in or out* (G.F.S.R., paras. 416 and 417).[1]

It is the duty of the commander of the outposts to see to the supplies for man and beast of his command, the iron rations only to be consumed in case of dire necessity (G.F.S.R., para. 454. As regards field kitchens, *vide* G.F.S.R., paras. 453 and 438).[2] Six companies and the cavalry being here quite close to Pouilly, these can be directed to requisition in that village (G.F.S.R., para. 466).[3]

[1] *E.F.S.R.*, Part I, sect. 49.—*Trans.*
[2] *Ibid.*, sect. 12 (7) and note page 26.—*Trans.*
[3] *Ibid.*, Part II, sect. 36.—*Trans.*

OPERATION ORDER No. 1
Copy No. 1.

BY

LIEUT.-COLONEL D., COMMANDING OUTPOSTS.

Reference: Main road north of **POUILLY**,
$\frac{1}{100,000}$ or $\frac{1}{25,000}$ *Ordn.* 1.7.00.

1. *The Enemy's* infantry is reported to have reached **SABLON**, and his patrols have been seen near **HAUTE-BÉVOYE, HORGNE-AU-SABLON, GRANGE-AUX-ORMES,** and south of **AUGNY**. *Our Army Corps* has occupied an outpost line extending from **ARS-LAQUENEXY** to the north corner of the **WALD VON CRÉPY** inclusive. *The Main Body* of our detachment is quartered in **VERNY, CHÉRISEY,** and **POURNOY-LA-GRASSE**, and the main guard in **FLEURY**. The cavalry of the main guard is reconnoitring west of the **SEILLE**.

2. *The I/Battalion* and *half the I/1st Dragoons* will take up a line of outposts extending from the north corner of the **WALD VON CRÉPY** to the **SEILLE**.

3. *The Cavalry* will take up a covered position at the south border of **POUILLY** and establish touch with the outposts east of the **WALD VON CRÉPY**. From **HAUT-GUENOT**, by hill 194·7 south-east of **MAGNY**, and **HAUT BOUTAN** it will observe the country towards **QUEULUE, SABLON,** and **MONTIGNY**. It will detail at once 4 orderlies to each of the following bodies: the 1st and 2nd companies, 3rd and 4th companies, and the outpost reserve. A patrol of 3 troopers is to be attached to the detached post on the **MARLY** bridge. Horses may be watered and saddles shifted in reliefs.

4. *Nos. 1 and 2 Companies*, under Major T., and posted near the hill 217·9 east of **POUILLY**, will hold a line extending from the north corner of the **WALD VON CRÉPY** exclusive to the **BOUILLON** brook inclusive.

   Nos. 3 and 4 Companies, commanded by Major P., and posted on the north side of **POUILLY**, will hold a line extending from the **BOUILLON** brook to the bend in the **SEILLE** west of **POUILLY**. A detached post is to be pushed to the **MARLY** bridge.

All the companies will patrol to the **ST. PETER** brook.

5. *The Reserve of Outposts*, consisting of Nos. 5, 6, 7, and 8 Companies, will bivouac immediately south-west of **POUILLY**. Captain X. is appointed officer on bivouac duty.

6. *In case of the enemy attacking*, the outpost companies will hold the hill 217·9 east of **POUILLY** to **POUILLY** inclusive.

7. *Supplies* for the 1st and 2nd Companies from the field kitchen; for the remaining companies and the cavalry by requisitioning in **POUILLY**.

8. *Reports* to the outpost reserve.

Verbally to the O.C. companies. In writing to O.C. squadron by Adjutant.
    2.15 p.m.

D.,
Lieut.-Colonel.

The commander of the outposts will ride round the outpost position, and confer with his subordinate officers *on the ground*. He will verbally arrange with the outpost company commanders any defensive measures, but these will afterwards be communicated to *all* in the outpost line. During this interval more detailed reports from the squadron will have arrived.

The outpost cavalry must be spared as much as possible; it may occupy during the night alarm quarters, *i.e.* be kept together in the biggest barns on the south side of the village which is least exposed to attack, steps being taken to ensure its turning out quickly, in case of an alarm, by preparing sufficient exits from the barns. The horses remain saddled. Such an arrangement, however uncomfortable, is preferable to a bivouac with the reserve. The commander of the outpost cavalry remains *responsible for permanent security* even *after* moving into the alarm quarters. It is his affair whether he leaves the parties he has posted during day in their respective positions during night.

It will, as a rule, not be enough for the cavalry to send the ordinary patrols in the direction of the enemy; stringent orders must be given to the cavalry, that it must maintain touch of the enemy under all circumstances by night as well as by day (*G.F.S.R.*, para. 269).[1] In the present instance the two directions in which it is most important to patrol are by Magny on Sablon, and by Magny on Queuleu. If you were to confine yourself to keeping touch of the enemy merely by patrolling, you would hardly succeed in doing so from Pouilly without unduly fatiguing the horses, owing to the long distances. In this case it is more practical to push out a detached post of cavalry, from which standing patrols are sent to keep the enemy under observation.

Copy No. 1.

OPERATION ORDER No. 2
BY
LIEUT. COLONEL D., COMMANDING OUTPOSTS.

Reference: *Bivouac south-west of* **POUILLY**,
$\frac{1}{100.000}$ *and* $\frac{1}{25.000}$ *Ordn.*   1.7.00.

1. Small bodies of *hostile* cavalry are posted at the southern outlet of **ST. PRIVAT**, at the bridge on which the main road crosses the **SEILLE** south of **SABLON**, and on the hill west of **HAUTE-BÉVOYE**. Some infantry are posted at the southern exit of **SABLON** on the road to **MAGNY**.

2. *The Cavalry* will occupy alarm quarters during the night in the southern portion of **POUILLY**. The **ST. PETER** bridge is to be occupied during the night by a detached post, which is to keep touch of the enemy towards **SABLON** and **QUEULEU**.

3. *The Reserve* may pitch tents, cook, and light fires.

4. Hill 217·9 east of **POUILLY** and the north side of **POUILLY** are to be *prepared for defence* at once. The bridges over the **ST. PETER** brook south of hill 194·7 are to be barricaded.

Dictated to the orderly clerks   D.,
of the companies and of the   *Lieut.-Colonel.*
cavalry.
     4.15 p.m.

I can well imagine that you think it rather dry work to detail every single sentry, etc.; but nobody who seriously wishes to study the subject of outpost duty of infantry and

[1] *E.F.S.R.*, Part I, sects. 89, and 90 (6).—*Trans.*

cavalry can afford to neglect it. The infantry officer knows the duties better from practical experience; he only needs to amplify his knowledge as regards the employment of the cavalry; but, from my experiences hitherto, the officers of other branches of the service are in a less favourable position for gaining experience.

The commander of the outpost cavalry will regulate the strength of his more advanced parties so that they can at once send off the necessary patrols, thus saving them fatigue; only special reconnoitring patrols he will send off from Pouilly. The cavalry will be distributed as follows:—

1. A post, No. 1, consisting of 1 N.C.O. and 6 troopers, will be stationed on the road at the eastern slope of Haut-Guenot (*G.F.S.R.*, para. 292). This will furnish a vedette (cossack post) of 3 men, and one patrol of 3 men to reconnoitre towards Crépy and to keep touch of the north corner of the Wald von Crépy.

2. A post, No. 2, consisting of 1 officer and 9 troopers (*G.F.S.R.*, para. 297), will occupy hill 194.7 south-east of Magny; it will furnish a vedette (cossack post—3 troopers) on the hill itself, one vedette (cossack post—3 troopers) at the northern outlet of Magny, and a patrol of 3 troopers to reconnoitre towards Queuleu and Haute-Bévoye.

3. A post, No. 3, consisting of 1 N.C.O. and 6 troopers (*G.F.S.R.*, para. 301), will be stationed at the north corner of the narrow strip of wood on the eastern portion of hill 186 which lies north-west of Haut-Boutan, to watch the Seille valley. Patrols are here not necessary.

The total number of men employed here is 1 officer, 2 N.C.O.'s, and 21 troopers.

There is no need, as a rule, for providing reliefs for the vedettes, since in the majority of cases they act dismounted, the horses resting, while the two men watch. Should it become necessary to relieve a vedette, it can be done by the troopers who acted previously as patrol. It is doubtful whether in the present instance the vedette at the northern exit of Magny can be allowed to dismount, owing to the

OUTPOST ORDERS

proximity of the enemy. If you feel any apprehension in that respect you must reinforce the post by three troopers.

During the time the remainder of the outpost cavalry is stationed at the south border of Pouilly it is guarded by a single sentry over arms. The position taken up must be reported to the outpost commander.

Major T., in command of Nos. 1 and 2 companies, will go on ahead, to select the most suitable place and to reconnoitre the ground with a view to finding a place best suited for resisting an attack by the enemy. He will place his companies on the east side of hill 217.9, concealed behind the north-west angle of the four-cornered copse there.

Before describing the disposition of the outpost companies in detail I wish to impress upon you the following principles which will have to be observed in connection with it :—

1. *All dispositions must conform to the network of roads.* In each part of the outpost line *every* road leading towards the enemy must be held by a body whose strength must be in proportion to the importance of the road ; *i.e.* either by a piquet, a detached post under a N.C.O., or a double sentry. The ground between roads is for the most part watched by patrols.

2. No double sentry, to be relieved from a piquet, should be posted more than 440 yards from it.

3. Especially *dangerous* or *important* points *in* the general line of observation, such as isolated farms, bridges, fords, and copses, should be held by piquets. Similar points *outside* the general line of observation by detached posts. If these latter are especially important, they will be commanded by an officer (*G.F.S.R.*, para. 240).[1]

4. The piquets and detached posts should not be more than 880 to 1100 yards from their companies. They are numbered *in each outpost company* without distinction between piquet and post.

5. Piquets and posts are guarded either by groups under a N.C.O., or by double sentries, and send out patrols.

[1] *E.F.S.R.*, Part I, sect. 83.—*Trans.*

Detached posts are often of greater strength than piquets.

From the right section of the outpost line three roads lead in the direction of the enemy:—

1. The track from Boiscarré, viâ 202 to Crépy.

2. The track along the east side of Haut-Guenot to Magny.

3. The track along the Bouillon brook to the St. Peter bridge.

The first track will be guarded by piquet No. 1 at the north-east corner of Boiscarré. Strength: 2 N.C.O.'s, 12 men. (Group under an N.C.O., pushed to point 202; 2 patrols, 3 men each, to keep up communication with the outposts at the north corner of the Wald von Crépy and to patrol as far as the St. Peter brook.) (*G.F.S.R.*, para. 243.)

The second track will be guarded by piquet No. 2, concealed behind the eastern slope of Haut-Guenot. Strength: 1 N.C.O., 12 men (1 double sentry pushed forward; 2 patrols, 3 men each, to patrol towards the St. Peter brook).

The third track will be guarded by piquet No. 3, posted on a level with St. Thiébault. Strength: 1 N.C.O., 14 men (1 double sentry pushed forward; 2 patrols, 3 men each, to patrol towards the St. Peter brook and along the Bouillon brook; 1 patrol, 2 men, to communicate within the sentry line with the left section of the outpost line). (*G.F.S.R.*, para. 265.)[1]

For the immediate protection of the outpost companies the *sentry over arms* will be posted on the road at the west corner of the copse east of hill 217·9 (*G.F.S.R.*, para. 236). Mounted orderlies (*G.F.S.R.*, para. 272).

Nos. 3 and 4 outpost companies will be posted in the northern portion of "Schl." (park) of Pouilly, the sentry over arms at the north-east corner of the park. These companies direct their attention chiefly to the main road, the field-paths west of it being of minor importance.

[1] *E.F.S.R.*, Part I, sect. 86.—*Trans.*

OUTPOST ORDERS

Piquet No. 1 will be pushed to the point where the road to St. Thiébault branches off the main road. Strength: 1 officer, 2 N.C.O.'s, 18 men. (A group under a N.C.O. pushed forward on the main road; a group under a N.C.O. in St. Thiébault; one patrol towards St. Peter brook; one patrol towards St. Peter brook west of the main road; one patrol on Magny; one patrol communicating with the right section of the outpost line.)

Piquet No. 2 on the field-path at the northern border of the vineyards. Strength: 1 N.C.O., 9 men (one double sentry pushed forward in the direction of Magny; one patrol along the Seille). It is all the same whereabouts on the path this piquet is, or how much west of Pouilly.

The outpost reserve will bivouac at the south border of Pouilly, but not on the meadow! (*G.F.S.R.*, para. 409.)[1] The officer on bivouac duty will post two double sentries from the colour guard, one on each entrance to the village.

In conclusion, I will ask you to frame the advanced-guard and outpost orders, and state how the whole of the outposts would be arranged, supposing that the enemy, instead of being already in Metz, were reported to be still at Diedenhofen, or somewhere between Diedenhofen and Metz. I will not discuss the matter in detail, but merely remark that there would be no need whatever for such a compact outpost line as above described (*G.F.S.R.*, paras. 202 and 213).[2]

TWENTY-THIRD EXERCISE.

(See general map, and maps Metz and Gravelotte.)

A detachment, consisting of 3 battalions, 1 squadron, 1 battery, and ⅓ light ammunition column, and operating in its own country, has crossed the Moselle at Metz on 2.12.00, after an exhausting march. As the head of the main body, at 1 p.m., reaches Maison-de-Planches[3] (on the road Metz–Maizières-bei-Metz), the commander of the detachment decides to halt for the night.

[1] *E.F.S.R.*, Part I, sect. 55.—*Trans.*
[2] *Ibid.*, sect. 75.—*Trans.*
[3] Close to the left margin of Metz map, 6½ inches from south margin.—*Trans.*

At the same hour the following report is received from the squadron which has trotted on ahead:—

"La Gillère, 12.50 p.m.—Enemy has withdrawn in two columns on Maizières-bei-Metz and on Semécourt. Small cavalry parties have halted at Amelange, Semécourt, and Fèves, and are patrolling on Metz. Hostile infantry remained in Hauconcourt and Maizières-bei-Metz."

A native of Mondelingen declares hostile infantry to have arrived during the forenoon at that village, coming from Diedenhofen.

After posting the outposts no fresh information is received concerning the enemy till the following morning.

Required:—
1. The orders of the commander of the detachment.
2. The orders of the advanced-guard and outpost commanders.
3. Show on the map the disposition of the outposts, indicating their strength.

TWENTY-FOURTH LETTER

OUTPOST ORDERS

OWING to the advanced hour of the day (it is December) the commander of the detachment does not wish to attack the enemy, who has evidently halted. He has the less occasion to do so, as the enemy has apparently been reinforced from Diedenhofen, which probably caused him to halt. The enemy seems to place outposts.

The commander of the detachment can billet at once his force in the houses of Devant-les-Ponts, east of the railway. The whole advanced guard, consisting of one battalion and one squadron, is detailed for outpost duty.

The country which the outposts have to watch can be divided into two regions, between which there is a marked difference—on the east the *almost level Moselle valley*, almost totally destitute of cover, and therefore very easy to watch; and west of a line joining Devant-les-Ponts and Semécourt, an *extremely broken* wooded and hilly tract. The former can be watched by comparatively few men; the latter requires careful observation, the more so as the enemy's cavalry extend westwards as far as Fèves, whence it is open to them to advance past the east side of the Wald von Woippy, or through Norroy-le-Veneur, or even through Saulny. Again, should the enemy purpose attacking our outposts with infantry in the night, he will obviously have a better prospect of success in the hilly and wooded region than on the bare flats near the river.

In view of the proximity of the enemy, comprehensive measures must be adopted; but the *degree of compactness* in both regions may *differ* greatly. *In the flat country the roads only* need be occupied ; *in the hilly country more must be done.*

Following on the map from south to north the course of the Metz–Maizières main road, the commander of the detachment will notice two groups of villages and farms: Maison Rouge, Maison Neuve, and Woippy to the south, and St. Remy, Bellevue, Ladonchamps, and Ste. Agathe further north. The first group is continued to the Moselle by St. Eloy and Thury ; the second group by the two Tapes, Franclonchamps, and Maxe. The first point, therefore, about which the commander of the detachment must be clear in his own mind is which of these two lines he will make use of for his outposts.

The last-mentioned line would entail a frontage, from the Moselle to the Woippy—Norroy-le-Veneur road, of about 4 miles, measured in a straight line ; the first-mentioned line, on the contrary, has scarcely 3 miles frontage. *For this reason alone* the position at Maison Rouge and Woippy is preferable. The other position has, besides, two great disadvantages : firstly, it would entail our having to observe a far larger arc of the more difficult country ; and secondly, it would be very close to the enemy, jeopardising thereby the night rest of the whole detachment.

The commander therefore *decides* to place his outposts in the nearer position, and, in case of the enemy attacking, to move up the detachment in support of the outposts.

He issues the following orders :—

Copy No. 1.

OPERATION ORDER No. 2

BY

MAJOR-GENERAL X., COMMANDING DETACHED FORCE.

Reference :   **MAISON-DE-PLANCHES,**
$\frac{1}{100,000}$ *Ordn.*   2.12.00.

1. *The Enemy* has received reinforcements from **DIEDENHOFEN**, has retreated on **MAIZIÈRES-BEI-METZ** and through **SEMÉCOURT**, and has occupied **HAUCONCOURT** and **MAIZIÉRES** with infantry ; **AMELANGE, SEMÉCOURT,** and **FÊVES** with small cavalry detachments.

2. *The Main Body of the Detachment* will at once occupy billets in the buildings of **DEVANT-LES-PONTS**, which are east of the railway. Major N. is appointed cantonment commandant.

3. *The Advanced Guard* will place outposts on the line from the **MOSELLE** to **WOIPPY**, reconnoitring towards **AMELANGE**, **SEMÉCOURT**, and **FÊVES**.

4. *In case of attack* the outposts will hold **THURY, ST. ELOY, MAISON ROUGE**, and **WOIPPY**. The main body will move up in support.

5. *The 2nd Line Transport* can join the advanced guard from **DEVANT-LES-PONTS**.

6. *Reports* to **MAISON-DE-PLANCHES**, where I shall be quartered.

Verbally to the assembled
O.C. units of main body
and advanced guard.
In writing to O.C. squadron
by orderly officer.
1.5 p.m.

X.,
Major-General.

As the whole of the advanced guard forms the outposts, there will be only one set of orders for both; there would be no object in detailing a main guard in the present case (*G.F.S.R.*, para. 204).

The outpost commander must bear in mind that, while the outpost cavalry may be expected to do good service in the open ground east of the Wald von Woippy, its action would be much hampered among the woods. I would allot, therefore, only the open country to the cavalry, and entrust the observation of the wooded country to infantry chiefly, to which, however, must be attached sufficient troopers for patrolling towards Fêves, Norroy-le-Veneur, and Saulny.

It is unnecessary to carry the line of observation further west, for although there is a possibility of bodies of hostile cavalry making a wide détour and attempting to advance on Woippy by the Amanweiler-Lorry road, the troops detailed to occupy Woippy will have to provide for their own security. There must be *some* limit to the doubling back the flanks of an outpost line.

In the level country the outpost infantry will defend as supporting points Thury, St. Eloy, and Maison Rouge; and opposite the woods, the village of Woippy, although only part of the north side of Woippy is suited for defence, the north-west and west portion being commanded by ground close in front, and having but a limited field of fire. In spite of this defect, however, Woippy must be defended, *because of the roads converging there*.

A suitable position for the outpost reserve is further back, at Maison Neuve, whence it can easily reach all parts of the line to be held. If you are afraid of being surprised by way of Le Chêne and Le Coupillon, the reserve can send a piquet direct to the western exit of Le Coupillon.

A hasty measurement with the compasses will show whether the whole position has sufficient depth.

Having thus *generally* decided the position of the outposts, Lieut.-Colonel A. will now consider the orders one by one. We will designate the troops at his disposal the II/Battalion and II/Squadron.

The squadron must be told the line of observation it is to occupy, but in the most general terms, so as to leave the officer commanding it the requisite freedom in regard to details; the more so as it must be assumed that he has already, in the course of reconnaissance, obtained a hasty view of the country towards the front, and so knows how the land lies in that direction better than the officer commanding the outposts, who has only the map to guide him.

In the month of December *nothing short of the direst necessity* should induce a commander to bivouac cavalry at night. There is no need for so doing here, for there is abundance of stabling in Woippy. One of the outpost companies will be in Woippy, as we shall see later on, so the squadron can go into alarm quarters, covered by the infantry, on the south side, the safest side of the village. For additional security the outlets towards Lorry-bei-Metz,

Le Chêne, and Le Coupillon may be occupied by dismounted men and barricaded at suitable places (*G.F.S.R.*, paras. 283, 284, 288). These precautions will protect the outpost squadron against enterprises on the part of hostile cavalry, and it is extremely unlikely that the enemy's infantry will attempt wide outflanking movements by night against the south side of Woippy, the more so as the enemy has hitherto been retreating, and there is nothing in the data to indicate the existence in him of any abnormally enterprising spirit; unless, indeed, you regard with suspicion the fact of his having received reinforcements.

Colonel A. has next to divide the line to be held by the outpost companies into sections. *Here again his arrangements have to adapt themselves to the network of roads.* Considering the time of year, it is highly desirable, and in the present instance compatible also with tactical considerations, to place all the outpost companies under shelter, if only in the uncomfortable form of alarm quarters.

Two outpost companies *must inevitably* be in Maison Rouge, the two most important main roads in the whole position, and the railway as well, joining at this point. *The position of these companies will form the basis for further arrangements.*

From Maison Rouge to the Moselle is about $2\frac{1}{4}$ miles as the crow flies, which, together with the two important main roads, is too much for one section of outpost line to be watched. Another section must therefore be formed, and two companies placed between Maison Rouge and the Moselle, either at Thury or St. Eloy. As a line of demarcation between the two sections Colonel A. will select the east border of the pasture-land between St. Eloy and Maison Rouge. If he places the companies at Thury, they will be about in the centre of this section, whereas at St. Eloy they would be towards the left flank of it; on the other hand, there is the disadvantage that Thury is too far ($1\frac{1}{2}$ miles) from the reserve at Maison Neuve, and therefore beyond the reach of ready assistance from that quarter. I therefore prefer St. Eloy as a position for the outpost companies, and would have a piquet at Thury, with orders to make an obstinate resistance. This should—the country being favourable for defence—check the enemy till the reserve can intervene.

From the east border of the pasture-land east of Maison Rouge to the washhouse on the road to Saulny is a little over 1¼ miles, a frontage which, taken alone, might be held by two companies, but not in the present case, where *four* important roads have to be guarded—besides which the country north of Woippy is *so very* difficult to watch. Two more outpost companies must therefore be sent to Woippy, to guard that village only; so there is no need to seek a special line of demarcation between this section and that held by the two companies at Maison Rouge. These companies will naturally be placed at the junction of the two roads from Norroy-le-Veneur and Saulny.

There are no difficulties as regards supplies in this case. Each company will find in the billets all they need; likewise the cavalry in Woippy.

Copy No. 1.

OPERATION ORDER No. 1
BY
COLONEL A., COMMANDING OUTPOSTS.

Reference:
$\frac{1}{100,000}$ *Ordn.*

MAISON NEUVE,
2.12.00.

1. *The Enemy*, who has received reinforcements from **DIEDENHOFEN**, has retreated on **MAIZIÈRES-BEI-METZ** and through **SEMÉCOURT**, and has occupied **HAUCONCOURT** and **MAIZIÈRES** with infantry; **AMELANGE, SEMÉCOURT,** and **FÈVES** with small cavalry detachments. *The Main Body of our detachment* is about to occupy billets in the buildings of **DEVANT-LES-PONTS** east of the railway.

2. What was hitherto *the Advanced Guard* will take up a line of outposts extending from the **MOSELLE** to **WOIPPY**.

3. *The* II/*Squadron* will occupy alarm quarters in **WOIPPY** and watch the enemy on a line running from the **MOSELLE** through **ST. REMY** to the **WALD VON WOIPPY** exclusive towards **AMELANGE, MAIZIÈRES, SEMÉCOURT**. The

OUTPOST ORDERS

officer commanding the squadron will at once detail 4 orderlies for Nos. 1 and 2 companies, 4 orderlies for Nos. 3 and 4 companies, 4 orderlies for the reserve, and 1 N.C.O., 12 troopers for Nos. 5 and 6 companies.

4. *Nos. 1 and 2 Companies* II/*Battalion*, commanded by Major B., will go into alarm quarters in **ST. ELOY**, holding a line extending from the **MOSELLE** to the eastern border, inclusive, of the meadow north-west of **ST. ELOY**.

   Nos. 3 and 4 Companies II/*Battalion*, commanded by Major C., will go into alarm quarters in **MAISON ROUGE**, holding a line extending from the east border of the above-mentioned meadow to **WOIPPY**, exclusive.

   Nos. 5 and 6 Companies II/*Battalion*, commanded by Major D., will go into alarm quarters in **WOIPPY**, holding a line extending from the east side of **WOIPPY**, inclusive, to a point 550 yards south of the washhouse on the **SAULNY** road.

   Infantry reconnoitring patrols are to go as far as the line **FRANCLONCHAMPS – TUILERIE-DE-VILERS**[1] **– CALEMBURG**.

5. *The Reserve of Outposts*, consisting of Nos. 7 and 8 companies II/Battalion, will go into alarm quarters at **MAISON NEUVE** and place a detached post at the western outlet of **LE COUPILLON**.

6. *In case of attack* the outpost companies will hold **THURY, ST. ELOY, MAISON ROUGE**, and **WOIPPY**. These places are to be put in a state of defence.

7. *Supplies* are to be obtained by requisitioning.

8. *The 2nd Line Transport* will move up to **MAISON NEUVE** and may join the outpost companies and the squadron. It will have returned to **MAISON NEUVE** to-morrow by 6 a.m.

9. *Reports* will reach me with the reserve.

Verbally to O.C.'s companies.
In writing to O.C. II/Squadron by Lieutenant and Adjutant Z.
    1.10 p.m.

A.,
Colonel.

---

[1] Probably "Zgl." on main road north-west of Woippy.—*Trans.*

Special Measure.

The following order will be issued to the outpost cavalry :—

"The II/Squadron in **WOIPPY** will make all necessary arrangements to secure itself during the night towards **SAULNY** and **LORRY-BEI-METZ**.
"A.,
Colonel."

The squadron will send :—

1. Piquet No. 1 (1 officer, 1 N.C.O., 15 troopers) to Grandes Tapes; it places a cossack post under the N.C.O. where the path branches off to Petites Tapes, and furnishes 3 patrols along the Moselle, on Amelange, and past west of Amelange.

2. Piquet No. 2 (2 N.C.O.'s, 12 troopers) to St. Remy; it places a cossack post under a N.C.O. where the road to Grandes Tapes branches off the main road, and furnishes one patrol along the main road and one along the railroad.

3. Piquet No. 3 (2 N.C.O.'s, 15 troopers) to La Gillère; it places a cossack post under a N.C.O. in advance at the washhouse, and furnishes one patrol along the Römerstrasse (Roman road), one towards Semécourt, and one towards Fêves.

Nos. 1 and 2 outpost companies, at St. Eloy, secure themselves by a double sentry on the road to Thury.

These companies furnish piquet No. 1, strength ½ company, under an officer, which goes to Thury. This piquet places group No. 1 (1 N.C.O., 9 men) on the road to the Moselle, about 440 to 550 yards in advance; group No. 2 (1 N.C.O., 6 men) on the road at the little copse 440 yards north-east of Thury; group No. 3 (1 N.C.O., 9 men) at the southern of the two "Abbaue zu la Maxe."

Piquet No. 2 (1 N.C.O., 9 men) on the road from St. Eloy to Franclonchamps about 550 yards north of the cross-roads marked 165.

Piquet No. 3 (1 N.C.O., 9 men) at the eastern border of the meadow; this piquet will keep in touch with Nos. 3 and 4 companies.

Nos. 3 and 4 outpost companies at Maison Rouge furnish piquet No. 1 (1 N.C.O., 9 men) on the road to Maxe about 800 yards in advance.

Piquet No. 2 (1 N.C.O., 9 men) on the main road to Ladonchamps about ¼ mile in advance.

Piquet No. 3 (1 section under an officer) at Ste. Adèle; it will place a double sentry No. 1 on the railway and a group under a N.C.O. on the road towards Ste. Agathe.

The companies secure themselves by a double sentry.

Nos. 5 and 6 outpost companies furnish piquet No. 1 at the road-fork 650 yards west of Ste. Adèle; strength, 1 N.C.O., 12 men.

Piquet No. 2 (1 N.C.O., 15 men), on the road to Norroy-le-Veneur.

Piquet No. 3 (2 N.C.O.'s, 18 men), on the road to Saulny.

The piquets are made stronger in this section because more security is obtained by lively patrolling in this difficult country than by sentries or groups, whose range of vision, especially during night, is much too limited.

No special sentry posts are needed outside Woippy.

TWENTY-FOURTH EXERCISE.
(See general map, and maps Metz and Verny.)

General Idea.

A Red Division, operating in hostile country, is retiring, after severe fighting west of the Moselle, through the unfortified town of Metz in the direction of Saarbrücken, pursued by a Blue Division.

Special Idea for the Blue Detachment.

The advanced guard of the Blue Division (4 battalions, 1 machine-gun detachment, 2 squadrons, 3 field-howitzer batteries, 1 field company R.E. with bridging train, 1 section field ambulance, 1 light ammunition column) reaches at 5 p.m. on the 1st April with the head of its vanguard the public-house (Krug) at the eastern outlet of Bordes. The enemy, apparently in great disorder, has retired by Lauvallière, Laplanchette, and Colombey across the Vallières brook, but some of his infantry are holding the two former places and the high ground west of Coincy and Aubigny, and are making preparations for defence. Some of the enemy's artillery has been ascertained west of Amitié brewery (Brauerei) and west of Coincy. Many cavalry patrols are in sight on the right bank of the brook. The Vallière brook is swollen by heavy rain, and impassable by infantry. The bridge at Planchette is blown up, and the other bridges over the brook—from Coupillon to Aubigny—are barricaded.

At the hour above mentioned the officer commanding the advanced guard received the following order verbally from the officer commanding the Blue Division:—

"The main body is going into quarters in **METZ**. The advanced guard will billet in the villages east of the **SEILLE** and provide for the security of the main body towards the **VALLIÈRES** brook on a line running approximately from **VANTOUX** to the **WALD VON BORNY**. The main body urgently stands in need of rest to-morrow. The advanced guard will actively continue the pursuit of the enemy to-morrow. For this purpose I am sending you 2 howitzer batteries, which will arrive at **BORDES** in about one hour. Further, 2 field batteries and $\frac{2}{3}$ light ammunition column, which will arrive at the road junction west of **PLANTIÈRES**, north of hill 189·0, at 7 p.m."

Ten minutes later an apparently reliable inhabitant of Montoy arrives and reports to the commander of the advanced guard the following:—

"Two battalions of the enemy have entered Montoy in great disorder about 4 p.m.; a strong body of infantry, perhaps 9 or 12 battalions, with several batteries, is said to have retired on Kurzel. At Laplanchette the enemy has placed several machine-guns so as to command the passage over the Vallières brook."

At the same moment Colonel M., commanding the R.A. of the division, reports "that he personally was placed at the disposal of the commander of the advanced guard for to-morrow, and that he would arrive at Les Bordes in 10 minutes."

Required:—

The orders of the commander of the advanced guard for the night; and show on the map all arrangements made by him to provide for observation and resistance, including the positions of piquets and groups, and the direction in which patrols are sent.

TWENTY-FIFTH LETTER

OUTPOSTS

THIS exercise well illustrates the fact that in connection with outposts, even more than in other tactical situations, it is impossible to lay down hard-and-fast rules, for in the present case it is quite out of the question to apply any fixed principles. In the last two exercises we had outposts in the customary form, but the present case will show the need of guarding against the use of any *set form in respect of the distribution of outposts on the ground, or the distances between the several fractions of the outpost system.* The *space* at one's disposal, *the nature of the country, the general situation, the intentions of the commander*, and *the object in view in taking up the outpost line* will in each individual case decide the measures to be adopted.

What, in the present case, is the purpose to be served by the outposts which the advanced guard has to throw out? Is it likely that the enemy, already beaten and thrown into disorder, will attempt a night attack on the main body, or even on the advanced guard?

The bulk of the Red Division, probably, is already retreating on Kurzel, so the force left at the Vallières brook cannot be a large one, though, of course, we have no accurate information as to its strength. It seems probable that the enemy will be only too glad to be left alone, so as to be able to give his troops in Montoy and at the Vallières brook some rest, and to restore order among them. With a view to checking the pursuit he is holding the line of the Vallières brook with such of his troops as are most fit for action. The fact that this rear guard is constructing entrenchments, and has blown up or barricaded the bridges, seems to imply that the *enemy entertains no idea of attacking by surprise or otherwise ;* he has, in fact, deprived himself of the power of doing so by rendering impassable the bridges over the swollen brook. Probably all he intends to do is to send out a few infantry patrols towards Metz, though purely in a defensive spirit, to give timely notice of a night attack. Your outposts have to prevent such patrols going too far, *nothing more is necessary. The measures to be adopted, therefore, for our own protection may be of the most simple nature.* In spite of the proximity of the enemy, it will suffice if on each of the two main roads a couple of companies be pushed out, which may find shelter in houses, and provide for their own security by posting a few guards.

Sebastopol and Belle Croix will answer this purpose. Let these two farms be occupied, and communication kept up between them by patrols, and it will be unnecessary to employ any more infantry.

Enough has been found out by the cavalry about the enemy to clear up the situation, and we are not likely to learn more by employing cavalry. Again, there is so little room between Sebastopol and Belle Croix on the one hand, and between these two farms and the Vallières brook on the other, that there is absolutely not space enough for outpost cavalry, such as we have treated of in the last two exercises.

It might be as well to have small bodies of cavalry placed *on the flanks* of the infantry line, which will endeavour by day, but more particularly by night, and *at daybreak next morning*, to work round the flanks of the enemy's position and find out all they can. This is in conformity with the principle which I have so often reiterated, that cavalry, if unable to make further progress straight to their front, must endeavour to work round an enemy's flanks (*G.F.S.R.*, para. 269).[1] This course is the more advisable here *as it is above all in pursuit that efforts should be made to*

[1] *E.F.S.R.*, Part I, sects. 89 and 97.—*Trans.*

worry continually the enemy's flanks (G.F.S.R., para. 186).[1] We must only employ *small* bodies of cavalry, however, in this way, because the advanced guard, and therefore the cavalry also, has heavy work before it next day. If you were to employ whole squadrons for this purpose, the horses, already used up by the exertions of the past day, could not be depended upon for the morrow. On the other hand, sufficient cavalry must be employed to drive in, if necessary, patrols or small bodies of the enemy. For these reasons I consider a troop on each flank sufficient, which I should place in Grigy and Vantoux.

A reserve for the outposts is unnecessary (G.F.S.R., para. 200).[2] Instead of it two companies in alarm quarters on the east side of Borny, and two on the east side of Bordes, will be sufficient to support readily the advanced companies should they (though it is most unlikely) be attacked by superior forces. Should any further support be necessary, it may be rendered by the infantry in Borny to the two companies at Sebastopol, and by the infantry in Bordes to the two companies in Belle Croix (G.F.S.R., para. 213).[3]

All the advanced companies must be placed under one commander of the outposts.

In framing the advanced-guard orders you probably took as your guide the model given in the twenty-first letter, but I dare say you soon realised that it cannot be followed implicitly in the present case, and that you can only in part copy the headings there given. In fact, it was my object in framing the general and special ideas for this exercise *to warn you against a too literal application of my models for orders*.

Taking into consideration the line which has been approximately fixed for the outposts by order of the officer commanding the main body, the following villages are available for billeting the advanced guard in—Queuleu, Borny, Belle Tanche, Plantières, and Bordes.

[1] *E.F.S.R.*, Part. I, sects. 72 (5), 112 (2).   [2] *Ibid.*, sect. 75.
[3] *Ibid.*, Part I, sects. 77 (2), 80.—*Trans.*

With regard to the distribution of the troops among the various villages, I must refer you to the advice given in the fourth letter. Should your distribution differ from mine, I shall not go out of my way to find fault, *so long as you have allowed for the next day's operations*. The mounted arms must, at any rate, be so provided for that the horses will find stabling; the artillery being, in addition, quartered in a place of security, and on no account in Borny. The orders below show how I propose to quarter the troops. I will here only observe that, *in accordance with the principle that the quartering for the night should, in a sense, be the beginning of the next day's work*, most importance must be attached to the Colombey road;—why this should be so I will explain afterwards.

In framing the orders take care to enjoin the necessity of never for a moment losing touch of the enemy, and do not leave it to the discretion of the officers commanding in Borny and Bordes respectively; for in a retreat, a defeated enemy often succeeds in stealing a march unobserved, profiting by the hours of darkness. In the present instance, certainly, the enemy's preparations for defence make a sudden retreat less likely, *but in war one is never certain that the enemy may not do something unexpected;* the advanced guard should therefore recognise that it is its duty to *strain every nerve to keep touch of the enemy. Any neglect in this respect may lead to the most fatal results.*

As explained in the twenty-second letter, it is sometimes advisable to notify to the troops, when dismissing them to their quarters, *what is to be done in case of an alarm*. If the orders say nothing to the contrary, each unit should provisionally assemble at its own alarm post. This will be the best arrangement in the present case. I do not consider it desirable to appoint an *alarm rendezvous* for the whole advanced guard, for, if the enemy attacks during the night, he must move by *one or the other* of the two main roads, but by which we cannot foretell. It is out of the question to assemble the advanced guard on *one* of the two roads;

OUTPOSTS

and there is no suitable place for assembling it *between* them. Under such circumstances the best thing the O.C. advanced guard can do is to direct the various units to await further orders at their several alarm posts.

The officers commanding units will be called together to meet at Belle Croix, where orders will be issued at once for the next day. You briefly make your arrangements for billeting the troops and then ride on to Belle Croix.

Copy No. 1.

OPERATION ORDER No. 2
BY
MAJOR-GENERAL A., COMMANDING ADVANCED GUARD.

Reference: *East side of* **BORDES,**
$\frac{1}{100,000}$ *Ordn.*   1.4.CO.

1. *The Enemy*, who has been defeated, and is in disorder, has retreated across the **VALLIÈRES** brook, which is greatly swollen, and is fortifying **AUBIGNY**—the high ground west of **COINCY**—**LAPLANCHETTE**, and **LAUVALLIÈRES**. The bridges are destroyed or barricaded. More than two brigades of infantry, with several batteries, are said to have fallen back on **KURZEL**. Two battalions are reported at **MONTOY**.

   Our Main Body is going into quarters in **METZ**.

2. *The Advanced Guard* will occupy billets as follows:—

   BORNY:
      I/Battalion, Machine-gun Detachment, I/Squadron.

   BORDES:
      II/Battalion, II/Squadron.

   PLANTIÈRES, northern half:
      III/Battalion, Field Howitzer Brigade (less 1 battery).

   PLANTIÈRES, southern half:
      IV/Battalion, 1 Battery Field Howitzers, Section Field Ambulance, Light Ammunition Column.

   BELLE TANCHE:
      Field Co. R.E. with bridging train.

   QUEULEU, northern portion:
      2 Field Batteries R.A. (18 pdrs.), $\frac{2}{3}$ Light Ammunition Column.

3. *From* **BORNY** a troop of cavalry will be sent out at once to the east outlet of **GRIGY** which will send patrols viâ **ARS-LAQUENEXY** to **AUBIGNY**. Two companies will be detached to **SEBASTOPOL**, which will guard the **COLOMBEY** road. Four troopers will be attached to these two companies. *From* **BORDES** 2 companies with 4 troopers will be advanced to **BELLE CROIX**, and will observe the roads to **LAPLANCHETTE** and **LAUVALLIÈRES**, and a troop of cavalry will be sent to the east outlet of **VANTOUX**, which will send patrols towards **NOUILLY**.

Commander of the Outposts: Major Z.

On the road through **COLOMBEY** and towards **LAPLANCHETTE** standing infantry patrols will keep touch of the enemy. At the eastern outlets of **BORNY** and **BORDES** respectively two companies will occupy *alarm quarters*.

4. *In case of an attack by the enemy*, **BORNY** and **BELLE CROIX** are to be held.

5. *The 2nd Line Transport* will be brought up to the troops, with the exception of that of the troops at **SEBASTOPOL** and **BELLE CROIX**.

6. *Reports* to the gasworks in **PLANTIÈRES**. Lieut.-Colonel N., III/Battalion, is appointed cantonment commandant in **PLANTIÈRES**.

7. Battalion commanders, excepting the officer commanding the outposts, and all other officers commanding units will *attend to receive orders* at 5.40 p.m. at **BELLE CROIX**.

Verbally to assembled commanding officers.
In writing to the advanced squadrons by orderly N.C.O.'s.
5.10 p.m.

A.,
Major-General.

You were further asked to show on the map all the arrangements made for observation and resistance.

The troop at Grigy acts as a piquet, and remains at the outlet from Grigy facing Ars-Laquenexy, covered by a double vedette (*G.F.S.R.*, para. 302). A Cossack post under a N.C.O. is pushed out to Grange-aux-Bois. This is, I admit, over a mile from the piquet, and it might possibly with advantage be nearer, say at the small road-bridge half-way between Grigy and Grange-aux-Bois. Patrols will go through Ars-Laquenexy towards Aubigny, and keep up communication with Borny. That is all that is wanted.

The two outpost companies at Sebastopol have a double sentry close to the farm. The two companies less one section are sheltered in the buildings, much the same as in alarm quarters. A piquet, strength one section, stands on the main road to Colombey, where the cross-road from Belle Croix runs in, and has a sentry over the arms for its own immediate security, besides the following:—Double sentry No. 1 down the road to Grange-aux-Bois, group (under a N.C.O.) No. 2 at the Franz. Denkm. Patrols keep up communication with Belle Croix, and go towards Grange-aux-Bois, and by Colombey and the northern part of the Todten Allee to the Vallières brook.

The two companies at Belle Croix have a double sentry for their immediate protection. A piquet, No. 1, strength one section, stands at the road-fork just east of Belle Croix, with a sentry over the arms, and throws out the following: group No. 1, under a N.C.O., at the north end of Todten Allee; group No. 2, under a N.C.O., about 220 yards down the main road to Lauvallières, where a lane goes off to Vantoux. Patrols go out from the piquet to Laplanchette and Lauvallières, and keep up communication with the piquet east of Sebastopol. A piquet, No. 2 (1 N.C.O., 12 men) is placed at the cross-roads about 800 yards northeast of Belle Croix, and sends out patrols towards Lauvallière and the Latour Mill, and keeps up communication with the cavalry in Vantoux.

The troop of cavalry in Vantoux is posted at the east outlet of the village, and acts as a piquet. It has a Cossack post under a N.C.O. in the Vallières valley, where the road to Méy branches off, and sends patrols towards Nouilly.

It would also be desirable for patrols to go through Méy towards Nouilly, but on account of the nature of the country and of the bad roads it is hardly feasible at night.

In rear of this outpost position the remaining troops of the advanced guard quartered in the villages must provide for their own security by *outlying piquets*. This measure is specially necessary in the case of Borny, which is nearest the enemy. Small infantry piquets will occupy the outlets facing Grigy, Sebastopol, and Bordes. I need not enter upon details here.

The local measures of security and the advanced companies are ample protection against any surprise of the enemy.

TWENTY-FIFTH EXERCISE.
(In continuation of the preceding Exercise.)

Give the orders of the commander of the advanced guard for the next day, assuming that no further information is received concerning the enemy.

TWENTY-SIXTH LETTER

ATTACK ON A FORTIFIED POSITION

IT appears likely that the enemy will be prepared next morning to dispute the passage of the Vallières brook, in the position which he has hastily fortified (high ground west of Coincy—Aubigny, Laplanchette, and Lauvallières). It is unlikely that he will fall back in the course of the morning, after the trouble he has taken in constructing field entrenchments, etc., unless you assume the enemy means to deceive you with these entrenchings. On the contrary, there is every indication that the object of the rear guard is to gain a day's rest for the main body, that has fallen back, much shaken, on Kurzel, to attain which the rear guard is prepared to *accept battle* on the line of the Vallières brook. To attack this position is the task which now devolves on the *advanced guard* of the Blue Division, which will have *to act independently in continuing the pursuit of the enemy.* The special idea tells us that " the main body of the Blue Division urgently stands in need of rest to-morrow," on which account it cannot continue the pursuit. The advanced guard cannot, therefore, look for any support —*though, but for this paragraph in the orders from headquarters, the data would give us reasonable grounds for counting on support from the main body.* The reasons for this exceptional procedure on the part of the main body do not come within the scope of our argument.

The brook, greatly swollen, constitutes a formidable obstacle, which the western troops would have great difficulty in surmounting in the course of any attack made in the *stereotyped* form. It is, unfortunately, *impracticable to slip past the enemy's flanks*, as to do so, whether on a northerly or a southerly line, would entail making too great a détour, with no certainty of success; though certainly it would be desirable to avoid attacking the position along the east bank of the brook. To move viâ Méy or Nouilly would mean crossing the deep valley at the latter place—an arduous undertaking—for there is hardly any doubt but that the enemy would succeed in moving troops from Montoy through Amitié in time to oppose us. On the other hand, an attempt to turn the position by way of Ars-Laquenexy would likewise involve heavy losses and severe fighting, in the all too probable event of the enemy rapidly moving on to the ground lying south of his line of retreat on Kurzel. In neither case would the advanced guard be pressing the pursuit *with the energy* which the situation demands, seeing that it is the intention of the officer commanding the Blue Division that *the enemy's rear guard should be crushed*.

The plan offering the *surest* prospects of success is to attack the enemy's position along the brook. This plan also promises the *speediest* results, as we shall not show the enemy the kindness of making a détour which will require a long time. In addition to this it is probable that the bridges are held only by small detachments, already disheartened by their recent defeat. I trust that you do not propose bridging the brook, with the aid of the bridging train; as such an undertaking would have but faint chance of success, especially as the bridge would in all probability have to be made under the fire of the defender.

It is unlikely that the bridges will be held in any strength because we have reliable information that the enemy's main body has already retreated eastwards; though, of course, it is impossible to say how far, but at any rate far enough to enable us to count on having only a rear guard to deal with next morning. Some clue as to the strength of this rear guard is afforded by the circumstance that there are only two battalions in Montoy during the night. Again, it is most unlikely that the whole line, from Nouilly to Aubigny, is held *as in a regular defensive position*, for it is about 2½ miles long in a straight line, which would require something like a whole division at least to defend it properly.

As, however, the enemy is concerned in defending a considerable extent of an unfordable stream, which can be crossed only at certain points, it is reasonable to suppose that he will be guided by the principles ordinarily governing *the defence of a river line of some extent*. The main thing for him to do is to check, by means of small detachments posted at the most likely points of passage, our attempts to cross, until a reserve (which should be as strong as possible), posted at a suitable road-junction in rear of the centre of the whole position, can intervene at the point threatened, and repulse the attacker by means of a vigorous counter-stroke. In pursuance of such a plan, the detachments holding the various bridges usually consist of infantry only, while cavalry patrol along the river-bank, and at the same time keep up connection between the several detachments. Artillery is seldom attached to such detachments, but may be employed when certain points of passage are so exceptionally favourable to the attacker as to make it almost certain that he will attempt to cross there. The reserve, consisting of infantry and artillery, maintains close communication with the various detachments by means of relays, mounted orderlies, signalling, cyclists, telephones, and telegraphing.

Let us now collate the information received concerning the enemy with the above principles of river defence which I have briefly run through. The bridges held by the enemy's infantry are spread over so great a frontage, that any outposts covering the troops in Montoy must necessarily be of a very sketchy nature. In fact, everything indicates that it is the enemy's intention to force you either to attack or make a wide turning movement, unless indeed his object be merely to retire, after having induced you to deploy for an attack on the stream line.

The troops in Montoy may be considered the reserve of the whole position. There being two battalions there, it is probable that another battalion is distributed along the Vallières brook. Artillery has been ascertained at two different points, and it is not impossible that there may be more artillery about; since, as you are aware, rear guards are, as a general rule, made *as strong as possible in artillery*. Of the enemy's cavalry all that is known is that it is actively patrolling along the brook. It will probably be employed next morning principally north of Nouilly and south of Aubigny, as its chief duty will be *to discover any attempt on our part to work round the flanks*.

We have seen, however, that the officer commanding the advanced guard cannot hope to pass round the flank of the enemy's position, neither can he attack it in the ordinary manner, on account of the heavy losses it would entail; he has now, therefore, to choose between two other methods of attack.

One is to make a *sudden attack* with his whole force *on one* of the points of passage, in the hopes of driving in the detachment on the spot before the reserve from Montoy can intervene. It is, to say the least, doubtful whether such an attack would not be patent to the enemy from its inception. If he realises it betimes, we should have to carry it out against his reserve, as it hurries on the scene, and should incur losses out of all proportion to the result obtained.

The other plan offers *more prospect of success*, namely, to attempt to induce the enemy, by means of *a feint vigorously carried out*, to bring his reserve into action, while we make the *real attack* at some *other* point. In such case the attacking force must be divided, and *two separate* attacks will have to be carried out; but the rôle of the feint is by no means the same as that of the " secondary attack " referred to in our previous orders for attack.

Such a feint should take in the enemy, and make him believe that he has to do with the *real* attack; it should, therefore, be carried out as if it were *intended to assault*

ATTACK ON A FORTIFIED POSITION 357

the point in question; *otherwise the enemy will not be deceived*, nor move his reserve to the point threatened. While the feint is being made, the troops for the main attack are being concentrated *under cover as near as possible* to the bridge to be assaulted; the main thing being *so to engage the enemy's attention* with the feint that he will not notice the true attack until the last moment. *The feint must, therefore, in* **time** *precede the real attack, and in* **place** *be as far distant as possible from the point selected for the real attack.*

In selecting the point for the main attack, the nature of the country *on the enemy's side* of the stream must be considered. Suppose you succeed in capturing the bridge, the *first troops* to set foot on the other side of the stream should find a good defensive position where they can *establish* themselves, and *hold their ground* against the enemy's reserve, when it arrives on the scene. Granted the existence of such a position, however, if the enemy's reserve finds out the main attack soon enough, it may succeed in driving back again over the stream the first troops who cross, who will probably be *in the minority*. It is, therefore, a great advantage if our *artillery* can, from a position on the near bank, come into action against such a counter-stroke. In selecting a point for our main attack, therefore, three things have to be considered: (1) *Where can a sudden advance be made from a position concealed from view?* (2) *where is it possible to ensure a firm hold of the further bank?* (3) *Where can the artillery best co-operate?*

The enemy would be most likely to believe in the reality of an attack on Laplanchette, because such attack would strike straight at his line of retreat; hence his machine guns there. We know, however, that the bridge there is broken, so that the enemy can feel fairly secure against attack on this quarter. Laplanchette, therefore, is *suitable neither for a feint nor for a main attack*, but we may there *occupy the enemy's attention* by a demonstration in small force.

We have next to institute a comparison, subject to the

above-mentioned requirements, between the other bridges, especially those at Lauvallières and Colombey. *Lauvallières will not do for the main attack.* The outlook is more favourable at Colombey. Troops can be concentrated under cover of the high ground at the Franz. Denkm., and will be sheltered by the park of Colombey while advancing on the bridge *supported by artillery fire.* A portion of the attacking force may rush the bridge south of the main road and seize Aubigny, thus gaining *the desired supporting point on the enemy's side of the stream.* The ravine between the main road and Aubigny will lend cover to the advance of the troops who have crossed at Colombey, and the enemy's troops in Aubigny will thus be in danger of being isolated, and will be induced to retire promptly from the village. Everything, therefore, points to the suitability of *Colombey for the main attack*, and of Lauvallières for the *feint*.

It follows from what has been previously said that, if the feint is to deceive the enemy, it must *not* be made *in broad daylight*, for from Amitié brewery every man in the attacking force could be counted as it leaves Belle Croix. The enemy would thus very soon see that he had only a small part of the advanced guard in front of him, and would want to know where the rest of it was. As the enemy is operating in a country hostile to him, he cannot be assumed to know that the main body is going to remain in Metz ; on the contrary, he probably expects *the whole of the Division* to attack the line of the Vallières brook. The employment of a probably small force to attack Lauvallières would, therefore, be certain to arouse his suspicions. Again, the less the enemy can find out concerning the strength of the feint, the more chance there is of his employing his reserve to repulse it. *The darkness will here be our best ally.* The feint must be made *just before daybreak*, the *main attack being made later, and by daylight.*

I am in this case opposed to making a night attack with the whole advanced guard, although such a plan may appear

ATTACK ON A FORTIFIED POSITION

to offer certain advantages. I need not go into the advantages and disadvantages of night attacks; well-trained troops can, of course, carry out a night attack, and how successfully it can be carried out the Japanese have shown us in the last campaign; but if we can avoid a night attack, then so much the better, for chance has too great a hand in it, and we know too little yet of the enemy's position.

It is another matter, however, when, as in this instance, an engagement is *begun* in darkness, the troops to deliver the *main attack assembling* before dawn, but *waiting for daybreak to advance*. The darkness covers the *assembly* of all the troops, *and the opening attack made by a fraction of the whole force;* but the main attack itself does not begin till it is broad daylight.

It is of no consequence that there is a *wide interval* between the main attack and the feint, that the whole attacking force is spread over a frontage far greater than usually admissible, or that it will be difficult, if not impossible, for the commander to control personally his whole force. This is a case of two *separate* attacks, and it is a *great advantage* that there is a wide gap between them, as the case with which we are dealing is *wholly exceptional*, and *cannot be gauged by any rules we have hitherto conformed to.*

The officer commanding the advanced guard therefore arrives at the following decision: *Main attack through Colombey on Aubigny; a feint (to be made while it is still dark) on Lauvallières; a demonstration in small force against Laplanchette.*

The commander of the advanced guard himself rides forward to Belle Croix, and turns over in his mind first how he could best employ his artillery in the attack next morning. He has at his disposal three batteries of light field howitzers, two batteries 18-pr. Q.F. guns, and two batteries heavy howitzers. First of all the *whole* artillery must be placed under *one* artillery commander, that is to say in our case under Colonel M. The commander of the advanced guard will *at once*, *i.e.* while it is yet light, confer with him and explain his intentions, so that Colonel M. can as soon as possible make the necessary preparations, reconnoitring positions for the batteries and approaches to them.

The heavy howitzers may come into action *at once*, and continue their fire during night (no billets have been provided for them for this reason). They are to harass the enemy's quarters, chiefly Montoy, but Coincy and Lauvallières as well. I need not point out to you what effect this will have on the enemy's nerves. Next morning they will engage the enemy's artillery at Amitié, and at Lauvallières too, so as to complete the enemy's deception; for, as a rule, a quantity of artillery is generally associated with large bodies of infantry. But as soon as the main attack is launched they will support it by firing on Aubigny. All this can be effected without moving from a position east of Bordes between hills marked 214 and 219·8.

The light field howitzers can be used against all targets, including those behind cover and in localities. They are to join in the fight against the enemy's artillery at Amitié, and take under fire the entrenchments at the Laplanchette and Colombey crossings. They will find for that object a position north of the Borny–Colombey main road.

The two field batteries 18-*pr.* will first engage the hostile artillery at Coincy; afterwards they will be used particularly against the enemy's reserve the moment he engages it.

The officer commanding the whole of the artillery will take direction of its fire next morning. He will immediately charge the commanders of the light and heavy howitzer batteries with reconnoitring minutely the ground for suitable positions, etc.; officers of his staff will do this for the field batteries 18-pr. arriving afterwards. As at the beginning of April the sun sets at 6.38 p.m., it will be dark only after 7 o'clock; there is, therefore, plenty of time for reconnaissance.

The machine-gun detachment is placed at the disposal of the officer entrusted with the main attack. But the commander of the advanced guard will see to positions being reconnoitred for these guns, from which at daybreak, they can effectively support the infantry fight at close range and from the flanks. A suitable position will be found at the copse south of Colombey.

The sun rises about 5.40 a.m.; it begins to dawn an hour earlier; the time of starting must be so calculated that the troops for the feint and the demonstration shall be deployed for the attack on Lauvallières and Laplanchette respectively before dawn. The distance to be marched being about 2 miles, the troops for the feint should move off at 4 a.m. The troops for the main attack will start at the same time, and proceed to the Franz. Denkm., where they will wait until the attack on Lauvallières is fully developed.

As two separate attacks have to be made, the form of the orders will have to be different from that of the orders given in preceding letters. The two portions into which the force will be divided will be named *after their respective commanders* (G.F.S.R., para. 98). As both columns should work in concert, it is essential that each should know precisely what the other is going to do; so one set of orders should be given for both. It would not do to issue first an order *for advance*, detailing in that march order a left flank guard—partly because the march is so short, and partly because there being no question of a guard on the flank, the expression "flank guard" might cause misunderstandings; nor should the troops be composed as if they formed a flank guard.

The bulk of the infantry and the machine-guns will be required for the main attack, and one battalion will do for the feint—six companies moving on Lauvallières and two on Laplanchette. The remaining three battalions, provided they succeed in rapidly crossing the stream, are sufficient to carry out the main attack—even if the enemy's reserve, contrary to our hopes and expectations, should be met by them.

In the orders for attack it is not advisable to say that

one attack is to be *a feint*. Avoid, therefore, the word " feint " in your order. In your reasons afterwards you can state that the attack on Lauvallières is to be a feint. The orders must also make it clear that the northern column must *lose no time* in beginning the attack. All details as to how the officer commanding that column is to dispose his force should be left to his discretion. On the other hand, it would be as well to state expressly in the orders that nothing more than a *demonstration* is to be made against Laplanchette, to prevent too many men being employed in that quarter.

The control of the southern column must be completely in the hands of an officer appointed to command it, so that the officer commanding the whole force may be free to *supervise both columns* and be relieved of the arrangement of details. The orders must leave no doubt that the southern column is not to attack until the action at Lauvallières has reached such a stage that there is some prospect of the enemy bringing up his reserve there. Meanwhile that column should take up a *position of readiness*, and be prepared to come into action at a moment's notice. The moment for beginning the main attack depends, however, on the development of the action at Lauvallières, and as opinions may differ as to its progress, I should, were I the advanced-guard commander, go *a step further, and reserve it to myself to order the main attack to begin*. In any case, the orders must clearly show the officer commanding the southern column the manner in which the column is to deliver its attack. It would be as well to distribute the ammunition of the S.A.A. carts before starting the attack, as there may be obstinate fighting.

Several tasks will devolve on the cavalry. *Part* of it may be employed dismounted against Nouilly, to pin the enemy to the ground there. In the semi-darkness of daybreak the enemy will be unable to distinguish whether he has cavalry or infantry to deal with. Should the enemy after a time withdraw from Nouilly, cavalry had better be employed on *one or the other of the enemy's flanks* there ; it will, therefore, be as well to attach one squadron to the northern column. The southern column will require some cavalry too, for it is especially desirable, in the event of the main attack succeeding, to threaten the retreating enemy from the south, and that thus our cavalry *pass round both his flanks*. The squadron which has detached a troop to Grigy must undoubtedly be attached to the southern column, so that it may be again united on the morrow.

I would so apportion the field company of engineers that a section of it is with the northern column, for the purpose of removing any obstructions on the road at Lauvallières, while the other sections of the company do the same in the case of the two roads at Colombey. There is nothing for the bridging train to do at the beginning of the action, though there may be later on. It may, therefore, remain at Sebastopol until the result of the action is decided, and may form part of the southern column as it assembles there. The section field ambulance may also be attached to the southern column, in which there will probably be the greatest number of casualties.

The officer commanding the machine-gun detachment will be given the following order :—

" Reconnoitre at once a position near the copse southwest of Colombey, with a view to opening fire at dawn on the Vallières valley at Colombey."

Colonel M., commanding the artillery, will be ordered :—

" Trot on, yourself, to Belle Croix, where you will receive orders verbally."

I would not fix the position of the *dressing station*, as it will depend entirely on the issue of the action. Suppose the main attack has little difficulty in crossing the stream, but has heavy fighting, say, between Aubigny and Coincy, the dressing station should be established at Colombey ; if, on the other hand, there are severe losses in crossing the stream, it would be better to have the dressing station at

Sebastopol. The field ambulance may, therefore, remain provisionally at Sebastopol; so placed, it can, if required, be brought up to the northern column as well.

The 2nd line transport should be so disposed as to be readily brought up in the event of the attack succeeding. It will naturally be collected *on the main road to Kurzel*. There being here two separate columns, the orders must detail whether the transport of the one or of the other is to lead the transport column. The 2nd line transport of the field batteries and of the heavy howitzer batteries is at the tail of that column.

The position of the officer commanding the advanced guard must be so chosen as to enable him to watch the progress of *both* attacks as far as possible.

Copy No. 1.

OPERATION ORDER No. 3
BY
GENERAL X., COMMANDING ADVANCED GUARD.

Reference:
$\frac{1}{100,000}$ *Ordn.*

BELLE CROIX,
1.4.00.

1. *Lieut.-Colonel B.'s column:*
   II/1st Dragoons.
   1 Sect. Field Co. R.E.
   II/Battalion.

2. *Colonel C.'s column:*
   I/1st Dragoons.
   Field Co. R.E. (less 1 section) with bridging train.
   I/Battalion.
   III/Battalion.
   IV/Battalion.
   1 Sect. Field Ambul.

1. No fresh information received concerning the *enemy. Our main body* will remain in **METZ** to-morrow.

2. *The Advanced Guard*, to which have been attached 2 more field and 2 heavy howitzer batteries, will attack the enemy to-morrow in two columns. Their commanders will at once reconnoitre roads and positions.

3. *The whole of the Artillery* is placed under the orders of Colonel M. The heavy howitzer batteries will come into action between the heights marked 214 and 219.8 east of **BORDES**, firing during the night on **MONTOY** and **COINCY**. The light howitzer and the field

ATTACK ON A FORTIFIED POSITION

batteries will be to-morrow, at 4.20 a.m., in the positions north and south of the **BORNY–COLOMBEY** main road, which have been reconnoitred to-day.—The light ammunition columns are placed at the disposal of Colonel M.

4. *The Machine-gun Detachment* will be in position at the copse south-west of **COLOMBEY** by 4.50 a.m. to-morrow.

5. *Lieut.-Colonel B.'s column* will march from **BORDES** at 4 a.m. and attack **LAUVALLIÈRES**, at the same time occupying the enemy's attention at **LAPLANCHETTE**. The cavalry with this column will dismount men to attack **NOUILLY**, and will reconnoitre viâ **MÉY** to **NOUILLY**.

6. *Colonel C.'s Column* will start at the same hour from **SEBASTOPOL** and take up a position of readiness west of the **FRANZ. DENKM.** It will attack (but not before I issue a special order to that effect) viâ **COLOMBEY** the heights west of **COINCY** and **AUBIGNY**. Patrols will reconnoitre through **ARS-LAQUENEXY**.

7. *The Outposts* will join their respective columns.

8. *The extra Ammunition* will be issued before starting. The *Section Field Ambulance* and the *Bridging Train* will await further orders at **SEBASTOPOL**.

9. *The Infantry Telephone Detachment* will, by 4.30 a.m., have established a line from the **TANNENWÄLDCHEN**[1] north of **COLOMBEY** to the **FRANZ. DENKM.** and to **LIMITE** (east of **BELLE CROIX**).

10. *The 2nd Line Transport* will be collected at 7 a.m. in column of route, with the head of the column at **SEBASTOPOL**, in the following order: Transport of Lieut.-Colonel B.'s column, of Colonel C.'s column, of field batteries, of light howitzer, and of heavy howitzer batteries.

11. *Reports* to the **TANNEN-WALDCHEN** north of **COLOMBEY**, where I shall be.

Verbally to assembled officers commanding units.
5.45 p.m.

A.,
Major-General.

You should now, by a slight effort of imagination, try and realise the effect this attack will produce on the mind of the officer commanding the enemy's troops in Montoy. His troops are already exhausted by the recent fighting and their retreat. On their arrival at the Vallières brook they were occupied till evening in constructing field entrenchments, barricading bridges, etc., and a considerable number have had to be on outpost duty during the night as well. The troops resting in the villages of Montoy and Coincy are being shelled all night by the heavy guns. All these circumstances will operate unfavourably on the already impaired *moral* of the enemy's troops, as their commander is only too well aware. Suddenly, at the first streak of daylight, hostile infantry in superior numbers

[1] Fir copse.—*Trans.*

make a determined assault on Lauvallières and Planchette, and, if the wind is that way, the sound of firing west of Nouilly may also be heard. The musketry fire is most intense at Lauvallières, on which point also a concentrated artillery fire is being directed by batteries in position on the high ground by Belle Croix, and by the heavy howitzer batteries. It is impossible, in the semi-darkness, to judge of the enemy's strength, but it appears likely that at any moment Lauvallières may be captured. At Colombey and Aubigny all is quiet. Would not the officer commanding the Red rear guard at once employ all his artillery to reply to ours at Belle Croix, alarm his infantry in Montoy, and hurry them up to support the defenders of Lauvallières? I fancy he would make strenuous efforts to drive back again over the stream our leading troops, should they have effected a crossing at Lauvallières.

You see it is very probable that the officer commanding the enemy's rear guard will be induced to act as I have described. But even if he does not, his attention will, at any rate, be occupied with the fighting at Lauvallières and Laplanchette, and consequently there is a good chance of a sudden attack on Aubigny and Coincy being successful before the enemy's reserve can reach the latter place. We shall gain a decided point even if the enemy employ only a portion of his reserve and his artillery to support Lauvallières, as that will weaken any support which he may bring up to the defenders of the high ground west of Coincy, and thus make matters easier for the main attack.

In continuation of the preceding exercise you might with advantage now imagine the following situation, and draw up the orders to meet it.

The enemy abandoned the whole position in disorder at 7 a.m., and is streaming back by the main road on Kurzel through St. Aignan, where three of his batteries have taken up a rallying position.

IN CONCLUSION.

Before concluding this series of letters I wish to impress upon you that you can set yourself other exercises on the basis of those we have worked through together, and thus get further practice in framing such orders as you do not feel yourself sure about. This will develop, more than anything else, a grasp of tactical principles, and the very process of solving your own problems will soon show you if you have made any mistakes in framing the exercises. I have therefore intentionally refrained from giving you exercises dealing with the opposing party. You must be able to do that now yourself.

I venture to hope that if you have thoroughly studied these letters, you have at any rate laid a foundation for your further tactical education. For more advanced study I advise you to work out some of the tactical Problems set at recent Staff College examinations.

Metz.

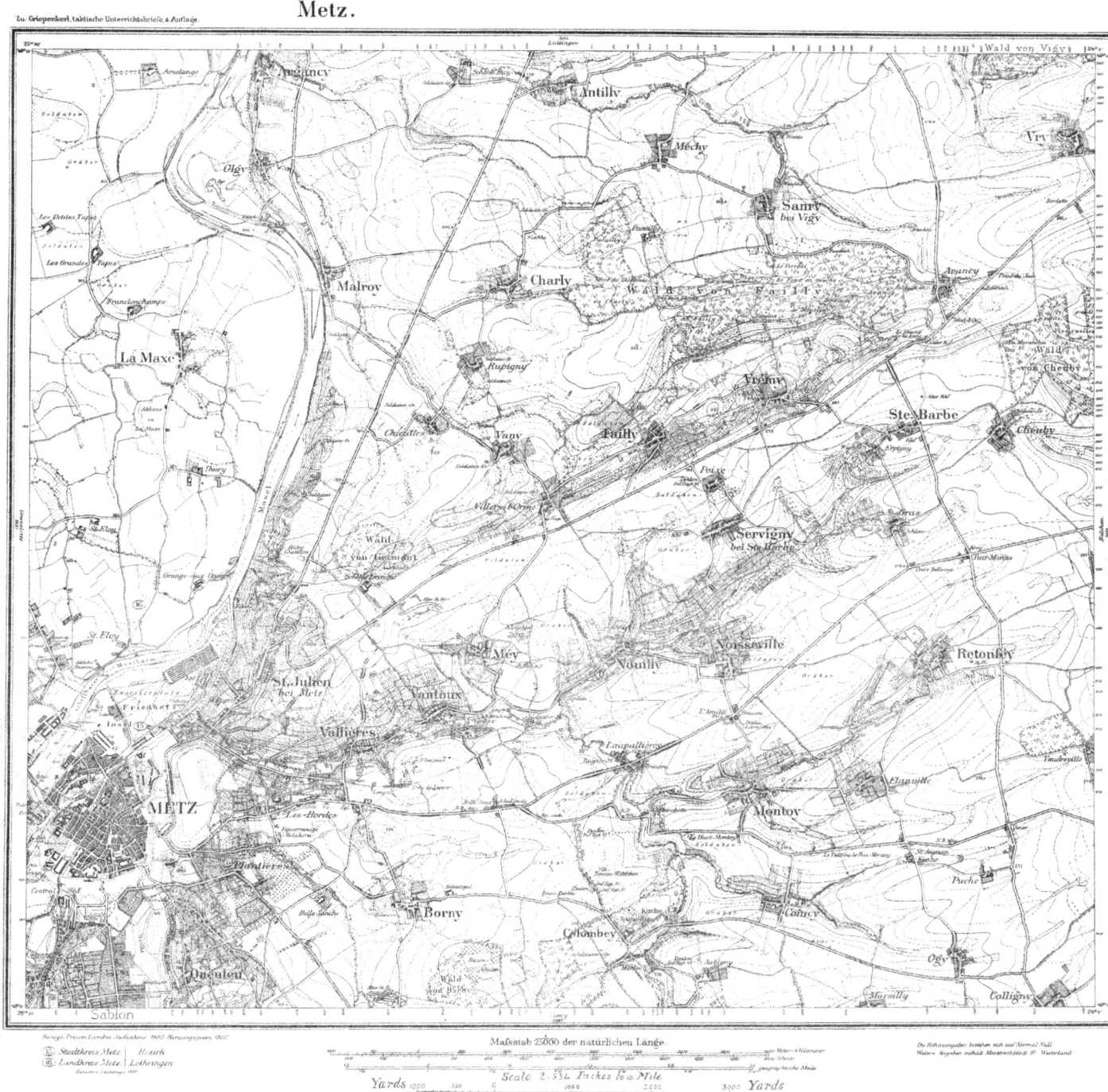

Metz.

Zu: Griepenkerl, taktische Unterrichtsbriefe, 4. Auflage.

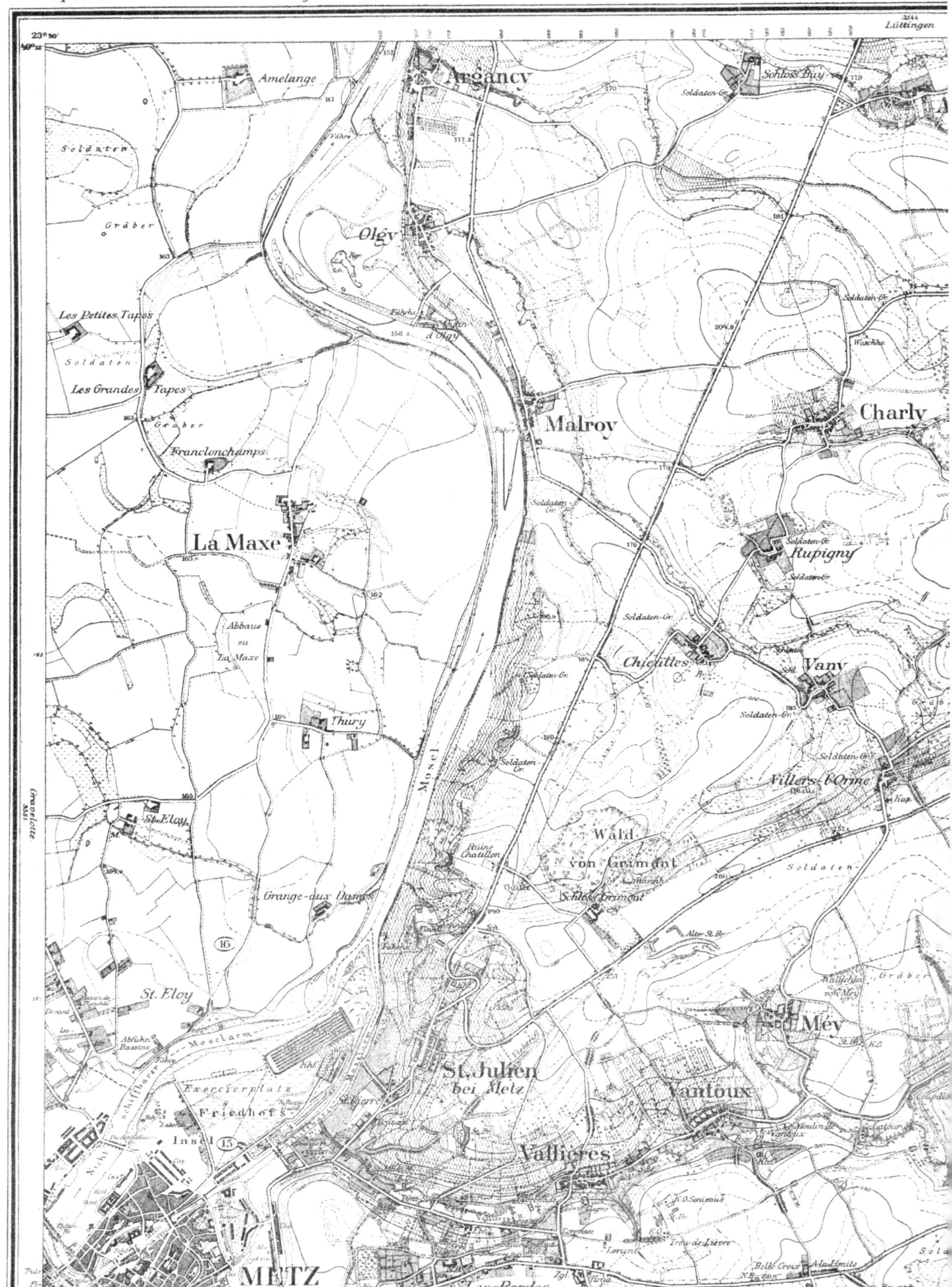

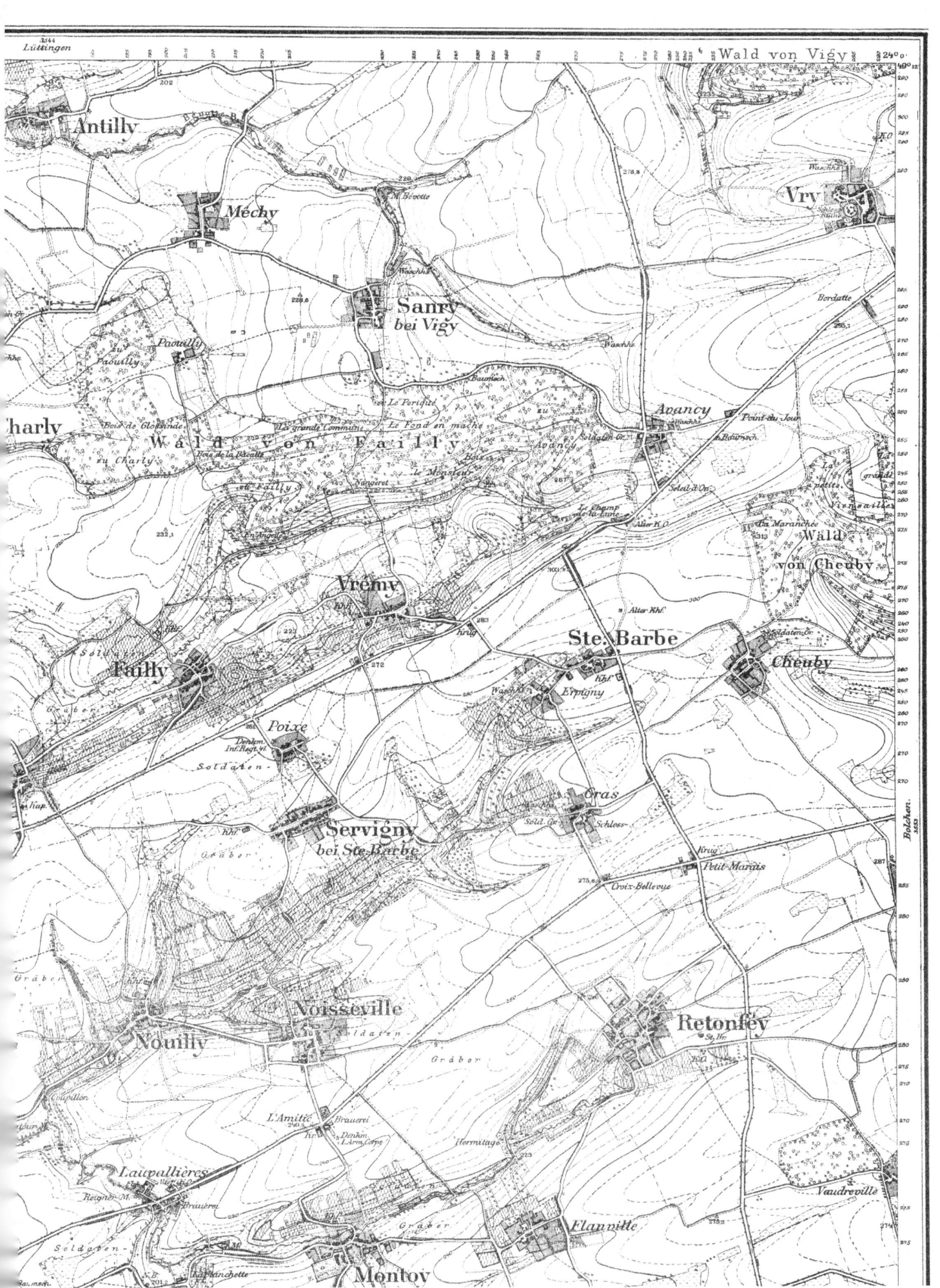

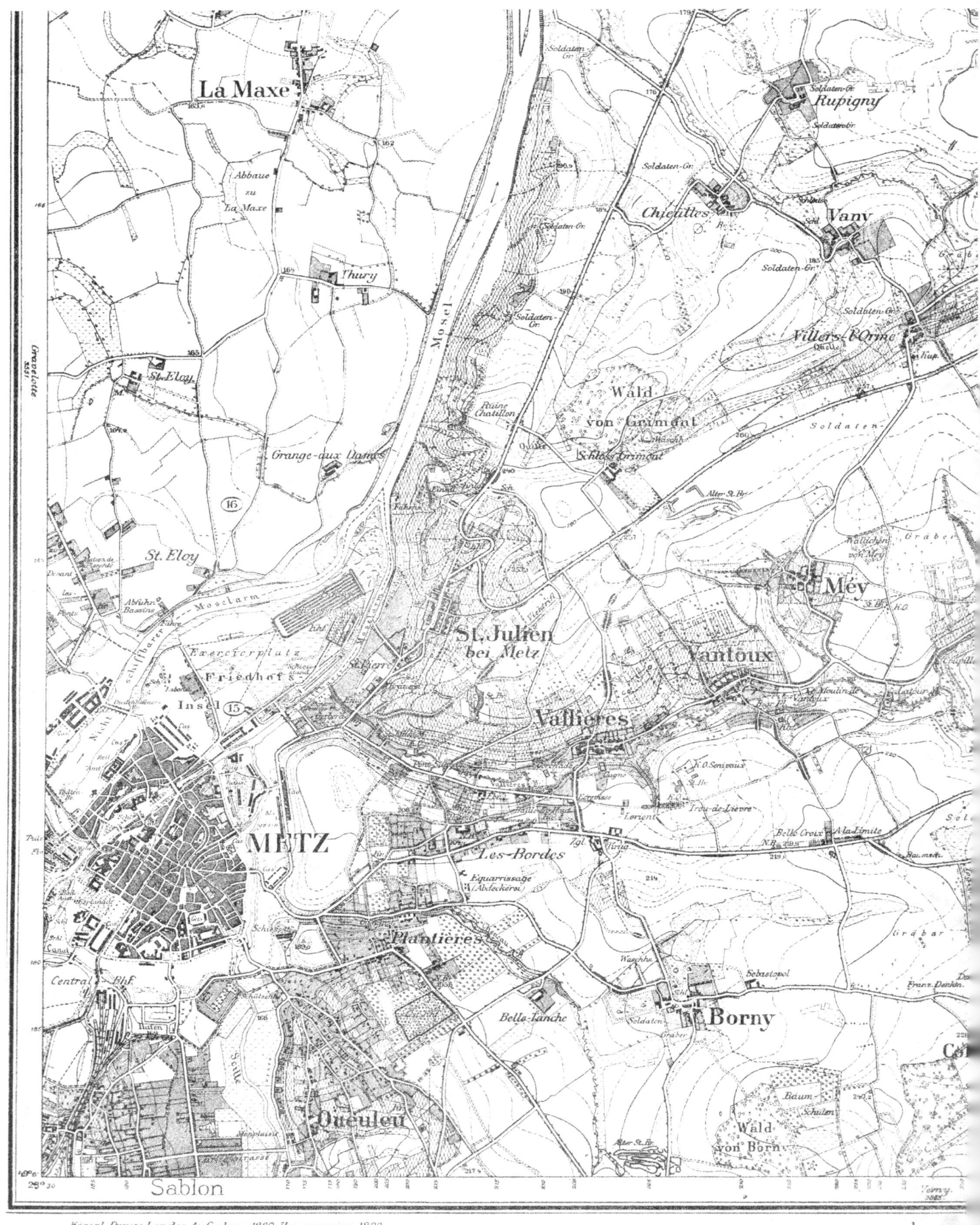

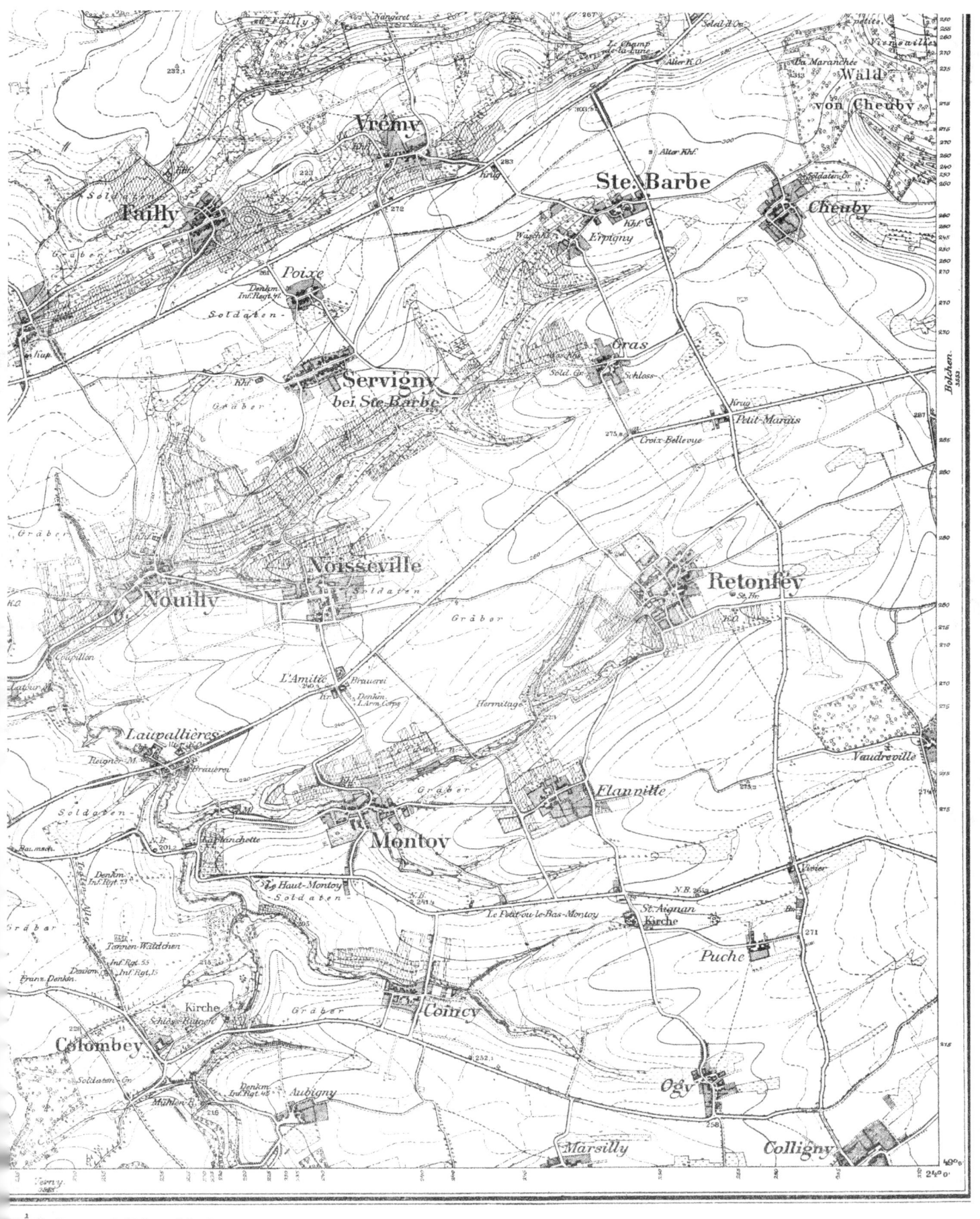

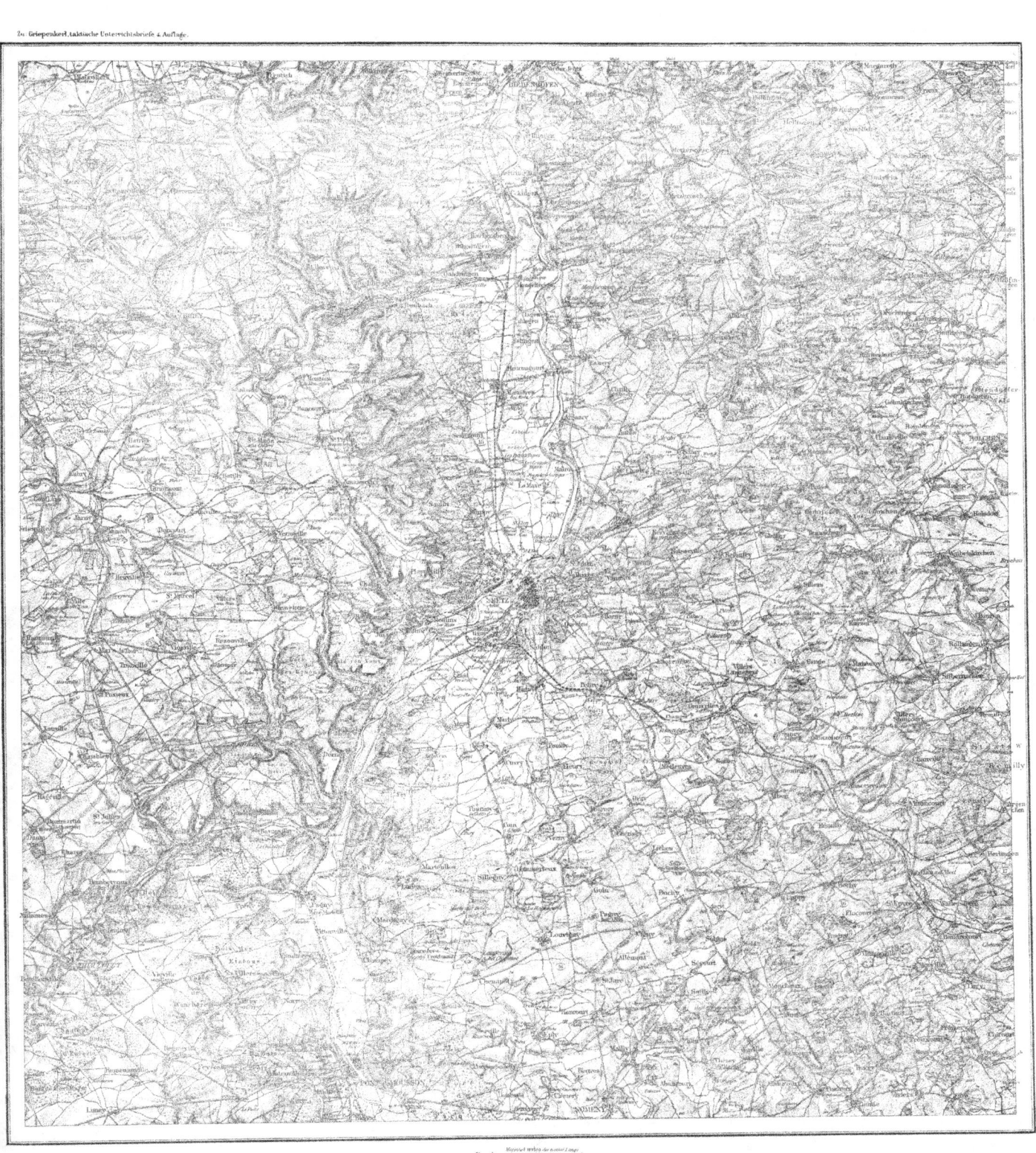

Zu: Griepenkerl, taktische Unterrichtsbriefe, 4. Auflage.

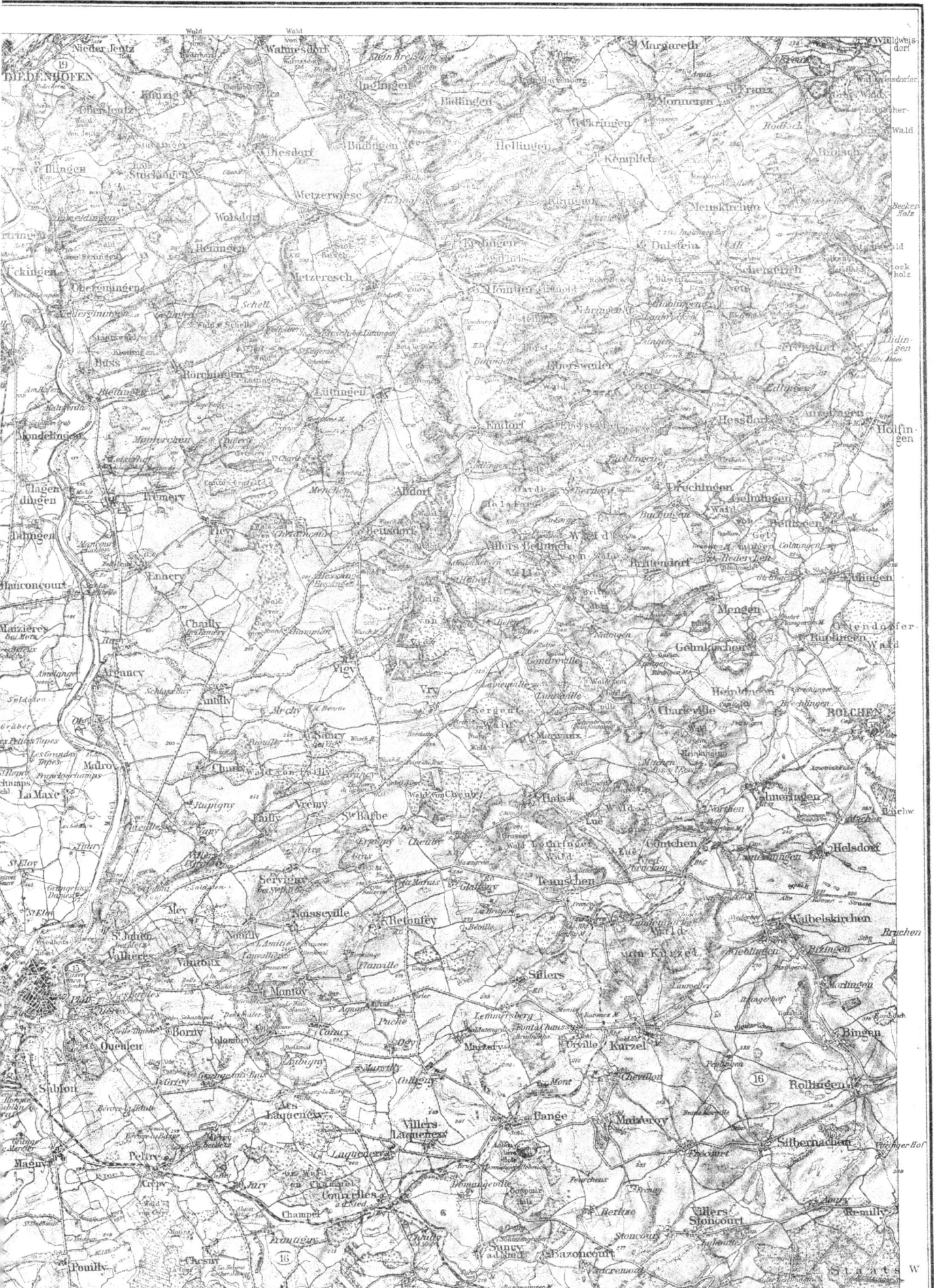

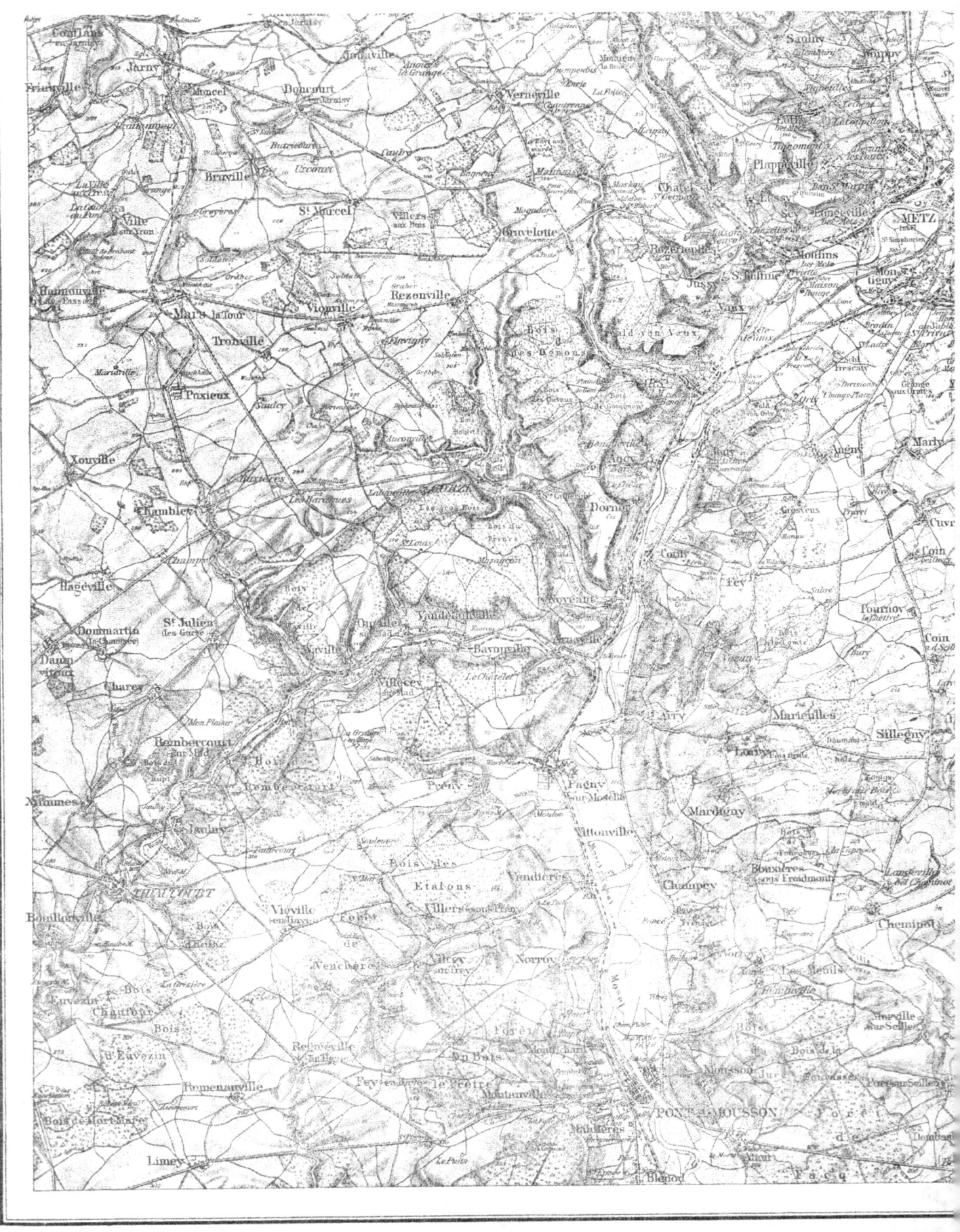

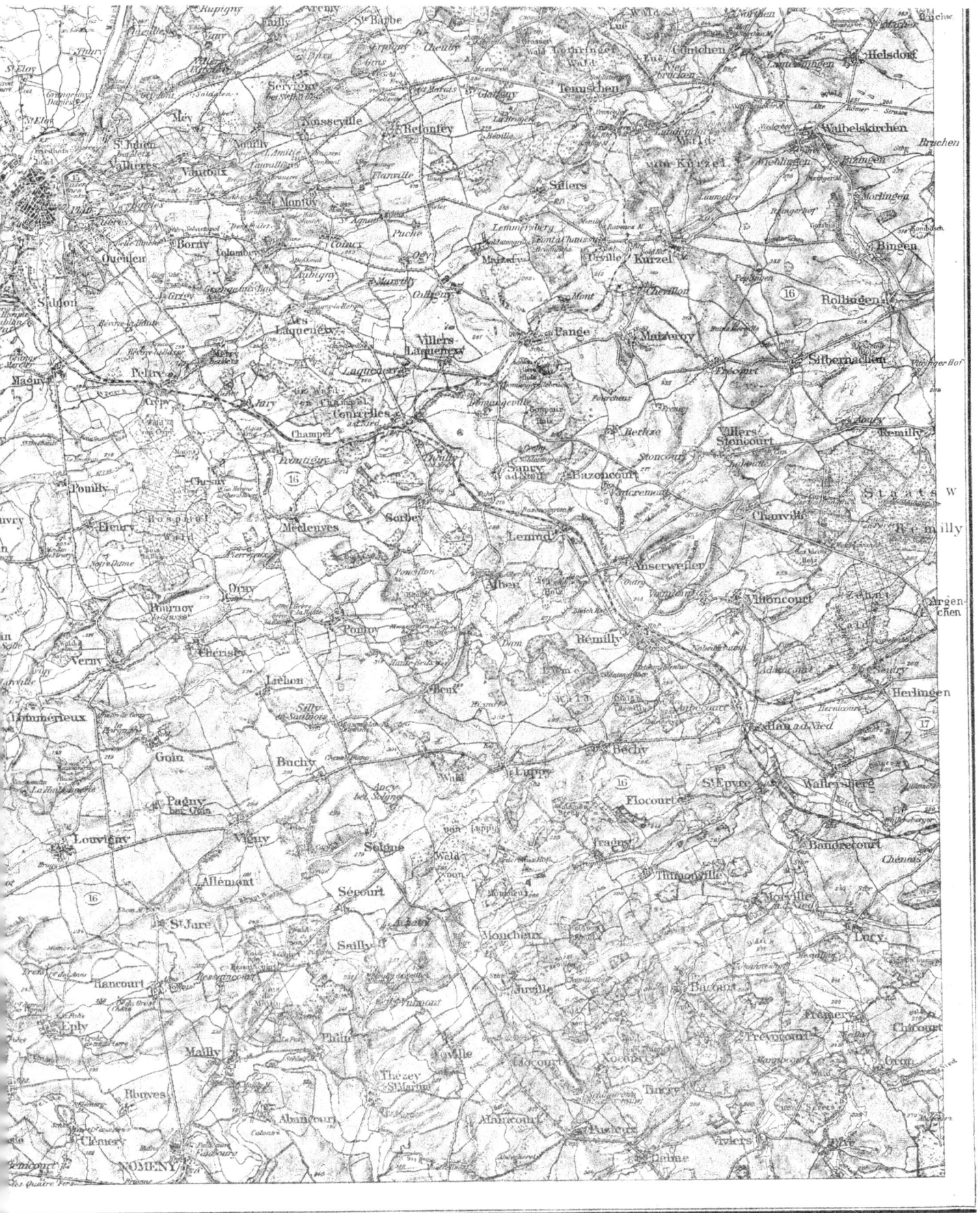

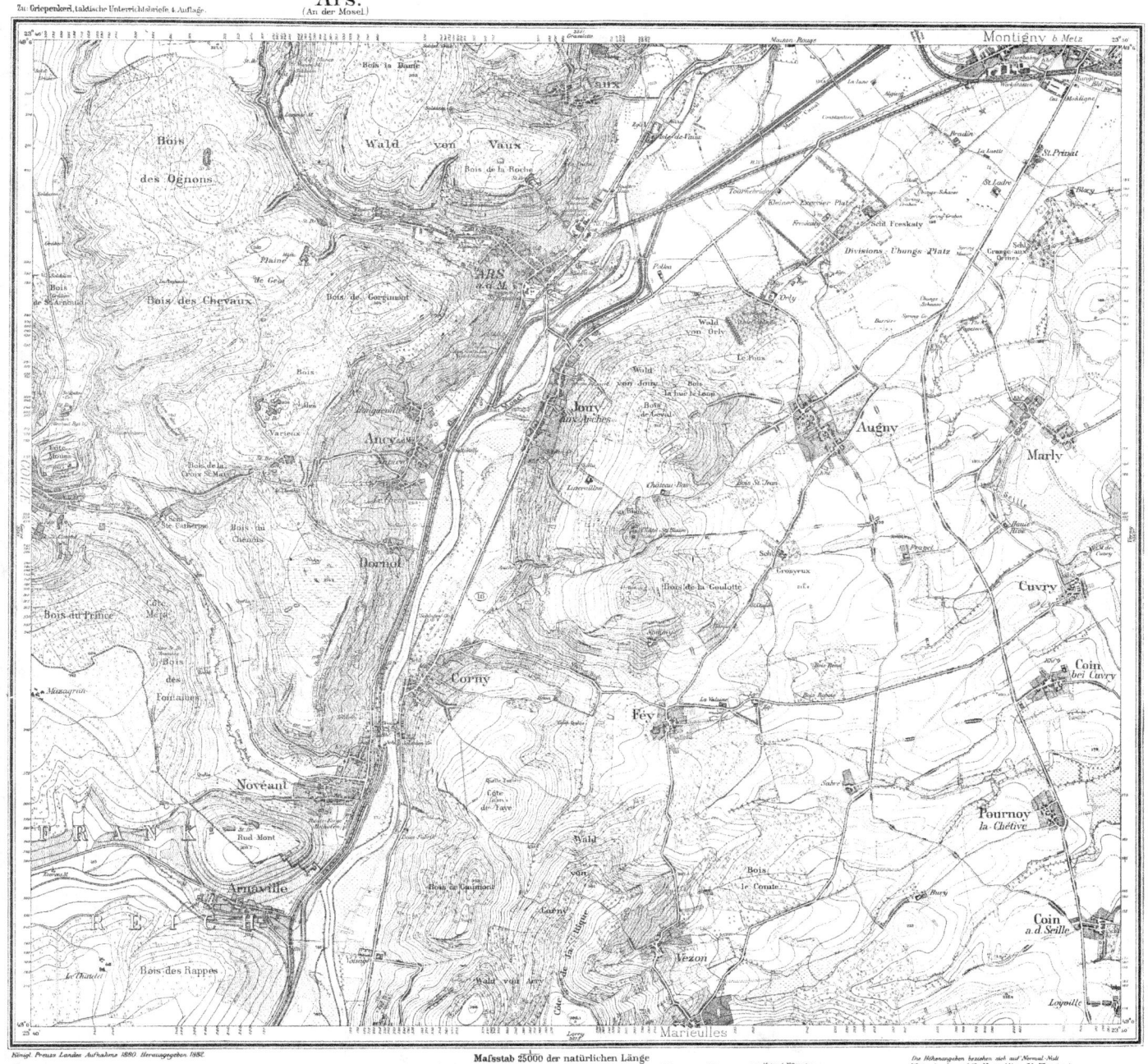

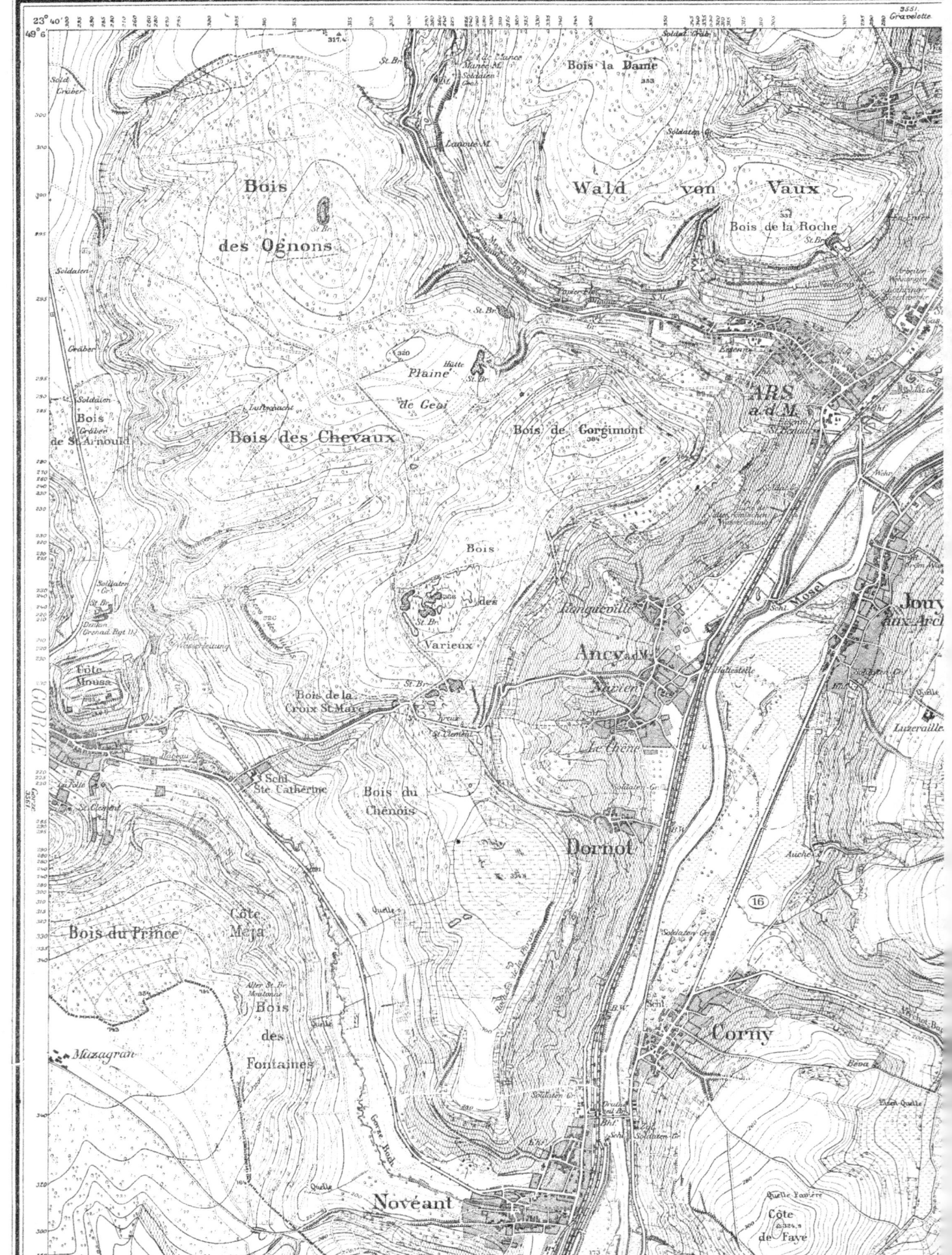

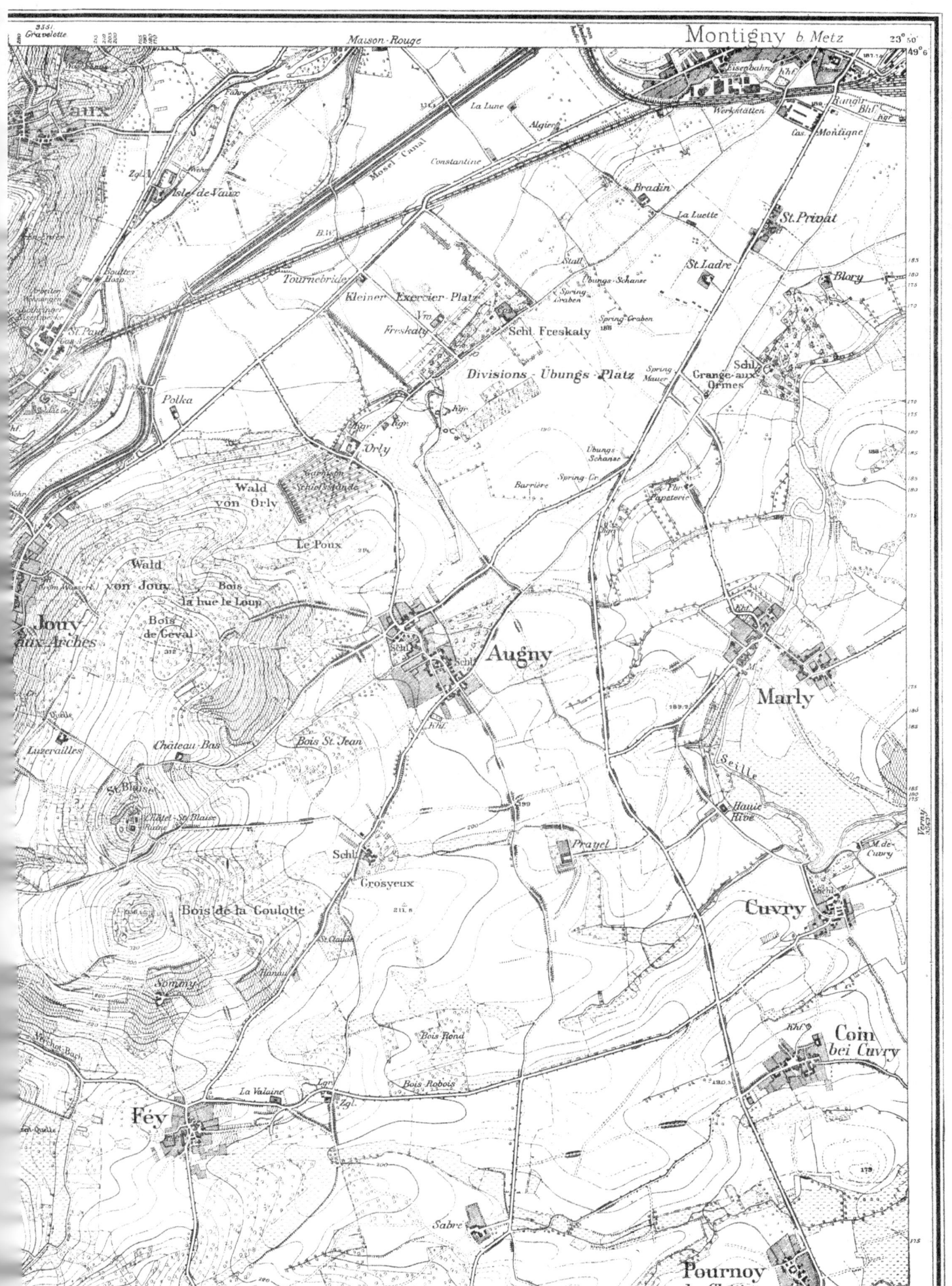

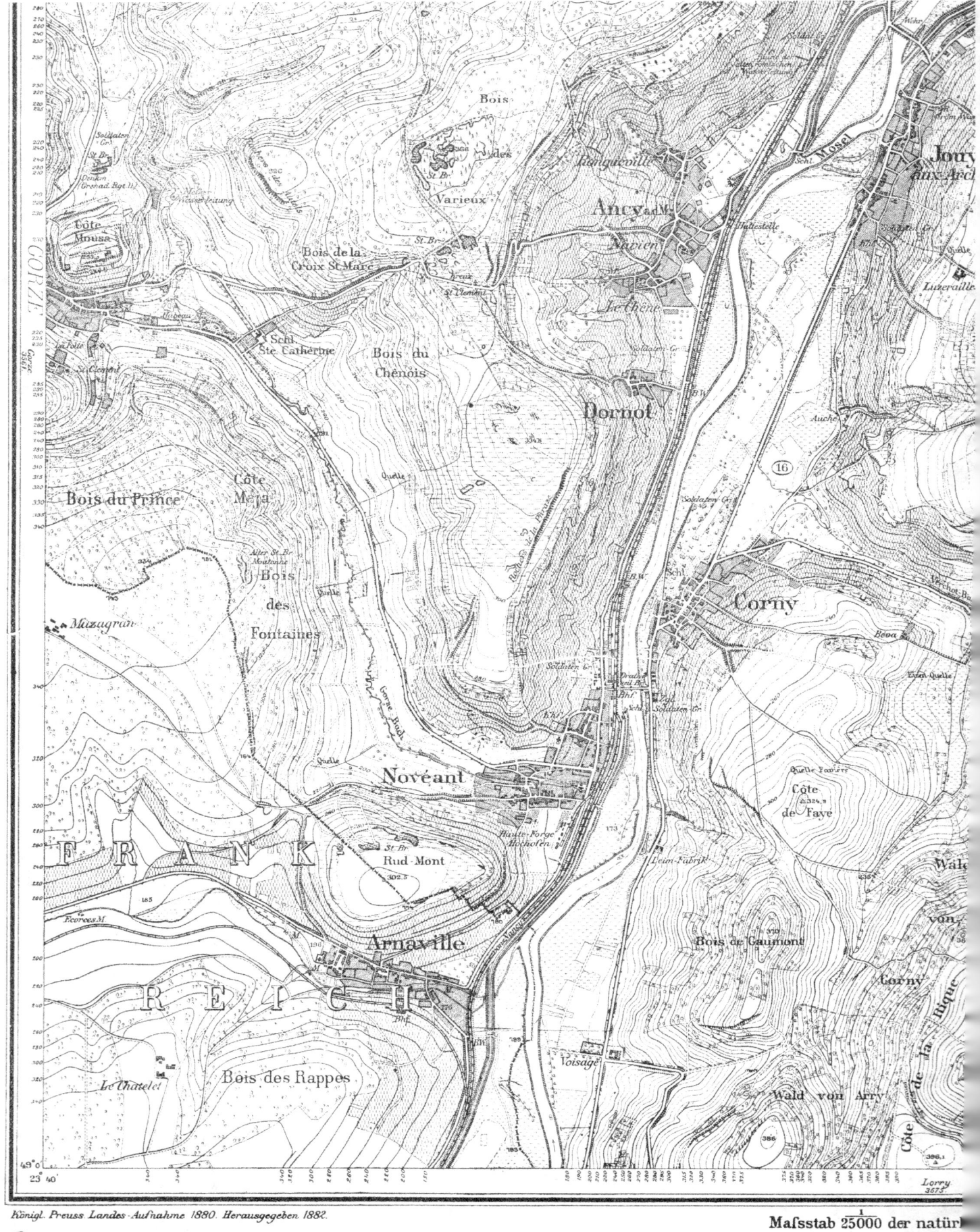

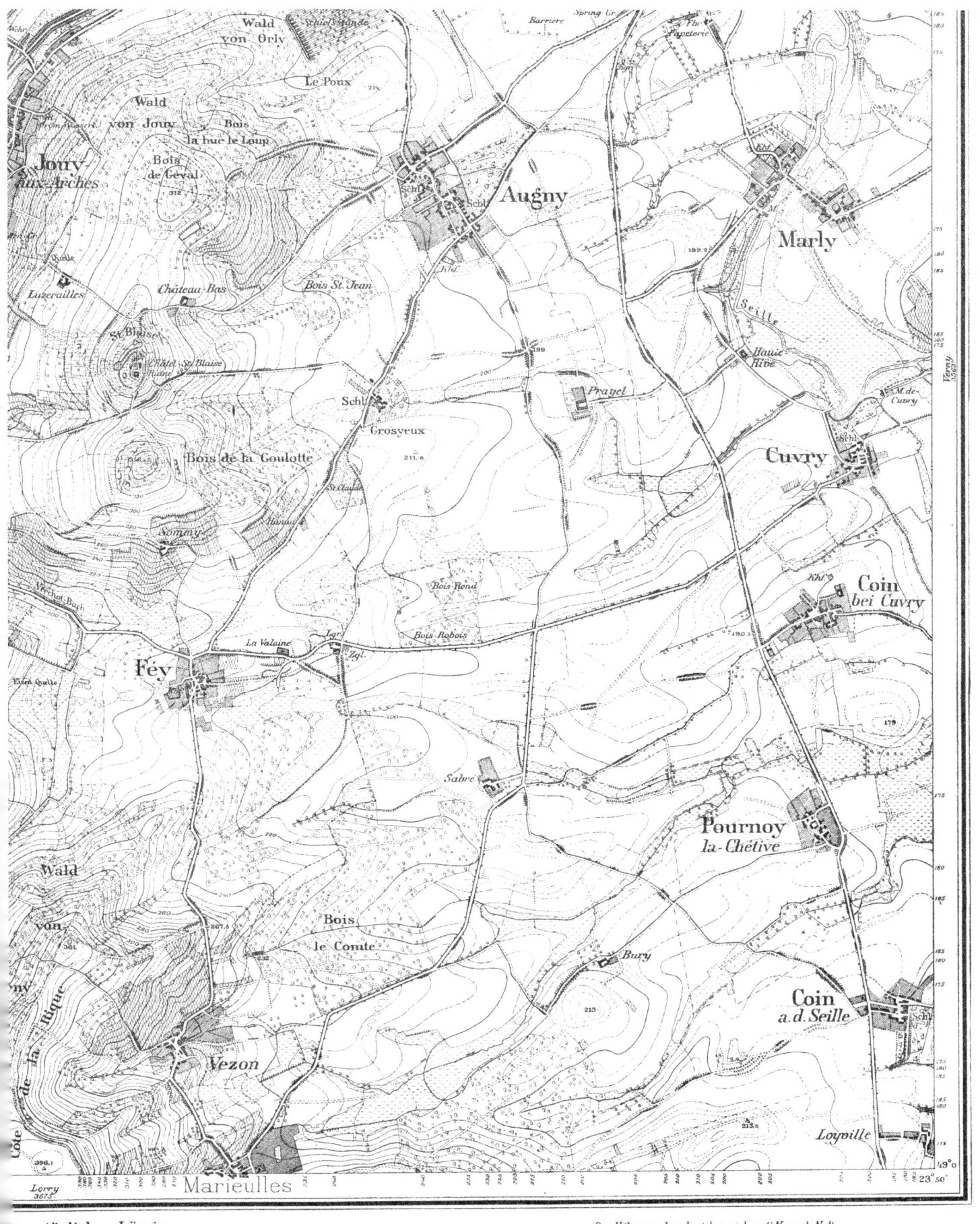

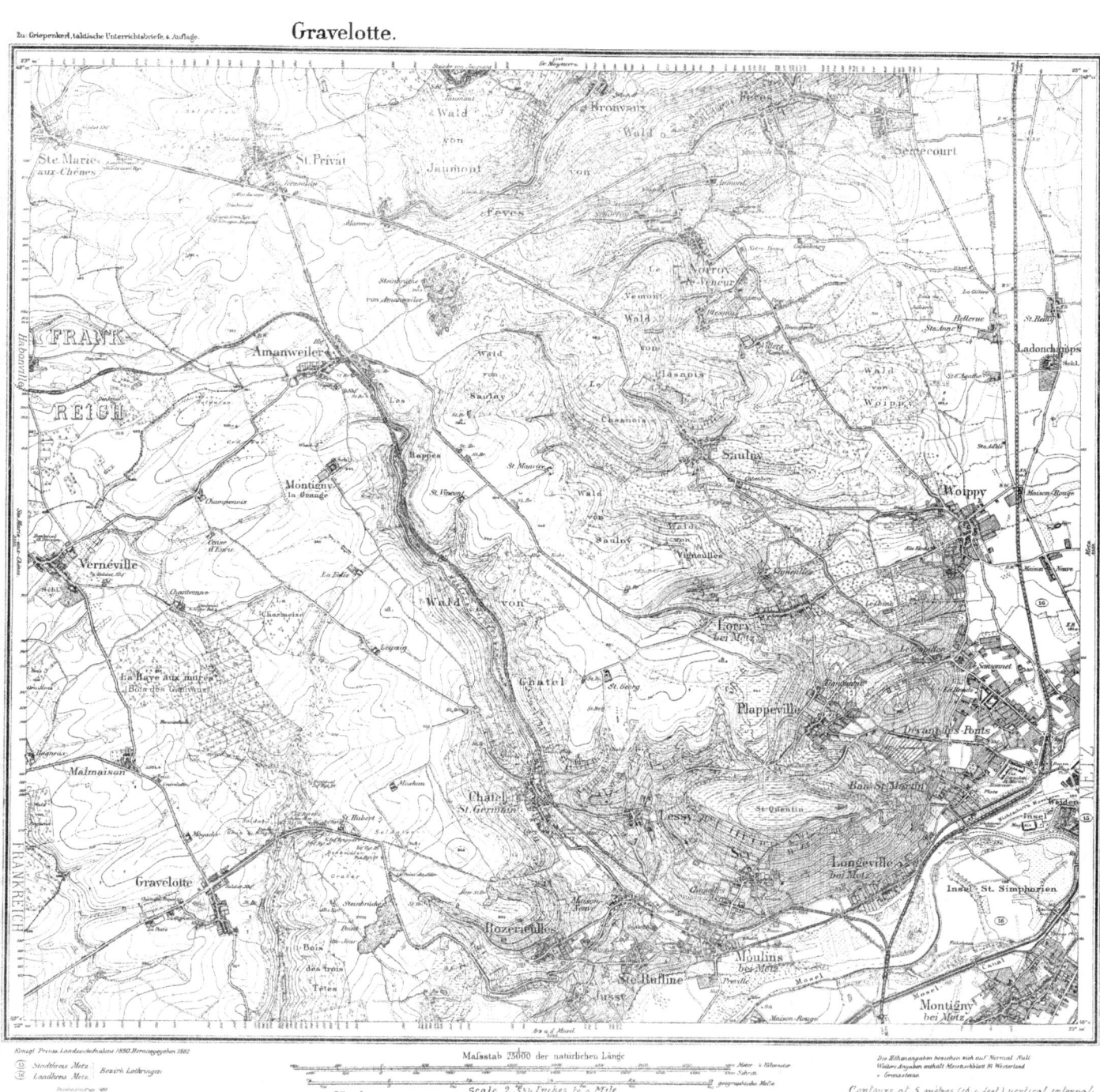

Gravelotte.

Zu: Griepenkerl, taktische Unterrichtsbriefe, 4. Auflage.

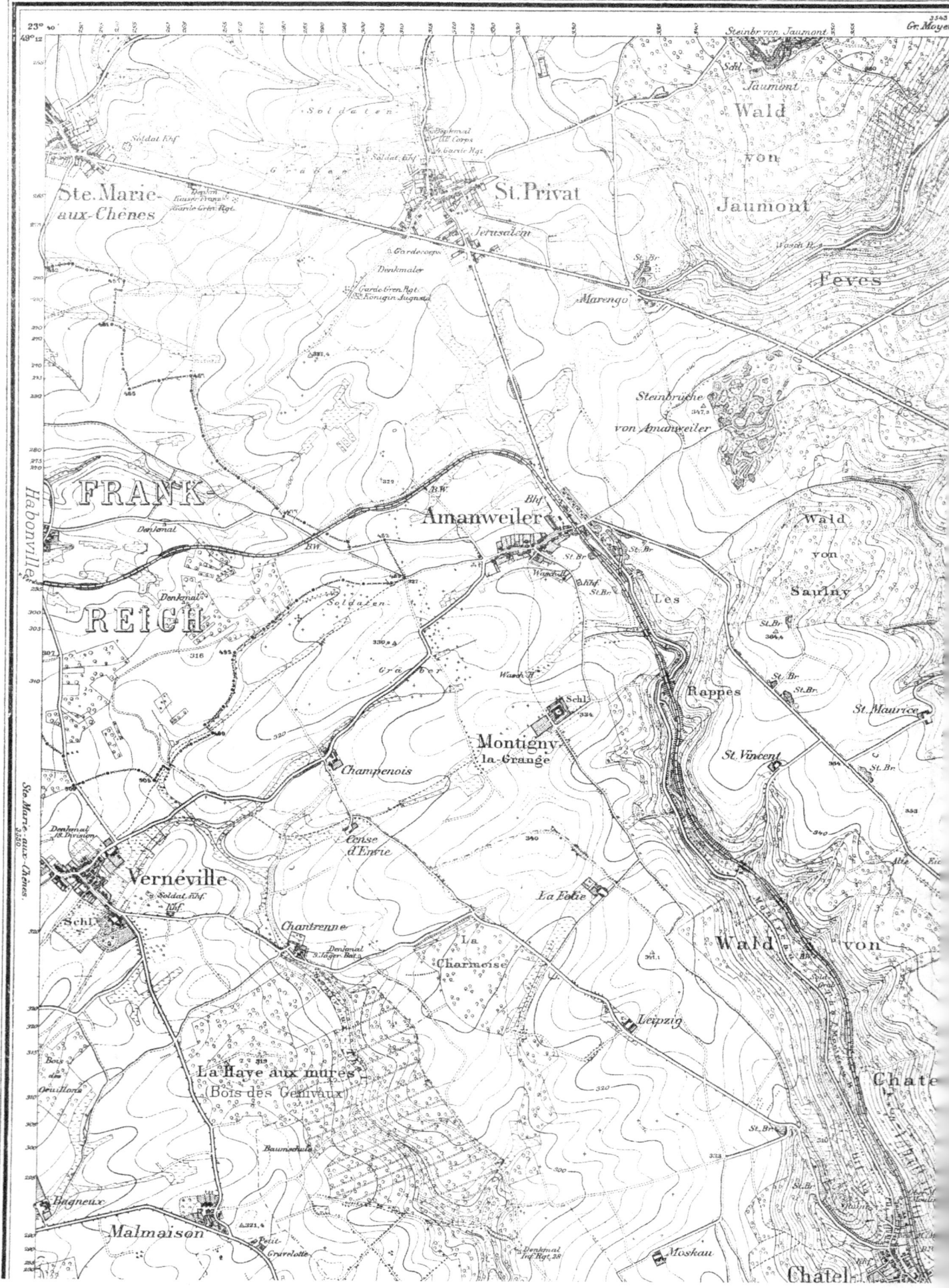

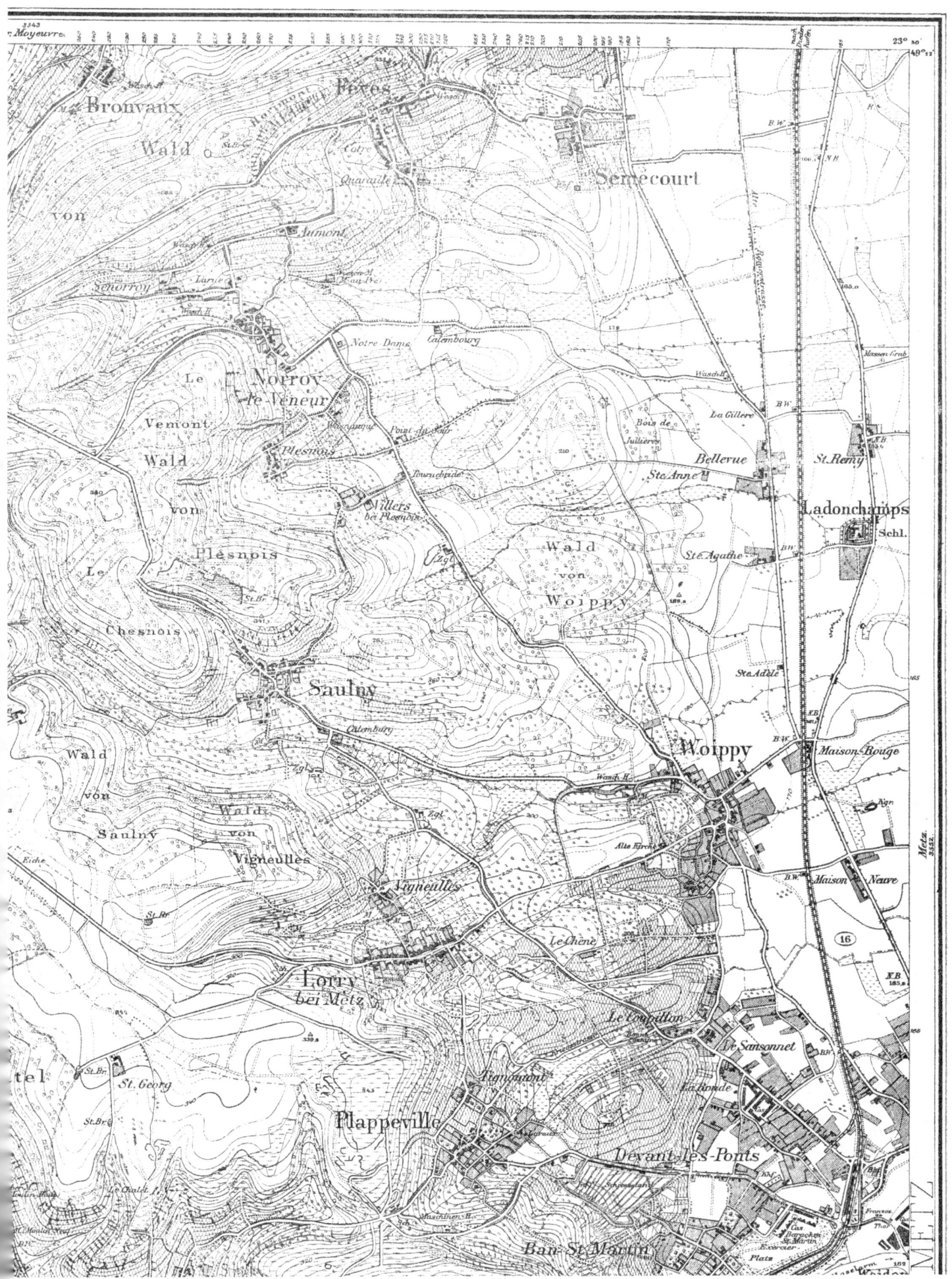

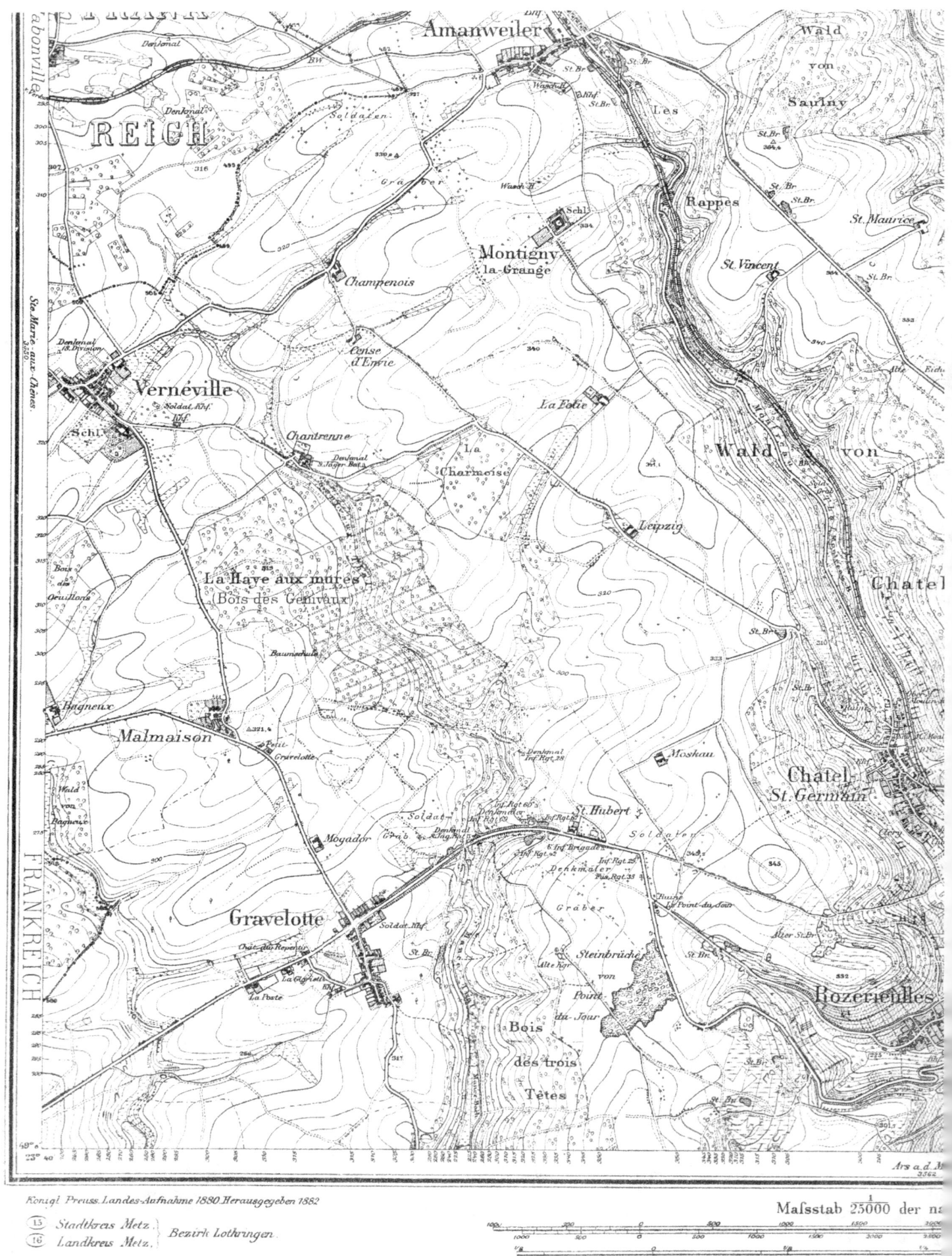

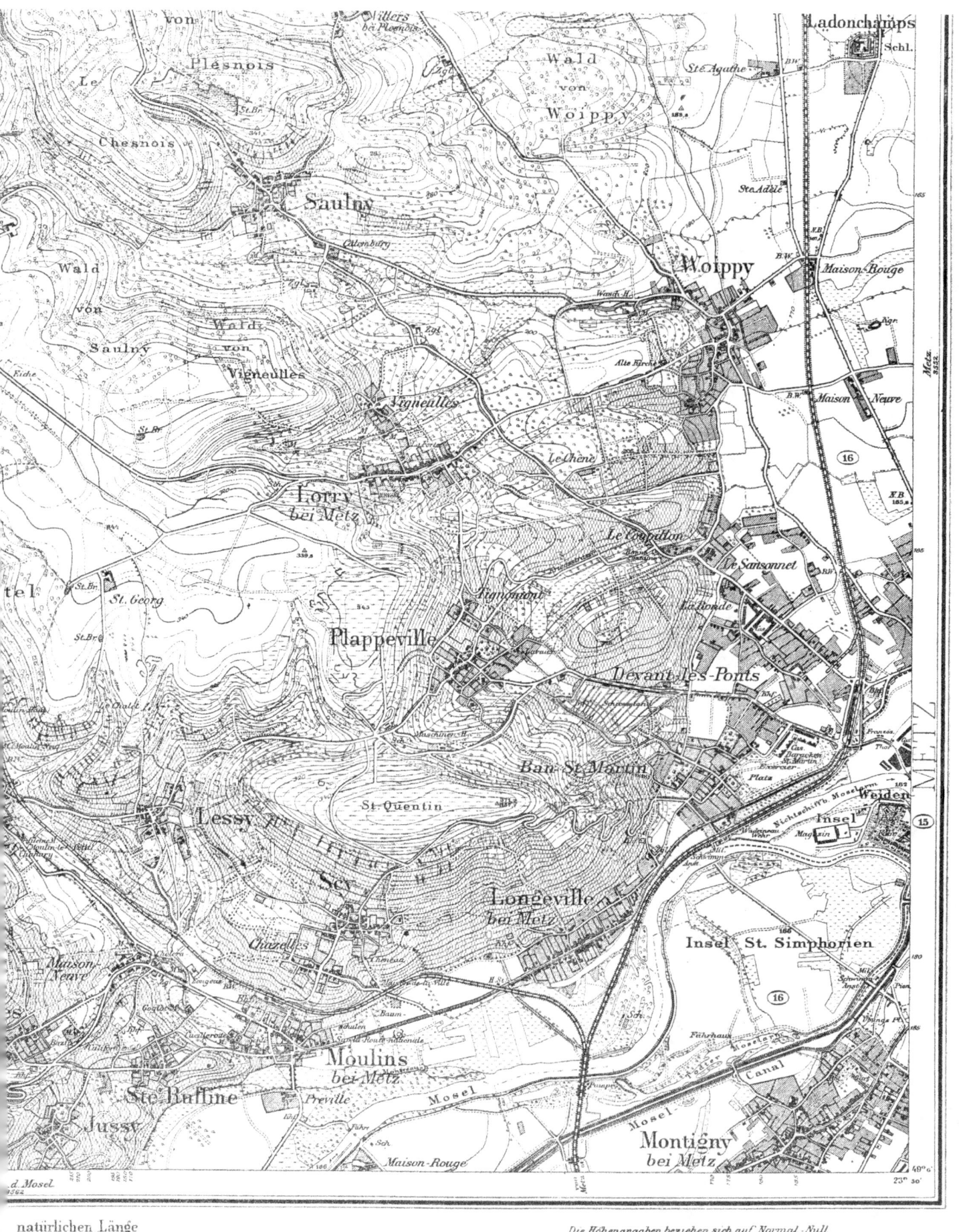

Verny.

Verny.

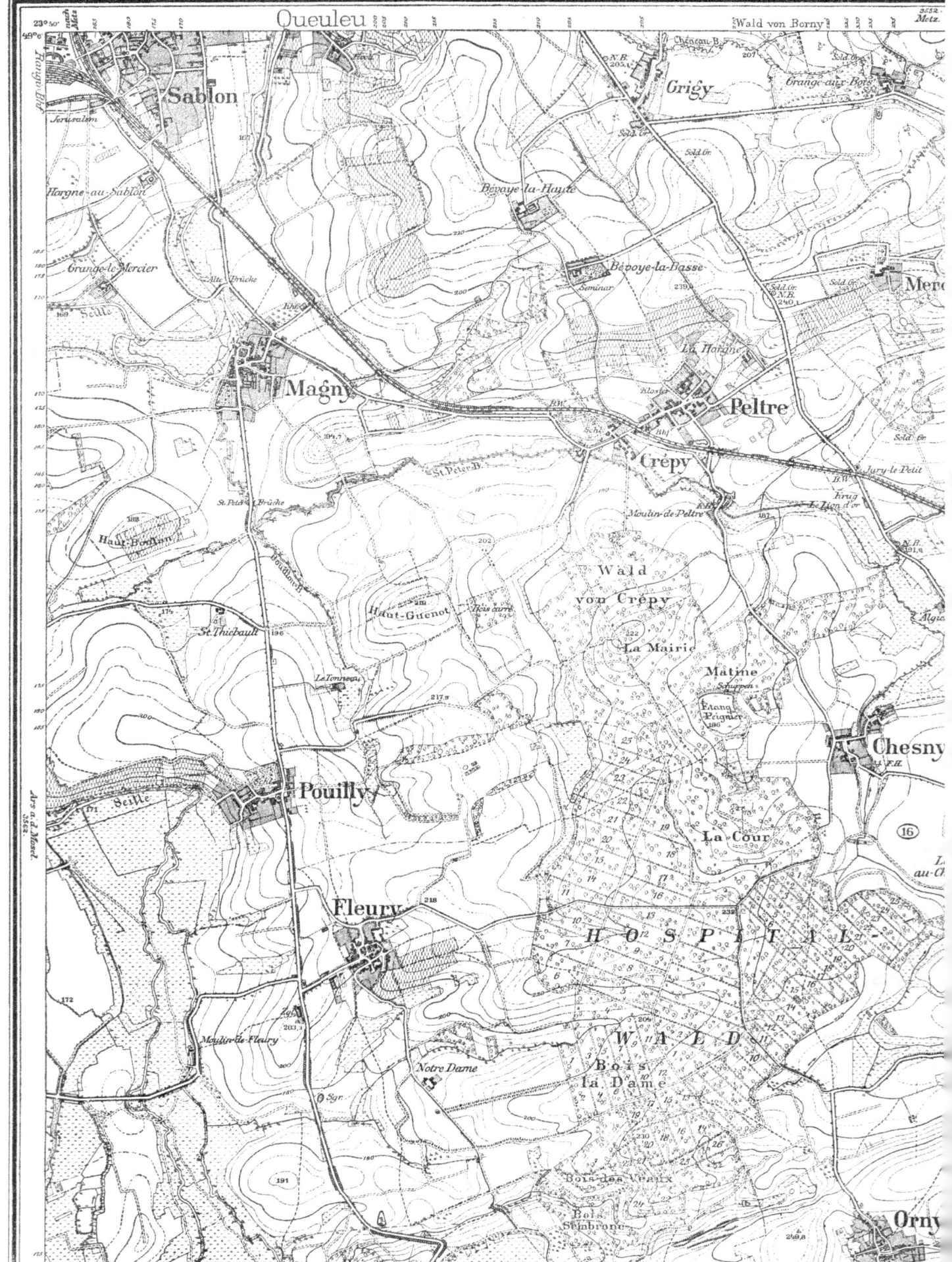

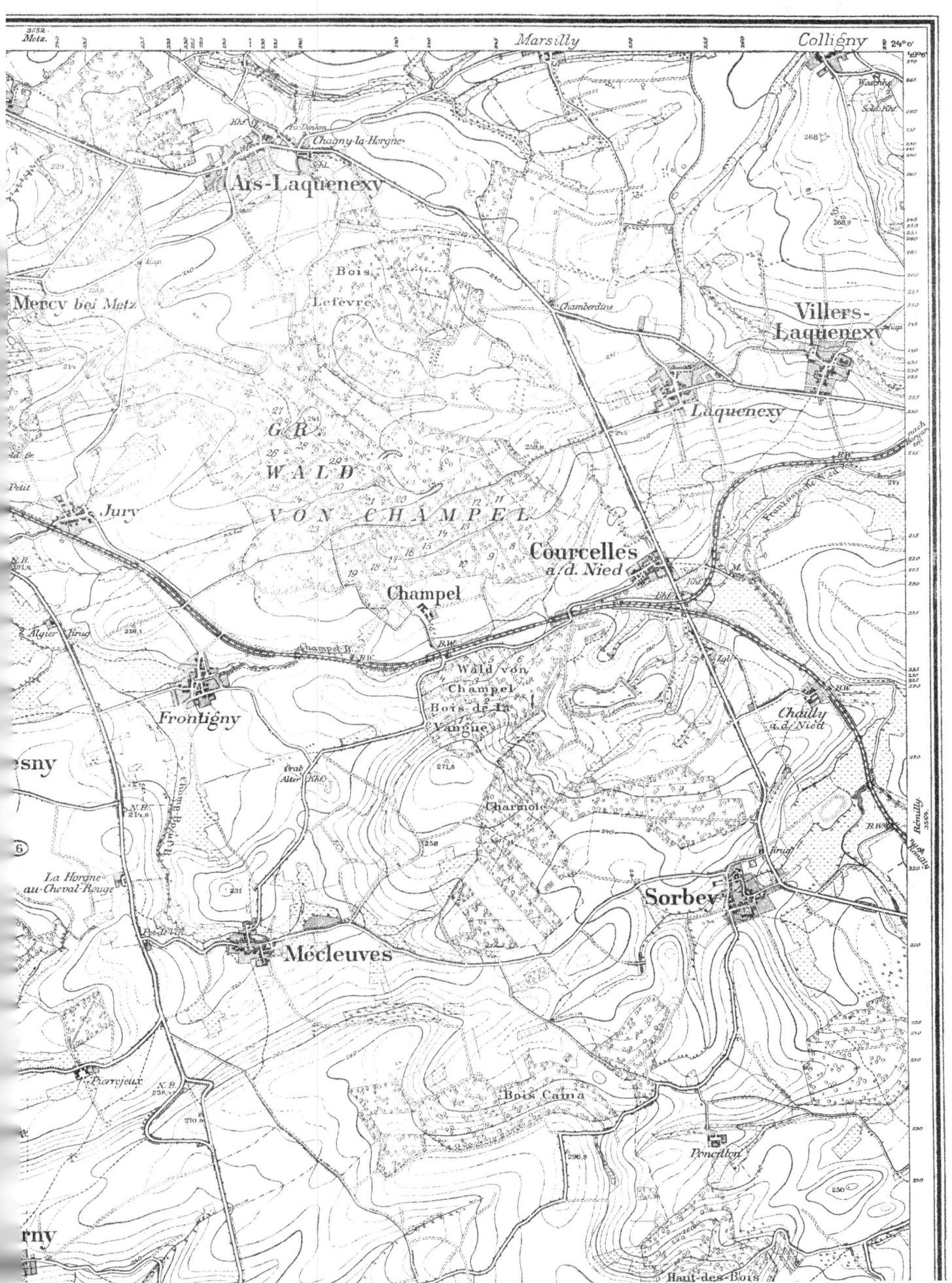

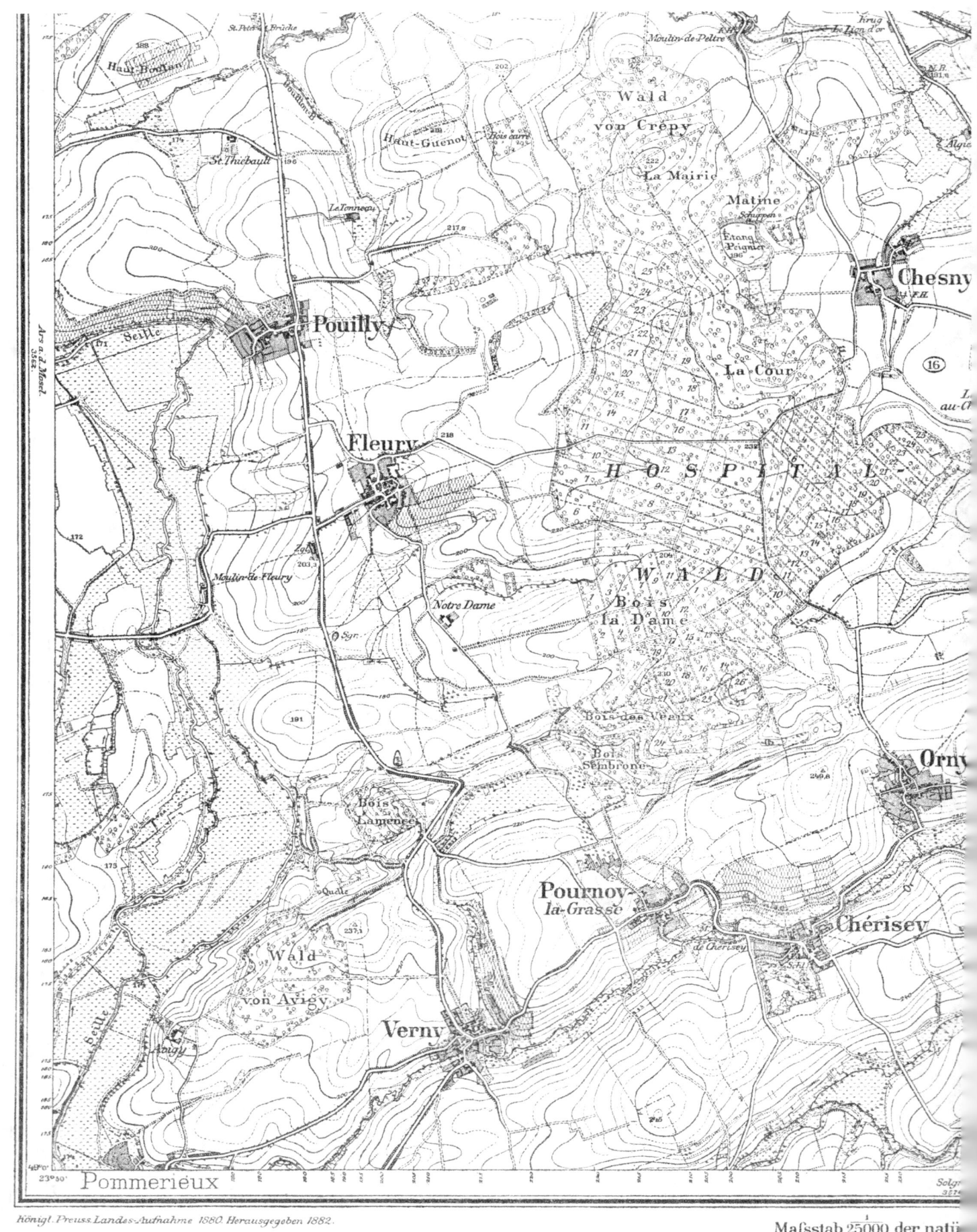

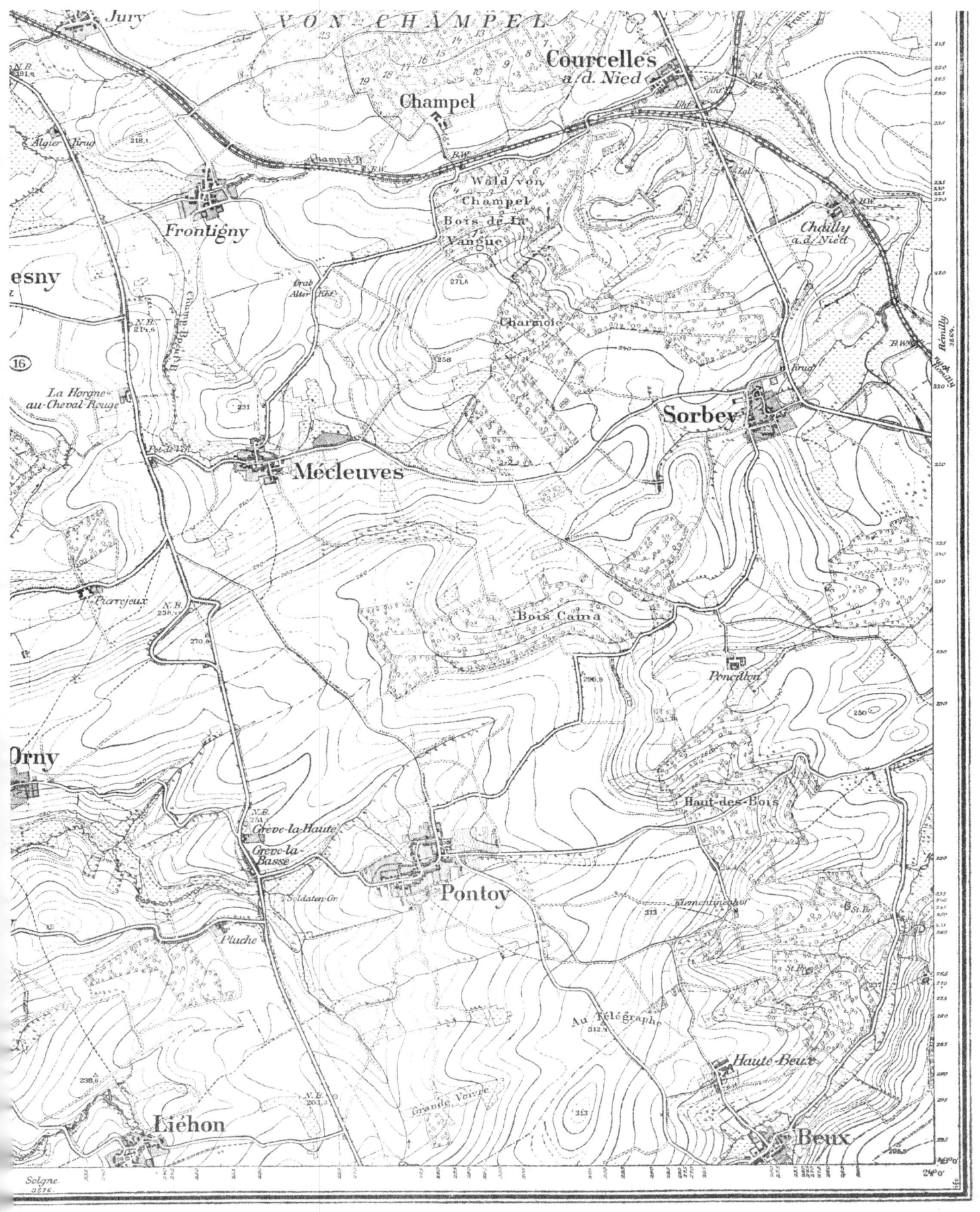

www.ingramcontent.com/pod-product-compliance
Lightning Source LLC
Chambersburg PA
CBHW080847010526
44114CB00018B/2392